ASPECTS OF
ELVIS

A S P E C T S   O F
ELVIS
TRYIN' TO GET TO YOU

EDITED BY
ALAN CLAYSON & SPENCER LEIGH

SIDGWICK & JACKSON
LONDON

First published 1994 by Sidgwick & Jackson

an imprint of Macmillan General Books
Cavaye Place London SW10 9PG
and Basingstoke

Associated companies throughout the world

ISBN 0-283-06217-7

1 3 5 7 9 8 6 4 2

A CIP catalogue record for this book is available from
the British Library

Typeset by CentraCet Limited, Cambridge
Printed and bound in Great Britain by
Mackays of Chatham PLC, Chatham, Kent

Contents

Contents

ALAN CLAYSON

Introduction

If Elvis Presley had shed most of his artistic load by 1960, he'd left such an indelible impression on the complacency of post-war pop that his own later capitulation to it was dismissed initially as the prerogative of glamour. Though the world has since become wiser to his failings, his omnipotence is such that veneration has yet to fade for countless fans in a languid daze from the fixity of gazing – figuratively anyway – on the bolted gates of his Graceland mansion. For them, the King – who would have been sixty in 1995 – still rules from the grave.

Certain humble folk still cling to the belief that he'd been spirited away, and that, alive and well, the once and future King would return to recover his domain. Among reported sightings are some in locations where you'd least expect to find him – shopping for groceries in an Essex supermarket; opening a bank account in Detroit, or, as Elvis himself informed one of the editors during a Radio Merseyside interview in 1989, 'with some Aboriginal friends of mine, eating raw meat and fish'. Joking aside, all ingredients of the Elvis-is-alive tales represent a profound human impulse – not peculiar to pop – that holds at arm's length a stark truth too grievous to be borne.

His passing was a boom time for those with vested interests – who regarded Presley's absence as no more of a hindrance than his spell in the armed forces had been. The final studio dates the previous October had spawned 'Way Down', a minor entry prior to that fateful day, but a chart-topper after he'd gone – and followed by a trail of swift repromotions. For the rest of 1977, Elvis was never off Top 40 radio. Given a rubbishing the week before the sands ran out in a *New Musical Express* review – which contained an unfortunate remark that he'd been dead for ages – Presley's *Moody Blue* finale was racing to Number One in the UK album list.

For that aged Tibetan monk who still hasn't heard of him, Mr E. A. Presley didn't start pop, but he got it going. Both the figurehead and during a long bout of seclusion in the '60s, the *éminence grise* of its brief history, he was of hillbilly parentage but spent most of his teenage years in the blues city of Memphis. In 1953, he turned up at Sun, a small local studio that provided record-your-voice facilities. He intended to sing 'My Happiness', an Ink Spots item, to his own guitar strumming as a gift for his adored mother. The Presley voice reached the ears of Sam Phillips, Sun's proprietor, who heard the fortune-making 'white man who could sing the blues' that he'd lost hope of ever discovering.

Though blues – later, rhythm and blues – and country and western were the main content, rock 'n' roll drew from light opera, folk song and all manner of trace elements in North America's musical spectrum: gospel, bluegrass, showbiz evergreens, Zydeco, vaudeville, Appalachian, and every branch of jazz, particularly when it touched on the frontiers of pop via, perhaps, the humour of Louis Armstrong, the orchestral euphoria of Count Basie, Ted Daffan and his Texans' Western Swing ('hillbilly jazz') or the vocal daredevilry of such as Anita O'Day and Frank Sinatra.

More explicit precedents may be heard in particular records. Examples include Hank Williams's 'Move It On Over', 'Boogie Woogie Bugle Boy' by the Andrews Sisters and Roy Brown's 'Good Rockin' Tonight' from 1947, plus any number of gutbucket Mississippi and Chicago blues offerings.

Most originated in the Deep South where, before television became a common household fixture, 'musical evenings' were a regular occurrence. In working-class homes like the Presleys', the essence of the entertainment issued from guitars, readily available from the Sears Roebuck mail-order catalogue since the early 1930s.

Home-made southern folk music lay at the bedrock of the 'western' in 'country and western'. Before the translation of C&W into this Coca-Cola century's commentary on the aspirations of middle America, C&W aficionados may once have made the excuse, 'I only had the wireless on. I wasn't listening to it'. 'Listening to it' used to suggest an affinity to ignorant, bigoted 'rednecks', parodied as unsophisticated, clannish and anti-intellectual. Yet Elvis was one of many who reached a wider public, initially via regional C&W radio.

White listeners might inadvertently tune in to static-laden bursts of what segregationalists reviled as 'the screaming idiotic words and savage music' on, say, Louisiana's KWKH station, where Stan the Man's No-Name Record Jive introduced the likes of 'Too Many Drivers' by Smiley

Lewis, the Midnighters' 'Sexy Ways', the Drifters' 'Such A Night' and 'Sixty Minute Man' from the Dominoes – all concerning sex and all banned from white playlists.

Nevertheless, with its cowpoke pessimism C&W is no more or less than white man's blues. The incorporation of blues into the stylistic *oeuvres* of C&W giants such as Jimmie Rodgers and Hank Williams was exemplified by vocals couched in rural black imagery and phrasing, an unusual preoccupation with rhythm, and an ineludible commitment to the spirit of their songs – and it was when contents of black and white music merged that Elvis Presley was able to advance beyond local popularity.

He was preceded by Oregon's Johnnie Ray, 'The Prince of Wails', whose melodramatic onstage exhibitionism was derived from black R&B. A pivotal onstage moment during a Ray recital was when he lurched into his 'cover' of 'Such A Night'. Such a whitewashing of an R&B hit for the mainstream pop charts was anticipated – even welcomed – by black recording acts of the early 1950s as it brought their music, if not their performances of it, to a parallel dimension of adolescent consumers with money to waste.

In the early 1950s, some unadulterated R&B crept into *Billboard*'s pop Hot 100, notably in the witty lyricism of Chuck Berry and Fats Domino's ambulatory lope. Though it owed as much to C&W for all its springing from a blues environment, some presenters weren't keen on scheduling such a racially integrated disc as Presley's first release – a jumped-up treatment of 'That's All Right, Mama' by black blues artist Arthur 'Big Boy' Crudup. Nevertheless, it rose high in the US country chart. Further smashes with similar material ensured that Elvis was both loathed and adored throughout the South. Everyone was talking about Elvis.

As it would over the Rolling Stones, the Sex Pistols and the attendant stylized delinquency in succeeding decades, so adult blood had run cold at Presley and the many other 'rockabilly' entertainers who flowered in his wake. Yet many teenagers were just as aghast as their parents when rearing up before them was everything that their upbringing had taught them both to despise and to fear. A hybrid of amusement arcade hoodlum and nancy boy, Presley's dress sense and hair style were as much of an issue as the shout-singing; his girly quiff and 'cat' clothes at odds with sideburns to the earlobes, and the hetero-erotic truculence in concerts where he didn't seem to care how badly he behaved – breaking

guitar strings, spitting out chewing gum, swivelling his hips in a rude
way, doing the splits, knee-dropping and crawling to the edge of the
stage.

'He told jokes that weren't funny, and his diction was real coarse like
a truck driver's,' observed a young Roy Orbison, who, with conflicting
emotions, also noticed 'the pandemonium in the audience because the
girls took a shine to him, and the guys were getting a little jealous'.
However, pulling out all the stops, and unfettered by slickness, Presley's
instinctive crowd control kept the mob just short of open riot – though
females continued to shriek and faint in defiance of their boyfriends'
sporadic barracking. Well before the first encore, all had tuned into the
new sensation and his backing trio's primeval rowdiness, unhinged go-
man-go sorcery and contagious backbeat.

Even those who heckled were tacitly sick of the corny stardust-and-
roses monotony they still had to endure at graduation balls, village hops
and other parched occasions supervised by grown-ups to keep them off the
streets. Let's dance – not hoedown or strict-tempo – let's rock 'n' roll.
Let's get real, real gone for a change.

Meanwhile, in 1954 too, Bill Haley and the Comets, a paunchy
northern dance combo, got lucky with a clangorous version of Sonny Dae
and the Knights' R&B original, 'Rock Around The Clock'. They publi-
cized it and many soundalike follow-ups with knockabout onstage antics
which, so Bill implied in the media, were less a pleasure than a duty to
humour the teenagers. What with this 'rock' nonsense going so well, it'd
be bad business not to play up to it, wouldn't it?

Elvis would make no such apologies when his time came after he was
spotted by Colonel Tom Parker, then Hank Snow's manager, who cajoled
Sun Records into auctioning Presley's contract to the mightier RCA in
November 1955. A few months later, the twenty-one-year-old entrusted
himself formally to the Colonel for as long as he lived – and beyond. From
then on, 'Elvis occupied every minute of my time,' said Parker, 'and I
think he would have suffered had I signed anyone else.'

There remains bitter disagreement about the Colonel. Was he a simple
funfair barker dragged into a situation he couldn't resist or the 'biggest
con artist in the world' according to movie director Sam Katzman?
Endorsing the latter opinion was his ruthlessness, which chilled those
used to the record industry's traditional glibness. 'Don't criticize what

you can't understand,' Elvis once said in his manager's defence, 'You've never walked in that man's shoes.'

'Heartbreak Hotel', Presley's RCA debut, reached Number 1 in the Hot 100, and global success followed despite – or because of – adult condemnation of 'this unspeakably untalented, vulgar young entertainer' (as a television guide would describe him) after an appearance on *The Ed Sullivan Show*, which would only risk screening him from the waist up. In the UK, Methodist preacher (and jazz buff) Dr Donald Soper wondered 'how intelligent people can derive satisfaction from something which is emotionally embarrassing and intellectually ridiculous'. Of 'Heartbreak Hotel' too, the staid *New Musical Express* wrote, 'If you appreciate good singing, I don't suppose you'll manage to hear this disc all through.' What more did Elvis need to be the rage of teenage Britain?

Whilst engineering his boy's conquest of an international 'youth market', the Colonel's blunt stance on behalf of his best-selling client compelled RCA to yield to his every demand, such as granting him around eight per cent of monies from non-vinyl goods officially associated with Presley, and the distribution of one million pressings of every Elvis 45. This latter judgement proved correct because, whether it was the sulky crooning of 'Love Me Tender' or the elaborated rockabilly of 'Blue Suede Shoes', every release sold by the ton, giving the King and his investors a magnificent self-confidence about anything he said or did.

When he started making films, he proved a better actor than most pop vocalists who fancy themselves as cinema attractions. However, although the films were worthwhile exercises financially, the quality of his celluloid output deteriorated after 1958's *King Creole*, partly because his directors took to dashing off an Elvis vehicle in less than a month. Each one was a quasi-musical of cheery unreality generally more streamlined and vacuous than the one before – and there would be worrying periods when Presley's records inclined the same way.

Their intrinsic worth aside, the King's unprecedented triumphs were the tip of an iceberg that would rake in more cash than had ever been realized since Edison invented the phonograph. Everywhere the hunt was on for more Presleys; every territory in the free world seemed to have put forward a challenger to the throne. Off-the-cuff examples include France's Johnny Hallyday, Mickie Most from South Africa and Australia's Johnny O'Keefe. In England, it was Tommy Steele followed by Cliff Richard and then Billy Fury who donned the mantle of domestic Elvis – while Scotland tried briefly with Andy Stewart(!) before he donned a kilt to host BBC television's *White Heather Club*.

Needless to say, most of these generally innocuous 'answers' emanated from North America, where innumerable talent scouts thought that all that was required was hot-potato-in-the-mouth vocals, 'common' good looks and a lopsided smirk. Some considered Jerry Lee Lewis merely an Elvis who'd swapped piano for guitar. There were also female Presleys in Janis Martin and Wanda Jackson; black ones in Little Richard and Chuck Berry, and an instrumental one in Duane Eddy. After Carl Perkins – an unsexy one – came bespectacled Buddy Holly and, bespectacled *and* unsexy, Roy Orbison with his eldritch cry and misgivings about the uptempo rockers he was made to record by Sam Phillips. A pair of quiffed brothers called Everly could be seen by their handlers, Acuff-Rose, as two for the price of one, but the Capitol label thought that it too had snared an Elvis in rough-and-ready Gene Vincent – 'The Screaming End' – who came down to earth after his breakthrough with 'Be-Bop-A-Lula'.

For various reasons, Vincent, Berry, Lewis, Richard and other dyed-in-the-wool wild men became commercially unreliable by the early 1960s when pop was at its most harmless and ephemeral with insipidly handsome boys-next-door like Bobby Vee, Bobby Vinton and Bobby Rydell in the ascendant. Elvis, however, survived by catching the overall drift of the Bobby era with Italianesque ballads, lightweight tunes with saccharine lyrics and jaunty rhythms, and infrequent self-mocking rockers.

A 1958 religious/Christmas album had been, perhaps, the first indication that even Elvis intended to drop raucous rock 'n' roll and get on with 'quality' stuff like his idol Dean Martin did. A more precise turning point had been his obligatory two years in the US army, from which he was demobbed in 1960 as a sergeant and 'all-round entertainer', a taming epitomized by the back-slapping presence of Frank Sinatra's 'Rat Pack' on his homecoming television spectacular from Miami – one of his last appearances before vanishing into the wings for nigh on eight years.

All the outside world knew of him then was what they saw in those rotten films and heard in stories of much the same veracity as those about Howard Hughes. Like the Rolling Stones, Bob Dylan and Frank Zappa would in the 1970s, he was racking up far heftier sales in the decade after he'd made his most prominent mark. Whatever he got up to in the years left to him then was barely relevant.

Nonetheless, the myth-shrouded King returned to the concert platform whether the Colonel liked it or not, via a 1968 television special. With rock 'n' roll revival in the air, he wore black biker leathers and focused on his 1950s repertoire – with miming to a token syrupy ballad as the sole concession to Parker. Yet, if rejuvenated, Presley displayed little ardour for all but the most conservative post-Beatles rock culture. In an amazing and ramblingly respectful letter to President Nixon, he requested enrolment as a Federal Agent in order to fight 'The Hippie Element' but, unconscious of their hero's reactionary tendencies, members of the Beatles, Led Zeppelin and other outfits who typified all that he evidently detested would troop backstage to pay their respects to the Grand Old Man when he began touring once more.

Selling out, say, twenty-thousand-capacity Madison Square Garden, he'd crank out the good old good ones but his stock in trade was now mainly country-pop – 'Kentucky Rain', 'Sweet Caroline' *et al.* – and bursts of patriotism like 'American Trilogy' and just plain 'America'. Many were taped in grandiloquent but self-indulgent cabaret pageants in Las Vegas, where the last most people would ever see of him would be in the white garb of a rhinestoned cowboy *sans* stetson.

Prey to hypochondria, paranoia and obesity, the King was nearing the end of his reign. He died on 16 August 1977 – with no successor named either then or since.

SPENCER LEIGH

Contributors

ALAN CLAYSON has written biographies of George Harrison, Roy Orbison, Ringo Starr and Steve Winwood, a history of British beat groups and the book of the film, *Backbeat*. He is also a musician and a performing artist of some note. He contributes a fictional piece about growing up in the late fifties, and an item concerning Colonel Parker.

Every week SPENCER LEIGH talks to musicians on his BBC Radio Merseyside programme, *On the Beat*. Conversation often turns to Elvis and he presents a selection of the most poignant and pertinent comments.

PETE FRAME's rock family trees usually work through the numerous line-ups of groups like the Byrds or Fairport Convention. For *Aspects of Elvis*, he's researched a genealogy of the King which goes back 200 years and delves into his American Indian ancestry.

In the sixties, you couldn't be hipper than PETE BROWN. He has made albums with his bands, Piblokto and Battered Ornaments, and he wrote the lyrics to such Cream classics as 'Sunshine Of Your Love', 'White Room' and 'I Feel Free'. Pete and Phil Ryan released *Coals to Newcastle* in 1993 and Pete is producing an all-star tribute album to Peter Green.

As a sixteen-year-old, actor/musician TIM WHITNALL played one of the three Presleys in Jack Good's West End production *Elvis*, in 1977. (The others were Shakin' Stevens and P. J. Proby.) Tim has supplied voices for *Spitting Image* and been in numerous TV and stage shows, including the West End productions of *Good Rockin' Tonite!* and *The Rocky Horror Show*. He is the voice of Elvis singing 'The Wonder Of You' on the Bovril ad.

BILLY BLACKWOOD's father, James, was the leader of the famed Blackwood Brothers Quartet, a gospel group which the young Elvis Presley admired (and nearly joined!). Billy has his own ministry and he and his wife, Kristi, have performed in the UK.

BOB GROOM edited *Blues World* for several years and wrote a book, *The Blues Revival*, in 1971. He contributed to *The Blackwell Guide To Blues Records*, which was published in 1989. He writes about Elvis Presley's links to the blues, and is excited about noticing St Elvis Farm and the Preseli District in Wales.

OSSIE DALES's speciality is popular music before rock 'n' roll and he contributes to *In Tune* and *Mitchell Music*. Elvis's links to country music and the blues are well established, but Ossie points out that he loved pop hits just as much.

For twenty-five years, BRIAN GOLBEY has been amongst the UK's top country performers and he writes for *Country Music People*. As he experienced service life for himself, he was commissioned to write about Elvis Presley's time in the US army.

It is doubtful whether there is a more informed person on the subject of UK and US chart positions than BARRY LAZELL, who has contributed to several rock encyclopedias and chart books including *40 Years of NME Charts*.

PETER DOGGETT is the editor of *Record Collector* and, as a writer, rivals John Tobler for productivity. He has written books on Lou Reed and John Lennon and his perceptive analysis of Elvis's recordings reveals many unknown facts.

KEITH STRACHAN wrote Cliff Richard's Number 1 'Mistletoe and Wine' and was the musical director for the West End successes *Elvis* and *Good Rockin' Tonite!* As he has trained singers to sound like Elvis, he is ideally placed to discuss the magic of his voice.

Now a Canadian resident, JIM NEWCOMBE continues to write for UK rock 'n' roll and country publications. Jim knows the Jordanaires well and he offers a detailed analysis of their contribution to Elvis's records.

MORT SHUMAN and his partner Doc Pomus wrote many great songs for Elvis – 'A Mess Of Blues', 'Little Sister' and 'His Latest Flame'. Mort came to Europe in the sixties, became a star in his own right in France and then settled in London. He was working on his contribution to *Aspects of Elvis* when he died and the finished product may well have been different from what is published here.

One of the UK's top horror fiction writers is RAMSEY CAMPBELL and his stories are sometimes combined with his love of film. Here he considers Elvis Presley's ability as a film actor.

HOWARD COCKBURN is a regular contributor to the rock 'n' roll magazine *Now Dig This*. We couldn't believe our luck when we found a good writer who wanted to defend many of his film songs, but Howard makes some very valid points.

BILL HARRY was the editor of *Mersey Beat* and *Idols* and he compiled *The Ultimate Beatles Encyclopedia*, which Virgin published in 1992. His fascination with lists – and show-business gossip! – makes him the ideal writer to discuss Elvis Presley's girlfriends.

TONY BARROW is the Beatles' former press officer. He was one of the few outsiders present when Elvis Presley met the Beatles.

The Official Elvis Presley Fan Club in the UK is run by TODD SLAUGHTER. Here he discusses his dealings with Elvis and the club visits to America. Those wishing to find out more about the club should contact him at PO Box 4, Leicester LE3 5HY.

A fan's-eye view of Elvis is provided by MARIA DAVIES. She saw him on stage and lovingly remembers every detail.

Say it One Time for the Brokenhearted was a passionate study of 'the country side of Southern soul' by BARNEY HOSKYNS. Here he looks at Elvis's return to Memphis for some memorable sessions in 1969.

ALAN BLEASDALE wrote about Elvis Presley in *Are You Lonesome Tonight?*, in which Martin Shaw played the King. Because a play cannot realistically extend beyond two and a half hours, many notable scenes had to be dropped. Alan Bleasdale gives us one of his outtakes. Imagine you're Elvis, alone in a darkened room, and read it aloud.

ADRIAN HENRI is one of the UK's leading poets and painters, also making his own contribution to the rock world with Liverpool Scene and Grimms.

MARK HODKINSON was born in Crumpsall, Manchester, in 1965. He worked as a journalist on several daily newspapers before turning freelance in 1989. He has since written four rock biographies, on Marianne Faithfull, Prince, Simply Red and the Wedding Present. He is currently writing his first novel and is on the lookout for a good agent.

The wildly eccentric and lovable CHAS 'DR ROCK' WHITE has written extremely colourful, and yet official, biographies of Little Richard and Jerry Lee Lewis. His contribution to *Aspects of Elvis* stems from his research in Memphis.

Many of you will know FRED DELLAR from Fred Facts in the *NME*. He writes for *Vox* and has many books on rock and country music to his credit.

For many years PATRICK HUMPHRIES was a feature writer for *Melody Maker* and he can now be found in *Vox*. He has written biographies of Bob Dylan, Fairport Convention, Paul Simon and Bruce Springsteen.

JOHN TOBLER co-founded *ZigZag* magazine with Pete Frame and writes for numerous magazines, including *Country Music People* and *Folk Roots*. His unique reference work, *This Day in Rock*, was published in 1993 and an inspiring choice on his record label, The Road Goes On Forever, was Ralph McFell's *The Complete Alphabet Zoo*. John is a controversial writer and is not afraid to defend Albert Goldman.

BRYAN BIGGS is the director of the Bluecoat Art Gallery in Liverpool. He has made a study of Elvis in art and also looks at the Elvis postage stamp.

STEPHEN BARNARD wrote wittily and perceptively for the much-lamented *Let It Rock* magazine and he has written rock histories and encyclopedias. He has provided teaching material for the Open University and lectured at City University in London.

MIKE EVANS played saxophone for several Liverpool bands, including the Clayton Squares, Liverpool Scene and Deaf School, and he organized an exhibition and wrote a book on *The Art of the Beatles*.

One of the leading academic writers on popular music, SIMON FRITH is Professor of English at Strathclyde University.

SPENCER LEIGH

You Don't Have to Say
You Love Me

Over the years I've spoken to hundreds of people in the music business, both in conjunction with magazine articles and with programmes for BBC Radio Merseyside. Sometimes the musicians have had specific connections with Elvis Presley and sometimes I have simply asked them about Elvis because I wanted their views. Here are over 100 quotes, all of which I hope are entertaining and revealing.

(1) RONNIE HAWKINS (one of the wildest rock 'n' rollers): 'Before Elvis hit it big, a bunch of us – and Jerry Lee Lewis was among them – used to meet on Beale Street. We told him that he would never go anywhere with a name like Elvis Presley: he'd have to change it. In 1954, Elvis couldn't even spell Memphis: in 1957, he owned it.'

(2) SCOTTY MOORE (Elvis Presley's lead guitarist): 'I would meet Sam Phillips every day. We would have coffee and discuss the business overall. His secretary said, "What about that boy who came in and did the acetate for his mother?" Sam told me to ask him over to my house to see what I thought before we took him into the studio. He came over to my house and he sang Eddy Arnold, Al Hibbler, pop, country, blues, stuff he had learned off the radio. Bill Black, who lived down the street from me, came over too, and we told Sam that he had a nice voice and could sing anything he wanted. Sam set up recording sessions at night 'cause Bill and I had day jobs. We were there to provide background music, just to see what his voice would sound like on tape, and tape hadn't been around that long. This was an audition and that was why the whole band didn't go in – it was just three of us. We tried anything anybody could think of and that he knew the words to, songs like "Blue Moon", and then after a couple of days, we came up with "That's All Right, Mama", by chance, by luck if you will, but Elvis heard it and knew he'd got something. It's refreshing to hear it now. It's so simple,

there's no production to speak of and it's just three guys doing the best that they could.'

(3) PAUL McCARTNEY: 'When I first heard Elvis's records, I had no idea what the roots of songs like "Milkcow Blues Boogie" were. For some time, I assumed that he'd written them himself. Then I found out it was the black guys like Arthur "Big Boy" Crudup.'

(4) SLEEPY LaBEEF (rockabilly performer since 1956): 'I loved the real, get-down-and-get-it, freight-train sound of Elvis on Sun Records. He got the beat from the old southern gospel songs and the only thing that was different was the lyrics. I'd had the same experience of singing in the southern churches, and they really put their body and soul into what they're doing.'

(5) B. B. KING: 'I saw Elvis at Sam Phillips' studio and he sounded very country to me. He didn't sound black to me at all.'

(6) SLIM WHITMAN: 'I'd heard "Blue Moon Of Kentucky" but all I really knew was that a fellow called Elvis Presley was going to be on the show. I could hear he was doing well so I went into the wings and I could see he had his own way of doing things. When he first came to Louisiana, he was singing to the same people that we were singing to, but the news got around and the teenyboppers started coming.'

(7) HANK SNOW (Canada's top country artist, writer of 'I'm Moving On'): 'Tom Parker suggested that we opened a booking agency together. We called it Jamboree Attractions and Hank Snow Enterprises, and he said to me, "I know a young feller who is working in Texas called Elvis Presley. He is tearing the hearts out of the teenagers in those clubs. We ought to bring him to the Grand Ole Opry." He did "Blue Moon Of Kentucky" on my late show on the Opry, but he didn't disturb the audience very much. They didn't understand what he was doing and he went away very discouraged. That was the only time he was ever on the Opry.'

(8) D. J. FONTANA (Elvis's drummer): 'When Elvis came on the Louisiana Hayride, he looked stranger than most with his purple shirt and sideburns, ducktail and greasy stuff. He was a good-looking kid and he had a charisma about him, but he didn't do too well the first time because it was a country-orientated older crowd. They saw him running across the

stage and decided he was a nut, but after a couple of weeks, they were telling their kids, "You gotta see this boy". The crowd changed completely – we got the young kids coming in and that helped him a lot.'

(9) MARTY WILDE: 'There's a wonderful album with him doing "Tweedle Dee" and "Maybellene" on the Louisiana Hayride. The magic aura comes across and you can tell that he desperately wants success. It's absolutely impossible to keep that fire in your belly all the time, and it's no surprise that he lost the buzz by the time he had got out of the army.'

(10) SLEEPY LaBEEF: 'Elvis was performing one night with Scotty and Bill – it was before D. J. Fontana came along with the drums – and it was dependent upon Elvis playing rhythm guitar while Scotty played lead and Bill the upright bass. He broke some strings on his guitar and he called to the wings for another. His reputation as to how he would work a guitar over had preceded him, so George Jones told him where to go, he wasn't borrowing his guitar. My wife was very tenderhearted and she lent him my guitar. He scratched it up and defaced it. If I'd known how big he was going to be, I would have kept the guitar, but I sold it for $90, and, even then, I only collected $50 of it.'

(11) WANDA JACKSON (country and rock 'n' roll performer): 'I wrote to my cousins who lived in the southwestern part of Texas that I would be working with Webb Pierce and someone called Elvis Presley. They wrote right back, they couldn't believe it, could they get backstage and meet him. Because I'm female, I was just like the rest of his fans. He was so great, he was so dynamic and he had such charisma. We dated for a little while and we became very good friends. Elvis never commented on my version of "Let's Have A Party" but it was his idea that I should start recording rock 'n' roll. It must be about the greatest rockabilly-type song that has ever been written. Even today, it really thrills people.'

(12) BRENDAN CROKER (Bradford singer/songwriter): 'Who in England would have said "Baby let's play house"? It's American language at its best and a beautiful description of a future sexual relationship.'

(13) BARNEY KESSEL (top jazz guitarist): 'Elvis Presley was an entertainer and he was really selling sex. He gained attention through being a white man who was able to emulate the body movements and the singing

of black artists. Also, he was extremely handsome and many women were attracted to his masculinity. What he did he did very well, but very little of it was original. This has led to a lot of other people doing the same, and the latest is Bruce Springsteen. He puts a bandana on his head and screams "Born In The USA" but I wouldn't walk across the street to see him. He's not my idea of a Boss. He's doing Elvis Presley, and so are Rod Stewart and a lot of others. Elvis Presley is doing the black artists, so people are responding to the third or fourth carbon copy of a letter, rather than the original.'

(14) JOE BROWN: 'The Sun records are amazing 'cause it comes straight from the heart. You can hear it, it's straight from the heart onto tape and that's the end of it. No highfalutin producer has got his greasy hands on it and mucked it around.'

(15) CHARLIE FEATHERS (Sun recording artist): 'Stan Kesler had a tune that he wanted me to show Elvis, "You Believe Everyone But Me", but I didn't think it was suitable. He then mentioned the title, "I Forgot To Remember To Forget", but he didn't have anything else on it. I said, "Man, that's an unusual title. Let's get on this song." We put it on a home recorder and took it to Sam Phillips, and he didn't like it at all. I took it on up to Elvis and he said, "You'll never write a song as good as this again."'

(16) RAY SAWYER (of Dr Hook): 'Elvis was the first country rocker. They booked him into a big honky tonk in Mobile, Alabama, and he was supposed to start at eight o'clock, but it was ten o'clock and he still wasn't there. Everybody was getting mad and cussing, and then a pink Cadillac pulls up at the front and everyone ran to the door. Scotty and Bill were in the front, and Elvis got out with a pink coat and that look that he had. Bill and Scotty went straight to the stage; all they had was one amp 'cause Elvis didn't play through an amp – he played acoustic guitar and Bill played upright bass. As they got ready, Elvis went back and forth through the audience, didn't say nothing, just walking, looking at people, 'cause this was before the people went nuts. He only had a few records out – "That's All Right, Mama", "Mystery Train" and "I Forgot To Remember To Forget", which was a country hit. Everything he did came from black music – Fats Domino and Joe Turner, "Shake Rattle And Roll"

and "Flip, Flop And Fly". We knew he was something special. I was nineteen years old and a drummer at the time, and he came to the end of the bar and ordered a beer and put a cigar in his mouth. He was only two people away from me, and I wanted to say, "Hey, man, do you need a drummer?" I often wonder what would have happened if I'd asked him. He might have said, "Yeah, boy, let's go."'

(17) D. J. FONTANA: 'Elvis had some shows in East Texas, which was only 100 miles away from Shreveport and the Hayride, and he asked me to play drums. He kept giving me work when they could afford someone else. They weren't making much money. I was the highest paid guy in the band at the time. I was getting $100 a week: they had to pay for the transportation and the rooms and they were splitting the rest three ways. Elvis, Scotty and Bill often didn't have anything left and I'd be loaning them ten bucks. It was that tight.'

(18) TOMMY COLLINS (witty country performer): 'In Jacksonville, Florida, someone had built a stage at the home place of the baseball team, the Diamonds, and the show was headlined by Andy Griffith with Ferlin Husky, Marty Robbins and myself. When Elvis performed, people started coming in from the bleachers and they were going crazy, they were trying to tear his clothes off. Andy Griffith said, in his North Carolina drawl, "It's an orgy", and even Colonel Parker was not prepared for this reaction. There was very little security, very few policemen, and I remember one woman who was in her forties trying to tear one of Elvis's shoes off, Colonel Parker just picked Elvis up, put him on his shoulder and started knocking his way through the crowd to get him to safety.'

(19) SONNY CURTIS (singer/songwriter, contemporary of Buddy Holly): 'He was wild, man, he was something else. I couldn't believe my eyes. There was so much magnetism there. We all just freaked and we all fell immediately in love with Elvis. Buddy Holly, in particular, fell in love with Elvis's style and the day after Elvis left we started playing his music. Buddy played the part of Elvis, and I was Scotty. I already had a Chet Atkins style, which is roughly what Scotty Moore was doing. That's where you employ the thumb to play the rhythm, and you play the melody with the fingers. You have rhythm and melody going at the same time, and so one guitar player can sound like two.'

(20) MARSHALL LYTLE (of Bill Haley's Comets): 'We did a show with Elvis Presley in Tulsa, Oklahoma. The newspaper said, "Appearing in person, Bill Haley and the Comets, the stars of 'Rock Around The Clock' "', with our photograph, and at the bottom of the ad it said, in small print, "Also appearing, Elvis Presley". He was a most down-to-earth young man with tremendous respect. He asked Bill if he could sing with us and Bill let him. Bill was very generous about sharing the stage with him.'

(21) PAT BOONE: 'We were two Tennessee boys and the first time we met he was my supporting act in Cleveland, Ohio. The industry people thought he was going to be a star, and I'd heard one of his records, (sings) "Blue moon of Kentucky keep on shinin' " on a country jukebox in Texas. He didn't sound like a rock 'n' roller to me, so I thought the promoter, a disc jockey called Bill Randle, had really missed this time. He went on ahead of me. He was shy until he got on stage, and then he just exploded. At first, the Cleveland high-school kids didn't know what to make of him with his turned-up collar and his long, greasy hair swooped down on his forehead. He looked like a guy that would be on a motorcycle or from the poor part of town. He'd sing his song and say, in a hillbilly twang, "Thank you very much and now I'd like to do another number for you . . .", and these kids would be covering their mouths and snickering. But when he began to sing again there was an electricity about it. They liked him very much and I had to follow him. I might have had a hard time with my narrow tie, little button-down shirt and white buck shoes, but I'd had a couple of hit records.'

(22) HANK SNOW: 'He was a good Christian boy, he didn't smoke, he didn't drink and he was very, very polite – a great example of the good, true, honest American boy. He and my son Jimmie were about the same age, so they would chum around together. He would sit in my home and play the piano and sing songs, just another great kid. We did several tours together and I could see he was headed for stardom. Regardless of any stories you may have heard or read, I was responsible for Elvis Presley getting his RCA Victor contract.'

(23) CHET ATKINS (top country guitarist): 'Steve Sholes conducted the buyout from Sun, and he was very smart as he bought all the masters. He

didn't get the demo of "My Happiness" but he didn't know about it at the time. He called me after he had got the contract and said that he was going to record Elvis and he wanted me to get a band together, which I did. We kept Scotty and Bill, as they gave him his sound, and we added Floyd Cramer, myself and a few others, along with a vocal group which was a couple of the Jordanaires and a couple of guys from another group. We went and recorded in the afternoon with Elvis on a couple of different sessions. I worked with Elvis quite a lot but I checked out when he went to recording at night, like from midnight to seven. I had to work during the day, and I couldn't afford to stay up all night.'

(24) CHARLIE FEATHERS: 'The Elvis that I knew died in '55. RCA didn't know how to record Elvis. "Heartbreak Hotel" sounds bad compared to anything he did at Sun. You listen to "Heartbreak Hotel" next to "Mystery Train", oh lordy, no. I wish you could have seen Elvis with Scotty and Bill: the band he had when he died was just a dime-a-dozen band.'

(25) CHARLIE LOUVIN: 'The show starred the Louvin Brothers and Elvis was one of the ". . . and many others". He was a good kid, but when he was on stage he got carried away and caught up in his music. I don't blame him for that – he pleased a lot of people.'

(26) TOM PAXTON: 'I was a student at the University of Oklahoma in the spring of '56 when Elvis was exploding. He came to Oklahoma City. The hall seated 5000 and he did two shows, totally sold out. Elvis was so new that the promoters didn't know what he was and so the entire supporting bill was of country and western acts, and I mean hard-core country and western. Hank Locklin was one of the artists. Well, nobody suffered the fate that these poor people suffered. They were playing to 5000 kids who wanted Elvis and nothing but Elvis, and it was simply awful for them. When Elvis came out, it was something that I'll never forget. The place went spare and what fascinates me in these days of sonic overkill, where the mistaken belief is that loud equals exciting, is that Elvis Presley's entire gear consisted of one microphone for his voice and none for his guitar. The Jordanaires had one microphone between the four of them, the standing bass had a microphone, the guitar player had a little suitcase amp, and the drums had no microphone at all. Elvis's mike was

through the PA and that was it, twenty-five watts or something like that, but, you know, it was adequate. He was so exciting even though you could only hear him in the odd seconds when the screams died down. It was an amazing performance, just fantastic.'

(27) CHARLIE LOUVIN: 'The first week we let him open, but the second week, after he had been on the Dorsey Brothers' TV show in New York, he was becoming a phenomenon. From the second week, there was just one big glittering sign from one side of the stage to the other that simply said, "E-L-V-I-S". They even dropped the name "Presley", and from that point on, nobody could follow him – you did good even to get through your show. His management got lots of kids to scream "WE WANT ELVIS!" from the start of the show until he came on. If you put a great performer with an extremely smart manager, you've got a winning combination. I knew Colonel Parker well. He would sell his mother if it would advance his artist: there was nothing that he wouldn't do to advance his artist. He wanted to make $50,000 a week from an artist, and if you couldn't make that, he didn't want to mess with you.'

(28) ALBERT GOLDMAN (author of *Elvis* and *Elvis: The Last 24 Hours*): 'I would say that Elvis would have made precisely the same impact with any competent manager. With an imaginative and innovative manager, he might have made an even greater impact and he certainly might have maintained higher-quality standards for his work.'

(29) TENNESSEE ERNIE FORD: 'I knew Tom Parker because he managed Eddy Arnold, who was known as the Singing Plowboy. Tom took Elvis and started that body motion and made it into a tremendous thing. I liked most of the things that he did, and he made great things out of "Heartbreak Hotel". Nobody can do that song like Elvis. It's like "It Was A Very Good Year" – you don't want to hear anybody else do it but Frank Sinatra.'

(30) GUY MITCHELL: 'When rock 'n' roll started, it was just uptempo country and western music. Elvis Presley, God rest his soul, sang country with a beat. I'll give you an example. Twenty-five years before Elvis, Ernest Tubb was singing (sings) "If you love your mama and you treat her right/But she keeps on hollering at you every day and night/She's going to

travel on you/They do it every time." Now listen. (Sings the first verse of 'Heartbreak Hotel'.) The arithmetic of the song is the same, right. You can't write four bars of music that you can't find someplace else, although I know "You ain't nothin' but a hound dog" isn't the kind of song Fred Astaire would sing to Audrey Hepburn.'

(31) TOMMY STEELE: 'The excess use of echo on "Heartbreak Hotel" gives you an idea of how primitive our music was then. We had to rely on atmosphere and this is a typical example. Some engineer decided to give it quality and atmosphere with this newfangled thing called echo. It sounds very amusing now.'

(32) CHET ATKINS: 'There's a lot of echo on "Heartbreak Hotel" but we weren't trying to be innovative, we were just trying to do our jobs. Really, we were trying to duplicate the sound that he had gotten on Sun Records. They probably used an Ampex tape machine. We had some old hand-built RCA machines and the playback head was at a different distance from the record head, which gives you the speed of the reverb.'

(33) SCOTTY MOORE: ' "Heartbreak Hotel" was a little different to what we were used to. It was a larger studio than Sun's and more regimented – they called everything by a take number and we weren't used to that at all. We would sit around at Sun, eat hamburgers and then somebody would say, "Let's try something". Sam used tape echo to make it sound like there were more of us than there really was, to give it a fullness. He also kept Elvis's voice close to the music, treating it like another instrument, and at that time the vocal on country and pop records was normally far out in front. RCA kept it that way, although he was more out in front on the ballads. Elvis liked it Sam's way: he kept saying, "Don't make me too loud, keep me back." '

(34) ALBERT GOLDMAN: "Heartbreak Hotel", which is an extravagant and highly exaggerated account of the blues, was more a psychodrama than a musical performance. As such, however, it was an extraordinary novelty and it moved rock music into another imaginative space. Had Elvis been able to continue in that genre, he could have been counted as one of the great creative forces of rock 'n' roll, rather than just its master image.'

(35) TONY CRANE (of the Merseybeats): 'The reason I like the early Elvis records is because the sound is so raw and so live. There were just a couple of mikes set up in the studio and he always sang live with the band. You couldn't make a record like "Hound Dog" with thirty-two tracks.'

(36) D. J. FONTANA: 'We were booked for two weeks in Las Vegas but we only did a week. We were opening for Freddy Martin and the stage show was "Oklahoma!". The people were eating $50 steaks and they didn't want to hear guitars and a loud set of drums, they wanted "Oklahoma!". The management said it was better if we left, but we heard "Hound Dog" in Las Vegas. Freddie Bell and the Bellboys were doing it in their act and we caught them every night for a week so that we could learn it. We copied his arrangement note for note and I guess Freddie Bell is still not too pleased about it.'

(37) JOHN STEWART (formerly with the Kingston Trio): 'I saw Elvis Presley at the Pan Pacific Auditorium in LA and that was right when "Hound Dog" was out. He still had the stand-up bass and the Jordanaires, and it was unbelievable. I was shaken by the concert. I had never seen anything like that in my life. There was so much energy coming from the stage, his voice was so strong and he was having so much fun.'

(38) TOWNES VAN ZANDT (singer/songwriter): 'Seeing Elvis Presley on *The Ed Sullivan Show* was the starting point for me becoming a guitar player. My sister had two or three of her girlfriends over to watch it, and they were screaming. I was a little kid, barely allowed in the room. I just thought that Elvis had all the money in the world, all the Cadillacs and all the girls, and all he did was play the guitar and sing. That made a big impression on me.'

(39) PAUL GAMBACCINI: 'Ed Sullivan is a key figure in American television history, although he was stiff. The guy had formaldehyde in his veins. Nowadays, they would not employ someone who is as physically unattractive and as vocally wooden as Ed Sullivan, but it is people like that who are distinctive. Look at Patrick Moore. If Patrick Moore was new, they wouldn't have him on, but he became famous in the days when they didn't have experienced television presenters who were also astronomers. He has personality and uniqueness, and Ed Sullivan was the same.

He had Bo Diddley on his show once and he was absolutely appalled in rehearsal when he saw him doing a song called "Bo Diddley". He said, "How can you sing a song where you mention your own name all the time?" and he told him to sing "Some Enchanted Evening" instead. Comes the live broadcast and Bo Diddley starts to play "Some Enchanted Evening" but in the middle he breaks into "Bo Diddley". Ed Sullivan is furious. He says, "I will never, ever have rock 'n' roll on my show again." Steve Allen, his competitor on NBC, signs Elvis, and Ed Sullivan realizes that he has to use Elvis in such a way that he will make the headlines, and take the momentum away from Steve Allen. The whole myth of Elvis being too sexy to be shot from the waist down was just Ed Sullivan's way of getting ratings. However, Ed Sullivan was very important for Elvis's career because there had been talk of him being this untamed sex object. Ed Sullivan put his hand on his shoulder and gave him a seal of approval. He said, "I want America to know that this is a good boy. This is a talented young boy." It was the seal of approval for him.'

(40) GORDON PAYNE (now with the Crickets): 'All week long there was talk in the paper about how Ed Sullivan didn't want him showing the lower half of his body. There was a lot of hoop-la about him being lewd and obscene, so it was really exciting to wait until that night when we saw him live. My whole family was sitting around the TV and my dad was saying, "That stuff will never sell" at first, but then he started tapping his foot and saying, "Hey, the guy's pretty good".'

(41) BEN HEWITT (Mercury rock 'n' roll performer): 'I saw Elvis at the Buffalo Auditorium and I had a seat about ten rows from the stage. I never heard him. From the time that Scotty Moore, Bill Black and D. J. Fontana walked out on that stage, I never heard a word. Maybe they were just up there going through the motions because I don't think anybody heard them. It was one continuous scream for the whole thirty minutes. I saw his mouth move and I saw the band's fingers working but you never heard the music.'

(42) WALLY RIDLEY (EMI record producer): 'RCA Victor sent me everything they released in America in the pop or country and western fields, and my job was to decide what should be released here on HMV. Steve Sholes, who was a real sweetheart of a feller, wrote to me one day

and said, "I'm sending you six sides. You won't understand a word but do yourself a favour and release two of them because this man is going to be very, very big indeed." He underlined the last words. I listened to the six sides and he was right, I didn't understand a word. I poked my ear into the set, I turned it up, I turned it down, nothing – the only two words I could make out on one of them was "Heartbreak Hotel". I released it and HMV got the worst reviews it had ever had for a record – the chief wanted to sack me for releasing it. Radio Luxembourg wouldn't play it and nor would the BBC. Jack Payne wrote half a page for the *Daily Express* saying, "How dare they release such rubbish".'

(43) TERRY DENE (early British rock 'n' roller): 'I was working as a record packer at the HMV shop, and every morning we used to listen to the new records. I saw the label with Elvis Presley's name on it and I thought, "What a strange name. I wonder if I'm pronouncing it right." We played "Heartbreak Hotel" over and over every morning until the management told us that we had to stop. I'd never seen a photograph of him, I didn't know whether he was black or white, but I knew he sounded great.'

(44) WEE WILLIE HARRIS (British rock 'n' roll eccentric): 'I used to go to a record stall down the market in Bermondsey. I was standing there one day when, all of a sudden, I heard this record – (sings) "Well, since my baby left me/I found a new place to dwell" – all very high-pitched. I thought it was Johnnie Ray with a new song but the guy said it was Elvis Presley. I said, "I like that. I'll buy it."'

(45) WALLY RIDLEY: 'Eventually, I got a call from Pat Doncaster at the *Daily Mirror*. He said, "We're doing a double-page spread about Elvis Presley." I said, "I hope it sells the record because nothing has happened so far." It did, and it was the first time that a record had sold because of the written word.'

(46) SCREAMIN' LORD SUTCH: 'I was young and wanted to get involved in rock 'n' roll, but Bill Haley didn't have the right image for me. As soon as I saw a photograph of Elvis Presley, I said, "That's it, that's the way I want to do it, just look at his hairstyle." He was amazing.'

(47) MARTY WILDE: 'There was a certain amount of excitement in skiffle music, but rock 'n' roll had a fire in its belly and some kind of

meaning. A lot of skiffle hits were silly songs that didn't make any sense – not that the early rock 'n' .oll hits were much better, but there was much more honesty and guts in "That's All Right, Mama" and "My Baby Left Me".'

(48) MARTIN CARTHY (British folksinger): 'I was fourteen or fifteen when rock 'n' roll came along, the sort of age where something is either going to leave you stone cold or knock you over – and it knocked me over. When I look back on Bill Haley, Lonnie Donegan, Elvis Presley and Gene Vincent now, I can see that rock 'n' roll and skiffle represented something very important – the idea that ordinary people could make music. For the first time, you didn't have to be a trained musician to make music.'

(49) PAUL McCARTNEY: 'There's much more glamour when someone's not from your country. Elvis was really glamorous to me, but I don't suppose he was glamorous to the people of Memphis at all.'

(50) PAT BOONE: 'Elvis and I were supposedly rivals, but that was not our doing – it was the record companies and the media. We came from the same state and had similar backgrounds, but he was the rebel and I was the conformist. We often appealed to the same fans but for different reasons.'

(51) DAVEY GRAHAM (British folk guitarist): 'By the time of *Love Me Tender*, Elvis was already going to the dogs. If he had wound up with Count Basie singing the blues, he wouldn't have expressed his sex appeal so broadly but he would have been a very good blues singer. His voice easily outstripped Joe Turner's, and I think he would have been the best there has ever been.'

(52) SCOTTY MOORE: 'We had gone through "Too Much" a couple of times: I had the solo down and it was in a strange key for a guitar. Elvis thought he could do it better and when we did it again I got lost, but we didn't stop playing. We didn't have multi-tracking and as we couldn't re-do a solo, I just kept going and somehow managed to come out at the letter A as I was supposed to. When Elvis heard the playback, he turned to me with a little smirk on his face and said, "You're gonna have to live with that for the rest of your life." He really liked that cut and he didn't choose it to annoy me.'

(53) GUS GOODWIN (presenter of *Rockabilly Party* on Radio Luxembourg): 'I've two favourite Elvis records. I just love the raunchy opening on "One Night" – you're hooked right away – and "All Shook Up", which just bounced along – really, that is rock 'n' roll.'

(54) DON BLACK (lyricist of 'Born Free', 'Love Changes Everything'): 'With anything good in the arts, it is truth and honesty that are important as opposed to the veneer and the glitz. I regard Bing Crosby's "True Love" and Elvis Presley's "Loving You" in the same way – it's an outpouring, a release of genuine feeling, and it comes from the heart.'

(55) WALLY RIDLEY: 'I never thought that Elvis Presley was a very good singer. He's a good deliverer in his own field, but that's a very different thing. Bing Crosby could mould and shape a note, he could hold a phrase and make it matter, and you'd have to go a long way before you find that in Presley. It's there occasionally but it's there by accident, rather than by design.'

(56) ALEXEI SAYLE: 'Elvis is incredible. He had enormous ability, and when you see those old films there's an incredible presence about him. Apart from anything else, he's so rude. The early Elvis with his sinuous hips is filthy, filthy but brilliant.'

(57) HANK SNOW: ' "A Fool Such As I" is one of my all-time favourite songs, and I hope I might have influenced Elvis on recording that song. I don't mean to brag but Elvis was a big fan of mine and he was always sitting around singing my songs, which tickled me to death. Maybe he heard my version of "A Fool Such As I".'

(58) DAVE MARSH (journalist and author): 'The implication of "Jailhouse Rock" is homosexuality. Number 47 says to Number 3 that he's "the cutest jailbird that I ever did see". As prisoners are segregated by sex, they must both be fellers. It's a joke and I think Elvis knew what was going on.'

(59) BOBBY VINTON: 'I used to sing Elvis's songs in my band, but it was the film of *Jailhouse Rock* that really impressed me. In that film, he starts his own record label and presses the copies up. That was a really neat idea and I wanted to do the same.'

(60) CHET ATKINS: 'Colonel Parker wouldn't allow anyone to be listed as Elvis Presley's producer. I certainly helped out but Steve Sholes was really the producer. He was a great man and I would never want to take any credit away from him. At first, we had quite a bit of input into what he would record. We could play songs for Elvis and he would say, "Yeah, I like that," and it was a great thrill when he did a song of mine, "How's The World Treating You?". Then, his publishing company got in on the act. Freddie Bienstock would come down with a lot of Hill and Range songs. He would play them on the phonograph and Elvis would say, "I like that" or "I don't like that". Then we would record the ones he selected.'

(61) BEN HEWITT: 'Clyde Otis asked me to do a demo for Elvis. We kept playing 'Doncha Think It's Time" in different keys until we found one where I sounded like Elvis, the band sounded like Elvis's recording band, and the vocal group sounded like the Jordanaires. That way, when Elvis heard it, he would more or less hear himself doing it, and it worked: Elvis recorded the song.'

(62) CHET ATKINS: 'He used to come in all the time with clippings from the newspapers. He was laughing about them because most of the time they were incorrect. A lot of the big-time gossip columnists didn't like him and made fun of him. He laughed at that but I'm sure it hurt him too.'

(63) TREVOR PEACOCK (scriptwriter, *6.5 Special*): 'I always remember Jack Good ringing up Colonel Parker, trying to get Elvis to appear on *6.5 Special*. They agreed some huge figure like £10,000, which today would be £100,000 and was, of course, totally unpayable. Jack said, "All right, ten thousand," and Parker replied, "Well, that's my cut. Now, regarding the fee for the boy himself . . ." It was a quarter of a million for one appearance, which was totally crazy. So, Elvis never did anything over here.'

(64) CHET ATKINS: 'Mr Sholes was aware of a lot of the old ballads with recitations, but I think Elvis had the idea to do "Are You Lonesome Tonight?" We recorded it at two o'clock in the morning and we turned the lights down low to get a good mood. It was very exciting when we did it. We all knew that he had cut a smash.'

(65) DOC POMUS (songwriter, often with Mort Shuman): ' "Surrender" was an assignment from Elvis Presley. It was the only time that he gave us an exact assignment. Following "It's Now Or Never", which was based on "O Sole Mio", he wanted something based on "Come Back To Sorrento". I thought that "Sorrento" sounded like "Surrender" so it worked out very well.'

(66) PAT BOONE: 'The album *Pat Boone Sings Guess Who* was done as a tribute to Elvis because I wanted to sing some of his songs, although I didn't want to do them exactly how he did them. I told the Colonel that I was going to make an album of Elvis's hits and that it was going to be called *Pat Sings Elvis*. He said, "Well, we'd better talk about the royalty." I said, "Royalty? Oh, we'll be paying the royalties to the songwriters." He said, "No, you've gotta pay a royalty to Elvis if you use his name." I said, "You're kidding. He publishes most of these songs. He's going to make a lot of money off this album anyway and, besides, it's a tribute." Colonel Parker didn't buy that. He said, "You're using his name. That's going to sell records, so you'll have to pay a royalty." I thought about it and then I decided to call it *Pat Boone Sings Guess Who*, and we never used his name once.'

(67) JERRY LORDAN (writer 'Apache', 'Wonderful Land'): 'Elvis Presley missed out on a lot of fine, original material because of cupidity on the part of his representatives. They thought that Elvis should be in on the songwriting royalties, and many songwriters regarded 50 per cent of something as better than 100 per cent of nothing. I think that it is totally wrong and so Elvis would never have had one of my songs.'

(68) BUNNY LEWIS (UK songwriter and manager): 'I met Elvis in Hollywood when he was recording the score to some ghastly film for Hal Wallis. I said to someone who worked for Colonel Parker, "I'm very impressed with Elvis in the recording studio because he knows just what he wants, but the songs are awful rubbish." I was told that was how it had to be as the Colonel took slices of the royalties and many writers wouldn't accept that. He didn't just want the publishing, which was a foregone conclusion, but half of the writer's royalties as well. I said, "Is there any chance of me writing a song for Elvis?", and as they said yes, I thought of his capabilities and what brought out the best in his voice. It was "The Girl Of My Best Friend", which was released as a B-side, but

the American jocks turned it over and made it a hit. That was just fortuitous.'

(69) BARNEY KESSEL: 'He had an unusual deal, which Colonel Parker had set up, in that although he worked exclusively for RCA Victor on record, he had two non-exclusive contracts to make motion pictures. He had one with MGM and another with Paramount. Instead of being exclusively with one studio, he guaranteed to make a certain number of movies within a certain time, but that didn't prevent him from doing something for someone else.'

(70) ALBERT GOLDMAN: 'Elvis had no say in the movies he appeared in, any more than he had a say in any other major decision in his career. He would get a script, he would examine it, he would be appalled by it, he would make devastating statements about it, and then he would go out and do it. There you have the essential Elvis Presley – he was a mule pulling a plough.'

(71) JOHN PHILLIPS (of the Mamas and the Papas): 'Elvis took me outside by his swimming pool. He said, "Look at the lawn, John." I said, "Very nice, Elvis." He said, "Know what it is? It's Astroturf. You never have to cut it." I said, "Very nice, Elvis."'

(72) VIV STANSHALL (formerly with the Bonzo Dog Band): 'Elvis Presley, Little Richard, Gracie Fields and Noel Coward are my strongest influences, and I recently recorded "No Room To Rhumba In A Sports Car". It comes from *Fun In Acapulco*, and you can't imagine such unfun in Acapulco. I mucked around with it and wrote new verses, but the song is absolute trash. I wonder what persuaded him to do that.'

(73) DOC POMUS: 'I thought some of his films were marvellous. I loved *Viva Las Vegas*, and *Wild In The Country* was very interesting. Okay, a lot weren't up to par but that's how it is with people who are singer/actors rather than actor/singers, you know, the motion picture becomes a vehicle for the singing.'

(74) BARNEY KESSEL: 'He was a very nice young man, who knew his manners. He had a problem in relating to people outside of his circle, which is why he kept an entourage from Memphis with him – he kept musicians he had worked with and he needed his home folks to feel good.

They felt strange at being in Hollywood, a very sophisticated town and far removed from their own natural settings. Elvis himself had very simple tastes: he would never have gone into a French restaurant. He liked fast, takeaway food. He used to drop peanuts into his Coca-Cola and he ate candy bars.'

(75) PETER NOONE (Herman of Herman's Hermits): 'I tried very hard to meet Elvis and I talked Colonel Parker into letting me meet him. I interviewed him at a press conference but it was a horrible interview: I'd cringe if I heard it now. Elvis was really nice and on his last tour, he sat down at the piano in Boston and played a bit of "Mrs Brown, You've Got A Lovely Daughter". He said, "That was written by a friend of mine", although I hadn't written it and I'd only met him once.'

(76) COLIN McCOURT (UK songwriter): 'I love everything Elvis did apart from the really rotten songs. Being a songwriter myself, I would love to know how some of those songs came to be recorded. I can't imagine someone saying to his producer, "I've got this song, 'Rotten Old Dog' or 'Song Of The Shrimp', and I think Elvis should record it." He had the pick of every songwriter in the world, so why did he record them? I was with Roger Greenaway when he got a call saying Elvis would record one of his songs if he could have the publishing on it. Roger said, "No", so there is more to it than just the song itself.'

(77) SCOTTY MOORE: 'The last time I worked with Elvis was in '68, which was also the last time I saw him. He'd been in the movies for so long, he hadn't done any concerts or television and so he really enjoyed making that TV special. He loved the people he worked with, he loved the crowds and he loved being back on stage. During that special, we had dinner at his house and he asked us to back him on a European tour. He'd been in Germany, he'd been in Paris, he liked the people and he wanted to go back. He really wanted to do it, but it never happened as he got caught up in Vegas. I can vouch 100 per cent that Elvis wanted to come to Britain. What happened then I don't know: I guess management and the bottom line stopped him.'

(78) GREIL MARCUS (author, *Lipstick Traces*, *Mystery Train*, *Dead Elvis*): 'The TV special was the first time he had performed in front of a live audience in nine years and you can see very clearly how nervous he

was, how uncertain he was, how scared he was, how he wasn't sure if he still had anything to offer people, but as the performance unfolded, he went from being tentative to singing with more passion and more life than he had ever sung before or since. I like "Tryin' To Get To You" and sometimes I like "One Night" even more than that.'

(79) D. J. FONTANA: 'The stage may look pretty big on that TV special, but it wasn't. They were having trouble with the cameras and the lights, and the hardware like my drums was reflecting off the cameras. It was one hassle after another, so Bones Howe said, "The drums are in the way, they're in the middle of everything, what can we do?" I said, "I'll play on the back of a guitarcase, who cares?" I'd done it before. That sound on "All Shook Up" is the back of a guitarcase, not a drum. I must've done about ten records like that.'

(80) JOHN STEWART: 'A friend of mine, John Wilkinson, was playing rhythm guitar for Elvis and he told me that Elvis used to sing "July, You're A Woman" in the dressing room before he went on stage. He never recorded it – and it would have been the high point of my life to have Elvis doing one of my songs – but the fact that he loved the song and sang it is enough for me.'

(81) LARRY GATLIN (country singer/songwriter): 'He was very nice to me. We sat together in his suite at the Hilton and we talked about philosophy and religion. He was very charismatic and I saw some wonderful shows. Later in his life when he was getting heavy, he was singing nearly as well but he didn't perform the way he did in Vegas. When I saw him, he was very healthy, keeping his body in shape and eating correctly, and he looked marvellous.'

(82) TOMMY ROE (American singer/songwriter who had a US Number 1 with 'Sheila' in 1962): 'When you met Elvis, the first thing you noticed about him was his looks. He had a charisma that you just couldn't imagine. He was off and on in his personality – sometimes he was very talkative and other times he wouldn't say very much. I think he was really a private guy.'

(83) JIMMY WEBB (songwriter, 'MacArthur Park', 'Up Up And Away', 'Wichita Lineman'): 'I used to go up and see Elvis all the time when I

was in my early twenties and he was at the Hilton International Hotel. I hung out with him a lot and got to know him quite a bit. Unless you have seen Elvis close up in live performance, it is impossible to understand the power that he had – it was a supernatural thing. He filled the air with a strange energy which I found palpable, and everybody felt it. He'd no idea what it was but he knew it was happening and he was amused by it, which I would have been had people been acting daft over me. There was definitely something special about Elvis but I wouldn't have to explain it to anyone who saw him in live performance.'

(84) ALBERT GOLDMAN: 'I was the music critic of *Life* and I went to see Elvis in Vegas, anticipating a wondrous performance, but he didn't make any impression on me. I had sat through a very lengthy performance by a very legendary performer backed by an enormous force of musicians, but I didn't feel a thing. It was like there was a wall of glass between myself and the performer. The only thing which could account for all the hysteria was that he was a male burlesque turn. He was very skilful at presenting himself physically but his performance was hollow and unworthy of serious attention.'

(85) MICHAEL OCHS (brother of Phil Ochs): 'To me, Phil stood for original songwriting and original ideas. I didn't think he should recycle the past, and it was dumb of him to put on a gold lamé suit. The idea in itself was clever: he thought that the only way to get any radical change in America would be to combine the intelligence of Che Guevara with the merchandising of an Elvis Presley. He thought that if Elvis had come out against the war, it would have ended a lot sooner.'

(86) BOBBY VINTON: 'Elvis and I were both in the same lounge after our shows and it's an awkward situation, who goes to whom – you know, in Hollywood, the big person comes over first. Well, he came over to me and he said that he liked my shows and my records. He said that he envied me for singing, dancing and playing instruments. He said, "I haven't done it for so long and I haven't got your confidence." I said, "Elvis, you only have to show up and they love you."'

(87) JOHN STEWART: 'I was playing in Las Vegas and I went to the lounge of the Dunes Hotel at about four-thirty in the morning. It was very dark and I was sitting at a booth having a drink and it looked like there

was no one in the place. The janitor had the electric broom going, just that sound of the whirling brush, and then I heard someone say, "Hey, Stewart, alone again, huh?" I turned round and there was Elvis with four girls in a booth right behind me, and I was so taken aback. I mean, there he was. When you saw Elvis Presley, there was no doubt that it was Elvis Presley. Jet black hair and this incredible face and he was very lean at the time and had the right outfit on. I had spent so much time looking at those album covers that I turned round and totally became Woody Allen. All I could say was nonsense. I turned back to my drink and he said, "See you later, John." I couldn't say anything and I'd missed this great opportunity to rap with Elvis.'

(88) ANTHONY NEWLEY: 'I had so many chances to meet Elvis and I missed them every time 'cause I never dug Elvis and he never turned me on as a performer. If he had, I'd have rushed over to the Hilton, which is where he was most of the time. If you asked me if I'd met Streisand, it's a different matter. I worship her and I would go to her reading the Yellow Pages. I appreciate what Elvis stood for and how much he was loved, but it would never have occurred to me to go and listen to him.'

(89) GLEN CAMPBELL: 'I was following Elvis Presley into the Hilton Hotel and I told him that I'd love to hear him sing "It's Only Make Believe". I didn't have anything to do with the publishing or anything, I just wanted to hear him sing it. He turned it round and said, "Why don't you release it, Glen? It'll be a hit for you." I have a gold record hanging on my wall and I give Elvis the credit for me releasing "It's Only Make Believe".'

(90) RONNIE HILTON (British balladeer of the 1950s): 'During the summer season at Blackpool in 1959, "The Wonder Of You" was in the charts and so it made my act that much stronger. It was like having an ace up my sleeve. When Presley brought his version out, I thought, "That's a bit of a liberty, you know, it's not much different to the way I did it all those years ago." Still, good luck to him, it was a good song and it deserved to get to Number 1.'

(91) KEITH EMERSON (of Emerson, Lake and Palmer): 'I saw Elvis at Lake Tahoe and the reaction was incredible. There wasn't a dry seat in the house. The curtains were closed as they played "2001" and they had

a huge shadow which was meant to be Presley, so he came out from the curtains as an extreme giant. He had his back turned to the audience with his head down on the guitar and when he turned round, they were all screaming. He forgot lyrics and that's what appealed to me. He could take the mickey out of himself and have fun on stage. I also saw him in Jacksonville about two weeks before he went. He was very laid-back and disappointing but the audience loved him. He was hung up on bass sounds and he spent ten minutes trying to harmonize with his backing singers, but the audience cheered and screamed their way through it.'

(92) BOBBY VEE: 'I met Elvis in Vegas in '73, and it had gotten to the point where it wasn't real exciting for him to be there any more. He was walking through his show. People came from all walks of life, and the opening was spectacular, everybody was on the edge of their seats waiting for something to happen, and then all of sudden he's on stage. For fifteen minutes, people are in shock, thinking, "Jeez, I am watching Elvis Presley, this is amazing." Although I felt he was walking through the show, he sang a great version of the Joe South song "Walk A Mile In My Shoes". I went back and met him afterwards and he was so approachable and friendly. He knew a lot of my old songs and he asked me about touring around America, "What is it like in Des Moines, Iowa?"'

(93) CLIVE GREGSON (British singer/songwriter): '"My Blue Suede Shoes" is about how people deal with being entertainers. It's easy to enter a twilight zone where nothing is real any more, and you switch off your responsibility and become "a rock 'n' roll star". People can become horribly insensitive and obnoxious: as long as they can get on the bus and get drunk and take drugs, they don't give a damn about anybody else. The song is about what it takes to be a professional entertainer and a real person. The two things are not mutually exclusive. It looks at Elvis, who went from being the greatest thing in rock music to a parody of himself.'

(94) JOHN STEWART: 'I got a call from RCA Victor: "Elvis wants you to write a song for him." He'd broken up with Priscilla and he was singing songs about breaking up with Priscilla. I guess it was so devastating for him that he wanted to sing what he felt, like we all do, I think. I wanted to write one like "Burning Love", you know, something with that "Mystery Train" feel. I wrote "The Runaway Fool Of Love", sent it in and never

heard a word. He never recorded it, but with all these sightings, I haven't given up hope.'

(95) PEGGY SEEGER (Ewan MacColl's wife and singing partner): 'Ewan's songs were very different from mine. He wrote political songs and he wasn't able to write the more personally emotional songs until the last years of his life. The exception is "The First Time Ever I Saw Your Face". He never sang it except for the one time he gave it to me. It was made for me and I sang it from then on. I first recorded it in 1963 and then Peter, Paul and Mary, Judy Collins and the Kingston Trio did it. A lot of them changed it because that last "lay with you" was too much for some pop singers. I didn't care for Elvis's version. Ewan used to say that it was like Romeo at the bottom of the Post Office Tower singing to Juliet at the top. There are better pop versions – Peter, Paul and Mary came closest to it, but I still think I sing it the best.'

(96) SID BERNSTEIN (US promoter, the Beatles at Shea Stadium): 'I worked with a company called Management Three, which exclusively did the tours for Elvis in the States. I didn't like Colonel Parker at first: the ego drove me nuts, but then I got to appreciate his value to Elvis. He pulled Elvis through every kind of scrape, he lived Elvis, and Elvis was his only client. If he did take fifty per cent of his earnings, he was worth it. I saw his brilliance and there hasn't been a manager like him.'

(97) GLEN CAMPBELL: 'When he introduced me to his audience on stage in Las Vegas, he said, "I understand you're doing an imitation of me in your act. I want you to know that it can only be an imitation." I said, "I'm not going to do it any more. I'd need to put some weight on first." Elvis could take the joke but the audience was against me. Nobody told Elvis he was fat.'

(98) HAL SHAPER (UK songwriter): 'People have their own vision of what songs mean to them. Elvis had gone to Las Vegas, where Jerry Vale was singing "Softly As I Leave You", and Jerry told Elvis a story about a man scribbling down this note on his deathbed. Elvis, who was psychically and mystically involved in everything, believed it to be true and the song became a great favourite of his. When I later went to Nashville and it became known that I had written "Softly As I Leave You", I became something of a hero and was taken out by all his friends.

I ended up on a Songwriters Hall Of Fame concert where I was asked to sing it to an audience of 1500 wonderful songwriters. I didn't know what terror and embarrassment was until I did that, but somehow I stumbled through it.'

(99) BARRY MASON (UK songwriter, 'Delilah'): 'Freddie Bienstock told Les Reed and myself that he would get our songs to Elvis. He said Elvis wanted some country songs so we gave him "Girl Of Mine". He was obviously ill when he recorded it, but I'm very proud of the record.'

(100) DAVID BELLAMY (of the Bellamy Brothers): 'Felton Jarvis, who was producing Elvis, got hold of our version of "Miss Misunderstood" and they cut the backing track for Elvis to add his voice. He was going to put it on his next album, and I'm mad at him for leaving before he cut it. After his death, Felton Jarvis brought Carl Perkins in for the vocal but it was in the wrong key for him.'

(101) CHAD STUART (of Chad and Jeremy): 'I only got to see Elvis after the decline had set in. This sad, overweight figure dressed like the Pope came out and went through everything in a daze. It was a terribly sad experience. I wish I'd never seen him because he was so incredible before that.'

(102) DON BLACK: 'I saw Elvis in Las Vegas in the last year of his life, and I was so disappointed. It was loud and echoey and you couldn't tell who was Elvis and who wasn't because he had a choir with him on stage. He didn't sing all that much and he kept giving things away – scarves, sweaters, pens – and he was blowing kisses. It was an embarrassing performance and it's a shame that I've got that memory of him.'

(103) ALBERT GOLDMAN: 'Many of the things about Elvis in my book had previously come out in the so-called bodyguards' book. They had provoked a sensation when they were first published, but the public has an enormous capacity to forget anything it doesn't wish to hear, and so the skin which had been torn off by the bodyguards had healed by the time my book came out. My book was treated as if it were some utterly unprecedented revelation, whereas it was simply a much deeper and more exhaustive treatment of the theme. I had also put a lot more work into my book, as theirs was a hastily conceived and concocted document.'

(104) GREIL MARCUS: 'I have encountered the question as to whether Elvis went to heaven or hell many, many times and in many different forms. I was in a seminar of women from the South, most of them middle-aged and all of them Baptists or Methodists, and this was a question that truly engaged them and worried them. They knew that Elvis had done, according to his religion and theirs, bad things, but they thought that he was a man of great decency, of great gifts and of great generosity. They took the question very, very seriously. This question has recurred again and again, sometimes seriously, sometimes satirically, but always I think with a sense of really wanting to know, did he do wrong or was he somehow lifted above his own failings by the music that he made and the way that he touched so many people.'

(105) ALVIN STARDUST: 'Elvis was totally let down by his friends. People were ripping him off all the way down the line and when he was under pressure, they just let him slip. That's what went wrong. And when he had been dead about half an hour, some clown phoned me up and said, "We're looking for someone to play in this thing called *Elvis*." I said, "I'm going to put the phone down and if you ever ring me again, I'll get a chair and wrap it around your neck. It is the most disgusting thing that I've ever heard of. The guy's only been dead a few minutes, and here you are cashing in." He said, "No, it's a tribute," and I said, "I don't believe in tributes. Someone's making money and it's going to go in your back pocket." I put the phone down and left it at that, but I eventually went to the Astoria to see it. Tim Whitnall who played the early Elvis was terrific but the fact that he was dressed in a clown's outfit annoyed me. I didn't like the taste of it, but when Shakin' Stevens came on, it was almost like watching Elvis.'

(106) JOE BROWN: 'I hate the way they start knocking people once they've died. If I see anything like that, I'm not interested in reading it. It's not only Elvis. Look at old Bing Crosby: as soon as he died, they said he was knocking his kids around. I hate all that gossip rubbish about people who can't protect themselves.'

(107) ALBERT GOLDMAN: 'As I got further and further into the story, I saw that the real Elvis had virtually nothing to do with his image. I was as

shocked, as startled, as appalled, as revolted as the readers of my book, but what they don't understand is that I had experienced everything they experienced years before: I came to terms with it and apparently they cannot. By the end of my research, I must concede that I did deliberately look for one thing, and that was something good to say about Elvis Presley because it seemed to me that I would be crucified if I couldn't balance the account. However, being an honest man, I have to admit that I never did find that balancing element in Elvis. Even his charitableness turned out to be illusory. For example, there was a very badly crippled boy, who had been the president of the Elvis Presley fan club in Memphis. Elvis had posed for photographs with him and we were led to understand that this boy was on some special terms with Elvis. When we finally got an interview with him, it turned out that he hadn't see Elvis for years. The photographs were typical Colonel Parker propaganda. A lot of fans don't accept my book but they are so besotted with the Elvis legend that no one could persuade them of the truth. I would say they were fools, and writers don't write for people whose minds are closed.'

(108) GREIL MARCUS: 'I think that Albert Goldman's book was written out of a spirit of hate and envy. It was meant to destroy a figure, not out of any true belief that this figure was evil and had done bad things to our culture that needed to be expunged, but simply for a contempt of people who are unlettered, who are from the South and who are not like him.'

(109) BRENDA LEE: 'Fortunately, Elvis Presley wasn't anything like the way Albert Goldman portrayed him, so that whole book can be discarded. He was a very nice, very kind human being, who loved his fans and his family. We should remember him for what he gave us and for the enjoyment he brought into our lives, and not the last couple of years of misery that he went through.'

(110) GEORGE HAMILTON IV: 'Elvis had his strange quirks and idiosyncrasies, but he was a country boy at heart and a good and generous man. I was on RCA for some years and I know that people like Chet Atkins wouldn't speak of him so highly if he was the monster he's been portrayed as in Albert Goldman's book. Elvis was kind to me – I know that – I was a nobody who happened to be on RCA, but he said, "Hi,

George, how are you doing?" I'm sure he did that to make me feel good 'cause he was a sensitive man. To my way of thinking, Elvis Presley was the greatest pop singer of all time and the musical genius of this century.'

(111) GREIL MARCUS: 'There is a deeply coded impulse in Western culture to refuse to believe that heroes who die prematurely and with their legacies unsettled have actually died. It goes back at least as far as King Arthur and probably further than that. Billy the Kid died in the 1880s when he was shot by Pat Garrett and in the 1920s you couldn't visit New Mexico without tripping over someone who was claiming to be Billy the Kid. The same thing happened with Amelia Earhart. The public don't want to let them go.'

(112) JIMMY WEBB (on his 1993 composition, 'Elvis And Me'): 'It's a diary entry but also a fan story – the fan who still believes he's alive, the fan who thinks he's in that empty chair, the fan who'll buy anything. In the last verse, I say, "And I know that it's wrong, but I just can't set him free", so on another level of perception, it's about the American mysticism of Elvis and the fact that every year, on the anniversary of his death, more and more people show up at Graceland, holding candles in a very eerie vigil, almost expecting a resurrection. Many thousands don't accept the fact that he ever died, so it's a new pop theology and who knows where that leads? How will this guy be perceived one hundred years from now? I see people on talk shows saying that they've seen him and playing the taped conversations. Okay, they're fakes, but it makes you think twice. The concept of Elvis being alive is more important than whether he is or not. If so many people want him alive, then he'll be alive. I'd love to be around in a couple of hundred years' time to see what this has mutated into. It's an amazing phenomenon and Elvis may be the leader of a new religion.'

SPENCER LEIGH

That's All Right, Mama

Much has been written about the relationship between Elvis and his mother, Gladys, and surprisingly little about Elvis and his father, Vernon. No matter how derogatory the articles and books may be, none of them questions Elvis's love for his parents, nor theirs for Elvis. Several writers, notably Albert Goldman, have attempted to make something more of it — did he have an unnatural love for his mother, did their intense devotion contaminate all his relationships with women? Or is this wishful thinking? Any writer wants to uncover something sensational in his subject's past, but he shouldn't distort the facts to do so.

Whilst the truth behind the relationship of Elvis and Gladys may be more commonplace, Elvis's family tree is remarkable. When he became famous, a reporter asked Vernon and Gladys about their background but they could only go back a few generations. There's nothing unusual in this: I couldn't tell you a thing about my great-grandparents.

Reviewers called Jerry Hopkins' biography, *Elvis*, 'thoroughly researched and meticulously detailed', but this 1974 biography contained little about Elvis Presley's antecedents. For all his faults, Albert Goldman was the first to document Elvis's Cherokee ancestry, while Elaine Dundy spent many months in Tupelo researching her unique *Elvis And Gladys*. Elvis, who had a tremendous sense of humour, would have been enthralled to read of his background, yet he died knowing little of his heritage. How sad that he didn't spend some of his fortune on acquiring the knowledge for himself.

Turn to the family tree Pete Frame has drawn for *Aspects of Elvis* and you'll see Morning Dove White, a Cherokee. In the early nineteenth century, there were not enough white southern girls to go round, so many hot-blooded males took Indian brides. That ancestry can be seen in Gladys Presley's dark, some say black, eyes and hair and in Elvis himself: consider how convincing he was as a half-caste in *Flaming Star*. No Cherokees infiltrate the Presley, possibly Pressley line. The first American Presleys had moved from Scotland to Ireland following the

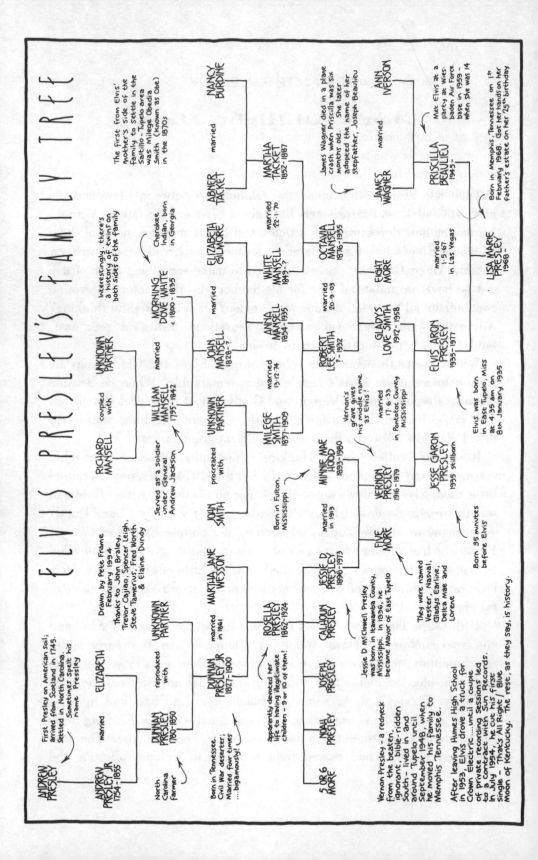

highland clearances, and from there to America because of the potato blight.

What a rum lot they are: they all seem as randy as hell and nobody knew about birth control. On Vernon's side, there's Dunnan Presley Jr, a civil war deserter who was married four times simultaneously, and Rosella Presley with her brood of illegitimate children. On Gladys's side, there's John Mansell, who abandoned his wife, Elizabeth, and his 'other wife' (her sister) and all their assorted children. Gladys's own parents were first cousins. Some Jewish blood was introduced into the tree by Nancy Burdine and this may have led to Gladys being buried with a Star of David on her grave – Elvis joked that she was 'covering her options'.

Despite Andrew Presley Jr making 101, there are numerous early deaths in the family tree. Two of Gladys's brothers, Travis and Johnny, died young, both heavy drinkers and given to brandishing knives and guns. Sexual promiscuity is rife throughout the family tree, so maybe Elvis had inherited this from his forefathers. Amongst the many children, there are three sets of twins (two on Gladys's side, one on Vernon's), so it is not surprising that Vernon and Gladys had twins.

Gladys Love Smith – the Love being a family name – was born on a farm in Pontotoc County, Mississippi, on 25 April 1912. She worked in the fields, she loved singing in church and she liked dancing. She was enraptured by Jimmie Rodgers' music, her favourite track being 'Mean Mama Blues'. Tiring of farm life, she moved to East Tupelo – the poor side of Tupelo – in 1932, stayed with relations and worked at the Tupelo Garment Factory for $2 a day.

Vernon Elvis Presley – the Elvis because his mother Minnie Mae liked the sound of the name – was born in Fulton, Mississippi, on 19 April 1916. Elvis was not a unique name, but it was not commonplace: bit like Spencer really. Oddly, it is an anagram of lives, veils and evils.[1] He dropped out of school and had no regular job when he met Gladys. They both liked singing in church and roller-skating and, after a two-month courtship, they were married on 7 June 1933. Because official record-

1. Anagram expert Bill Tasker tells me that Elvis Aron Presley can be transferred into 'Loveless yearn RIP' for his sad fans. Elvis Presley becomes 'silvery sleep', assuming he was buried in his stage gear, while the last order to his staff may have been 'Yes, serve pill'.

keeping was poor, they were able to lie about their ages – on the marriage certificate, Vernon is twenty-two and Gladys nineteen. In reality, Vernon was seventeen and Gladys twenty-one, which, in that time and place, was quite old for a first-time bride. Elvis himself didn't know Gladys's real age until after she had died. And, in keeping with this bizarre family tree, Vernon's brother, Vester, married Gladys's younger sister, Clettes, in 1935.

Vernon, with Vester's help, built their first home on the Old Saltillo Road. They did a good job because it survived a tornado when Elvis was one and is still standing as *the* tourist attraction in Tupelo. The outhouse has not survived and there's not much to see: a two-room shack with each room measuring 15 feet by 15 feet. Still, the Tupelo Mississippi Flash was born there.

At 4 a.m. on 8 January 1935, Gladys Presley gave birth to Jesse Garon, the Jesse being after Vernon's father. Jesse Garon was already dead by the time his twin brother came into the world thirty-five minutes later. It was typical of that time and place to give twins matching names – hence, Jesse Garon and Elvis Aron, and Elvis's second name was after the minister at the First Assembly of God church.

In 1937 Vernon sold a hog to his landlord for $4. Unhappy with the price and egged on by Gladys's feckless brother Travis, he altered the cheque to $14. Even in later life, Vernon had difficulty in signing autographs, so presumably the forgery was none too good. He was caught and he, Travis and another friend were sentenced to three years apiece.

You must have seen the picture of the three-year-old Elvis with his parents. Elvis wears a hat and overalls and even then has that trademark curl to his lips. The picture is posed but no one is smiling and it has the same stark reality as Grant Wood's *American Gothic*, which was painted in 1930. Why do they look so sad? Why is Gladys gripping Vernon's shoulder? Why is the background a cement wall? Possibly the picture was taken at the police station as a keepsake for Gladys.

Vernon was taken to Parchman, an infamous penitentiary in Sunflower County, and the subject of a well-known song by Mose Allison. Coincidentally, the black blues singer Bukka White was serving time there for assault. Although Parchman had a strict regime, it allowed prisoners conjugal rights, presumably to cut down on homosexuality within the institution. So, each weekend Gladys and Elvis travelled for ten hours to visit Vernon. Much has been made of the fact that Elvis didn't wave goodbye to Vernon but, hell, he was only three and how would you feel if you'd been left with a warden whilst your parents went to the married quarters.

Going to prison was a very unfair sentence for Vernon's crime and fortunately he was released after a year, in February 1939. Gladys had moved out of their house and moved in with a cousin who looked after Elvis while she worked in a laundry. As an ex-jailbird in a small town, Vernon found it hard to get work.

In 1942 Vernon found work building a prison, actually a prisoner-of-war camp 200 miles away. Then he found factory work in Memphis. Around that time Gladys had a miscarriage and was not able to have further children. As their only living child, the solitary Elvis looks out of place in that heavily populated family tree.

Another misinterpretation: Gladys walked Elvis to school every day and this continued until he was in his teens, so was she overly protective towards him? She might have been but this is not evidence of that. Vernon saw no value in book learning: you learned your trade from working with others. Gladys, on the other hand, appreciated the advantages of being educated and wanted to be certain that Elvis didn't abscond. She was determined that Elvis would eventually graduate, which he did. Although Gladys walked him to school, Elvis became his own man on the way home.

No one needed to force Elvis to go to church. His earliest memories are of gospel singing and it became the foundation of his work. He recorded many gospel songs and began recording sessions by singing old-time hymns. On a more superficial level, he got his wiggle from the emotional outpourings of the Pentecostal preachers.

Elvis befriended the local celebrity, country singer Mississippi Slim. When only eight, he was performing with him on local radio in Tupelo. His parents gave him an $8 guitar for his tenth birthday – significantly, he had wanted a rifle. When some jealous school children cut the strings, others clubbed together to buy new ones.

The country singer Red Foley had written and recorded a doleful song about the life and death of his dog, Old Shep. Elvis loved 'Old Shep' and performed it at every opportunity. In 1945 a teacher entered him in the Mississippi–Alabama Fair and Dairy Show. It was Elvis's first large audience – up to 2000 people – and Elvis tugged at the heartstrings and won second prize. The winner, Shirley Jones, was from the same school and Elvis sang duets with her on school shows.

Because of the lack of opportunities for Vernon in Tupelo, the family moved, with his paternal grandmother Minnie Mae, when Elvis was thirteen. Elvis, sounding like a Steinbeck character, said, 'We were broke, man, and we left Tupelo overnight. Dad packed all our belongings and put them on top and in the trunk of a 1939 Plymouth. We just headed to Memphis. Things had to be better.' Well, it wasn't that good. Vernon found work loading cans in a paint factory, but a bad back put him out of action. Gladys, however, revelled in a job as a hospital orderly. This was ideal for her friendly and sympathetic nature and it was even suggested that she train as a nurse.

The Presleys lived in a housing project: they had one room with a toilet down the hall. Again, many have said that it was unnatural that Elvis should sleep with his parents, but what else could he do? I should think that thousands of families were in the same position.

Although he kept on with his schooling, Elvis was working in a cinema in Memphis from 1950. Memphis was a city that was strong on blues music. He became infatuated with the music, hanging out on Beale Street, soaking up the fashions and buying garish pink and black clothes. He experimented with dyeing his hair black.

In May 1953, during his last days at school, Elvis hitched 250 miles to Meridan and won a guitar in the first Jimmie Rodgers 'The Father of Country Music' Festival. After graduating from Humes High, he worked as a deliveryman for Crown Electric, significantly driving the same truck as singer Johnny Burnette had driven the year before. He yearned to be a professional musician like Johnny but his father told him, 'I never met a guitar player worth a damn', which is identical to Aunt Mimi's admonishing John Lennon, 'The guitar's all right, John, but you'll never make a living from it.'

Sun Records, primarily a blues label, allowed the public to make one-off, two-sided records for $4 each. This kind of facility is often seen at fairgrounds – see Graham Greene's *Brighton Rock* – but I've never heard of any other label that did this. It interrupted the day-to-day work as Sun's manager, Sam Phillips, usually cut the records himself. Maybe, and this is quite possible, Sam knew that the local talent would want to hear themselves and he was effectively getting them to pay for their own auditions.

There's the much-quoted story of Elvis making a record for his mother's birthday, but as his mother's birthday was in April it is more likely that it was for their wedding anniversary. In any event, he wanted to hear his voice and, more to the point, wanted to sound his best for Sam Phillips. As it happens, Sam wasn't there but his secretary Marion Keisker told him of Elvis's potential. I'm not surprised – the eighteen-year-old Elvis gave convincing performances of 'My Happiness' and 'That's When Your Heartaches Begin' to his own guitar accompaniment. He sounds so confident, so assured and so unmistakably Elvis. Elvis had it altogether before any record producer had worked on him.

So Sam Phillips put Elvis with Scotty Moore and Bill Black and they worked out Arthur Crudup's 'That's All Right, Mama' for their first release. Commentators have had a field day with this recording: after all, the 'mama' in the song switches from a mother to a girlfriend. Is it so significant? Elvis, Scotty and Bill had been experimenting with numerous songs, including other blues by Arthur Crudup. This one happened to lend itself to a new interpretation: there is no deep social significance in its title and the fact that it became Elvis's first record, although there's no doubting the perfect symbolism.

At first Elvis was playing on country shows but he needed a different audience. Colonel Parker signed him to a demanding contract: demanding because all the onus was placed on Presley: 'As a special concession to Colonel Parker, Elvis Presley is to play 100 personal appearances within one year for the special sum of $200 including his musicians.' As Elvis was under twenty-one, the contract had to be signed by his parents. Vernon approved but Gladys was suspicious and there are no known photographs of her with the Colonel. Having signed Elvis, Colonel Parker negotiated a profitable deal with RCA and when Elvis received $5000 in cash, he bought his mother a pink Cadillac even though she couldn't drive. 'You may have a pink Cadillac, but don't you be nobody's fool,' warns Elvis in 'Baby Let's Play House'.

Once with RCA, Elvis's anti-authoritarian image was exploited to the full: he wasn't the first young rebel but, unlike Marlon Brando and James

Dean, he could sing. Rock 'n' roll was promoted as rebellion – rebellion against existing forms of music, rebellion against authority, rebellion against the older generation, rebellion against one's parents.

This must have sat uneasily with Presley. He loved country music, rhythm and blues and even crooners like Dean Martin. He was law abiding and a regular churchgoer. He was polite to his elders, addressing them as 'sir' or 'ma'am', and he was devoted to his parents. Ironically, most of the major rock 'n' rollers – Elvis, Buddy Holly, Jerry Lee Lewis, the Everly Brothers, Ricky Nelson – not only loved their parents, but also received their wholehearted support. No star was antagonistic to his parents until Bob Dylan.

Gladys didn't mind Elvis's gyrations, although she feared the fans would get out of hand at his concerts and injure him. Elvis told her, 'Mama, if you feel that way, you'd better not come along to my shows because that stuff is going to keep right on happening – I hope.' Gladys can be seen in the audience of the 'Got A Lot Of Livin' To Do' sequence in *Loving You*. She is in a blue dress, has put on weight and sits behind the woman who has her feet in the aisle. Some prints of the film also have a shot from the stage in which both Vernon and Gladys can be seen.

Although jokingly referred to as Elvis the Pelvis (with a twin brother Enis), he was only re-enacting what some southern preachers had been doing for years. However, a wiggling torso on a sexy twenty-one-year-old had a completely different effect. Gladys would smart when she heard her son being denounced as obscene and was bitterly hurt when ministers rose to attack him: one described him as 'a new low in spiritual degeneration'. Elvis recorded gospel songs ('Peace In The Valley', 'It Is No Secret') to no avail: his best-selling 'Elvis' Christmas Album' was banned by many radio stations as being sacrilegious. Incidentally, Vernon and Gladys loved singing gospel songs with Elvis: somewhere there must be a tape of them all singing together, and sooner or later, someone is going to find it.

Gladys appeared to have no trouble with her son's succession of girlfriends, although she did once tell him to settle down, get married and open a furniture store. She and Vernon had been hoping that he would marry a local girl, Dixie Locke, but he was on the road so much that she found another boy. When she wanted to break it off, she asked Gladys to inform him.

Although magazines like *Confidential* blew the gaff on film personalities, there were few attempts to discredit rock 'n' roll stars. In the week I write this, Axl Rose's tempestuous home life is making the headlines, but Chuck Berry's indiscretions, which landed him in jail, were hardly mentioned by the press of the day, so much so that Berry was able to deny it for many years. A *New Musical Express* journalist told me that, although he was aware of Gene Vincent's drinking habits and wild living, he wrote blander pieces because that was what the readership wanted.

An investigative journalist could have had a field day with Elvis Presley's background. Elvis would have been discredited if his father's prison sentence had come to light – and there might have been a series of revelations as Jerry Lee's father had also done time. And Elvis daringly flaunted the family secret by making *Jailhouse Rock*. Maybe signing Elvis for *Jailhouse Rock* was one of the Colonel's jokes: perhaps he was saying to Vernon, 'Don't you dare cross me.'

Maybe it was another of the Colonel's jokes that Vernon became Elvis's personal business manager. Vernon paid the staff, including Elvis's schoolboy friends, the Memphis Mafia, and no doubt did his best to keep Elvis's expenditure in check. Like Gladys, Elvis was impulsive, a costly quality when you have the money to give away cars and expensive jewellery on a whim.

In 1957 Elvis bought a former Christian church, Graceland, a beautiful building on thirteen acres of land. He chose the decoration with his parents and it displays the tastes of people who have recently come into money. A lot of it was tacky and I wonder how someone who had such great taste when making records – at least, up to that time – could have bought such things as red phones with rhinestones. Maybe he had seen them in the homes of country stars and thought that was the way it was done. Certainly he envied Webb Pierce's guitar-shaped swimming pool.

One look at the photographs of Gladys from that time reveals how unhappy she was. Like Vernon at Parchman, she felt like a prisoner and she rarely saw her son, although he rang her every day. A return to Tupelo for one of Elvis's concerts made her realize that she preferred the old days. She started drinking heavily, mostly beer and vodka, and became bloated and fat. Nothing was to annoy Elvis more than accusations that his mother drank: one fan outside Graceland gave him Jerry Hopkins' book to sign. Elvis threw it across the road, saying, 'These people who write about me don't know nothing.'

In an attempt to transform his image, Prez allowed himself to be drafted
into the US army. It would have been easy to escape the draft, but Colonel
Parker thought this was a good career move. And those who say that
Colonel Parker was always shortsighted are wrong: he knew that being
with Uncle Sam would pay off in bucketfuls once he'd been demobbed.

Whilst Elvis was undergoing his basic training, Gladys became ill with
chronic hepatitis. The army was reluctant to let him go but they relented
when he threatened to go AWOL. He rushed to her bedside but she died,
at the age of forty-six, on 14 August 1958. Colonel Parker took control
and, in what can be seen as a dry run for 1977, allowed hundreds of
mourners to file past and all but turned the funeral into a circus.

According to Jerry Hopkins' biography, 'Elvis's world collapsed like a
sandcastle in the burning sea'. Maybe it did for a short time, but, come
on, he was in the army and he had to return to the job in hand. After
becoming a sergeant, he returned to music, often accompanied by his
father. Generally they got on well together, but allegedly he disapproved
of his father's marriage in 1960 to Dee Stanley and certainly took
exception when she began to redecorate Graceland. The couple were
divorced in 1977. Vernon basked in Elvis's glow: he loved the limelight,
he loved being introduced on stage (always as 'Daddy') and he loved
talking to the fans. After Elvis's death, he would even talk to the press –
for $25,000. He must have been taking lessons from Colonel Parker.

Vernon's health had not been good for many years – at one stage, he
and Elvis had been in adjacent hospital beds – and he died of a heart
attack on 26 June 1979 at the age of sixty-three. He was buried in
Graceland between Gladys and Elvis: some have said that he shouldn't
have been in the middle, but he was, after all, the head of the family.

Rocking in the background and taking her snuff whilst all this was
going on was Elvis's grandmother, Minnie Mae. She, Vernon and Elvis's
daughter were the only beneficiaries under Elvis's will. Elvis did not leave
anything to Colonel Parker, but what can you give a man who already has
your soul? Minnie Mae outlived Gladys, Vernon and Elvis, eventually
dying in 1980 at the age of eighty-six.

Graceland is now a major tourist attraction. Some parts of it are out of
bounds, including the upstairs room which contains several trunks marked
'Mrs Presley'. In them are Gladys's clothes, clean and neatly pressed,

almost as though she is going to return one day. The pink Cadillac, too, has been lovingly restored and is in immaculate showroom condition.

Elvis loved his parents and was devastated by Gladys's early death, but I don't think it was an unnatural relationship. If he had been so devoted to his mother, would he have gone on tour: wouldn't he have stayed home and sacrificed everything for his mother. Mind you, I can't think of a single performer who has sacrificed everything for his mother. It's a contradiction in terms. You can't become famous unless you leave the house.

ALAN CLAYSON

Snowmen: The Manager and
his Client

Who is Colonel Tom Parker? His very genesis is shrouded in mystery. All that is certain is the date – 26 June 1910 – but was he Thomas Andrew Parker, born in West Virginia, or Andreas Cornelis van Kuijk, a teenage runaway from Breda, Holland?

The plot becomes less vague by the 1930s when he was employed by the Royal American Carnival, the Union's top itinerant funfair. As general factotum, his duties ranged from palm reading to preparing refreshments. Over the next two decades, he developed into a cigar-gnawing entrepreneur prone to Goldwynesque homilies and eye-stretching initiative epitomized by his practice of trapping sparrows, staining them yellow and selling them as canaries.

He felt an inverted pride in such escapades. To intimates, he boasted that he was less a 'showman' than a 'snowman' – US slang for a con merchant – and that they were welcome to join his Snowman Society. Subscription was free but it cost $10,000 to leave. Most amusing, I'm sure.

For a while, a capacity for selfless action surfaced in a post in a Florida charity organization. The most potent source of fund-raising, he discovered, were presentations headlined by a popular country-and-western entertainer. In parenthesis, one such artist, Jimmie Davis, became a close pal who, on gaining the governorship of Louisiana, elevated Tom to the honorary rank of colonel.

Inevitably, Parker committed himself full-time to C&W, initially by exhausting but lucrative 'round robin' productions whereby a show would play twice in one evening at venues up to 100 miles apart. Moving to Nashville, he stepped up a few rungs on becoming personal manager to 'Tennessee Plowboy' Eddy Arnold, who had already notched up two late 1940s million-sellers. 'When Tom's your manager,' remarked Eddy, 'he's all you. He lives and breathes his artist.'

After he and Arnold parted amicably, the Colonel took on Hank Snow – and it was in a guest spot on a Snow tour of the southeastern states that the wheels of the universe came together, and Parker's most famous client was first seen by his future Svengali – who had, nevertheless, been aware of Elvis Presley's activities for many months.

Presley's guitarist Scotty Moore and, next, promoter Bob Neal had been acting in a quasi-managerial capacity. However, both realized that Elvis needed someone with more clout than they, who could give him that extra push up the ladder – all the way up if necessary. In March 1956, therefore, it came to pass that Tom Parker, trusting his instinct, took formal charge of the young man's professional life – and afterlife.

The Colonel was no Dutch uncle to Presley. Their relationship was always based at least as much on profit as friendship. You may read what you will from a Christmas card dedication from client to manager that read: 'To the Colonel. You know how I feel so there's no need to make this a snowjob. Elvis.'

Any reservations that Presley's father and adored mother had about Parker taking their only child in hand dissolved as his imagery of a dotage rich in material comforts smouldered into form. Elvis himself had a few disagreements but eventually he stopped bothering with circular and half-understood discussions about work and finance with Parker. After all, he only had to ask and the latest make of flashy car, a wardrobe of the fanciest clothes or even a new house was his. 'I always knew he had a million dollars' worth of talent,' smiled Colonel Tom, 'Now he has a million dollars.'

This fortune – and those that followed – was made through the single-minded – some might say bloody-minded – dedication that Eddy Arnold had observed, combined with Tom's hard-nosed certainty about everything he did and said. In the first instance, he'd decided that both Sun Records and the Louisiana Hayride-type showcases were less than an artist of Elvis Presley's calibre deserved. Nothing else would do but a long-term deal with the Record Corporation of America – RCA – and exposure on the nationally televised *Ed Sullivan Show*. Via connections nurtured during proceedings concerning Arnold and Snow, Parker brushed aside obstacles like demos and auditions as he persuaded RCA to contract his new find. Likewise, he overcame an initial reluctance to feature the boy on *The Ed*

Sullivan Show – and, ultimately, Sullivan had to shell out three times more for Presley than the previous record fee.

Thanks to the Colonel, there Elvis was, a country hick broadcasting to fifty million viewers. The plug had been pulled and he'd been sucked into a vortex of events that hadn't belonged even to speculation once upon a time. Zigzagging round the continent in tour bus and train before graduating to jet and limousine, he'd no sense of acting of his free will, and, at the same time, no thought of resisting the force that had effectively finished off his old life of poverty and a dead-end job. Instead, he was pushed in whatever direction fate and the Colonel ordained. If he'd found himself in front of an audience of Martians, it might not have seemed particularly odd.

'It all happened so quickly,' gasped Elvis, 'I got a call from Colonel Parker. He signed me, and we just drove from town to town, wherever the Colonel got us bookings. Then he arranged for RCA to hear my records. They paid $35,000 to buy my contract from Sun. It was a lot of money. I had $5000 too. I went out and bought Mama a pink Cadillac.'

Over the years following the global breakthrough, Parker made some strange decisions, but he accepted full responsibility for them. While advised by publicity managers and other courtiers, he was not to be RCA's marionette – very much the opposite. With Elvis responsible for sixty per cent of RCA's net takings in 1956 alone, the Colonel was the biggest ape in the pop jungle. In his half-nelson, RCA felt compelled to accede to Parker's every desire, regardless of positioning research. Thus a ghastly corporate smile was fixed as he took an intense and often unwelcome interest in every link of the chain from pressing plant to deletion rack.

Only the brave incurred his wrath, and attempts were made to hold it at arm's length with plaques and similar official citations for 'non-artistic artistic help' – meaning that he'd been more tractable than expected. Otherwise, he contributed simply by, for example, making sure that only pictures of the star appeared on Elvis LP sleeves. Producers or auxiliary musicians were hardly, if ever, credited.

Nothing was left to chance. Later, just in case any reviewer dared to make disobliging comparisons, Tom Jones was warned against actually duetting with the King when the two boon companions back-slapped and horsed around on stage during one of the King's seasons in Vegas. The

Colonel also nipped in the bud Presley's interest in recording 'Golden Years', composed by David Bowie – also on RCA's books. The actual song was neither here nor there, but Parker didn't want this ineffable Limey's image to rub up against that of Elvis, projected constantly as the most heterosexual of men. Generally, however, Parker seemed to have little interest in Presley's music *per se* – rather like the cold fish of a lawyer recruited by the convict-turned-pop-singer played by Elvis in *Jailhouse Rock*.

Controlling every aspect of his charge's celluloid enterprises for MGM too, Parker was billed as 'technical adviser' for such input as endeavouring to ensure that no other male actor was particularly handsome or charismatic and, therefore, unlikely to divert attention from the romantic lead. In turn, no low-budget Presley film was up to the fighting weight of, say, *Ben Hur* in terms of quality, but that was beside the point. The idea was to rake in the most loot with the least effort by accommodating thousands of movie-going fans in one go, and plugging the songs on the soundtrack album.

The Colonel occupied five rooms – some with trademark snowmen woven into the carpet – in MGM studios, where he entertained prominent figures. These included members of the Senate.

Unconvincing though most of the King's 1960s silver screen vehicles were, each usually reached a profit position within weeks – and it was only in the last year or so of the decade that the customers finally grew tired of them. The same quality control and law of diminishing returns applied to licensed spin-offs like Elvis Presley wallpaper, Elvis Presley ironing-board covers, Elvis Presley chewing-gum, Elvis Presley fizzy drinks, Elvis Presley biros, Elvis Presley teddy bears, Elvis Presley lipstick and, of course, the Elvis Presley fan club. The Colonel also oversaw the marketing of both 'I Love Elvis' and 'I Hate Elvis' lapel badges.

More insidiously, he patented the publicity stroke that everyone from Gene Vincent to Bestial Vomit (of Death Metal combo Sore Throat) was to pull: that the most depraved rock 'n' roller could be 'A Nice Lad When You Got To Know Him'. With Parker's manipulation of Elvis setting the sir and ma'am standard, pre-Beatle North America became used to a pop star being relatively devoid of independent opinion, having been put in motion by his handler as a walking digest of truth, justice and the

American way. Subliminally, through the medium of teen magazines and even in the piffle he started to release in the early 1960s, Elvis would parrot stolid middle-aged dictums – your parents' word was law, don't talk dirty *et al.* – and parade an apparent dearth of private vices. With the gentlest humour, he'd answer questions about his favourite *color*, preferred foodstuffs and the age at which he hoped to marry.

The Colonel's smoothing of his rough diamond began with the stressing of an uncomplaining diligence while Elvis was on national service. The post-army 'Do The Clam'-type chart potboilers, the long absence from the stage, and the churning out of more conveyor-belt family movies: all were part of Parker's repackaging of Presley as an 'all-round entertainer'. Into the bargain, Parker was, arguably, the arbiter of the King's reactionary leanings, demonstrated after he recommenced concerts in 1968.

When these expanded to full-scale tours, the Colonel was often encountered out in the foyer, hustling merchandise. However, in the accompanying semi-documentaries such as *That's The Way It Is* and 1972's *Elvis On Tour*, he chose to be an unseen *éminence grise* hovering over the operation with an authority as absolute as that of a Grand Vizier over a boy-sultan's palace.

In the late 1970s, there were rumours of internal ructions. Certainly, there was concern that the King's coffers weren't as full as they had been. He was apt to overspend despite no longer being able to take big hits for granted. Moreover, the Colonel was, reputedly, allowing a reduced rate – with interrelated pruning-down of costs – for his concert extravaganzas. Yet an occurrence just before the record industry's 1977 Yuletide sell-in got underway gave Tom Parker an unlooked-for bonanza.

Elvis Presley's sudden death in August of the same year precipitated a boom time for the Colonel, who regarded the more absolute absence as no more of a hindrance than when Elvis was square-bashing in Germany. Throughout that autumn, record-store windows bloomed with the late King's splendour. He was scarcely off pop radio, and was swamping many national charts six or seven singles and albums at a time. His final LP, *Moody Blue*, and its attendant 45, 'Way Down', raced to the top of their respective lists, trailed by a retinue of repromotions.

The dust had barely settled when tabloid hearsay had it that the Colonel would be devoting himself professionally to Rick Nelson – who'd come into his own during Presley's patriotic chore – but, though Parker advised the late Nelson briefly, only Elvis's posthumous career disturbed a virtual retirement in Palm Springs.

In title and appearance, Tom Parker was, to some, uncannily like Fort Baxter's Commanding Officer Hall in television's *Phil Silvers Show*. His character, however, seemed closer to that of Hall's *bête noire*, Sergeant Bilko. Elements of Del Boy of *Only Fools and Horses*, Bradley Hardacre of *Brass* and *Dad's Army*'s spivvy Private Walker were also reminiscent of some aspects of his character. As such, the question remains: was the Colonel, as one critic wrote, 'the hardest manager since Cardinal Richelieu' or merely a sly hoop-la pedlar confronted by temptations he was unable to withstand. Is he to be praised for concentration on the possible or vilified for overcaution? Has he proved the best or worst role model for many pop managers since? These have varied from Don Arden, Gordon Mills (who took care of Presley's great friend, Tom Jones), Allen Klein and Shakin' Stevens' mentor, Freya Miller, nicknamed 'The Colonel' by the tabloid press in the early 80s.

What will be history's verdict on the real Colonel? Mention of him still brings out strange stories of what people claimed they saw and heard, but the following two vignettes are true. Firstly, he made an anonymous payment for a pew in the Elvis Presley Memorial Chapel, adjacent to the Mississippi shack where Presley was born. Many years earlier, a well-known English impresario gained an audience with Parker to discuss the possibility of bringing Elvis over to Europe for two concert spectaculars. 'What kinda money are you offering, son?' enquired the Colonel. 'A million bucks! Well, that just about takes care of me. How much are you gonna give the boy?'

PETE BROWN

Separate Ways

Sometimes when I'm looking through old photographs I find the ones of me aged fourteen at the school holiday camp in the summer of '55 looking very Elvis-like and macho. The pictures are black and white, so you can't see the casual jacket I'm wearing is red, signifying my allegiance to James Dean. Another thing you can't see is the awesome ignorance and terror of matters sexual festering inside the jacket.

Did Elvis single-handedly bring sex out from under the carpet where it had been hiding since World War II? He certainly wasn't responsible for my sexual liberation, unlike that of countless others – most of whom, it seems, were men. No, my personal sexual liberation, when it eventually came to me as a young beat poet, had a lot more to do with James Dean.

Now I liked girls in 1955 right enough, but I wasn't convinced they liked me. An aggressively possessive mother, who tried hard to convince me girls were no good, didn't help. That's when I began assuming aspects of James Dean's screen persona, at the same time as beginning to write poetry, both desperate ploys to attract female attention.

Not liking Elvis, though it was easy, posed a problem. The more macho Elvis followers seemed initially to have more sexual success, consisting mainly of seducing or being seduced by Butlin's redcoats after marathon bouts of beer drinking, a scenario both seductive and repellent. James Dean was never part of such brutality, and, despite Elvis's 'sensitive' roles in some of his films, he never fooled me.

Though I spent my first ten years in a village twenty-five miles outside London (which London has now swallowed), I was always a city and suburban animal. It was much easier for me, as a teenage mess, to identify with Dean in *Rebel Without A Cause* than any of Elvis's personae, most of which were determinedly lumpish/yob/yokel and carried undertones of violence, ignorance and racism, later adopted to Nazi effect by the black-leather-jacketed and drape-suited gangs who occasionally menaced the local Jewish youth clubs.

Another strike against Elvis and the early Brando, whose moral confusion I admired, was their motorbike image. In the fifties, the only place to have sex, apart from Butlin's or getting married, was in a car. I loved big cars for that reason, although I never had one, never even had a driving licence; the nearest I got to my goal was almost losing my virginity outside a party in the back of a friend's Morris Minor, which was tragically driven away before consummation.

Furthermore, I knew even then that motorbikes were dangerous, and though I drank like a whale and ate speed pills like they were going out of style (some of them did), I hated danger. I didn't love fighting, either, and Elvis was always fighting. He was the rock 'n' roll John Wayne.

I happen to come from a long line of pacifists. Elvis joined the army; James Dean did not.

How on earth did I, let alone anyone else, turn out to be as normal as I now am (of course you have to take my word for it) after being exposed in my most impressionable years to the media megablast from those two supremely fucked-up icons? Thank Something we were not as enlightened as we are now, and that we didn't know anything near the truth about them.

In the Beatles era, kids copied clothes, religion and Liverpool accents. With Bowie, they began to copy sexuality. Imagine all those fifties teenagers exposed to two sexual pathologies that would have made Freud turn in his grave! The words of the great blues singer and writer Victoria Spivey come to mind:

> *I done it in a passion,*
> *I thought it was the fashion.*

Musically, it's another story. I always preferred survivors to fly-by-nights. Especially the great swing era survivors like Ellington and his band, Red Allen, Coleman Hawkins, and great singers like Joe Turner and Billie Holiday.

Bowing to peer pressure, I once bought a 78 of 'Heartbreak Hotel', but I knew it couldn't compare to the records of Sidney Bechet, Armstrong, Gerry Mulligan or Sonny Terry and Brownie McGhee that I began my collection with.

For me the real thing was always nine-tenths black, although I liked the Californian cool school for a brief period.

My suspicions about Elvis were confirmed many years later when, having become a songwriter, I met the legendary Otis Blackwell. He gave me an album that he'd just recorded which included songs he'd 'given' to Elvis, including 'Don't be Cruel', 'Return to Sender', and 'All Shook Up.' The album is called *These Are My Songs*, and he sings them a lot better than Elvis did. He gave up half his royalties to have them record by the so-called King.

I believe Elvis was the first great pop manipulation. His fame is not unlike Hitler's. There was no need to manipulate or fake Nat 'King' Cole (one of the first real spearheads of popular music), Sinatra, or even Frankie Laine and Doris Day. They had all paid their dues and achieved solid musical credentials. Elvis, beginning an illustrious line which culminated in the likes of Bryan Ferry and Kylie Minogue, only had style – though unlike Ferry, he couldn't play, he couldn't write, and he wasn't really a musician. However, creating a precedent for the hordes of gullibles to follow, he was ignorant and mostly did what he was told, rebelling only by killing himself. So, he became the biggest success of all time.

Elvis always smelled of corruption to me, though in fairness a lot of that smell was the Colonel's. The only time I ever heard Elvis sounding sincere was singing a gospel song in a documentary film. I fear that, like a lot of drugged and desperate people, Elvis believed in some form of god – or that possibly he was one, but it didn't work.

As much as some people, even James Brown, say that Elvis helped popularize black music, I believe he got in the way of it, delaying its progress and recognition.

As a songwriter, I have to admit that Elvis, a non-writer, was useful to the careers of such great writers as Mort Shuman and Doc Pomus, Leiber and Stoller, and Otis Blackwell; albeit, at a price.

In the end Elvis, for me, was just a piece of commerce, with none of the vision or artistry of other popular pioneers such as Chuck Berry or Little Richard.

Why do I feel so angry about Elvis after all these years?

Probably because he occupies too much space in the history of the cosmos; and because James Dean is dead.

Elvis versus James Dean. It would have happened one day, in an alternative future. Like Mothra versus Godzilla. A film, maybe. Or an album – Dean would inevitably have taken up warbling, actors always do.

But as the images fade I mourn Dean's tiny spark of sensitivity, especially when placed against today's brutal street culture. I can't help feeling that he made things better for a short time, while Elvis made things worse for a long time.

TIM WHITNALL

Real, Real Gone

MEMPHIS, TENNESSEE, AUGUST 1991

Elvistown asserts the title in shocking pink – a glossy guide to all matters Presley in the 'city Elvis called home'. The hand-tinted cover depicts the young rocker in his prime, all '56 lip-curl and collar, squinting into the sun with the trademark quiff sprayed loose over his right eyebrow.

It's ninety degrees and Elvistown swelters. The sunburnt pavements downtown are curiously devoid of pedestrians, and on the wide streets an occasional vehicle drags by in the afternoon heat. The pictures of old Memphis show a bustling city centre, sidewalks crammed and the roads full of cumbersome saloons, but that was then. Now, a chrome-wheeled low rider cruises Front Street, windows wide open as the hi-fi booms out its punishing hip-hop message to the world. All around, the tall buildings impose on the skyline. Several sport the broken or boarded-up windows of obsolescence, while others gleam with obvious prosperity. The Peabody Hotel shoots twelve storeys up into the blue, the fancy red and yellow brickwork restored to Victorian splendour. Down on the forecourt, the out-of-towners are greeted by a smart bellhop who delivers a polished welcome as he unloads their cases onto a golden trolley. 'MEMPHIS, TENN-E-SSSEEE!' he proclaims. 'It all started here, and, hell, its gonna *end* here!' His voice rises to a soothsayer's tremor, and then, with a knowing wink and an alligator grin, declares his love of the blues and tells you proudly of his own guitar, 'A black and white Fender, yessir black and white, just like the *world*.' He bids the folks a good stay in the city and, with tongue firmly in cheek, reminds them to keep an eye out for the 'howlers, prowlers and growlers' that haunt Beale Street after dark. It is an impressive performance.

As in many cities, a character often emerges born of both its history and an indigenous humour. 'Memphis, always a haven for eccentrics and individuals,' wrote Peter Guralnick in *Lost Highway*, 'is the only locale I know that actually boasts of its craziness.' You know what he means. It doesn't take long to get a feel of the place, a feel that permeates the whole city, something of the streets that can only be truly understood by being there. It can be felt on the banks of the Mississippi and looking back up to the painted signs fading with age atop the old cottonsheds that face the very river that brought the first settlers here. All over the city there are similar reminders of the good old days. The infamous Beale Street, alive with sin, danger and the Devil's music for the first half of the twentieth century, now resembles a movie set, with well-scrubbed cobblestones and smartly painted storefronts – some merely a façade propped up by cleverly concealed steel braces.

Back in the early fifties when Elvis Presley was a teenager (and by all accounts a brave one) he'd hang out on Beale soaking up its wildness, ducking in and out of the clubs and dancehalls and latching on to a secret culture that would directly influence his own persona. He learned the walk and talk of jive, watched how the blues could turn a club crowd, and bought his outlandish loose-fitting outfits from Lansky Brothers men's shop. Today, on the street that they used to call the 'Murder Mile', a solitary policeman breezes by on a mountain bike. A statue of W. C. Handy – 'The Father of the Blues' – stands with his trumpet, looking up the street that inspired him as it later would the young Elvis. Just behind him on the slabs known as Handy Park, a guitarist plays a gentle bottleneck blues under the sycamores. Sometimes it seems that everybody here is a musician, and that is perhaps where the spirit of Memphis exists at its strongest. The city's vast musical legacy, as diverse as its own character, would fill a book of its own, and there can't be a city elsewhere that has affected the texture of popular music in so many ways. The field-hollers and worksongs at the turn of the century, minstrel shows and jugbands, jazz and big-band swing, country, gospel, blues, rhythm and blues, hillbilly, the birth of rock 'n' roll, and the emergence of funky Memphis soul. It is a legacy regarded by some with an almost holy reverence, and there are still those, including artists, who come here in search of a blessing. When you weigh up this musical past with the current variety of music on the bandsweep of local radio you can't help feeling that, one day, Memphis might just do it again.

It was back in 1954 that Memphis really did it. Sam C. Phillips and his Memphis Recording Service had been heading towards legend long before the release of 'That's All Right, Mama', the first-ever record by Elvis

Presley. In the spartan set-up in a converted radiator shop on Union Avenue, Phillips – a radio announcer, engineer and self-confessed capitalist – used his guile and skill to capture some of the best post-war blues on wax, including sessions by B. B. King, Howlin' Wolf, and Sleepy John Estes. The tapes were then released to labels like Chess in Chicago, and in 1951 a chance recording made by Ike Turner's band, fronted by his youthful cousin Jackie Brenston, became a number one smash. More importantly 'Rocket 88', a saxy eulogy to the snazzy new Oldsmobile coupé, earned acceptance as the 'first-ever rock 'n' roll record'. By 1952 Phillips felt confident enough, despite frequent pressure on his health and his bank balance, to launch his own label – Sun Records – taking raw, primarily black talent off the street and, like a demon scientist at work in his laboratory, coaxing performances rich in feel and spontaneity in his alchemic quest for pure gold. In an interview with Paul Jones for BBC Radio 2 in 1988, Phillips outlined his chemistry. 'I wanted to capture that person as nearly in their "habitat" as possible,' he remembered. 'It was kept *very* simple, honest, straightforward . . . the elements of keeping it native was the primary thing I had to do . . . That, if anything, is what made me. I didn't want to mess with the *good earth*.'

You can comprehend the science if you listen to early Sun records like 'Take a Little Chance' by Jimmy DeBerry or 'Easy', the moody duet he cut with the harmonica player Walter Horton. It's also there in the humour and high energy of Rufus Thomas's 'Bear Cat' and 'Tiger Man', and the smokier atmosphere of Junior Parker's 'Mystery Train'. The sun was rising fast for Phillips and his maverick operation, but his eyes and ears were sharpened towards an even bigger potential. Aware of the growing market in teenage record buyers, he sensed that the time was right for a product that would exploit it. He recalled in that same radio interview, 'You had children's records, but you then jumped to the adult, big-band sort of thing. So there was – in the most formative and most active years of a person's life – nothing. They began to listen to rhythm and blues, or as it was known then 'race records'. I just thought this may be a great opportunity, but I didn't want to find somebody that's trying to sound like a Negro or a black man. That I did not want. I wanted someone with an innate natural feel, and I knew that had to come solely from somebody white, out of the South, if in fact we could achieve it.'

When it came, not even Phillips could see it. The eighteen-year-old

Elvis Presley travelled the long ribbon of Union Avenue on a Saturday afternoon in the summer of 1953, clutching a cheap guitar and four dollars to finance a vanity record cut on the Memphis Recording Service's sideline business – 'We record anything – anywhere – anytime' said their motto. Nobody could have known that the adolescent husk crooning a tender version of the Inkspots' 'My Happiness' down onto the Presto lathe would change history. Elvis must have liked the result for he returned to the studio a short while later to try another personal recording. Bitten by the boogie disease, he put his face about at Sun and eventually persuaded Sam Phillips to try him out on session work. Phillips teamed Elvis up with Scotty Moore, a guitarist whose unique style blended country and jazz, along with the bass-slapper Bill Black, a hyped-up joker whose long-suffering fiddle was held together with piano wire. After weeks and months of jamming and trying out ideas, this curious trio was eventually given studio time. They achieved some average ballads like 'Harbour Lights' and 'I Love You Because' (complete with Elvis's whistling solo), but to Phillips, who had seen the likes of Howlin' Wolf and Rufus Thomas practically tear off the acoustic tiles with their towering performances, it must have seemed directionless. After a long session in early July 1954, he was about to turn off the power in the control room when he heard the sound that he had almost lost hope of hearing. The trio were kicking around an old tune, 'That's All Right, Mama', recorded in 1946 by the Chicago bluesman Arthur 'Big Boy' Crudup. Elvis's frantic A-major guitar strum carried his voice to the edge of its range as it taunted and mocked the blues. Bill spurred him on, slapping the bass strings and making them chug on the offbeats, as Scotty filled in any gaps with a fluid figure, way up high on the neck of his big Gibson guitar. Phillips made them do it again, got a balance and switched on the two Ampex 350 recorders. It was the stuff that Sun Records and the early career of Elvis Presley were made of – a collection of lucky accidents that came together at the right time. To Sam Phillips, as he watched the VU meters flickering before his eyes, this was the rock 'n' roll eureka, a white boy singing the blues, and the rest, as they say . . .

Union Avenue begins at the waterfront and then undulates away from downtown Memphis, travelling out east until it leaves the city. Past the big hotels and the Greyhound terminus, it passes the tyre shops and exhaust centres and a well-manicured lawn behind which stand the plush offices of the *Memphis Appeal*. Across the street an old Dodge pick-up, similar to the one that Elvis drove for the Crown Electric Company before he turned professional, rusts to death on airless tyres. These are the streets where rock 'n' roll grew up, and a little further along, where Union rises slightly to its junction with Marshall Avenue, stands the small storefront building where it was born. Set back from the road at forty-five degrees, the red-brick and white-boarded façade with its big windows faces the blistering southern sun. 706 Union now looks much the same as it did in its heyday. With Sam Phillips' guidance the former studio has been restored to its original guise, both inside and out. They've jazzed it up with a little neon, and there is a huge replica of the famous golden Sun label, with its dozen sunbeams and the crowing rooster, adorning the side of the café next door where, back in the fifties, Sam and his artists would talk business over cups of coffee. Back then three or four dollars would have bought you a private session and your name stamped on the label of your very own shellac 78 – even if your name was Elvis Presley. Today the same price secures you a yellow ticket and a twenty-minute look inside the 'cradle where it rocked'.

You pass through a tiny reception, overcrowded by a couple of desks, and into the recording area, some six yards by ten, with a raised control room at the far end sealed behind a big rectangular window. The walls are covered with pictures of all those associated with the studio, from Sun's earliest days, through Elvis and those that followed, like Jerry Lee Lewis, Carl Perkins, Johnny Cash and Roy Orbison, to recent visits by U2 and Rufus Thomas. Several antiquated glass lights hang down from the crock-backed ceiling and, despite an abundance of white acoustic tiles that line the whole space, the room has an eerie, slightly gloomy aura. The coffee-brown floor gleams, its polished lino giving off an antiseptic aroma. 'The floor-tiles are original,' says Randy the tour guide to the visitors who congregate in front of a sparkly blue drumkit, 'so y'all are standing right where Elvis stood.' Indeed we are. You can do the same all over Memphis, from the place where Elvis bought his motorcycles to the hospital where he was pronounced dead, but there is something more believable here where Elvis lived out his last days of a 'normal life', creating the monster that turned him into a phenomenon. His five singles for Sun and the tracks that he laid down at the Memphis Recording Service represent Elvis and his music at their most unaffected, and some would say their finest. You can sense the simplicity behind it all when you look around the old studio. Shortly afterwards, rock 'n' roll would become an untameable beast, and the music business would become the music industry. In his later years Elvis never really discussed his early career and if asked would shrug off the subject as if it embarrassed him. As with many artists, his best work was often achieved without him realizing it. Way back before the final grim days of his life, the opulence and the trappings of something called 'success', before the movies, mansions and gold records, the bodyguards and private aircraft, Elvis Presley was a very real person – a young white southern boy from poverty, living with his parents and training to be an electrician as he harboured a crazy dream that maybe, just maybe, he could make a go of it as a ballad singer. That's what walked through the door at 706 Union all those years ago.

Back out on the street, the heat hits you hard once again. The tour guide locks up the studio and disappears, leaving you on the deserted sidewalk. Next door, the café offers shade and a freezing beer. The first thing you hear as you enter are the opening bars of 'Milkcow Blues Boogie'. There is something genuinely thrilling knowing that it was recorded, albeit some thirty-seven years earlier, on the other side of a wall now covered in memorabilia. 'Hold it fellas! . . .' orders the cocky kid Elvis to his band as they saunter through the slow blues intro. '. . . that don't move me.' You can see him, hand in the air like a traffic cop, his guitar slung loose and that greasy sneer crossing his skinny face. 'Let's get real, real gone for a change . . .'

And gone they got. Real, real gone, and now of course Elvis is gone forever. In the souvenir shop the stickers on the albums say 'Elvis in the '90s', marketing a commodity as if the man himself were here today. It doesn't seem right. Elvis belongs to another time and that is where he'll always be should you wish to find him. It shouldn't be a sad thing either – it would be far worse to expect to avail yourself to the ghost of Elvis Presley because, even in Memphis, he won't show. But listen to 'Good Rockin' Tonight' or 'Baby Let's Play House' and there he is, wild and dangerous, singing as if he had three minutes left to live, and young forever. *That* is where Elvis belongs.

The sun begins to set on Beale Street. There's a band now in Handy Park playing 'Green Onions' with a flautist taking the lead breaks. As you stroll back towards the riverfront the clubs and bars are getting ready for the evening. A splendid neon sign invites you into B. B. King's swanky nightclub. Further along, where the street climbs up the bluff, there stands the nine-foot bronze of Elvis, his back turned on Beale as he gazes out towards the Mississippi. 'It's got a cute ass,' quips a tourist to her friend, 'but it ain't Elvis.' I look up at the graffiti-covered statue, trying to find the likeness. Just then an old hobo dressed in torn camouflage clothing seizes a chance to talk. 'I KNEW'D HIM!' he bellows. 'Eh-vis was a GOOD BOY, good to everybody black or white!' He moves inwards, a little too close for comfort, as if to confide a great secret, and his voice assumes a sad whisper. 'That's why they came for him. You be good, and they'll whup yo' ass, but you be bad . . . YOU'RE GONNA LIVE FOREVER.' The brown eyes go right through you and his expression freezes sternly as the message sinks in. 'I'd better start being bad then,' I reply, all credibility shot down there and then by an English accent. The old man's face cracks and a wheezy laugh full of the blues wracks his entire frame. He slaps his chest as if to rid himself of some demon, but he can't shake the laughter which mutates into a hacking cough. He turns back to Beale Street, dragging his belongings behind him in plastic bags and I watch him fade away.

BILLY BLACKWOOD

His Hand in Mine

An hour's drive south of Tupelo on the Natchez Trace Parkway takes one through the heart of Choctaw County, Mississippi, where, in the early 1930s, four young men from the same family began to catch the ears of their neighbours with their musical harmonies.

Singing songs they had learnt growing up in church they began to capture more and more attention and, in 1934, they officially formed the Blackwood Brothers Quartet. That original group included three brothers, Roy, thirty-three, Doyle, twenty-two, James (my dad), fifteen, and Roy's son, R.W., thirteen.

They sang in churches and county fairs throughout northeast Mississippi gaining increasingly enthusiastic audiences with their blend of uptempo spirituals including their theme song for many years, 'Give The World A Smile', and more familiar traditional hymns of the church such as 'Amazing Grace'.

The following year the man whose name and picture adorn this book was born and, in all likelihood, he, or at least his parents, became familiar with the music of the Blackwood Brothers during his childhood.

In 1950, after a steadily growing popularity had taken the Blackwood Brothers over much of the United States, they moved to Memphis, Tennessee, and began daily programmes on WMPS Radio, frequent television appearances, and a monthly concert at Memphis's Ellis Auditorium. Those concerts would have a profound influence on the young Elvis Presley, whose family had also moved to Memphis.

During the early 1950s Elvis was a frequent face in the crowds that came from west Tennessee, eastern Arkansas, and northern Mississippi to listen to an evening of alternately rousing and solemn gospel music at the Ellis. His unusual hairstyle and general appearance made him easily recognizable and, in fact, my father *did* recognize him hanging around the backstage door one evening, by himself and looking a little disappointed. Asking him why Elvis wasn't inside listening to the concert, Elvis told him that the price of the ticket was more than he could afford at the moment. My dad, knowing how often Elvis had been to their monthly concerts there, and having grown up poor himself, let him in the stage door that night and gave him a standing invitation to use that entrance at any of their concerts.

There was one night, however, that my dad missed seeing him but later spotted him among the crowd. Asking Elvis how he got in, the young man said he had bought a ticket. My dad wrote a cheque reimbursing him for the ticket and as long as Elvis was living, that cheque hung in a frame in Elvis's awards room at Graceland along with the accompanying note my father had written.

Our family visited Graceland in October 1991 and the revamped awards room no longer had the cheque and letter on display but somewhere in the collection of memorabilia it still testifies to the influence of gospel music and my dad on Elvis's early years.

In 1951 the Blackwood Brothers signed a recording contract with RCA Victor Records, a company that would be their home for the next twenty-one years. After Presley's rise to popularity established their friendship on a professional level my dad would send Elvis a copy of each Blackwood Brothers album as it was released and often received notes of appreciation for them. In that visit to Graceland in October 1991, downstairs in the yellow-and-black den I spied an album called *At Home With The Blackwoods*. Released in 1963, it contained six songs by the Blackwood Brothers, four by my brother's group, the Junior Blackwood Brothers, and two songs by a group my cousin Mark and I sang in called the Blackwood Little Brothers. The cover picture featured all the members of the Blackwood Brothers and their families and was taken in my parents' living room.

When the Blackwoods settled in Memphis in 1950 they began attending First Assembly of God Church, which was also the church of the Presleys. The pastor was Rev. James Hamill, whose son, Jim, with R. W. Blackwood's younger brother, Cecil, had a part-time gospel group called the Songfellows. Elvis had expressed interest in singing with them but his somewhat radical appearance and style of singing were not thought to be complementary to the conservative pastor's son's group image. The early fifties in the United States were characterized by chaste mores; customs and standards which Elvis would challenge and begin to change in the not-too-distant future.

It was about that time that my dad's two brothers, Roy and Doyle, retired from the strenuous travelling of the quartet and stayed in Memphis to manage the Blackwood Brothers Record Shop, a gospel music retail outlet and distributorship the brothers had established in downtown Memphis. (It later moved to 209 North Lauderdale, just a couple of blocks from Lauderdale Courts where the Presleys lived during their first years in Memphis.) Different personnel took Roy's and Doyle's places in the late forties and early fifties and the Blackwood Brothers changed faces several times but always around the nucleus of my dad and his nephew, R.W.

In 1954 the quartet included those two, with Bill Lyles singing bass, Bill Shaw singing tenor, and Jackie Marshall playing piano. By that time, television had found its way into many American homes and one of the three major networks, CBS, had the most popular show on TV at the time, *Arthur Godfrey's Talent Scouts*. Mr Godfrey featured entertainment of various kinds from around the United States. The Blackwood Brothers had had great success in their comparatively small world of gospel quartet music and were asked to appear on the *Talent Scouts* show; their first opportunity to present their unique brand of music to a nationwide audience. An appearance, and particularly a win, would immediately catapult one's career to new heights. Anita Bryant, the McGuire Sisters and Pat Boone were among those whose careers benefited greatly from an appearance on *Talent Scouts*.

In June 1954 it was the Blackwood Brothers. As they concluded their rousing version of 'Have You Talked To The Man Upstairs' the thundering audience applause registered a win for the Blackwoods! After investing twenty years in their career they had arrived at the top of their profession.

Two weeks later everything literally came crashing down around them. They had begun to fly to some of their engagements in their own private plane and one day, while rehearsing an approach to a small landing strip in Clanton, Alabama, the plane crashed, killing R. W. Blackwood and Bill Lyles. My dad, others in the group, and their families and friends watched in horror as the plane burned in flames a few hundred feet from the hangar where they stood.

The crowd for the combined funeral was so great that it was held in Ellis Auditorium in Memphis and was the largest funeral in the city's history. It held that honour for twenty-three years, until 1977, when another city funeral attendance record was set. That funeral was Elvis Presley's.

As my father sought to recover from this earlier tragedy he found replacements for R.W. and Bill. R.W.'s younger brother, Cecil, took over his brother's position, and replacing Bill Lyles was a thirty-year-old bass singer from the Sunshine Boys, J. D. Sumner, who, many years later, became Elvis's bass singer.

In 1956 the new Blackwood Brothers Quartet was invited back to New York by Arthur Godfrey and again appeared on *Talent Scouts*, and won.

Elvis, meanwhile, had some notoriety of his own on Steve Allen's and Ed Sullivan's television shows. He, too, signed a recording contract with RCA Victor and was on his way to superstardom.

Elvis's and my dad's paths crossed at least twice during those hectic late fifties. When Elvis's mother died, the Presleys asked the Blackwood Brothers to sing at her funeral, and when Elvis received his discharge from the army and returned to Memphis, one of his first calls was to my dad. He invited the quartet to Graceland to sing around the piano with him, which they did until the wee hours of the morning.

J. D. Sumner sang bass in the Blackwood Brothers during those years and in 1960 he and my dad bought the Stamps Quartet Music Company, inheriting the Stamps Quartet name. In 1965 J.D. left the Blackwoods to manage and sing bass with the Stamps, and he still holds those positions today.

When J.D. went to the Stamps, my brother, Jimmy, left the Junior Blackwood Brothers and joined J.D. The following year I joined them as their drummer. Also in the group was J.D.'s nephew, Donnie, who was a very talented musician/arranger and contributed greatly to the Stamps' sound.

During the late sixties, Elvis made his much-celebrated comeback and among the entourage he took to the Las Vegas Hilton International showroom was another gospel group, the Imperials. My cousin, Terry, whose father, Doyle, was my dad's brother and an original member of the Blackwood Brothers, sang lead in that group and, as their vocal arranger, was largely responsible for the Imperials' sound, which won them many awards and established them as the premier gospel quartet of their day.

When the Imperials decided to leave Elvis's show, Elvis called his bass-singing friend J. D. Sumner. J.D. and the Stamps became his backup quartet and held that position until Elvis's death. It is J.D.'s voice that creates the memorable sounds on Elvis's recording 'Way Down'.

My brother and I had left the Stamps in December 1969, which was before they began their association with Elvis. Donnie left a few years later to pursue his own musical career and formed a group called Voice with Tim Baty, a former Stamps bass guitarist, and Sherrill (Shawn) Neilsen, who had sung in gospel groups for several years and was recognized as one of the great tenor voices in the industry.

After doing some backing work on the Grand Ole Opry in Nashville the group got a chance to try out for Tom Jones's show in Las Vegas. Tom and Elvis were appearing at different hotels there and Tom mentioned to Elvis that he needed a backing group. Elvis called Donnie and asked him if they wanted to audition for the spot. Donnie's group flew to Las Vegas and met with Elvis, who wanted to hear them before they tried out for Tom. He was so impressed he hired them on the spot for his own show, promising to make room for them as an opening act.

Meanwhile, as my musical tastes were growing considerably more contemporary than my dad's and the Blackwood Brothers', I decided to leave them in pursuit of my own career. I was to perform with them for the last time at the National Quartet Convention in Nashville in October 1973. The NQC was the brainchild of J. D. Sumner and has become the biggest event on the southern gospel music calendar.

When I arrived in Nashville the convention was abuzz with the news that Voice, Donnie's new group, had signed to open the shows for Elvis. Having worked with Donnie and Tim in the Stamps and having known Sherrill for years, I was anxious to see them and congratulate them on their new position. Little did I know I was about to be caught up in their success.

When I first saw Donnie in the halls of the Municipal Auditorium in Nashville I ran to meet him. He immediately asked if the rumour he had heard about my leaving the Blackwood Brothers was true and I told him it was. He then stated that as an opening act they were going to need a drummer and asked if I would be interested. I accepted and the next month I was sitting in Elvis's living room in Palm Springs, California, as our part of the show was discussed.

All my life I had known Elvis as my dad's friend. The Christmas after

Lisa Marie was born, Elvis invited us to Graceland to see her. I also remember several times his coming to the gospel concerts in Memphis, still through the backstage door but with a huge entourage and tremendous security. I knew him as the obvious superstar he was, but to be sitting in his living room in his employ and soon to be sharing the stage with him was quite an experience for a young twenty-year-old.

The next year and a half was a tremendous opportunity and education for me. As we opened the Elvis show with our uptempo gospel and pop numbers, not only in the showrooms of Las Vegas and Lake Tahoe, Nevada, but also on tour across the United States, I saw first hand the adulation and mania that followed Elvis everywhere he went.

We were also guests in his homes in Memphis, Palm Springs, and Beverly Hills, California, at parties and between tours. I was alone in a room with him on only one occasion; with him and one or two others a few times, and during those more intimate times the topic of discussion was religion. He never got too far away from his religious beliefs and his love of gospel music.

Elvis often included a gospel song in his shows; most frequently, 'How Great Thou Art', which was often met with the longest applause of any song in the show. And, of all the albums he recorded, the only ones to win a coveted Grammy Award were his gospel albums *His Hand In Mine* and *How Great Thou Art*. My personal favourites of Elvis's gospel recordings are from another gospel release, *You'll Never Walk Alone*, and include that song as well as 'I Believe'.

I left the show in 1975 after a spiritual rededication of my own and saw him alive on only two more occasions, at shows in Murfreesboro, Tennessee, and Louisville, Kentucky.

I was playing drums on a recording session in Nashville when my dad telephoned me with the news of Elvis's death.

As I viewed his body lying in state at Graceland I thought of the times I had enjoyed his company at home and as part of his show but, more importantly, of the fleeting value of fame and fortune. At that moment those things became glaringly insignificant.

At his funeral my dad sang Elvis's favourite song, 'How Great Thou Art'. I remember thinking how fitting it was that the music Elvis really loved and one of the men who helped introduce him to it, would be his final tribute.

BOB GROOM

Tiger Man: Elvis and the Blues

Stalking across the stage, yelling out the ferocious lyrics, 'I'm the king of the jungle, they call me the tiger man,' Elvis Presley, arguably the greatest white blues singer, had returned to his musical roots for the all-important television special that marked his return from the wilderness. The celluloid pussycat that had wandered for years in Hollywood's cotton candy land was once again the hard rocking tiger that had electrified audiences in the fifties. Elvis was back . . .

27 June 1968 marked a watershed in the career of Elvis Presley, the second coming of the singer universally acknowledged in the late fifties as the King of Rock 'n' Roll. Following his return from army service in March 1960, he had reached even greater heights of popularity by changing his musical focus to ballads and lighter beat numbers and presenting a more clean-cut image. The quality of his material steadily declined, however, as the movie production line churned out soundtrack album after soundtrack album. Eventually he rescued his recording career by outflanking Colonel Parker and performing what *he* wanted to on the 1968 television special.

Significantly, the first filmed session included a rousing rhythm and blues number that had been popularized by Rufus Thomas (on Sun 188) in 1953 as a follow-up to his big hit 'Bear Cat', which borrowed heavily from Big Mama Thornton's 'Hound Dog'. Although 'Tiger Man' didn't make the national R&B charts it must have had considerable impact in Memphis for Elvis to revive it fifteen years later, even using the insistent guitar riff originally played by legendary Memphis bluesman Joe Hill Louis (who wrote the piece with Sam Burns). Full of raw power and excitement, Presley's 'Tiger Man' was first released on a special LP put out by the Singer Sewing Machine company, who sponsored the TV special, and later re-released by RCA Victor.

Aided and abetted by producer Steve Binder, who had expressed his intention to present the *real* Elvis Presley, Colonel Parker's wishes notwithstanding, Elvis chose several R&B and early rock numbers for the informal sessions at NBC's Burbank studios. Several versions of Chicago blues singer Jimmy Reed's 'Baby What You Want Me To Do' (a 1960 R&B hit on Vee-Jay 333) were recorded, with Elvis playing acoustic guitar and obviously enjoying the work-outs, as well as 'Big Boss Man', another Jimmy Reed number (a 1961 R&B hit, Vee-Jay 380, that also entered the Hot 100) which had been a modest hit for Elvis in 1967.

Simply the most influential, and for many years the biggest-selling solo popular singer of the post-war era, Elvis Presley stands alone as the most charismatic synthesizer of white and black popular music in the middle fifties. He may not have launched the rock 'n' roll revolution single-handedly, but he overwhelmed the media in 1956 and ensured that it became an internationally popular form of music. Sam Phillips may have nourished the vital spark and Tom Parker groomed Elvis for stardom, but where did the unique Presley sound come from? Partly, it is true, from the gospel and country music that he grew up with, but I submit that the strongest strand in his musical development was his love of the blues.

In retrospect, it could be said that Elvis was born to sing. Although neither of his parents were musicians they were both regular churchgoers in Tupelo, Mississippi, when Elvis was a child and he sang with them there and at revivals and camp meetings. Born in a shack on the 'wrong side of the tracks', his early years were probably spent in circumstances little different to that of any poor family, black or white, in the South. It is known that the Pressley (original spelling) family originally hailed from the Carolinas, where a David, or possibly Andrew, Pressley (of Anglo-Irish extraction) landed in the 1740s, as revealed in Albert Goldman's thought-provoking but extremely unsympathetic biography *Elvis*. The family name may well, however, originate in Wales, the 'Land of Song'.

In the hinterland of the old county of Pembrokeshire in West Wales is the Preseli district, a wild area which takes its name from a range of hills known variously as the Prescelly, Preseli or Preseley mountains. Intriguingly, a few miles to the west, on the coast near the village of Solva, is an area known as St Elvis, centred on St Elvis Farm! It seems that St David, patron saint of Wales, was baptized by Elvis, the Bishop of Munster (who had recently landed from Ireland) soon after AD 500. Elvis's mother bore a first name, Gladys, which was always very popular in Wales. All this suggests that Elvis's distant ancestors may have come

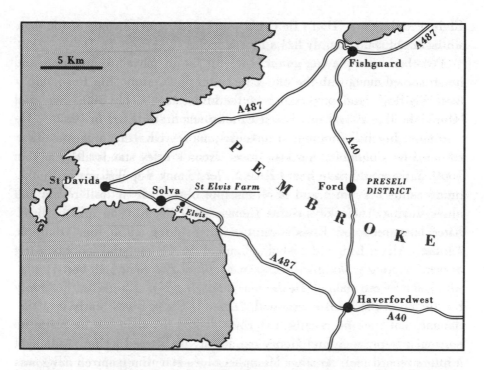

from Wales. Certainly, Elvis always showed a particular camaraderie with Tom Jones and affinity with his singing, so perhaps he himself felt that he had Welsh roots!

Elvis was thirteen when his family moved to Memphis. That year, 1948, a song called 'Good Rockin' Tonight' was at the top of the black R&B charts, pointing the way towards the rock 'n' roll era still to come, in which the young Mississippian was to play a key role. Elvis was soon expressing his individuality by shopping for clothes down on Beale Street, copying black dress and growing his hair long, despite the opprobrium that this inevitably attracted at Humes High School, where crew cuts were still the norm for young males. Down on Beale Street Elvis would soon have become acquainted with the current R&B hits as well as the harder blues sounds of the previous decade. What his parents thought of his musical tastes at this time isn't known but they were probably happier with his interest in country music and gospel than the raunchy blues he heard on radio stations like WDIA or along Beale Avenue (as it is more correctly known). However, in her youth Gladys loved the black-inspired 'Blue Yodels' of Jimmie Rodgers and danced to his records. Her favourite

Elvis recording was 'Don't Be Cruel', an Otis Blackwell composition that, whilst not blues, certainly has a bluesy feel.

Elvis had been playing guitar since his family moved to Memphis and he strummed along with the music he heard on the radio. He was familiar with 'Big Boy' Crudup records from the forties like 'Cool Disposition' and 'Rock Me Mama' and numbered Crudup amongst his top favourites. He also liked Big Bill Broonzy, whose early forties OKeh records were later reissued by Columbia, his last 'race' records being cut for Mercury in 1949. Elvis would have heard Rice Miller (Sonny Boy Williamson No. 2) broadcasting his own brand of Mississippi blues over station KWEM and blues-singing disc jockeys Rufus Thomas and B. B. King on WDIA. (B. B. King later recorded Elvis's multi-million-selling 1956 hit 'Love Me Tender'. Albert King did a whole album of Presley material for Stax: *King Sings The King's Thing* also known as *Blues For Elvis*.) Robert Henry, who had a record shop on Beale, was managing B.B. King when he finally hit the top of the R&B charts with 'Three O'Clock Blues' early in 1952. Around that time he recalls that Elvis visited his shop but he made no particular impression and Henry can hardly be blamed for failing to spot a future record idol. Another Memphis blues star who inspired Elvis was the ill-fated Johnny Ace, whose 'Pledging My Love' (Duke 136), recorded in January 1954, was a huge R&B hit after his premature death at the end of that year. (Elvis recorded this blues ballad in 1976. It was issued as the B-side of 'Way Down'.)

As far back as 1947, Elvis had appeared on the radio, with Mississippi Slim on WELO, Tupelo, singing numbers like 'Old Shep'. He sang this again at his triumphal appearance at the Humes High School Christmas Concert in 1952. By the summer of 1953 he had the confidence to record his voice, using the facilities of the Memphis Recording Service, run by Sam Phillips. It has been a long wait but we can now hear what he sounded like on his very first recording, the ballad 'My Happiness'. The aural evidence shows that at eighteen, although far from polished, he had already developed his distinctive vocal style and that, whatever Sam Phillips subsequently achieved in the Sun studio, it was not to teach Elvis to put over a song his own way; he could already do that.

The story of the first Sun recording session in July 1954 has been recounted many times. When Elvis was trying to sing like the popular singers of the day, he didn't cut the mustard: he was competent, but not distinctive enough. An intermission jam session put him at ease and he turned instinctively to the black music that had intrigued and excited him through his teenage years; the blues. 'That's All Right, Mama' had been a good seller for its composer, Mississippi-born blues singer Arthur 'Big Boy' Crudup, who recorded it under that title in 1946 for Victor (20-2205), reissued in 1949 (50-0000), and at the same session cut an alternative version, 'I Don't Know It' (Victor 20-2387). Elvis's version is at the same tempo (and none the worse for that) but charged with that special musical energy that characterized all his best recordings. As the A-side of his first record (Sun 209) it sold rapidly following exposure on WHBQ, Memphis, hitting Number 3 on the local C&W chart. A blues song in the country bestsellers lists was nothing new, however. Artists as diverse as Bob Wills, Bill Monroe and Jimmie Rodgers had all achieved this. Just as Hank Williams changed from a Roy Acuff imitator to a great original when he gave free rein to the blues feeling in his songs, so Elvis abandoned his pretensions to become another Dean Martin when he had recording success with the rhythm and blues he loved. It has to be significant that such country greats as Jimmie Rodgers, Bill Monroe and Hank Williams, as well as (white) rock greats like Elvis, Carl Perkins and the Everly Brothers (partly through father Ike), were all initially influenced by black blues performers.

On 30 July 1954 Elvis gave his first public concert, at the Overton Park Shell in Memphis, in the sixties and seventies a venue for blues festivals featuring such legendary artists as Bukka White and Furry Lewis. Slim Whitman was the headliner and his smooth country pop performances contrasted sharply with the raucous and raunchy rock and blues that Elvis was performing at this time, almost certainly including 'Good Rockin' Tonight', which Elvis recorded in September 1954 and which became the A-side of his second Sun record (210). It was tailor-made for Elvis and he really rocks it up, accompanied by Scotty's electric guitar, his own acoustic guitar and with Bill Black frantically pumping his string bass. Originally written and recorded by Roy Brown (DeLuxe 1093) in July 1947, a rumbustious version by Wynonie Harris (King 4210) had been a major R&B hit in 1948. At the same session Elvis recorded the blues ballad 'Tomorrow Night', which had been a huge hit (reputedly a million seller) for veteran bluesman Lonnie Johnson in 1948 (King 4201). His version is slightly faster than Lonnie's but otherwise very similar. When first released, on *Elvis for Everyone* in July 1965, it was swamped with overdubs which obscured the vocal in a misguided attempt to 'update' the sound. Fortunately, the original, undubbed version, on which he is backed solely by Scotty Moore's guitar, was at last released, thirty years later, in the April 1985 collection, *Reconsider Baby*.

In December 1954, Elvis, Scotty and Bill were back in the studio to cut four more sides. Their third Sun record (215) featured 'Milkcow Blues Boogie', an exciting version of an old blues which opens at a slow tempo and then is rocked up after those immortal words, 'That don't move me, let's get real, real gone', illustrating in miniature the progression from blues to rock. 'Milkcow Blues' was originally recorded by Tennessee blues singer Sleepy John Estes in May 1930 (Victor V-38614). Kokomo Arnold speeded it up when he recorded his much-changed version in September 1934 (Decca 7026) and it was a big hit. Decca reissued it a decade later to initiate their 48000 series, in the wake of several jazz (Bob Crosby, 1938) country/western and swing (Johnny Lee Wills, 1941; Moon Mullican and Bob Wills, both 1946) versions. Elvis would have been familiar with the Arnold record, and probably also the white versions. The strength of the theme is illustrated by the excellent rock 'n' roll versions by Ricky Nelson (Imperial, 1961) and Eddie Cochran (Liberty), the former featuring a James Burton guitar solo.

At a February 1955 session, Elvis apparently tried out the 1954 Ray Charles R&B smash 'I Got A Woman' (Atlantic 1050) and a song that had been recorded, also in 1954, by a vocal group called the Eagles, 'Tryin' To Get To You' (Mercury 70391), but neither interpretation was released. 'I Got A Woman' was re-cut for RCA Victor in January 1956. Elvis tackled 'Tryin' To Get To You' again at a July 1955 Sun session and produced one of the most powerful performances of his career. A much-underrated recording, not a blues song as such but imbued with so much blues feeling that it surely qualifies as R&B, if it must be categorized. Scotty Moore takes a memorable guitar break midway through, and the edge on Elvis's voice is sharpened up still further on the RCA reissue. The February session did produce one side of Elvis's fourth Sun record (217), a rocked-up version of Arthur Gunter's 'Baby Let's Play House' (Excello 2047) which had been recorded a few weeks earlier and was achieving some success in the South. (Gunter may have taken the idea for his song from a 1951 country hit by Eddy Arnold, 'I Want To Play House

With You'.) With this record, released on 1 April 1955, Elvis finally broke into the national country charts.

Elvis's final recording session while still under contract to Sun took place on 11 July 1955. 'Mystery Train' had been an R&B hit for Little Junior Parker (Sun 192) in 1953 before he switched to the Duke label. (A vintage photo of Elvis with Junior Parker and Bobby Bland adorns the sleeve of *The Original Memphis Blues Brothers* on Ace CHAD 265.) Elvis took the song at a faster tempo but his vocal is drenched in blues feeling and he achieves an ominous, almost doomy effect: 'That long black train, took my baby and gone.' Coupled with 'I Forgot To Remember To Forget' on the fifth and final Sun record (223), 'Mystery Train' climbed steadily up the country charts, eventually providing Elvis with his first Number 1. (After RCA purchased Elvis's contract in November they hastened to issue 'Mystery Train' themselves on 78/45, even though the Sun issue was still climbing the charts!) Probably at the same session, Elvis recorded the first version he made of 'When It Rains, It Really Pours', which had been written and recorded in 1954 by Billy 'The Kid' Emerson (Sun 214). On this and 'Mystery Train' drums complemented the regular two guitars and bass line-up. The Sun version remained unissued until 1983 but Elvis recorded the song for RCA in February 1957 and this version surfaced on *Elvis For Everyone* in 1965. Elvis gives the song a straight, most effective blues treatment.

January 1956 saw Elvis, Scotty and Bill, with the addition of Chet Atkins (guitar), Floyd Cramer (piano) and D. J. Fontana (drums), participating in the first of many recording sessions for RCA Victor, this one being held in Nashville. Between a convincing re-cut of 'I Got A Woman' and a rousing rendition of 'Money Honey', previously an R&B hit for Clyde McPhatter and the Drifters on Atlantic, they tackled a new song with sombre lyrics and gave it a very bluesy treatment. 'Heartbreak Hotel' proved to be the most important recording Elvis ever made. Rush-released at the end of the month, it entered every chart and in April climbed to the top of the Hot 100, staying there for eight weeks and selling over a million copies. It enjoyed similar success overseas and established Elvis as an international star. RCA had struck gold at the first attempt.

A few days later Elvis was in RCA's New York studio to record eight titles, including two 'Big Boy' Crudup blues. 'My Baby Left Me' had been recorded by Crudup in November 1950 (Victor 22-0109) and its fast tempo made it ideal for Elvis's rocking treatment. 'So Glad You're Mine', first recorded by Crudup in February 1946, with Jump Jackson on drums (Victor 20-1949), is more of a slow burner, with Elvis relishing the lyrics, declaring exuberantly, 'My baby's long and tall, shaped like a cannon-ball.' 'Shake, Rattle And Roll' illustrates the difficulty in distinguishing between early rock 'n' roll and rhythm and blues. A hit for Bill Haley and the Comets (Decca) in 1955, it might be thought that this prompted Elvis to record it, but a listen to his version on the Dorsey Brothers' television show makes it clear that he was familiar with the Big Joe Turner original (Atlantic 1026) from 1954 as he uses the original lyrics ('She wears those dresses, the sun come shining through . . .') – one wonders what the sponsor thought – and he even adds verses from Turner's 'Flip, Flop and Fly' (Atlantic 1053). The studio version was as toned down as Haley's but constitutes a marvellous slice of vintage rock 'n' roll. Coupled with a strong reading of Lloyd Price's 1952 Number 1 R&B hit 'Lawdy Miss Clawdy' (Specialty 428), it was issued as a single in the autumn. (At this period Elvis's stage movements caused considerable controversy, particularly when seen on television. Much of what he did came naturally but it has been suggested that he was visually influenced by Bo Diddley, whom he saw on stage in New York in 1956.)

In July 1956 Elvis recorded his biggest selling version of a previous R&B hit. 'Hound Dog', an early Jerry Leiber and Mike Stoller composition, was waxed by Big Mama Thornton for Peacock (1612) in 1952 and topped the R&B charts the following year. Elvis's version was faster and fiercer, with machine-gun-like drum rolls and two great Scotty Moore guitar solos. Coupled with 'Don't Be Cruel' from the same session, it soared to the Number 1 position in the Hot 100 in August. Within a few months its world sales approached five million, and the Presley phenomenon was well and truly rolling. By the time 'Mean Woman Blues' was recorded in January 1957, the transition from R&B to rock 'n' roll was complete. Elvis didn't entirely desert his blues roots, however. In February 1957 he recorded a sanitized version of a Dave Bartholomew and Pearl King composition that had been recorded by New Orleans R&B singer/guitarist Smiley Lewis in 1956 (Imperial 5380). 'One Night' soared up the charts when released as a single in October 1958. It wasn't until the '80s that RCA felt able to release the unbowdlerized 'One Night of

Sin' that Elvis had recorded a month earlier. Also in February 1957, Elvis successfully recorded Billy 'The Kid' Emerson's 'When It Rains, It Really Pours' but this was another track that had to wait for release until the *Elvis For Everyone* compilation.

Back in December 1956 Elvis had, unknowingly, been taped participating in an informal session at the Sun studio with Carl Perkins, Jerry Lee Lewis and (possibly) Johnny Cash, later dubbed the Million Dollar Quartet. Thirty-nine recordings from this session have now been issued. Mostly country, gospel and pop material there is little indication of the blues element that all four artists had in their musical make-up, except for near R&B like Chuck Berry's 'Brown Eyed Handsome Man'. Jerry Lee Lewis didn't hesitate to record blues for Sun and during a recent television interview for *Arena* stated his preference for the music. 'We listened to black artists mostly, down in Louisiana where I come from. I loved the blues, singing blues – I *still* think that's the best music.' Listen to his 'Hello, Hello Baby', 'Deep Elem Blues' or 'Big Legged Woman' (ultimately derived from a 1938 Johnny Temple blues, 'Big Leg Woman' on Decca 7547), at the end of which he exclaims, with his usual modesty, 'That's a hit!' As a teenager, Lewis frequented Haney's Big House in Ferriday, Louisiana, where he could hear black blues first hand. Jerry Lee's first big hit, 'Whole Lotta Shakin' Goin' On', a 1957 million-seller, had originally been recorded by R&B singer Big Maybelle in March 1955 (OKeh 7060). After regularly using it in concerts, Elvis himself recorded it for RCA in September 1970.

Several of the songs in Elvis's 1958 film *King Creole* – 'New Orleans', 'Hard Headed Woman', 'Trouble' (which uses the same riff as Muddy Waters's 'Hoochie Coochie Man') – have a strong blues feel but he was now recording such material less frequently. However, he still used his 'blues voice' on suitable songs like 'Santa Claus Is Back In Town', recorded in September 1957 for *Elvis' Christmas Album*. In June 1958, soon after his induction into the army, Elvis cut a few sides in Nashville, including a song written by Ivory Joe Hunter and Clyde Otis, 'Ain't That Lovin' You Baby'. (It is completely different to the Jimmy Reed R&B hit of the same title or Bobby Bland's 'Ain't That Lovin' You' on Duke.) The original seems to have been the version by Eddie Riff for Dover Records but its recording date is unknown and it may not predate the Presley version. However, Elvis's 'Ain't That Lovin' You Baby' stayed in the can until 1964. It made the US Top 20 late that year. A previously unissued alternative take – rather too frenetic – was included in the 1985 album *Reconsider Baby*.

On his return from the army in March 1960, Elvis recorded, if not 'a mess of blues' certainly several very relevant pieces: 'Fever' (a Peggy Lee pop hit in 1958 but originally an R&B Number 1 for Little Willie John on King in 1956), 'Like A Baby' (later an R&B hit for James Brown, also for King) and 'Such A Night' (a pop hit for Johnnie Ray in 1954 that had earlier been an R&B smash for Clyde McPhatter and the Drifters on Atlantic). The highlight of that April session in Nashville was, however, an incredible blues performance of Lowell Fulson's 'Reconsider Baby' (a 1954 R&B hit on Checker 804) with Elvis in his best 'growling' voice and Boots Randolph blowing the blues as if he'd been born to it. It was rightly chosen as the title track for a collection of Elvis's blues and R&B recordings issued in April 1985 that I can heartily recommend as the next best thing to the blues album that Elvis should have, but never did record.

During a March 1961 session otherwise devoted to ballads and beat numbers, Elvis recorded 'I Feel So Bad', which had been a 1954 R&B hit for its composer, Chuck Willis (OKeh 7029). Elvis's version made the R&B charts and reached Number 5 on the Hot 100, a surprisingly good placing for such material at that date. Despite this success, he recorded very few other such numbers during the 60s. Mixed in with the often mediocre film soundtrack songs were items like the 1959 Ray Charles hit 'What'd I Say' (July 1963), Chuck Berry's 'Memphis, Tennessee' (January 1964) and 'Too Much Monkey Business' (January 1968), and Jesse Stone's 'Down In The Alley' (May 1966), first recorded by the Clovers in 1957. Keeping faith with his roots, Elvis cut Jimmy Reed's 'Big Boss Man' and Tommy Tucker's 1964 hit 'High Heel Sneakers' (included on *Reconsider Baby*) at a September 1967 session and the bluesy 'All I Needed Was The Rain' in October.

The June 1968 television special included a version of 'That's All Right, Mama' but it was not shown when *Elvis* was screened by NBC on December 3. However, it featured in concert medleys of his early hits (some of which appeared on LP), but usually received perfunctory treatment. It's interesting to note that Bob Dylan also recorded a version of this song (electric rather than acoustic) as early as November 1962, but it wasn't released. Dylan freely acknowledged Elvis as a major early inspiration and shared with him an interest in rhythm and blues. (With the difference that Bob went right back to country blues sources for his material. Hear his excellent blues interpretation 'Meet Me In The Morning' on *Blood On The Tracks* or his Spivey recordings with Big Joe Williams, on which he played harmonica.)

'I'll Hold You In My Heart', a very bluesy treatment of a non-blues song, was one of the highlights of *From Elvis In Memphis*, released in June 1969 that drew from January/February sessions in that city, as did one album from a double LP set released in November. This included a memorable version of Percy Mayfield's 'Stranger In My Own Home Town' that the composer had recorded in 1963 (Tangerine 941). An alternative mix can be heard on *Reconsider Baby*, allowing the listener to savour his low-register 'blues voice' in context.

Although Elvis rarely returned to the blues in the seventies, when he did the results could be memorable. Chuck Berry had had some success in late 1958 with a revival of Charles Brown's 1948 hit (with Johnny Moore's Three Blazers) 'Merry Christmas Baby' (Exclusive 63X) and Brown himself recut it several times in the 60s. Elvis picked up the song for a May 1971 Nashville session and it was later released on an uneven album, *Elvis Sings The Wonderful World Of Christmas*. He was in tremendous form, both vocally and dynamically, and James Burton's brilliant guitar work serves to enhance the blues effect. A seven-minute edit is available on *Reconsider Baby* and rarely did Elvis relish his material so much: 'Dig it, James!'

Muddy Waters's theme song was his voodoo-influenced 'Got My Mojo Working'. The best of several recordings was the two-part version at the 1960 Newport Jazz Festival, his voice full of power and great support (Chess LP 1449). Elvis included the song in a lengthy June 1970 Nashville session and a couple of years later it appeared (somewhat inappropriately) on *Love Letters From Elvis*. Another Chicago blues artist, harmonica ace Little Walter, had a tremendous R&B chart success with a Willie Dixon composition, 'My Babe' (Checker 811) in 1955, reissued in 1960 with overdubbed chorus (Checker 955). Ricky Nelson's rocking version, with tasty helpings of James Burton guitar, was the B-side of a 1958 hit single on Imperial. Elvis sang it on stage, a recording from an August 1969 International Hotel, Las Vegas, concert being issued by RCA on *From*

Memphis To Vegas. (Conway Twitty also recorded 'My Babe', plus 'Big Boss Man' and 'Got My Mojo Working'.)

'See See Rider' or 'C. C. Rider' featured in many of Elvis's concerts and the February 1970 International Hotel recording of it was released as a single in the UK during 1970. This was credited to Ma Rainey, whose 1924 recording 'See See Rider Blues' (Paramount 12252) with Louis Armstrong (cornet) was extremely popular. ('See See Rider', 'C. C. Rider' and 'Easy Rider' are all variations of a traditional blues beginning:

> *See, see, rider, see what you have done,*
> *See, see, rider, see what you have done,*
> *You made me love you, now your man (or girl) done come,*

the term 'rider' being a euphemism for lover. Another early recording beginning with this verse is Blind Lemon Jefferson's 1926 'Corinna Blues', Paramount 12367.) Elvis was probably familiar with the 1957 revival of 'C. C. Rider' by Chuck Willis (Atlantic 1130), an R&B hit which also did well in the Hot 100, and LaVern Baker's faster 'See See Rider' (Atlantic 2167), which had some success in 1962.

Recording at the famed Stax studios in Memphis in July, 1973 Elvis recorded 'Just A Little Bit', which Rosco Gordon had recorded (Vee-Jay 332) and had some success with in 1960, and 'Three Corn Patches', a Leiber and Stoller composition which veteran bluesman T-Bone Walker had recorded for Reprise in 1973. Not many Presley recordings were made between 1974 and 1977, partly because of recurrent illness, and blues did not feature much on the agenda for the few sessions that did take place. However, it is fitting that amongst the songs performed at two of his final concerts that were used for a television film released after his death were 'That's All Right, Mama', 'Hound Dog' and 'See See Rider', all links with his R&B roots. Some rumoured Presley blues recordings remain unheard, notably his interpretation of 'Stormy Monday Blues' (memorably recorded by composer T-Bone Walker for Atlantic in 1956 and by Bobby Bland for Duke in 1962, although Elvis may instead have tackled a different song with this title that had been recorded by Billy Eckstine for Bluebird in 1943), and the fabled demos with Phineas Newborn's band, supposedly cut at a Memphis radio station, circa 1954.

Elvis Presley died at Graceland on 16 August 1977. Exactly 39 years before, on 16 August 1938, Robert Johnson – arguably the greatest and most influential country blues singer – died, near Greenwood, Mississippi. The King of Rock 'n' Roll and the King of the Delta Blues Singers had each influenced a generation of musicians and had a profound effect on the course of popular music. There was Elvis the 'Good Ole Boy', Elvis the rocker, Elvis the sublime ballad singer, Elvis the devout gospel singer and, least well known but for me the most exciting, Elvis the blues singer. Should you doubt his abilities in the field, take a listen to the 1985 compilation of Elvis R&B interpretations and prepare to *Reconsider Baby*!

I Did it My Way

As you become older, you relate more and more to the music from your early teens. Beatles enthusiasts were by and large born in the fifties, rock 'n' roll fans in the forties, and for those born in the thirties, the music from their formative years was a goodly supply of 'standards' and the corny but catchy hits of the late forties/early fifties. Almost every artist of the fifties included some standards and cover versions of those hits in their repertoires, and Elvis Presley was no exception. Time and again in his career, he chose songs from the period 1948 to 1954. Those years from the decline of the big band to the advent of rock 'n' roll are overlooked in the history of popular music, yet they were the years when the vocalists took the spotlight and would never return, after performing their solos, to sit demurely with the orchestra. Presley turned the music scene on its head – and yet, at the same time, he was singing standards just like Nat 'King' Cole, Rosemary Clooney, Frankie Laine and Joni James. Additionally, in later years Elvis also chose to record and perform successes by his contemporaries: cover versions, in fact. Here we look at some of his numbers which weren't original songs or from the rock 'n' roll, R&B or country fields – the standards and the covers – and find out who wrote them and who made them successful.

There can be little difficulty in deciding what constitutes a standard. By the time Presley was making records, nearly every number that had been written in the thirties or forties – or earlier – that was still being played, providing it wasn't too silly, was a standard. 'Pennies From Heaven' and 'Stardust' were standards; 'Mairzy Doats' wasn't! The same yardstick applies today. 'Bridge Over Troubled Water' and 'Yesterday' are standards: 'Chirpy Chirpy Cheep Cheep' isn't.

A cover version is more difficult to define. Nowadays, there is generally only one version of a current hit song, but go back to the fifties and nearly every song that showed signs of becoming a hit would be assigned to at least one act on each of the major record labels. In May and June of 1955, there were nineteen versions of 'Stranger In Paradise' issued in the UK.

Tony Bennett had the biggest seller, but six versions made the charts. Were the remaining thirteen cover versions of the Bennett hit? But then 'Stranger In Paradise' came from the musical *Kismet*, where it was sung by Doretta Morrow and Richard Kiley and also issued as a single. They sang it first, so in reality Bennett's recording was a cover of the duet version. Going back further still, the song itself was a cover – the music was adapted from Russian composer Alexander Borodin's *Polovtsian Dances*. In effect, someone originates a recording – not necessarily the hit version – and all recordings afterwards are covers.

Pleasing Mom with a copy of her favourite song is as old as the hills – most of us have bought records to do just that. What I never realized in the fifties was that it was possible to go one step further and *record* Mom's tune. Presley knew, though, and recorded 'My Happiness'. (Barbra Streisand also knew, and in 1955, as a thirteen-year-old, she recorded 'You'll Never Know', but she also took along her mother who aired her own tonsils with 'Second Hand Rose' – a song from *her* teenage years!) 'My Happiness' has music by Borney Bergantine and words by Betty Peterson and the copyright originates from Kansas City in 1933. The song met with little success then and it was only on 15 May 1948 that a recording by an unknown husband and wife team, Jon and Sondra Steele, on the equally obscure Damon label, entered the American charts. The disc sold over a million copies and became the year's biggest seller. Jon and Sondra had no further hits and so qualify as one of the biggest and earliest 'one hit wonders', although their follow-up, 'I Want To Be The Only One', also had lyrics by Betty Peterson.

Following the success of Jon and Sondra, there were other chart versions of 'My Happiness'. Ella Fitzgerald sold well, and her 'backing' vocals were by the Song Spinners, who became her instrumentation as this version was recorded at the time of union action by musicians. Some artists, and record labels, anticipating the strike, had recorded a stockpile of numbers in advance. The B-side to Jon and Sondra's hit was, appropriately, 'They All Recorded To Beat The Ban'! Another vocal group, the Pied Pipers, who were one of America's hottest acts at that time, also had a smash with 'My Happiness'. They had originated in the early forties with the Tommy Dorsey Orchestra and for a while their girl vocalist was Jo Stafford. By 1948 she had gone her own way and been replaced by June Hutton. Any one of these versions could have influenced a thirteen-year-old Elvis – he could hardly have missed the song on either the radio or the juke box. In November 1953, the number returned to the US charts, albeit briefly, for a harmonica-playing group, the Mulcays, who recorded for Cardinal. It was the label's only success out of the fifty singles they issued. A good percentage of their releases were by the Mulcays – and several of the rest were by, wait for it – Jon and Sondra Steele.

Nineteen forty-eight was also the year that 'Blue Moon' became a hit again. This standard is on so many vocalists' lists that it might be easier to name those who haven't sung it. The song dates from 1934 and was composed by Richard Rodgers and Lorenz Hart. They wrote mainly for the stage and the cinema and 'Blue Moon' is their only hit not to be associated with either medium. The lyrics you hear are the third set for the tune. The first version was called 'Prayer' and the second, 'The Bad In Every Man', occasionally gets an airing – usually as a comparison to the version we know today. Lorenz Hart wrote with Richard Rodgers until the early forties, and the partnership produced such hits as 'My Funny Valentine', 'The Lady Is A Tramp', 'With A Song In My Heart' and 'Where Or When'. Hart died in 1943, aged 48, from pneumonia, but by that time Rodgers had commenced writing with Oscar Hammerstein II. 'Blue Moon' provided several of the thirties bands with a hit, most notably those of Glen Gray and Benny Goodman, and the 1948 revival was in the hands of two men, both with big band associations, who became stalwart singers on the jazz scene in the fifties and beyond. They were Billy Eckstine and Mel Tormé, and Presley is likely to have recorded 'Blue Moon' on the strength of remembering either of these versions. Richard Rodgers may not have been entirely happy with Presley's treatment, although it clips-clops along quite nicely, as he was possessive about his material. When he heard the revival of 'Blue Moon' in 1961 by the R&B group the Marcels, he reached for his lawyer's phone number and probably some Panadol! However, the record wasn't withdrawn from the market – unlike the Robins' earlier version of the Cole Porter 1944 standard 'I Love You' from the Broadway show *Mexican Hayride*, which offended both composer and publisher. Possibly the royalties from the sales of the Marcels' adaptation mollified Mr Rodgers.

Presley dipped into the Rodgers catalogue again when he had a small hit in 1968 with 'You'll Never Walk Alone'. The song from Rodgers &

Hammerstein's *Carousel* had been popular at the end of 1945 when it reached the Top 10 via Frank Sinatra. Judy Garland also garnered some sales, and a cover by Roy Hamilton sold briefly during 1954. However, the song never meant a great deal in the USA – it certainly never had the impact, regard or sporting connotation that it has had here since Gerry and the Pacemakers completed their hat-trick of consecutive Number 1 singles with the number: indeed, the redoubtable Mr Marsden only reached Number 48 in America.

Another song which provided Elvis with a hit was definitely a cover version, though the song itself is a standard. Presley's 1966 version of 'Love Letters' owes everything to the Ketty Lester hit, especially by cribbing the outstanding piano accompaniment which helped to make it a big hit in 1962. The original hit version in 1945 had been by Dick Haymes, who was Frank Sinatra's replacement with the Harry James Orchestra and a popular crooner of the forties who vied with Sinatra and Crosby to be the decade's most popular male vocalist. The song itself had words by Edward Heyman, a very competent lyricist who wrote 'Blame It On My Youth' and 'I Cover The Waterfront', and music by Victor Young, who was a musical institution in himself. As well as violinist, conductor and arranger, Young was a prolific composer who had more than 300 themes and scores for the cinema to his credit. His numbers include 'Around The World', 'When I Fall In Love', 'My Foolish Heart' and 'Golden Earrings'. 'Love Letters' has both verse and chorus on some recordings – for instance, the Nat 'King' Cole version. Fashions change: to write a song without an introduction – a verse leading into a chorus – was almost unheard of during the first half of the century, but by 1950 it was a dying art, and many standards were being sung and recorded as chorus only. The big bands started the trend by dropping verses during the war years – not to help the war effort, I hasten to add! However the advent of the LP did slightly halt this trend. Richard Rodgers was extremely fond of the verse; some of his numbers had longer verses than choruses! Sinatra, bizarrely recorded the verse and not the song of 'Stardust'! Frank Loesser, composer of the show *Guys and Dolls* and such hits as 'Baby It's Cold Outside' and 'Standing On The Corner', had his finger right on the button, though, when he wrote his late forties hit 'On A Slow Boat To China', which declared, 'There's no verse to the song because I can't wait too long' to get you on a slow boat . . .

Another cover was Presley's version of Johnnie Ray's 1954 hit 'Such A Night'. Play the original (the original 'copy' by Ray that is, for even he was covering an R&B number by the Drifters) and then play Elvis and dare to disagree. What is more important, however, in this instance is not the song that was covered, but rather the singer. Johnnie Ray showed many rock 'n' roll singers the direction in which to go – there is no greater role model with whom to compare Elvis. Johnnie Ray hit the scene in 1951 and, like Presley, many listeners at first assumed he was a coloured performer. Not only is there a vocal similarity to Presley, but the electrical excitement that Ray created was the same – though much much more intense. The crowds that mobbed and sobbed with Johnnie Ray in the UK were young, with their emotions readily on display. There hadn't been a singer like him before. True, there had been Sinatra and his bobbysoxer fans in the USA, but Britain didn't take to Sinatra so readily and he never had a young following here. Britain's first singing idol of the post-war years was Donald Peers, a middle-aged pipe-smoking Welshman who became the hottest item around via his BBC series and theatre appearances, singing such songs as 'Dear Hearts And Gentle People' and 'Lavender Blue Dilly Dilly'. The American invasion started with the wholesome blond cowboy Guy Mitchell and his jaunty singalong ballads, 'The Roving Kind' and 'Belle Belle My Liberty Belle', and Frankie Laine who belted out 'Mule Train' and 'That Lucky Old Sun' and started the adrenalin pumping as he bent notes and wooed the audiences with 'The Girl In The Wood' and 'Jezebel'. By the time Johnnie Ray appeared, sobbing, wailing, clutching the microphone and tearing his heart out in public, the 'new' fans had arrived. Their only remaining need was the appearance of Presley and rock 'n' roll. Donald Peers' female fans would have loved to have gone to the cinema with him and strolled home hand in hand. With Guy Mitchell, they'd have expected a kiss on the doorstep. But with Johnnie Ray it was all that and 'bed'! Such was the sexual innuendo in Ray's 'Such A Night' that the BBC slapped an immediate ban on its broadcast – probably before the record had finished spinning. To hear it you had to buy it or hope that reception on Radio Luxembourg would be good that night! Also banned at the same time was Jo Stafford singing 'Make Love To Me', and the title alone did it! What a sheltered life those in the UK led, courtesy of the BBC.

'Old Shep', which charted in the UK as a track on the *Strictly Elvis* EP shouldn't really get a mention here, for the song doesn't fit the content under discussion – however, the composer warrants inclusion. Red Foley, who wrote the song, a particular favourite of Elvis's, in 1947, was a famous Grand Ole Opry star with numerous crossover hits, which, in turn, were covered by easy listening stars. When Elvis recorded 'Old Shep' he was following in the footsteps of Bing Crosby, who covered 'Chattanoogie Shoeshine Boy', Perry Como, with 'Don't Let The Stars Get In Your Eyes', Kay Starr, with 'Mississippi', and Teresa Brewer, who covered 'Cincinnati Dancing Pig'. The only difference – he waited ten years to cover the number! But if all this isn't worth Red getting a mention, then how about the fact that his daughter Shirley married Presley's main rival of the late fifties, Pat Boone?

Nineteen fifty was a good year from which Elvis chose material, the most famous of all being 'Are You Lonesome Tonight?'. The song's success was due to Blue Barron and his orchestra. The song originally dates from 1926 and was written by Roy Turk (composer of 'I Don't Know Why', 'I'll Get By' and Bing Crosby's theme, 'Where the Blue Of The Night Meets The Gold Of The Day') and Lou Handman. There were recordings then, long since vanished into the mists of time, by such as Henry Burr, one of America's top ballad singers during the first quarter of the twentieth century, and Vaughn Delcath, who despite the butch sounding name was in fact Leonore Vonderleath and, to boot, the first woman to sing on American radio. Al Jolson also recorded the song, but his version wasn't the hit that people have since implied. Blue Barron, the man with the hit in 1950, led what was described as a 'sweet band'. The type of music played by Barron and bands such as those of Guy Lombardo, Sammy Kaye and Kay Kyser, constituted, in the main, pop hits of the day and standards, as opposed to the big band music of the Woody Herman, Les Brown, Artie Shaw, Benny Goodman, Duke Ellington, Tommy and Jimmy Dorsey orchestras. As on the Jolson recording, Blue Barron featured the famous narration, but with a difference. Although Barron's current male vocalist Bobby Beers was entrusted with the vocal, along with a group called the Blue Notes, the recitation was given to John McCormick, a local disc jockey. Obviously, Bobby hadn't a lot going for him in the acting department! Play the Barron disc – if you ever manage to find this elusive MGM 78 rpm issued in August 1950 – and then play the Presley disc and you will find that although the tempo and scenario were changed very little, the dramatic content was considerably improved by Presley.

Nineteen fifty was also the year that 'Harbour Lights' enjoyed renewed popularity. With seven versions making the American Top 20, it is little wonder that Elvis chose this number for one of his Sun recordings. Sammy Kaye made it to the top, Guy Lombardo reached Number 2, Ray Anthony and his Orchestra Number 4 and Ralph Flanagan, with a sound not far removed from Glenn Miller's, was Number 5. Bing Crosby docked at Number 8, and at 11 was an instrumental by organist Ken Griffin, whilst a combination of steel guitars and harmonicas by Jerry Byrd and Jerry Murad's Harmonicats also sailed into the harbour at Number 19. Originally written in 1937, 'Harbour Lights' had words by celebrated English songwriter Jimmy Kennedy, whose lyrics also included 'Red Sails In The Sunset', 'My Prayer' (both of these, along with 'Harbour Lights', were hits for the Platters), 'Isle of Capri' and 'South Of The Border'. Vera Lynn had the British hit in the 1930s, whilst the honour in America fell to Frances Langford. By 1980 the song had become a country song and provided Rusty Draper with a chart entry.

Two country numbers became popular enough crossover hits to warrant inclusion here. Whether Elvis covered them as pop hits I leave to your choosing. In 1950, 'I Don't Care If The Sun Don't Shine', which didn't break into the C&W charts, became a Number 8 pop hit for Patti Page. Utterly different in treatment to the Presley version, Patti's starts with a slow bluesy verse which leads into a bouncy orchestrated chorus. Miss Page was one of the new breed, a singer with no big band experience, of the kind who were taking over as the favourites of entertainment. Later in her career she would be found singing ballads, standards, novelty songs, alongside cabaret and film work; she could put her voice to any kind of number and come out on top. 'How Much Is That Doggie In The Window?' may have been a hiccup in 1953, but the sales and publicity did her no harm whatsoever. Already in 1950 she had been involved in new recording techniques, when she was multi-tracked singing along with herself – four Pages for the price of one – and guitarist Les Paul and his vocalist Mary Ford would take this 'gimmick' to even greater heights. Patti also covered several other country numbers and can be described as the first easy listening vocalist to introduce country music to the national charts.

'Tennessee Waltz', originally a B-side to a Christmas number and a cover of Pee Wee King's 1948 hit, sold six million copies and made her the biggest-selling female artist to date. She may be overtaken by Madonna in sales – but never in repertoire! 'I Don't Care If The Sun Don't Shine' also became a hit for two other vocalists with the same surname, Martin. Tony had been around since the thirties, and he possessed a fine singing voice and starred in many film musicals. He also had the good fortune to be married to Cyd Charisse, whose well-known legs stretched from Monday to Friday. The other Martin was Dean, who possessed a great 'crooning' voice and had enough comic timing to suffer the indignities of Jerry Lewis throughout a series of movies in the early fifties.

The second country crossover hit, '(Now And Then) There's A Fool Such As I', written by Bill Trader, dates from 1953 and was a success for performers Tommy Edwards and Jo Stafford (as well as a country hit for Hank Snow): Edwards had made it big in 1958 with a re-recording of his minor 1951 hit 'It's All In The Game', and Jo Stafford was 'the girl with perfect pitch'. Tommy's version is a slow gentle ballad similar to Nat 'King' Cole's recording of it, whilst Jo's rendition is much slower and blues tinged. Jo gives of her best in phrasing and emotion: Elvis gives it all that too – and then some! By 1953 Jo Stafford was married to conductor/arranger Paul Weston and had moved from the Capitol label to Columbia. Columbia was *the* pop label of the early fifties, as it had many big American stars on its books. Although it lost Sinatra to Capitol, it boasted Frankie Laine, Guy Mitchell, Doris Day, Rosemary Clooney, Johnnie Ray and Tony Bennett, and a combination of these artists was invariably in the charts. Nineteen fifty-three was also the year that the Dutch company Philips, having acquired US Columbia which had previously been issued through EMI's UK Columbia label, began issuing records in Britain, and because of this roster became one of the most popular labels. Strange to relate, Philips was the last major label to issue records at 45 rpm, and had Elvis signed for Columbia rather than RCA Victor, all of his releases on Philips prior to 'Jailhouse Rock' would have been on 78 rpm only, other than 45s specially produced by the company for juke boxes. As well as Columbia and RCA Victor, the other major labels were Capitol and Decca. Coral, King, Mercury and MGM, though strong, were second division. Jo Stafford's 'A Fool Such As I' was the first American record released on Philips, but failed to make any impact in Britain despite her being the first female vocalist to top the newly introduced UK record charts when 'You Belong To Me' unseated the first Number 1 of all, Al Martino's 'Here In My Heart' – and what a fine cover Elvis could have made of that song.

Nineteen fifty-three was also the year from which Elvis took 'Crying In The Chapel', a song that had proved to be a hit on each of the three US charts. Written by Artie Glenn for his seventeen-year-old son Darrell and inspired by the little church in Fort Worth, Texas, where Darrell taught Sunday School, it became their one and only hit when the father and son team made it one of the year's big country numbers. Covered by the Orioles, it made the R&B chart and the pop versions included those by Ella Fitzgerald, June Valli and cowboy singer Rex Allen. Doubtless, had there been a religious chart, it would have made that too, especially as one of the cover versions was by the Sunshine Boys on a label called Bibletone. By the time of his recording, Elvis was an old hand at semi-religious numbers – maybe it was a good middle-of-the-road move on his part to widen audience appeal. Artists such as Bing Crosby, Tennessee Ernie Ford, Jo Stafford and Louis Armstrong all found a good market for religious and spiritual numbers. American Decca even had a separate numbering series on its label. A Christmas album was also considered a good move but Elvis's came too early in his career. The resultant ban by some radio stations and the actual sacking of a DJ in Portland, Oregon, created a furore of publicity and an even stronger pro-Presley lobby from listeners.

'Rags To Riches' was another song from 1953, and it provided Tony Bennett with a big-seller. This uptempo ballad was the work of composers Richard Adler and Jerry Ross, who were to have Broadway musical hits with *The Pajama Game* and *Damn Yankees*, which produced several popular songs, including 'Hey There', 'Hernando's Hideaway', 'Heart' and 'Whatever Lola Wants'. Tony Bennett was one of many early fifties balladeers with an Italian background, renamed from Anthony Dominick Benedetto by Bob Hope who had caught his act by accident. The Italian school of singers had a very strong influence. The advent of rock 'n' roll changed that, but for the first half of the 1950s there were hits for Sinatra, Perry Como, Frankie Laine, Dean Martin, Vic Damone, Joni James, Al Martino, Julius La Rosa, Jerry Vale, Lou Monte, Alan Dale and Toni Arden. Strangely enough, once rock 'n' roll had its feet firmly under the table, there was a second Italian school emanating from the East Coast, with Frankie Avalon, Connie Francis, Fabian and the two Bobbys – Darin and Rydell.

At the time of the second 'Italian Renaissance', there was a popular song which provided the first hit for twenty-year-old singer Ray Peterson called 'The Wonder Of You'. This was a pleasant ballad sung with little fervour and there were British versions, recorded in 1959, by Ronnie Carroll, Ronnie Hilton and Sheila Buxton. When Elvis recorded it live at Las Vegas eleven years later, he made such a *tour de force* of it that no other version could live alongside it. Play the Presley version and either of the two Ronnies and argue if you can.

Perhaps we could describe the third Italian revival as the time when Elvis recorded 'It's Now Or Never' and 'Surrender'. Both of Presley's huge-selling singles were adaptations of Italian compositions – 'It's Now Or Never' was originally written in 1901 as 'O Sole Mio' – and had become one of the staple songs of tenors the world over: even in the days before 'Just One Cornetto'! Presley talked of hitting a note like Mario Lanza at the end of the song and he even brought a Lanza record to the session. 'Surrender' was an adaptation of 'Torna A Sorrento' (from 1911) and, once again, a feature in the repertoire of every tenor who drew breath and also of those Italian singers from the early fifties: Frankie Laine, Al Martino, Dean Martin, Vic Damone all gave it the once over. Very often they would sing it half in Italian and then half in English under the title of 'Come Back To Sorrento'. None of them handled it like Presley, so none of them sold five million copies!

As the sixties turned into the seventies and Presley moved to the Las Vegas circuit, his repertoire grew to include many songs from his contemporaries – some of whom, such as Tom Jones and Engelbert Humperdinck, were singing them just down the road from him! 'Release Me', 'Gentle On My Mind', 'You've Lost That Lovin' Feelin'', 'Hey Jude', 'Bridge Over Troubled Water', 'It's Impossible', 'Yesterday' and more appeared in his shows and on his albums. The one song that sums up the international star/cabaret artist which Presley had become by the mid-seventies is 'My Way'. Some regard the song as an epitaph to superstars who have come along the long and winding road to fame and, like the man of La Mancha, 'fought the invincible fight' and 'dreamed the impossible dream'. Not quite true of course. 'My Way' is just another song of personal glorification which happens to fit a few stars like a glove – give or take a little poetic licence. A glance at the current catalogue reveals that many versions are available, including those by Paul Anka, Sid Vicious, Vera Lynn, Acker Bilk, Eartha Kitt, Doctor Feelgood, Mantovani, the Platters, Hank Snow and the Treorchy Male Voice Choir – all of whom obviously believe that they did it their way. Some may well have done so, some have already faced the final curtain, but there are plenty more artists doing the rounds and singing the songs who never will. The song is French in origin, with words by Gilles Thibaut and music by Claude François and Jacques Revaux, and it was known as 'Comme d'habitude'. Claude François was a popular singer in France – his sole UK chart success coming in 1976 with 'Tears On The Telephone' (who remembers that?) – who also did it his way when he changed a lightbulb whilst standing in the bath, and thereby became the late Claude François! The English lyrics to the tune came from Paul Anka: David Bowie had looked at the song but his lyric was not recorded. From Paul Anka it was but a short step to Frank Sinatra, who is reported as saying that if he didn't get an exclusive on the number there would be a horse's head at the foot of Mr Anka's bed. He was given the song and it did suit him down to the ground; Frank certainly did it – and is still doing it – his way. Never can a number have served one star for so many retirements and returns as 'My Way' did Francis Albert. In Britain the number became a personal triumph for Dorothy Squires, a popular female vocalist since the forties who had also done it her way. Miss Squires had been married to the prolific songwriter Billy Reid ('The Gypsy', 'Tree In A Meadow', 'I'm Walking Behind You') and 007 Roger Moore. She had also been shunned during the middle part of her career by most variety agencies but triumphed over this adversity by booking the London Palladium herself and selling out in an acclaimed comeback. Other stars wisely chose their own 'My Way'-type songs: Matt Monro with 'If I Never Sing Another Song' and Shirley Bassey with 'Nobody Does It Like Me'. The defiant 'I Am What I Am' from La Cage Aux Folles became the 'My Way' of the eighties.

Why, then, did Presley choose to record 'My Way' when it might have been better to have had his own similar type of number? In hindsight, he picked the right song, so did he choose the number with a certain amount of foresight? Was it just because it was such a good number? Could it have been a tribute to Frank Sinatra? They knew each other. In 1957 Sinatra stated that rock 'n' roll 'fosters almost totally negative and destructive reactions in young people' (conveniently forgetting his record-ing of 'Two Hearts, Two Kisses', a cover of the Charms' rock number) – but by 1960 he was hosting a TV spectacular to welcome Elvis home from Germany. Elvis's reason for choosing 'My Way' will never be known, but all the standards and covers that Elvis performed and recorded – just as Crosby, Como and Sinatra – had that extra-special quality added to them. From 'My Happiness' to 'My Way' is a great musical journey.

There was a time when I was young, when everything was new and life was for living, in a brave new world that seems so long ago now. The 1940s, with all that they implied, were over; and when Harold Macmillan pronounced that we'd never had it so good, few doubted it. Then, as often now, politics meant little or nothing to the youth of the time. The war was receding in the minds of people who just wanted to get on with their lives with as little hassle and as much fulfilment as possible. True, there were other conflicts around the world; but from what I remember, they had little or no effect on kids of our age group. This is not surprising, as the sages tell us: 't'was ever thus.'

The youth of Britain were filled with optimism, and rock 'n' roll was the catalyst. Everything was new, with more and more consumer goods appearing every day. The medium of television was gaining momentum and so, for the first time, it was possible to see the new idols as well as hear them. Rock 'n' roll, more than anything else, gave a fresh hope and impetus to youth. It had helped to destroy the dogma that you followed your parents without question into a lifestyle that had been laid down by previous generations, to become their younger clones. For the first time the world was your oyster, anyone's oyster – or at least it would be when it was all sorted out and had finally settled down. This born-again generation stood up and began to take its first faltering steps on a journey which questioned everyone and everything.

There was, however, one area where the old order held total, ultimate power, the one thing that hung like the sword of Damocles over every young man in the land: National Service.

It was always there. From early childhood every boy knew that this was what awaited him at the threshold of manhood: two years away from hearth and home. And this would come hard to a great number of those summoned, for, unlike today's high-flying youth, hardly anyone but the richest or the most foolhardy lived away from the family until that other inevitability, marriage. Strange as it may seem now, and especially in the context of those times, it was amazing how much individuality was retained in the face of a system that was designed to induce conformity – this initiation to 'make a man of you'. The Establishment went to great lengths to ensure that very few escaped the net, so the rich and the poor, the famous and the anonymous found themselves thrown together for what would be, probably, the only time in their lives.

Amongst the anonymities such as myself, there was the odd professional footballer and minor pop star; but nothing like the United States army, which boasted none other than Elvis Presley himself among its ranks. In common with Britain and, indeed, most countries that were lined up against each other at the height of the cold war, America also retained conscription: 'the draft' in their terms. The same sense of the inevitable occupied the minds of the boys on the other side of the Atlantic in the way it did ours. In fact, the USA would continue to call on their young men, throughout the tragic conflict of Vietnam, long after National Service in Britain had been consigned to history.

Elvis was almost an exact contemporary of mine; we both were called into the service of our respective countries within six weeks of each other. Though he was blissfully unaware of my specific case, I am sure he was acutely sensitive to the fact that his call-up did help to salve the indignation of many National Servicemen. After all, if the hero of the generation had to do his bit, then it must be OK for everyone else. I remember the disgust that was voiced when our own aspiring Elvis, Terry Dene, 'threw a wobbly' and was declared unfit for service. He had let the side down as far as the lads were concerned. This seriously damaged his career; his popularity waned, and a couple of years later he was virtually forgotten. Elvis, in the meantime, went from strength to strength. Because he served his time like everyone else, he gained a respect among the male population that he would not otherwise have had. Had Elvis not realized so for himself, I am sure his management team would have recognized the value of this sympathetic association with the experience of the generation worldwide.

Elvis reported to Fort Chaffee, Arkansas, to begin his basic training. I, along with some 250 other guys, reported to Aldershot, 'Home of the British Army', secure in the knowledge, acquired from my two grand-fathers, both Boer War veterans, that it had not changed much since their day (which was almost certainly true). In common with Elvis, I passed my induction medical A1 – this was not particularly creditable, I don't know anyone who didn't. (Due to the standards of the army medical, many who should not have been called up at all found themselves in the armed forces. I recall one colleague passed as A1 who had the sight of only one eye. He was eventually discharged on the recommendation of an army doctor who was in command of more faculties than the initial medical board, all of whom apparently served in the Boer War.)

Everyone came into the forces proudly sporting DA hairstyles, and wearing Italian suits with the latest winkle-picker shoes; but these were the last dying moments of freedom before the issue of the infamous khaki uniform with the texture of a coconut mat, and about as much style. The culture shock really began when we stood in line outside the barber's shop, a couple of hundred of us, and waited in trepidation for a team of sadists to run up the vertical sides of our craniums with electric clippers that had been in constant use for hours. They were so hot they could have burned our hair off without even being switched on. It was noted, however, from the pictures to be found in the newspapers and magazines of the day, that not only did Elvis's uniform seem a better fit than ours but his hair, attended to by one Karl Heinz Stein, also had some semblance of style, which we thought a bit unfair. But then, the Yanks always had it better, didn't they? Anyway, that's what the old sweats told us. Herr Stein is still in the hairdressing business in Freiburg, while our barbers probably went back to their old occupations as sheep shearers after National Service was abolished and the number of recruits declined.

It is well documented that Elvis's first meal as a conscript consisted of milk, a sandwich and the inevitable apple pie, which he is reported to have enjoyed. Our first meal was, I recall, steak, chips and peas. While we were eating, and I suspect being lulled into a false sense of security, officers walked amongst us, enquiring after our welfare and inviting comments on the repast. Come the dawn, however, the whole world changed. The officers of the night before were as unrecognizable as the food we were to consume for the next two years. There does not appear to have been a follow-up story for Elvis, but I like to imagine it might have been a similar tale.

Our first full day in the army was very like Elvis's. We were 'processed', as they aptly called it, allotted a number and issued with a bewildering number of items which were referred to as 'kit'. We were then given stencils and ink pads, and instructed to mark all the kit with our army number. Almost every piece of equipment confounded the stencil, which would move just as the ink was applied. A further application of the pad, in an effort to repair the damage, resulted in a great inky smear which made identification completely impossible. This rendered the original object of the exercise obsolete in one, or rather several, strokes.

The number which is assigned to you on induction into the services is like an invisible tattoo, you never forget it. I recall mine, 23563906, as if it were burned into my soul. It is, of course, of no interest to anyone else except those who trot their number out in pubs and the like as if it were a feat of memory to recall it. It always amazes me, therefore, that Elvis Presley must be the only serviceman in history whose army serial number, 53310761, is known to millions who can reel it off in a manner that suggests they personally had been issued with it.

Some time during the first full day, our squad corporal appeared. He had not been in evidence earlier due, I suspect, to having had something of a struggle extricating himself from beneath a large stone somewhere close by. Resplendent in his uniform and sporting a magnificent orchard of closely shaven acne, he volunteered the information that, in the event of us losing any of Her Majesty's property, not only would we be required to purchase replacements but he would personally subject the miscreant to punishment of an unsavoury, if not downright impossible, nature into the bargain.

Squad corporals apart (or possibly not), the next few weeks would have been the same for Elvis as for all new recruits. These were referred to as 'rookies' in the Americn army and, for some unknown reason, 'goons' in our mob. We were shouted at from dawn to dusk, subjected to inoculations and indoctrinations, marched till we dropped and then marched some more. Like a latter-day trial of Hercules, we marched hundreds of miles whilst remaining in the same place. Most of us wore out the soles of our boots during basic training, and when we were not wearing them, we were polishing them. We carried our rifles till our collar bones felt as though they had been thumped with a lump hammer; and then fired them until our ears sang for hours afterwards. Slowly and painfully, we were gradually transformed from a bunch of individual misfits (their terminology) into a single well-oiled unit (ditto). Those six weeks were the hardest and the longest of my life. The culmination was our 'passing out' parade, and then we all got our first weekend pass. Along with everyone else, I had never looked forward so much to anything in my life. It was only forty-eight hours, but I can still taste it now.

After that first weekend pass, virtually everyone was posted to a new unit: some were sent abroad to Germany and the like, while others stayed in Britain. On the completion of his basic training, Elvis was posted to Germany. I stayed in Aldershot.

With basic training out of the way, we were allowed the luxury of some of the accoutrements of everyday life. Everyone assumed, probably rightly, that Elvis had taken his guitar with him into the srvices. So a great many of our lads did the same. After all, it seemed the right thing to do, to emulate the King as much as was feasible. (It also gave me some sense of normality seeing my guitar lined up beside the old .303 rifle in my locker.) Then we more or less settled down in the knowledge that it was, after all, only for two years. Two years? My God, that is a lifetime when you are only nineteen.

These were the times when repeated obedience to mindless orders engendered a stoic emotional front. But when news came through of the plane crash that killed Buddy Holly, the Big Bopper, and Ritchie Valens, I saw grown men cry openly in the mess. That was the power of the fifties' pop heroes.

In common with most young men of his age, the opposite sex were starting to play a more important role in Elvis's life: indeed, it was while serving in Germany that he met his future wife, Priscilla. The subject in the barrack rooms always seemed to revolve around girls: how many, how often and . . . well, you know how it goes. There used to be what were officially termed 'unlicensed vendors', but which were referred to by the lads as 'Johnny Men', who would haunt the barracks of the new recruits. They were a most persistent species, hawking bits of lace-edged taffeta they referred to as table mats with 'Dear Mum and Dad' embroidered on them together with the regimental shoulder flash. They managed to gain access to the unsuspecting and homesick squaddies by bribing the junior NCOs with packets of condoms, hence the sobriquet. One unsavoury corporal had between thirty and forty packets in his locker. With monotonous regularity, at least half a dozen 'packets of three' were flashed to his mates prior to a weekend pass. He would then proudly display the empty packets on his return some forty-eight hours later. We were easily impressed, and we all envied his supposed sexual prowess.

After the completion of basic training, all trained soldiers were entitled to apply for a permanent pass. This meant that, with a stamp in the back of your pay book, signed by the company commander, you were not required to obtain a leave of absence from the barracks for a period up to thirty-six hours. In order to get this much sought-after passport to relative freedom, the applicant had to parade before the CO in regulation 'civilian dress' for his approval. This entailed the usual smart suit, collar and tie, all of which most guys had already kicked into touch and did not, or would not, admit to owning. The solution, however, was very simple. There was a certain lance corporal who did actually own such attire. For a small consideration, this suit (which was, luckily, of an average fit) appeared many times on many personages before our worthy Colonel, and was given the seal of approval. Once armed with his pass, the individual turned to his own threads, which were more in keeping with the times. As far as I can remember, no one was ever brought up on a charge for wearing his Italian-style, instead of the establishment, suit. I can still remember that much-borrowed civvy uniform: grey suit, striped shirt, a canary-yellow tie, and lace-up black Oxford shoes. Evading it scored yet another victory for the new ways.

It was while serving in the forces that many of us suffered the personal loss of someone close. Many of us lost a grandparent during this time and, in some cases, a parent. Elvis lost his beloved mother and although he was able to see her before the end it was, nevertheless, a very traumatic experience. It was another sign that our lives were changing and the innocence of youth was passing.

Because of the sheer number of men in the services on both sides of the Atlantic (or in any country where conscription was in force for that matter), the chances of promotion were that much greater. These advancements were of the paid/acting variety, where your substantive rank remained private. I am not sure how this worked in the American army but that is how it worked in ours. I was one of thousands who were promoted to NCO rank, though my true status still remained private. Most 'celebrities' in our lot were promoted at some stage of their service, and this was usually to give them more clout when pursuing what had been their civilian occupation. It might be a professional footballer working for the benefit of the battalion football team. The recipients of such promotions were able to avoid the more menial tasks, such as cookhouse duty, which were difficult to dodge if one remained the lowest of the low. Elvis made the rank of sergeant, perhaps for the same reason. In any event, his promotion to five-star general would have been greeted no less enthusiastically.

Eventually the two years passed away and we were thrown back into the real world again, and Elvis spiritually left us too to resume his career. Nothing was ever the same again. We went in as boys and came out as entirely different people. Viewing it all now from over thirty years later it seems such a short time, but the camaraderie is still there. From time to time, I have run across mates from those days and I can attest to the truth of it. Although Elvis served in a different army, he too was viewed as one of the boys and I imagine he would have greeted his old comrades no less warmly on the occasions that he ran into them – because it must have been a similar experience for him too. We were in the prime of our lives and those friendships were unique and never to come our way again.

BARRY LAZELL

King of the Whole Wide World

Elvis Presley died in mid-1977, which in pop music terms is a couple of careers ago, but, remarkably, he still holds the record on both sides of the Atlantic for the most hits in both the singles and albums charts. In the US, his tally of around 150 singles entries is more than half as many again as second-placed James Brown, and over double the total of third-placed Ray Charles, while his ninety hit albums similarly constitute half as many again as second-placed Frank Sinatra's score. Elvis is unlikely to be caught up with or overtaken in either case.

In the UK, his one-time imitator Cliff Richard is only now closing the gap in the singles stakes, a decade and a half after Elvis's death. Both artists have topped 100 hit singles, while nobody else has had more than fifty UK chart singles. Even with his current run of successes, and taking several duets into account, Cliff is a couple short of drawing level. On the album chart, with Elvis again topping ninety entries, second-placed James Last has to find another forty to turn the tables. Not, you'll agree, very likely. It will be a long time, if ever, before Elvis is replaced as the all-time charts champion.

AMERICAN CHART FEATS

Number Ones

Elvis had more US Number 1 singles than any other solo artist (and more than anyone at all, bar the Beatles), though the actual total is a movable feast, dependent upon which charts you consult. For starters, seventeen singles – 'Heartbreak Hotel', 'I Want You, I Need You, I Love You', 'Don't Be Cruel', 'Love Me Tender', 'Too Much', 'All Shook Up', 'Teddy Bear', 'Jailhouse Rock', 'Don't', 'Hard Headed Woman', 'A Big Hunk O' Love', 'Stuck On You', 'It's Now Or Never', 'Are You Lonesome Tonight?', 'Surrender', 'Good Luck Charm' and 'Suspicious Minds' –

topped the *Billboard* Best-Sellers in Stores chart and its successor (from mid-1958) the Hot 100. However, the rival chart from *Cashbox* magazine offers a few bonuses: 'Hound Dog', 'Return To Sender', 'In The Ghetto' and 'Burning Love' also reached Number 1; 'Hound Dog' for four weeks, and the latter three for a week apiece.

The question of 'Hound Dog' needs looking at more closely in the chart context, since it was, of course, coupled with 'Don't Be Cruel', and this double-sider was Elvis's biggest-ever seller in the US, topping a staggering six million copies. *Billboard*'s Best-Sellers chart coupled the single as a double A-side, giving it a record eleven consecutive weeks at the top. The same magazine's Top 100 of the time, which was a survey of song popularity rather than sales, divided the two sides, and placed 'Don't Be Cruel' at the top for seven weeks, with 'Hound Dog' sitting behind it at Number 2 for most of that time. (This, of course, was unprecedented in itself.) The *Cash Box* chart, compiled from a mixture of sales and jukebox plays, was able similarly to divide the sides up and, in this way, gave 'Hound Dog' its four-week spell at Number 1, to be replaced by 'Don't Be Cruel', which topped the chart for a further six weeks. The comparative weekly *Cash Box* placings in 1956 for both these titles are fascinating: never before or since have two sides of one single so dominated the top of the chart (the Beatles came closest in 1969, when 'Come Together' and 'Something' also climbed to Number 1 and Number 2 in *Cash Box*). The table below shows both sides' chart progress, plus the departure and arrival of the previous and next singles 'I Want You, I Need You, I Love You', and 'Love Me Tender'. One or the other of 'Hound Dog' and 'Don't Be Cruel' was in the Top 10 for seventeen weeks; they were there simultaneously for eight weeks. Note that 'Love Me Tender', which entered the chart the week 'I Want You, I Need You, I Love You' left, replaced 'Don't Be Cruel' at Number 1.

Elvis's second-biggest Number 1 seller was 'It's Now Or Never', in 1960, with three million copies sold in the US. The chart-toppers with the biggest advance orders were 'Love Me Tender' – for which 856,237 orders from record shops had been received by release date: half a million were before he had even recorded the song, but after he had previewed it on TV's *Ed Sullivan Show* – and 'Stuck On You', his first post-army single, which racked up an astonishing 1,275,077 orders, and thus qualified for a gold disc before it was even shipped.

	'I Want You . . .'	'Hound Dog'	'Don't Be Cruel'	'Love Me Tender'
4 Aug	4	6		
11 Aug	5	2	29	
18 Aug	8	1	13	
25 Aug	12	1	5	
1 Sep	14	1	4	
8 Sep	13	1	3	
15 Sep	15	2	1	
22 Sep	19	3	1	
29 Sep	28	2	1	
6 Oct	43	5	1	
13 Oct		6	1	40
20 Oct		14	1	2
27 Oct		13	2	1
3 Nov		14	3	1
10 Nov		19	4	1
17 Nov		22	7	1
24 Nov		25	5	1

B-side Hits

Elvis is also the all-time US record-holder for individually charting both sides of a single. In fact, it was almost an exception to the rule for both sides of a Presley 45 *not* to make the Top 100. A survey of both *Billboard* and *Cash Box* charts shows that no less than fifty-seven B-sides featured along with their A-sides, with 'Hound Dog'/'Don't Be Cruel' obviously being the supreme example. Other cases of both sides of a single hitting the US Top 10 were 'Don't'/'I Beg Of You', 'One Night'/'I Got Stung', 'A Fool Such As I'/'I Need Your Love Tonight' and 'Little Sister'/'His Latest Flame', while a further five singles placed both sides in the Top 20.

EP Hits

A strong format during the 1950s, the EP died very rapidly in the US during the early 1960s. Elvis bucked the trend by not only putting EPs into the Top 30 as late as 1962, but still charting them in the Top 100 in 1965, by which time the format had virtually vanished in America altogether. The use of radio and jukebox plays in US chart computations meant that, just as both sides of singles charted in their own right, so could different tracks from EPs. This was particularly so with Elvis's most successful EP, the first four-track excerpt from his second album *Elvis*, in 1956. The lead track 'Love Me' reached Number 6, helping the EP to its unprecedented million-plus sale, but 'When My Blue Moon Turns To Gold Again' also made the Top 30, and a third track, 'Paralyzed', climbed to Number 59 in *Billboard*. Almost simultaneously, 'Old Shep', lead track on the second EP taken from the album, also reached the Top 50, and 'Poor Boy', the most popular track on the *Love Me Tender* soundtrack EP, reached the Top 30. Earlier in 1956, Elvis had quickly followed his 'Heartbreak Hotel' chart debut with a Top 20 EP in the form of 'Blue Suede Shoes', which gave Carl Perkins' original hit single heavy opposition.

It was after he came out of the US Army that Elvis continued to have hit EPs when everyone else was failing to sell them. Early in 1961, *Flaming Star* climbed to Number 14 in *Billboard*. RCA didn't actually call this an EP: it was a four-track seven-inch 33 rpm disc in stereo, rejoicing in the description of 'Compact 33 Double' – to most people, nonetheless, it was still an EP. Its chart achievement was almost matched a year later by the *Follow That Dream* soundtrack EP, which made Number 15 in *Billboard*, and by the six-track EP from *Kid Galahad*, which reached Number 30 later in 1962. The latter again charted on the strength of one of its tracks – 'King Of The Whole Wide World' was the title which got the chart listing. The last Elvis EP – and the last EP ever – to enter the US Top 100 was the five-track selection from *Tickle Me*, which climbed to Number 70 in July 1965.

BRITISH CHART FEATS

Number Ones

In Britain too, Elvis has had more Number 1 singles than any other solo act. Again, different references (particularly the *Guinness Book Of Hit*

Singles, which sabotages many important statistics, some of which we'll unravel below) make it necessary to shop around to get the full total. Taking the *New Musical Express* chart (by far the most widely consulted during virtually the whole of Elvis's chart career) as first reference, there is a total of seventeen Number 1s – 'All Shook Up', 'Jailhouse Rock', 'One Night'/'I Got Stung', 'A Fool Such As I'/'I Need Your Love Tonight', 'It's Now Or Never', 'Are You Lonesome Tonight?', 'Wooden Heart', 'Surrender', 'Wild In The Country', 'His Latest Flame', 'Good Luck Charm', 'She's Not You', 'Return To Sender', 'Crying In The Chapel', 'In The Ghetto', 'The Wonder Of You' and 'Way Down'. However, the charts published by *Disc* and *Melody Maker* both gave 'Stuck On You' a week at the top in 1960, and the *Record Retailer* chart (the one used by the Guinness book) bestowed the same on '(You're The) Devil In Disguise' in 1963. Both these singles peaked at Number 2 in the *NME*. Also, every chart but the *NME*'s placed the 1962 double A-side 'Can't Help Falling In Love'/'Rock-A-Hula Baby' at Number 1 (we'll discuss the reason for this later on). This gives a grand total of twenty UK singles-chart-toppers, precisely the same number scored by the Beatles in a similar aggregation of the different charts. This is streets ahead of Cliff Richard's third-placed total of thirteen, while no other act has ever taken their British chart-topping tally into double figures.

Some of these singles actually entered the chart at Number 1. 'Jailhouse Rock', in January 1958, was the first record by any performer to attain this feat. It did so after being held back for a week, when Decca's presses proved unable to meet the 250,000-plus advance orders by the official release date of 10 January. By the time it did make the shops on 14 January, that demand had doubled (the film opened in London on the 16th), and half a million copies were sold over the first three days.

Almost exactly a year later, 'One Night'/'I Got Stung' similarly debuted at Number 1 in *Record Mirror*'s chart (though at Number 2 in *NME*), while in the autumn of 1960, 'It's Now Or Never' entered at the top, again after a delay in release. In fact, the song had been delayed for months because of a copyright hassle (RCA had put out the US B-side 'A Mess Of Blues' as an A-side in its own right instead), and once it did make the shops, it sold a million in six and a half weeks, to become Elvis's all-time best-selling UK single. The follow-up, 'Are You Lonesome Tonight?', was another instant Number 1 in the *Disc* chart (though a Number 2 entry in

NME), and in mid-1961, 'Surrender' debuted at the top, to make five first-week chart-toppers in all. Only the Beatles were to manage more.

B-side Hits

As in the US, Elvis charted more B-sides of singles in the UK than any other act, and again the *Guinness Hit Singles* book doesn't list several of them, because the chart it uses from 1960 onwards combined the sales of double-sided hits.

The first B-side to make it alone was, inevitably, 'Don't Be Cruel'. Although for some reason this didn't show in the *NME* chart, it reached Number 17 in the *Record Mirror* listing. In the UK, it definitely played second fiddle to 'Hound Dog', which reached Number 2. 'I Don't Care If The Sun Don't Shine', B-side of 'Blue Moon', was next to make it in its own right, towards the end of 1956, and four more flips – 'Rip It Up', 'Loving You', 'Got A Lot O' Lovin' To Do' and 'Trying To Get To You' – all followed their A-sides into the Top 30 during 1957.

'One Night'/'I Got Stung' and 'A Fool Such As I'/'I Need Your Love Tonight' were both given single entries in all the UK charts. In both these cases, their relative popularity was pretty well neck-and-neck, and it was therefore hard satisfactorily to separate side from side.

In 1960, as mentioned above, 'A Mess Of Blues' appeared in the UK as an A-side, when 'It's Now Or Never' was delayed. 'Girl Of My Best Friend', from the *Elvis Is Back* album, was selected as its B-side, and a highly profitable choice it proved to be. While 'A Mess Of Blues' climbed rapidly to its peak of Number 3, 'Girl' started off in the lower regions of the Top 30, but by its sixth week had joined its A-side in the *NME* Top 10. They rode the Top 10 simultaneously for four weeks, and 'Girl Of My Best Friend' peaked at Number 6 in its own right (while 'Mess' was still at three). In 1961, two chart-toppers, 'Wild In The Country' and 'His Latest Flame', were accompanied briefly by their B-sides: 'I Feel So Bad' reached Number 20 in a three-week Top 30 run, and 'Little Sister' made Number 18, also charting for three weeks.

Elvis's final charting UK B-side was actually a double A-side – the 1962 'Can't Help Falling In Love'/'Rock-A-Hula Baby' coupling referred to above. By requesting its dealers to log carefully which title buyers were asking for, the *NME* chart managed to show the comparative popularity of

	'Rock-A-Hula Baby'	'Can't Help Falling In Love'
3 Feb	4	30
10 Feb	2	19
17 Feb	3	18
24 Feb	3	9
3 Mar	7	5
10 Mar	8	7
17 Mar	8	5
24 Mar	13	3
31 Mar	18	3
7 Apr	26	6
14 Apr	24	8
21 Apr	28	9
28 Apr	25	16
5 May	16	16
12 May		20

both these titles throughout the single's sales run. This procedure prevented either side from overtaking Cliff Richard's 'The Young Ones' to gain Number 1 status in the *NME*, but it did make the coupling Elvis's biggest two-sided success ever. As with 'Hound Dog'/'Don't Be Cruel' in the States, it's fascinating to see their parallel week-on-week chart progress.

Note how the faster side of the single was initially the favourite, with the ballad creeping up on it after the first month, and eventually proving the more consistent side. The two sides peaked at 2 and 3, a double-side peak only ever beaten by Cliff Richard's Numbers 1 and 3 placings with 'The Next Time' and 'Bachelor Boy' at the end of 1962.

EP Hits and LPs in the Singles Chart

Only a week after 'Jailhouse Rock' entered the UK chart at Number 1, the soundtrack EP from the film charted too. It had not done so, surprisingly, in the US, where presumably the compilation method had caused the sales on the title song of the EP to be added to those of the single. In the UK, it became the highest-yet-charted full-price EP, reaching Number 18 in the *NME* and 15 in *Record Mirror*.

In February 1960, the EP *Strictly Elvis* made Number 26 in the singles chart, mostly on the strength of the track 'Old Shep', which had been off the market for two years in this country at the time, and was being clamoured for by fans. It was Elvis's only EP to make the Top 30 that year, but extraordinarily, two of his albums also sold in sufficient quantities to hit the singles lists during 1960 (this was before the LP chart carried any significance, albums still ordinarily being a tiny minority market). *Elvis Is Back* crashed in at Number 20 in the *NME* a week after release in July, and went even higher, to 17, the following week. Just before Christmas, Elvis repeated the trick with the *G.I. Blues* soundtrack, which made Number 25 in its first week of release.

The 1961 US chart-making *Flaming Star*, to the consternation of fans at the time, was not released in the UK, largely because Decca here was not geared to issue RCA's Compact 33 Doubles, and presumably either US RCA or Colonel Parker refused to allow it to appear any other way. However, the following year Elvis had his biggest UK EP success with *Follow That Dream*, which sold like a hit single during the summer of '62. The *Record Retailer* chart gave up logging it after two weeks, as indicated by an apologetic note quoted in the *Guinness Hit Singles* book. To view the EP's true achievement, it is necessary once again to check the *NME* chart, where 'Follow That Dream' debuted at Number 19 on 16 June, and went on to an eleven-week run in the Top 30, peaking at Number 11, a new high-point for a full-price EP. It wasn't the end of the EP run for 1962, either. In November, along came the six-track soundtrack to *Kid Galahad*, which fared only slightly less well: it reached Number 15 in a five-week Top 30 run.

There is a little-remembered coda to the Elvis singles chart EP entries, too. In 1965, RCA, in a fit of corporate idiocy, failed to issue either of the US singles ('(Such An) Easy Question' and 'I'm Yours') which followed the chart-topping 'Crying In The Chapel' – both reached Number 11 in the US and would surely have sold equally well here. Nevertheless, they were paired instead (with their B-sides) on an EP which celebrated their inclusion in the film *Tickle Me*. This release, different from the *Tickle Me* EP which was Elvis's last US chart EP (though that too was issued here, as *Tickle Me, Vol. 2*), sold well enough to make the *Melody Maker* singles

Top 50 in August 1965, when the *Record Retailer* Top 50 was still excluding EPs. It made Number 39, and charted for three weeks, sharing singles chart space with other big-selling EPs – Manfred Mann's *The One In The Middle*, the Rolling Stones' *Got Live If You Want It*, and Donovan's *The Universal Soldier*. Not a lot of people know that, but it's just another of Elvis's myriad extraordinary chart achievements.

ALL-TIME CHART CHAMP?

It would be premature to suggest that Elvis's chart feats are over. Single releases by him now are few and far between, and usually appear as a taster for a new compilation album, with little or no promotion, and so he is not currently adding to his singles-chart tally. While impossibly far ahead of anyone else in the US, he could be overtaken by the still chart-active Cliff Richard in the UK during the next year or two (a fact of which the Bachelor Boy is well aware, as he has indicated in interviews). However, with Presley recordings finally being made available for TV advertising music ('Stuck On You' in 1988 was the first – in a glue ad! – and 'Good Luck Charm' and 'The Wonder Of You' were both used in 1992), there is a possibility that such a track could appeal to a non-Elvis audience and suddenly top the chart. Suppose Levi's were to use an Elvis song, for instance? Meanwhile, on the album chart, frequent compilations still provide hits. The TV-promoted ballad set released for Valentine's Day, *From The Heart – His Greatest Love Songs*, has given Elvis a Top 5 album in the UK. It will not be the last.

PETER DOGGETT

I'm Counting on You:
Elvis by Numbers

Victorian collectors so loved the sight of butterflies flitting innocently through the air that they killed them and pinned their bodies to display cabinets. I felt the same air of sacrilege turning to the pocket calculator, rather than the thesaurus, in an attempt to understand the mysterious beauty of Elvis Presley's music.

Accountancy is more suited to the science of the production line, where numbers are everything, than to the realm of art. But with Elvis, we're left midway between inspiration and industry, with the quandary of a genuine artist whose raw materials were often the crassest products of the commercial song factory. It's easy to recognize art, or inspiration, or genius, or passion, or whatever you want to call it, in the epochal Elvis recordings – the rockabilly sides he cut at Sun in the mid-fifties, the initial swagger of his rock 'n' roll epics at RCA in 1956, the sheer relief that is recognizable in his voice when he escapes the twin prisons of the army (in 1960) and Hollywood (in 1968), and the stunning combination of craft and reflex which shaped his 1969 recordings in Memphis.

But what of the rest – the formula rockers of the pre-army days, the cutesy pop songs of the early sixties, the barren wastes of the Beatle-era film songs, even the drab conventionality of the middle-aged ballads which became his refuge in his final years – what do they have to do with art? How do they fit into our idea of Elvis as a musical genius? And what do they tell us about the man, and the overpowering framework of financiers, leeches and sycophants that surrounded him?

Facing an enigma, I reached back for the safety of numbers. If I couldn't comprehend what it was to *be* Elvis, sleepwalking his way through 'Petunia The Gardener's Daughter' or 'Yoga Is As Yoga Does' in the knowledge that he had once changed the world, I could at least document what happened to him as his career lurched beyond his control. So I went back to the beginning. Elvis Presley was primarily a recording artist: what did he record? The answer is not only 'Baby Let's Play House' and 'Suspicious Minds', but over 600 songs, divided unfairly between pop, blues, country, rock 'n' roll, gospel, ballads, and a special category of tunes that can, at best, only be classed as novelties. By itself, the division between each genre is pretty meaningless: it's mildly interesting that Elvis recorded more novelty tunes than gospel, but nothing more than that. Take this obsessive approach to the limits, though, and the year-by-year breakdown of Presley's song selections gives an uncannily accurate history of his multi-personalitied career. How much did Elvis decide his own artistic destiny? Was he a pawn of the money-men or an erratic judge of his own best potential? Was the real Elvis a balladeer, a rock 'n' roller or a child of the Hollywood musical? The bare figures come some way to answering all these questions. They also highlight the damning failure of Elvis, or his support team, to keep pace with the rapid-fire changes in the American music business, and the American psyche, over the twenty or so years when he was an active recording artist.

By 1956, when Elvis signed to RCA Records and began to gather the baubles of international, rather than merely regional, fame, he had already fractured the cosy progress of music history. The million-selling records of the next few years were simply a consolidation of what Elvis, Scotty Moore and Bill Black had achieved in the cramped quarters of Sun Records at 706 Union Avenue, a mile out of downtown Memphis. The common equation reads: R&B + C&W = R&R. That wasn't the whole story – in 1954, Elvis was as much a student of Dean Martin or the Blackwood gospel quartet as a unique mingling of blues and country. Elvis's genius wasn't just that he mixed styles. His achievement was to take the voices of black and white working-class Americans and produce music that crossed international boundaries, acting as a declaration of independence for all those who responded to its call.

So it's no surprise to discover that over half of the songs Presley cut at Sun came from either the blues or the country traditions, while another quarter were conscious attempts to milk the union of the two. The rest, appropriately for a man who loved songs of sentiment as well as of rebellion, were ballads, delivered with an almost spiritual air of respect for all that they implied.

The move to RCA – a company with national, even international, ambitions to consider – in 1956 signalled an immediate shift of emphasis in Elvis's work. Only one-third of the songs he recorded that year came from blues and country sources; another third were purpose-written rockers which turned Elvis's rockabilly revolt into style. Weakening the brew even more were the pop tunes, which borrowed the trappings of Elvis's stance as a rebel, and applied them to music which could just as easily have been written for Doris Day or Guy Mitchell.

Until the moment when Elvis was banished to Germany, and his recording career was halted for eighteen months, this uneasy balance was maintained. It allowed RCA and Colonel Tom Parker to market their boy as an all-round entertainer in the fullest sense of the cliché. On one level, Elvis appeared as a sneering, pelvis-thrusting delinquent promising a big hunk o' love; on another, he was a tender romantic, whose quavering baritone suggested an unholy alliance of seduction and safety; at the same time, late fifties Elvis was a spiritual, family-orientated man, who respected his mother, the church, and the conventional expectations of the idealized working-class. And there was more: the film actor, the growling bluesman, the hillbilly, the carol-singer, the devil, the saint. Even without the 'authenticity' of his initial rockabilly recordings, which was lost the moment Elvis reached RCA, Presley in 1958 was a sea of potential, each thrilling scenario on the verge of being fulfilled.

'Elvis died when he went into the army,' John Lennon commented when the body was finally entombed twenty years later. Lennon was wrong: Elvis didn't die, but the rudest of his artistic personalities were discreetly smothered. He returned to recording in 1960, and his music that year was a strange, almost cruel, clash of opposites. In keeping with the style's commercial collapse, rock 'n' roll was effectively excised from the menu. Instead, Elvis voiced his protest in the blues, cutting sides like 'Reconsider Baby' and 'Such A Night' with a raw, open emotion that was often hidden in the pre-army years.

Alongside this defiantly black music, Elvis offered the common currency of white middle-class pop, in the first of what would become a weary recital of emasculated songs tailored for his feature films. The movie music came in three kinds: ballads, which at least recognized one of the pivots of Presley's musical synthesis; pop songs, which occasionally mocked the style, if not the heart, of Elvis's fifties recordings but made no pretence of innovation; and novelties, which were simply vehicles whereby Elvis could advance the plots of his films, or establish himself as a cuddly Yuletide companion for all the family.

Elvis's final musical statement of 1960 was double-edged. By recording an album of gospel songs, he confirmed his allegiance to the values of the American nation. Yet at the same time, his passion for the affairs of the spirit inspired him to a depth of artistic and emotional commitment that was eradicated from his mainstream work. Gospel took the place of rock 'n' roll as Elvis's means of rebellion, at the same time as it conformed to the unquestioning acceptance he was rebelling against. Significantly, Elvis recorded no more gospel tunes until 1966, by which time the very notion of him as a rebel seemed laughable. The years in between were the darkest, and at first the most successful, of his career. Through 1961 and 1962, the diet of safe pop tunes, soundtrack novelties and gentle ballads occupied ninety per cent of his time in the studio. 1962 was a landmark: the first year in which Elvis recorded nothing which even approximated country, R&B or rock 'n' roll. The percentages slipped a little in 1963, but only because a new element was introduced to the stale recipe: Latin-flavoured tunes, which were true to some vision of America as a cultural melting pot, but had no emotional link with the child from Tupelo, Mississippi.

In 1963 and 1964, rock 'n' roll was allowed a tentative return – though in almost unrecognizable form. There were moments, on Chuck Berry's 'Memphis Tennessee' or the title song to the movie *Kissin' Cousins*, when Presley's music felt, from a distance, like a continuation of the sound of '58. What was missing was emotional involvement: with all corners rounded, all surprises barred, this was Rock by Numbers, backed by musicians who might as well have been recording 'No Room To Rhumba In A Sports Car'.

Nineteen sixty-five was the nadir: a year of three sets of soundtrack recordings, and not a single song which bucked the established movie formula. Untouched by the enterprise of Phil Spector, the Beach Boys, the Beatles, the Stones, the Byrds or Bob Dylan, Elvis's career dawdled in artistic limbo, timeless, pointless and grimly self-enclosed. The fans, painted in the master-plan as unquestioning consumers of Presley product, began to grow restless. They didn't have the opportunity to complain to Elvis in person, as the Beatles did during their much-hyped summit meeting with their fifties idol that summer, so they made their point with apathy. Movie revenues dropped; so did sales figures and chart placings. Significantly, Elvis only enjoyed one major hit in 1965, and that was 'Crying In The Chapel', recorded five years earlier during the post-army gospel sessions.

The NBC-TV special *Elvis* in 1968 was greeted as a rebirth of the 'old' Elvis, a transcendental moment of self-discovery. In fact, the television special merely confirmed a subtle drift which had begun in 1966. That year, a quarter of Elvis's recordings were, for the first time since 1960, gospel tunes. His sublime interpretation of the ballad 'Love Letters' debuted the mature, adult style which he perfected at the end of the decade. Rock 'n' roll made a faltering return, with some half-convincing songs on the *Spinout* and *Double Trouble* soundtracks. And Elvis signalled his first nod of recognition to the new spirit of American music by recording Bob Dylan's 'Tomorrow Is A Long Time', in a voice which ached with the knowledge of what he had been avoiding since he'd left the army.

On the surface, 1967 was a return to bad habits: two-thirds of his recordings that year were hapless film songs or unfelt ballads. For the first time since 1963, however, Elvis cut a country tune – and this wasn't a sentimental weepie he remembered from the fifties, but a brilliant new Jerry Reed song, 'Guitar Man'. In its lyrics, Presley must have recognized the man he might have been: over the next three years, he *became* him.

Nineteen sixty-eight evokes the TV special, with its revivals of classics from Presley's past, sung in a voice that blended hunger and coy self-mockery. The special closed with a song every bit as significant as 'Guitar Man', or anything else Elvis had recorded since the fifties: 'If I Can Dream'. Its democratic vision of universal harmony and respect was unreal in a year of political assassinations and inner-city riots, but just as 'Guitar Man' had connected Elvis to his past, 'If I Can Dream' allowed him to take a few steps into the world outside the airtight sanctuary of Graceland.

And so to the dilapidated shack of American Studios, on the fringes of Memphis, in January 1969, for the sessions which transported Elvis from a Hollywood dreamworld to a melting pot of contemporary musical styles. In two sets of extended sessions, Elvis returned home – not just to the city which he had set on fire in 1954, but also to the twin traditions of black and white music which he had been the first to entwine. At American

Studios, Elvis Presley also came of age as a performer. His recordings that year were spread across the spectrum, from gospel to harmless novelties, blues to country. Most numerous, though, were songs of maturity – 'adult pop', if you will – which moved beyond teenage scenarios to deal with the bitter-sweet magic and loss of grown-up love. That could be found as easily outside the marriage contract as within, but always had to be constructed within the borders of guilt and responsibility. Into this category slipped 'Suspicious Minds' and 'Kentucky Rain', both of which would have been inconceivable vehicles for the Elvis who played romantic lead to a procession of models in his movies.

Ultimately, 1969 was the first year since 1955 in which Elvis eluded any attempt at neat compartmentalization. A song like 'Long Black Limousine', which dealt with the ironies and disappointments of adult life, came from the country tradition and was sung with a raw emotion and control that epitomized soul music. For the first time since he invented rockabilly, Elvis's music crossed all boundaries.

Typically, the American Studios experiment wasn't repeated. For two more years, Elvis gave himself over to marathon studio sessions, in between his concert commitments, but the location was switched to the more familiar and homely RCA Studios in Nashville. In 1970, Elvis cut *Elvis Country*; the following year's project was *Elvis Sings The Wonderful World Of Christmas*. The latter was irrelevant, but the country album confirmed which of 1969's potential routes Elvis had chosen as his own. Equally important were the songs which didn't fit into either category. The *That's The Way It Is* album was Elvis's first – possibly only – full-blooded venture into adult pop, albeit with most of the passion safely removed. A year later, during the Christmas sessions of 1971 (recorded in May, with the studio decked in seasonal decorations to put the maestro in the mood), Elvis at last touched his own experience, with the first of a series of songs that reflected the imminent collapse of his own marriage. 'I'm Leaving', 'Until It's Time For You To Go' and 'It's Only Love' only hinted at what was to follow: the pathetically small output of 1972 rammed the message home.

That was a year of retreat for Elvis, who began to suffer from the health problems that dogged him till his death and also opted to keep away from the studios as much as possible. When he could be enticed in front of a

	1954/55	1956/58	1960/61	1962/65	1966/68	1969/71	1972/77	Total
Rock'n'Roll	22%	31%	4%	7%	8%	3%	4%	9%
R & B	40%	23%	10%	3%	8%	8%	13%	10%
C & W	16%	10%	3%	1%	5%	20%	27%	10%
Ballads	22%	17%	30%	25%	20%	12%	29%	22%
Teen Pop	—	11½%	30%	32%	20%	10%	11%	20%
Novelties	—	2½%	7%	22%	14%	7%	—	10%
Adult Pop	—	—	—	—	4%	21%	11%	6%
Soul	—	—	—	1%	—	6%	5%	2%
Gospel	—	5%	13%	—	20%	12%	—	8%
Latin	—	—	3%	9%	1%	1%	—	3%

Elvis Presley's Recorded Output by Musical Category

microphone, he was drawn to songs of regret, like 'Always On My Mind' and 'Separate Ways'. He found them on the country charts, and in ballads specially written for him by country composers.

Twice in 1973 Elvis attempted to rekindle the spark of the 1969 sessions by returning to Memphis and its soul capital, Stax Studios. But Stax was on the verge of bankruptcy, and so was the Presley studio formula. Elvis toyed with soul during those sessions, and even cut his last great rocker, Chuck Berry's 'Promised Land'. But more than half the songs were elegaic ballads and contemporary country laments like 'Good Time Charlie's Got The Blues' and 'You Asked Me To'. As if to lend pathos to the situation, Elvis even began to lose his vocal tone, which gave his Stax recordings a slightly desperate air.

From then on, studio work was an unwelcome obligation. Elvis recorded so little between January 1974 and his death in August 1977 that analysis is almost irrelevant. Let the record show, however, that on his final albums – which had to be completed with live tapes, as session after session was cancelled for reasons of illness – Elvis mixed recent country hits with the songs of his youth: classics like 'Unchained Melody', 'Softly As I Leave You' and 'Pledging My Love', 'He'll Have To Go' and 'She Thinks I Still Care' from the country songbook, a histrionic cover of Timi Yuro's hit

'Hurt' with a vocal that was one final bellow of anguish, even 'America The Beautiful' and 'Danny Boy'. The voice was leaden and inflexible, the pitch uncomfortable, the spirit battered and worn: only copious overdubs and Elvis's desperate need to communicate with his public salvaged these sides for release.

Given such waste, such potential, such abuse, maybe the bare, clinical figures of Elvis's recording career convey it all. The greatest rock 'n' roller of them all recorded more novelty songs than rockers – and only nine per cent of his studio time was devoted to rock 'n' roll. The vocalist who epitomized soul, whether directed through blues or country, spent the years of his prime – from twenty-six to thirty-three – recording synthetic pop and insipid, empty ballads. And having found, in the '68 Comeback Special and the '69 Memphis Sessions, music that was equal to the depth of his talent and power, he turned his back on self-discovery and wrapped himself in the drudgery of the road, a type of protection from the outside world that became every bit as cocoon-like and enervating as the inane movies of the sixties. The simple arithmetic tells that sad story; the explanation – wilful self-destruction, baleful outside influence, or perhaps simple ennui – remains obscure.

KEITH STRACHAN
A Voice to Die For

Late in 1977, shortly after Presley's death, I was asked by the producer Ray Cooney to be the Musical Director of a theatrical tribute to Elvis Presley, titled, simply, *Elvis*. It was like winning the pools. 'El the Pel' had been my childhood hero. Out came the old record collection, *Elvis' Golden Records* in the original (now somewhat dog-eared) picture album sleeve, 'Jailhouse Rock' on 78, those precious EPs and countless singles on 45. It brought it all back. I have been a professional musician for most of my working life and it was listening to those early Presley records plus those of Jerry Lee Lewis, Little Richard and Fats Domino that was my first inspiration.

I had my first taste of Elvis in 1956, at the tender age of twelve, when I heard 'Heartbreak Hotel' for the first time. It was a revelation – the cool string bass, that raw guitar solo, those Floyd Cramer piano fills that took me hours to work out, but most of all that *voice*. I'd never heard that kind of singing before. The popular artists of the time were 'crooners', the Top 10 was full of them. Rosemary Clooney, Dickie Valentine, Ruby Murray, Tony Bennett, Alma Cogan and Jimmy Young had all been Number 1 in the British charts in 1955.

For me Elvis's greatest contribution to popular music was his rendition of songs in this 'rockabilly' style. It was a raw blend of country music and rhythm and blues (as Carl Perkins put it, 'blues with a country beat') and Presley sang it like no one else could with an abandon and a joy of life that gave the music a prominence it might not otherwise have deserved. Most of the early records with Sun were covers of songs from black blues artists: when he left Sam Phillips to record for RCA the recordings and the songs had a greater sophistication but his voice retained that same vibrancy and spontaneity. Hence, the recordings of 'Jailhouse Rock', 'King Creole', 'Treat Me Nice', all written by Jerry Leiber and Mike Stoller, were, and still are, classics. Indeed, his voice on all the recordings before he went into the army in 1958 had an earthiness, a sexuality and that indescribable quality we call charisma. 'Heartbreak Hotel', that first major hit in 1956, changed the course of 'popular music' forever.

Which brings me back to 1977 and my job as Musical Director on the West End musical *Elvis*. The show had been written and was to be directed by Jack Good whose reputation I knew from *6.5 Special* and *Oh Boy!*, TV shows I'd watched in my teens. Jack, it turned out, was a stickler for accuracy and insisted that the guitar solos were note perfect and that the songs sounded exactly like the originals. It was my job to study the original records and write down the arrangements for the musicians in the band. Of course, getting the music to sound right is a bit of a wasted exercise if you haven't got someone to sound like the man himself. We auditioned about 2000 hopefuls for the part and it was my responsibility to judge their singing ability. It was a daunting task but I need not have worried, we ended up with three Elvi (the plural of Elvis in Jack's terminology) and they were played by P. J. Proby (who had recorded demos for Elvis and had been a big star himself in the sixties), Shakin' Stevens (who went on to be a recording success in his own right) and a sixteen-year-old schoolboy, Tim Whitnall, who sounded more like the young Elvis than I thought possible. Jack was looking for performers that had something of the charisma of Elvis rather than Elvis impersonators, and he chose well. The whole experience forced me to be much more analytical about that voice that had impressed me so much at the age of twelve. For instance I found myself asking such technical questions as 'What was his singing range?', 'Was Elvis a tenor or a baritone?', 'Did he support his voice as a trained singer should?', 'Did he breathe properly?', 'Did he always sing in tune?', 'Did his voice mature over the years as is usual in the classical field?' and 'How did he compare with other acknowledged singers of the time such as Roy Orbison?'

Of course, in rock singing (unlike classical singing) some of these considerations are thought to be irrelevant. Certainly, by the seventies singing to the upper extremes of your range was considered to be the key to good rock singing for both sexes, and if it roughed up your speaking voice a little, all the better. Surely, a rock singer who sounded as though he/she smoked 200 Woodbines a day and drank a bottle of whisky before breakfast had 'the right stuff'. Well, Joe Cocker, Bruce Springsteen, Janis Joplin and Rod Stewart did all right, but they all abused their voices in some way or other. Joe Cocker, in particular, has virtually no voice left after years of abuse. On the other hand, Elvis, in the main, looked after his voice. He had an innate musical intelligence, and an instinctive understanding of his own singing voice. He was a natural.

Yehudi Menuhin once said, 'Above other arts, music can be possessed without knowledge. Being an expression largely of the subconscious, it has its direct routes from whatever is in our guts, minds and spirits, without need of a detour through the classroom.' These words of wisdom are particularly appropriate to Elvis and his singing talent. He had no formal training. What we had was a young white boy from a poor family who had been brought up singing white gospel music and now was listening to music ranging from country and western to black rhythm and blues, but who wanted to sound like Dean Martin. An odd combination, but, over the years, you can hear all these influences in his various recordings. The R&B influence is the most obvious – it's what makes him sound black on all those great tracks like 'Hound Dog', 'All Shook Up', 'One Night', 'Party', 'King Creole' and 'Trouble'. The early ballads were often of country and western origin, e.g. 'I Want You, I Need You, I Love You', 'Love Me', 'That's When Your Heartaches Begin', 'Anyway You Want Me', and 'I Love You Because', and the title track from his first film 'Love Me Tender' was based on a traditional folk tune. He recorded two albums of gospel music, *His Hand In Mine* and *How Great Thou Art* and the songs 'It's Now Or Never' and 'Surrender' were even based on Italian operatic arias. 'Can't Help Falling In Love With You' shows the Dean Martin influence. Listen to that vibrato!

As for the question 'Is he a baritone or tenor?', the answer has to be baritone. A baritone singing voice is defined chiefly by its range low G to high G – two octaves. (A tenor is C to high C – again two octaves.) The other consideration, in this respect, is the natural sound of the voice: a baritone sounds richer, especially in the lower range. Elvis fits all the criteria for a baritone, his natural range is from low G to high G and his voice has a natural richness. The lowest note I can find Elvis singing on record is in the verse of 'King Creole', a low F which is really too low for him and sounds more like a sexy groan than a note. His low G, which occurs in numerous songs, e.g. 'Teddy Bear' and 'Don't', is much more comfortable. His highest note is at the end of 'Surrender', a high B flat. No mean feat for a baritone.

He did support his voice correctly for the most part (he did it instinctively), but there were exceptions in his later recordings. On 'If I Can Dream', recorded in June 1968, his voice sounds tired. He is straining to reach notes well within his range, he tends to sing flat and, although the recording has elements of excitement, it doesn't do him justice. With 'Burning Love', a studio recording from March 1972, it's difficult to believe it's Elvis at all: he sounds like a cheap impersonator. He's not supporting his voice at all and sounds strained on notes comfortably within his range. 'Always On My Mind', recorded the next day, is a much better performance.

He did sing in tune on almost all of his recordings, both studio and live. I've heard criticism of his singing of 'Love Me Tender' on the grounds that he's flat. Well, if we're being really pedantic he is a touch under the note here and there but the overall performance is so full of yearning and emotion that it is hardly noticeable. One recording that does offend me, though, is 'The Girl Of My Best Friend'. It's unusual to hear him sing out of tune but he's all over the place on this one. Even the Jordanaires sound sour.

In the main, his voice matured during those early years before the army: it sounds richer and his range was extending. In 'Jailhouse Rock', which is in the key of E flat, unusual for a rock 'n' roll song, he sings in the top of his range, the highest note being G flat. We hear the contrast in 'Don't', also written by Leiber and Stoller. His voice sounds much richer in this soulful ballad, ranging from a low G to his high D, a big range for a pop song. 'One Night' is a wonderful, animal-like performance and he hits a powerful high G sharp at the end.

While in the army he experimented with operatic arias. He was impressed by Mario Lanza, a popular operatic tenor of the fifties, and it seems he was trying to emulate him in these efforts. In 'It's Now Or Never', a Latin American treatment of the Italian classic 'O Sole Mio', he is going for the big tenor sound. The big high note at the beginning is only an E, but he does reach a G sharp for the big finish. The original 'O Sole Mio', it has to be said, is in the key of A, a full fourth higher than 'It's Now Or Never', and features a high B to show off the voice of the classic tenor. (Listen to Pavarotti's recording of 'O Sole Mio' to hear the song sung to perfection.) In 'Surrender', Elvis repeats the same trick with another Italian classic, 'Torna A Sorrento'. This recording, another Latin

American treatment, is only a semitone lower than the original (E flat instead of E) and he hits a high B flat, a full tone higher than anything he's recorded before. It's impressive all right, but with the benefit of hindsight, Elvis was treading dangerous ground. I liked it in 1961 but now it sounds like an academic exercise. So he manages to hit a B flat, but what happened to the charisma? Where's that animal sexuality? We should have been worried. The writing, I'm afraid, was on the wall.

After the army, he did rather go into decline as a performer and a singer. The hits kept coming for two or three years, largely because of his reputation, but I hardly think he is remembered as the King for 'Wooden Heart', 'His Latest Flame', 'Rock-A-Hula Baby' and 'Good Luck Charm'. We struggled to keep our faith when he was making those awful movies, but neither the material nor the performance of that material did him any justice. However, in the seventies, when he returned to live performances, he managed to rediscover some of the old magic. The better recordings of this later period are 'In The Ghetto' (using the low baritone area of his voice) and 'Suspicious Minds', recorded two days later using his upper range. He doesn't hit the high G with as much ease as he would have done before but it still has an earthiness true to his origins. 'Don't Cry Daddy', from the same time, is a country song performed with feeling in spite of its mawkish sentimentality. 'The Wonder Of You', a live recording from 1970, was his biggest hit in the years before he died. His voice sounds tired but he gives it all he's got. A better rendition of a better song is 'I Just Can't Help Believin'' a year later. Its strength is in its understatement, you always feel he has a little in reserve and the gospel choir is terrific. His performance of 'Polk Salad Annie' was dynamite, and then in a live recording from February 1972 he stirred our souls with the classic 'American Trilogy'. Just listen to the richness and control of his voice on the low notes at the beginning and then the power of his top A at the end. He sounds for all the world like a trained baritone with 'added street cred' on this recording, which encompasses a range of over two octaves. A great vocal performance full of dignity and passion. Compare and contrast this performance with 'Burning Love', recorded a month later. It's hard to believe it's the same person.

How does Elvis compare with other 'acclaimed' singers of the period? Elvis once said that Roy Orbison was 'the greatest singer in the world' and it was generous of him to say so. Orbison was after all named 'The

Caruso of Rock'. The thing about Orbison that sets him apart from Elvis is that he wrote his own songs. He was a tenor and he developed the falsetto part of his voice (the high part) and used it to great effect in many of his recordings. Orbison had a range of about two and a half octaves (much the same as Presley), but being a tenor he could reach higher (easily a C) but not quite so low. He wrote most of his songs so that they started at the bottom of his range and ended up really high. These songs, in the main, were anthems of pain and longing and some of them, such as 'Only The Lonely', 'In Dreams', 'It's Over' and 'Crying', remain classics. But, from a technical viewpoint, Roy never had quite the vocal control that Elvis had and as a result his intonation (tuning) wasn't as secure. He made some great records, and the voice was unique but, for me, it never had the charismatic quality of Presley's. And in the 'sex' department, even Roy's most ardent fans would have to accept that Elvis had a slight edge! Perhaps the only singer who deserves to be compared to Elvis in that department is Tom Jones. Although he emerged some years later and came from this side of the water, Tom had, and still has, a huge voice and an undoubted charisma as a performer. His influences were probably American soul music and he excelled in this area. The problem for Tom Jones is that he learned his trade on the British cabaret circuit and never quite got it out of his system. Unfortunately, in rock music 'street credibility' is everything and all too frequently Tom didn't have it. Consider, however, 'It's Not Unusual', 'Green Green Grass Of Home', 'Delilah' and, most recently, 'Kiss'. Some voice! But, compared to Elvis, the earthiness and sexuality in the voice seemed to be part of 'the performance' rather than being purely natural. Presley's sexuality was as natural as life itself.

And in the end that's what it comes down to. That's what set him apart from the pack. Elvis was a natural. He had it all. He had the look. He had sex. He had charisma. *And* he had a voice to die for.

JIM NEWCOMBE
Bop, Bop, Ahhh . . .

I was never fortunate enough to see Elvis on stage but one evening, at the Ontario Place Forum in Toronto, I got a taste of how it might have been when Don McLean did Presley's 'Don't' with the vocal backing of the Jordanaires. As they sang the breathy intro 'Don't, don't . . .' you could have closed your eyes and expected Elvis's impassioned plea to cut through the night air. It must have been magical to have seen him do this type of song 'live' and it's a pity that he didn't do more television shows or filmed performances. I have twice seen the Jordanaires with Presley imitators but I was distracted by the over-emphasized movements or vocal take-offs: the McLean treatment was simple and honest but it was the Jordanaires who made the song so special. Elvis and the Jordanaires had a rare chemistry together that other artists and producers tried to emulate by using the quartet on their own sessions.

The original Jordanaires were formed by the four Matthews brothers in Springfield, Missouri, but we move on a few years and a few changes in line-up before we get to 1949, when Gordon Stoker, who played piano for the quartet, took over as first tenor. The Grand Ole Opry was the place to be and so the group was working in Nashville. Stoker did a show with Hank Williams. As usual, Hank had turned up late.

Gordon Stoker from Gleason, Tennessee, had known Kentuckian Hoyt Hawkins most of his life and had sung with him when they were in their early teens. They both attended Peabody college in Nashville and Hoyt joined as baritone. Neal Matthews returned to his hometown, Nashville, after a stint in the armed forces and became second tenor. The bass singer was Colley Holt, but sickness forced him to quit and another Nashville native, Hugh Jarrett, who had already filled in with the group, took over. They became regulars on *Eddy Arnold Time*, a television show beamed out of Chicago for twenty-six weeks in 1955. The group would drive back from the Windy City on Friday night so that they rehearsed at the Opry on Saturday afternoon. By the time they recorded with Elvis, they were experienced performers with their own contract on Capitol Records.

When Elvis first met the Jordanaires, he told them that if he made it big on records, he'd like them on his sessions. Gordon Stoker recalls, 'When we first cut a session with him in 1956, which was at the old RCA studios in Nashville, he reminded us that he had met us. I vaguely remembered him because of the way he was dressed – he had white shoes, black pants and either a pink coat or a pink shirt – and he had long sideburns. It was out of character for a boy from Memphis, Tennessee, at that time, and that's what made him stand out at first. One of the secrets of his success is the fact that he looked different from anyone I've ever met. He had a period from about the mid-sixties to mid-seventies when he had the best-looking face that I've ever seen.'

Presley had the looks but underneath his shy exterior was a driving ambition and he was keen to learn more about the music business and to make contacts. Much has been made of the influence of black performers on the young Elvis, but he was also taking in country and pop acts. Stoker is sure he knew why Elvis came to say hello: 'He'd been hearing us on the Grand Ole Opry – we were on the network portion called the *Prince Albert Show* – nearly every Saturday night and we would sing a spiritual. He'd also heard us sing behind Red Foley and Hank Snow, people he dearly loved.' The tapes from the *Million Dollar Sessions* confirm this, with Elvis imitating Snow's nasal delivery. Stoker continued, 'He'd also heard records we had done with Red Foley and Hank Snow and he really liked the sound of the Jordanaires.' The young man they had met backstage had ambition and talent and when 1956 came around Elvis was hot enough to get on a major label, RCA.

The first RCA session produced a major hit, 'Heartbreak Hotel'. It didn't feature backing vocals but the B-side 'I Was The One', did, although it was Gordon Stoker, with Ben and Brock Speer, who provided the backing and not the Jordanaires. Why? Gordon explains: 'When RCA signed Elvis he asked for the Jordanaires through the Colonel, who already knew us through Eddy Arnold. The Colonel told Chet Atkins to get us, and we thought we would be called, but Chet Atkins said, "Gordon, would you mind working with Ben and Brock Speer instead of the rest of the Jordanaires? RCA has just signed the Speer Family: they need money and you've known them for years." I did kinda grow up with them, and I said, "Brock is a bass and Ben is a lead and I'm a first tenor, so who is gonna sing baritone?" Chet said, "Don't worry, it won't make any difference."'

Perhaps this indicates that Atkins thought Elvis was going to be a flash in the pan and did not merit a full commitment on the first session. Elvis, naturally, asked where the rest of the Jordanaires were and Stoker made up an excuse – 'If I'd told him the truth, it would have made him mad and he'd have told Chet off even though he wasn't in the habit of doing that. He didn't say anything except "Ah, ah, ah, the next time I want the Jordanaires".' 'Heartbreak Hotel' established Elvis and Elvis got what he wanted.

Even though 'Hound Dog' and 'Don't Be Cruel' were recorded in New York, the Jordanaires, rather than a local group, were on hand, but Gordon Stoker remembers the New York session for another reason: 'Shorty Long played piano on "Don't Be Cruel" and "Anyway You Want Me" and we went thirty minutes over. He said he had to go to another session, so I had to play piano as well as sing on "Hound Dog". If you play "Hound Dog" and listen to the instrumental, the "aahs" we sang were horrible. It was the worst sound we ever got because they didn't have a pick-up on the piano. We were not on different tracks, so we couldn't fix it.'

Gordon also recalls that it was in New York that Elvis asked if he could use their name on his records. 'We had never been asked that by an artist before, but that's the way he was, he always wanted to give people credit. Elvis Presley was the first artist who insisted the engineer, the musicians, the producer and the background singers were listed. It is a beautiful thing that he did.' Certainly, the Jordanaires were credited on Elvis's second album and the musicians were listed on the *Loving You* album. The Jordanaires were on Capitol and their producer, Ken Nelson, saw the wisdom of letting their name be carried into the homes of millions of fans.

The session that produced 'Hound Dog' took place in July 1956 and, from then on, the names of Elvis and the Jordanaires would go together like ham and eggs. Elvis felt comfortable with familiar faces around him and the Jordanaires found themselves being recognized in popularity polls in the pop magazines of the world. They scored high in the vocal group and instrumental sections of *Record Mirror*'s annual polls in the sixties: some people obviously thought that the Jordanaires was a collective name for all the musicians. Gordon Stoker has said, however, that they did play on some of Presley's first sessions – Neal playing guitar, Hoyt bass and Gordon piano.

The theory goes that a happy worker is a good worker and the

Jordanaires remember those sessions fondly. Gordon tells it like this: 'We thoroughly enjoyed every session 'cause Elvis was a big delight. He'd walk in with a big smile, he'd go to each person and shake hands and say something funny to everyone, like "Hey, man, I dig that shirt. Are you getting many laughs with it?" or "Where did you get that haircut? Did they fit a bowl around your head?" He wasn't putting you down: he just wanted to warm up to you and warm up to the session. He was trying to relax. He always wanted to have a lot of fun and he always did have a lot of fun.'

In Nashville in 1963, I saw George Jones cut four songs in a standard three-hour session with the Jordanaires, and I remember George taking off a little duck from a cartoon show. Before each song, George and the Jordanaires would sing the song together and they would work out their parts. It happened so incredibly fast that it left me bewildered. One minute the musicians were milling about, tuning up and talking, and then the next minute they'd deliver an incredibly good first take. This, then, was the kind of atmosphere Elvis worked in but no one watched the clock. Every record was going gold, so what if he did take longer than most? Gordon comments: 'He would come in and sit down at the piano or pick up his guitar. Most of the time, he'd start playing the piano like mad and singing, often religious songs, but you never knew what he might do. He might sing for two hours before we cut the first side.' Neal remembers an occasion when Elvis's good humour wore thin on the producers. 'We were called for a six o'clock session and Elvis played around and we sang spirituals and we were kidding and telling jokes. Of course, the longer we sang the more tired we got, and we reached a point where we were pretty well worn out. Elvis was just getting fired up and so, about three o'clock in the morning, he said, "Come on, guys, let's cut 'Crying In The Chapel'" and we only spent forty-five minutes on the song. It was one of the best records he ever did and he just did it because he was in the mood to do it. When he was ready, we had to be ready.'

The many out-takes which have been released since Elvis's death show him laughing and having a ball. He had a sharp ear, too, and you often hear him commenting on the music: he was in charge and, despite Gordon giving Elvis credit for his name checks, there was never a producer shown. Elvis worked with the Jordanaires on their arrangements. 'He made suggestions but most of the time he left it to us though,' says Gordon, 'but if he didn't like what he heard, he would say, "Would y'all try it this way, I think I might like it better."' Gordon recalls, ' "Don't" was one of Elvis's very favourite recordings. Maybe it was because it was the first session we used Millie Kirkham, the high soprano. We'd been using Millie in Nashville on a lot of country hits and he called me and asked me to bring her to Hollywood. Millie continued to work with him in Vegas after we quit.'

I also asked Gordon about the tours. 'The first concert we did with Elvis was in Atlanta, Georgia, in 1956, and to be onstage with him in front of many, many thousands of screaming people was a thrill I'll always treasure. Elvis said one time in the dressing-room, "I bet if I burped they'd scream." We were in the middle of the second song and he looked over at us, winked and burped real loud into the mike. They screamed. In Toronto they threw eggs at the stage and one hit Elvis's guitar, which he didn't like at all. He said, "One more egg and we walk off the stage." Another time in Kansas City, Missouri, the police lost control and Elvis said, "Everybody run. Run for your lives." We got in the cars just in time and that's an experience I'll never forget. We lost our guitars, drums and arrangements because the crowd took everything they could get their hands on.'

The Jordanaires not only did the backing vocals on the film soundtracks, but they appeared in some of them too. They are seen prominently in the final song of *Loving You*, where Elvis cuts loose on a television show. They're singing in a carriage of a train in *G.I. Blues* and in the nightclub scenes in *King Creole*. Filming was lucrative and, thanks to the Colonel's shrewd dealings, the group still receive royalties, although the schedule affected their main income from Nashville sessions. Lee Gillette of Capitol advised them that a career in the background would last longer than scrambling for a hit record themselves. Life in Hollywood was good with evening sessions and Elvis held parties almost every other night. Gordon reflects, 'Take *King Creole*: we stayed in Hollywood seven weeks to do just the little bit you see us in. His mother and his dad were there for *Loving You*. His mother was happy, all smiles, and he'd bought her a little dog to make her feel at home. She's sitting in the audience in the movie. He dances down an aisle and she's sitting on the end of a row. He would never look at the movie after her death.'

While they were in Hollywood, the Jordanaires got offers to do sessions and they recorded with many stars, including Ricky Nelson, a rival in

Elvis's record stakes. Gordon Stoker: 'Many times I would ask Elvis if he minded us working with various people and he said, "No, man, if I don't have anything cooking, I don't care." He wasn't happy, though, when someone had told him we cut with Tab Hunter the night before. Boy, fire flew in his eyes! He said, "I don't mind you cutting with other people, but I didn't know it was gonna be Tab Hunter."' Gordon never discovered the reason, but, as they were the most eligible bachelors in Hollywood, a woman was probably the cause.

So here was Elvis on top, with hit records and hit movies, when Uncle Sam called in 1958. Here we have the only change in the Jordanaires line-up throughout their association with Elvis. Hugh Jarrett left the group as his work as a disc jockey interfered with his group commitments, so a new bass man was needed. Ray Walker had studied at a Nashville college and sung in various quartets and he came out of the auditions best. Having a great sense of humour and being born in Mississippi like Elvis, he was soon in the firing line as Elvis cut some tracks just prior to going overseas for army service. Ray was given the juicy bass intro to 'A Fool Such As I'.

On his return, Elvis worked with the Jordanaires on one of his best albums, *Elvis Is Back*. I particularly favour the great blues, 'Like A Baby', the Jordanaires taking what would normally be the instrumental break and filling it with a vocal pattern that finds Elvis soaring in. And 'Girl Of My Best Friend' features a very distinctive intro by the boys. If you listen to other country and pop records from the same period, the vocal backings often sound dated, but not so the Presley classics. When he needed the Jordanaires just to bubble along in the background, as on 'I Beg Of You', that's what they did, but they are up-front on 'Return To Sender' and 'Teddy Bear'.

The Jordanaires also worked with Elvis on his television appearances. Gordon relates, 'TV appearances did not make him happy at all, and he was always very nervous. That's why he liked us so close. We're right behind him on *The Ed Sullivan Show* appearances. Now, the producers and directors did not want us that close, so it was always a struggle between Elvis and the producer! He wasn't happy on *The Steve Allen Show*, because they made him wear a tuxedo, in which he was very uncomfortable. They referred to him as a country boy, a hick, a hillbilly or whatever, and Elvis wasn't that at all. They thought that because he was from Tennessee, and they made a skit with Andy Griffith. It was Ed Sullivan who saw what a genuine person Elvis was, what a sincere person he was. He also did *The Milton Berle Show*, but he didn't do too many because the Colonel asked for too much money.'

It is no surprise that Elvis often wanted to record gospel songs. He did record an EP early in his career with the Jordanaires featured prominently, Neal Matthews singing some solo parts on 'Peace In The Valley'. As Stoker says, 'He trusted us to carry these songs, many of which he heard on Jordanaires' albums. We told him about "How Great Thou Art", he'd never even heard the song. We started singing it to him and he loved it so Ray said, "Hey, if you want to record this song, I'll go out and get the religious song book for you." He taught it to him and that's how that record came about and it has got more recognition than any other gospel album. The only Grammy Elvis got was for a religious album, ain't that something! This album, incidentally, was the first one on which Elvis used Felton Jarvis as producer. Felton told me that, as Elvis moved around a lot when he was singing, he sometimes gave him a handmike to get "the performance out of him".'

The gospel work is so different from Elvis the rocker and he immerses himself into the group so much, often sounding like he's just the lead singer. Listen to 'Man In The Sky', where the group sing one part and Elvis flits in and out in a high voice. Gordon says of 'Working On A Building', 'He didn't even know this song and he kinda leaned on us as he did on many recordings. It's amazing that anyone can listen to "Joshua Fit The Battle Of Jericho", just listen to it a few times and do all those words by memory, which is absolutely incredible, but we loved his leaning on us.'

Love is a word Gordon uses often to describe their relationship with Elvis, and I saw J. D. Sumner on a chat show about a year ago and all he talked about was the gifts, the jewellery Elvis had given him. Stoker says Elvis didn't have to buy their friendship, he had it already and they loved him like a brother. It was not easy for them to turn down the offer to resume stage work when Elvis made his comeback in Las Vegas, but their recording schedule was three sessions a day, five days a week. If they had gone to Vegas, then producers left without their services for six weeks would have found other groups. All the Jordanaires had done well financially, with interests in property and businesses all over Nashville and they couldn't give this up. Gordon says that with more notice of the comeback and better communications between Elvis's office and them, it might have been a different story. They continued working with him in the studio after his comeback but often their voices were blended with the Imperials, the first group he took to Vegas. Elvis was beginning to go for a bigger sound.

Gordon says the last session, in 1972, stands out for the wrong reasons. Like the first session, it was not the full Jordanaires but a mixed crew. Neal was on holiday and Hoyt was sick when the call came. Gordon called in Bergen White, who had done some arranging for Elvis but who had never met him. This in itself did not please Elvis as he disliked changes. 'I could tell he wasn't feeling good when he came in very late with something on his mind. He tried to play a demo record for us but the record player at RCA wouldn't play it very well. He got mad and kicked the record player and cussed RCA for not having a better one. He had three girls on one mike, the Jordanaires on another, and he was on one mike. The first number was a song like "My Wish Came True" – one of those numbers where Elvis came in and sang a few words: we would answer him and then maybe the girls would answer us. It was two or three hours before he put his headphones on and by that time the plugs had been pulled out of the wall. He couldn't hear us on his headphones, so he threw them on the floor and said, "Sorry, fellas, I shouldn't have come in tonight." He walked off and that was the last session we did with him. It upset me so much that I didn't go to sleep for three hours after I got home.'

The Names in Brackets

Elvis Presley's career can be divided into chronological sections: the rock 'n' roll years when the records predominated, the insipid years centred around films, and the performing years, often in Las Vegas. The varying aspects of these phases can be seen most clearly in his choice of songs.

Even Elvis's most savage detractors would admit that, throughout it all, he could actually sing. He was singing well in 1961 and he was singing well in 1968, so he was perfectly capable of doing just that in the intervening years. And yet he did little to stretch himself either vocally or intellectually. Outside his last few months, any deterioration in Elvis Presley's music had nothing to do with the quality of his voice. The problem lay in what he chose to do with his very considerable abilities.

Despite what the credits tell you, Elvis was not a songwriter. His name appears alongside Mae Boren Axton and Tommy Durden on 'Heartbreak Hotel' and Otis Blackwell on 'All Shook Up', but he didn't write them. It was common practice in the rock 'n' roll era but usually involved the managers and promoters taking credits, for example the DJ Alan Freed claiming a half-credit for Chuck Berry's 'Maybellene', Norman Petty a third share for 'That'll Be The Day', and Murray the K's mother sharing 'Splish Splash' with Bobby Darin. In light of that, it's surprising that Colonel Parker didn't claim some for himself. The most bizarre credit concerns the *Love Me Tender* soundtrack. The songs are supposedly composed by Vera Matson and Elvis Presley. Elvis didn't write them and nor did Vera. She was married to music arranger Ken Darby and, for tax reasons, he put his compositions in her name. As 'Love Me Tender' itself is based on a nineteenth-century tune, 'Aura Lee', the true credit is anyone's guess.

So, despite claims that he wrote some great songs, there is no evidence that Elvis ever wrote a note of music: it was all part of the publishing deals. Elvis himself said that the credits must stop, but the deals continued. Presley would record your song *if* he could also publish it and *if*, in many instances, you would agree to a reduced royalty rate.

This hadn't happened at Sun. All the songs he recorded there, whether new or old, were immaculately chosen and each Sun single combined two fine sides. The songs were from a variety of sources and yet none of the writers were to influence his subsequent career.

Elvis's first RCA record was 'Heartbreak Hotel', a power-packed, emotional song, but the record was as much a parody of Johnnie Ray's 'Cry' as Stan Freberg's 'Try'. It was written by Mae Boren Axton, but none of her subsequent songs was even recorded by Elvis, which is hardly surprising as they are mostly mediocre country. She was a songwriter with one true flash of inspiration. Still, Elvis returned to the Axton family in 1972 when he recorded her son Hoyt's song 'Never Been To Spain', an ideal song for Elvis as, compared to most stars, he had hardly been anywhere. (Travel might have broadened Elvis's mind and stopped him from becoming the most self-centred person on the planet.)

In July 1956 he had a session which introduced him to two major songwriting sources. He revived Big Mama Thornton's 'Hound Dog', which was written by Jerry Leiber and Mike Stoller. They worked as songwriters and producers for the Atlantic label and around the time of the recording Mike Stoller was aboard a sinking liner, *Andrea Doria*, and almost lost his life. When he returned to New York, Jerry Leiber met him on the quay. Ignoring his friend's experiences, Jerry exclaimed, 'Elvis has recorded "Hound Dog" and it's a hit!'

Although Leiber and Stoller were hardworking producers and songwriters for the Atlantic label, creating hit after hit for the Coasters and the Drifters, they tailored many songs for Elvis. Mike Stoller plays piano in the film *Jailhouse Rock* and they wrote the title song, 'Treat Me Nice', and two others, 'I Want To Be Free' and 'Baby I Don't Care' for that film alone. Their songs ranged from the whispered ballad 'Don't' to the seasonal R&B of 'Santa Claus Is Back In Town'. In later years, they wrote 'Is That All There Is?' for Peggy Lee and 'Pearl's A Singer' for Elkie Brooks. Their versatility was such that they could have given Elvis songs in whatever direction he wanted to go.

The other side of 'Hound Dog' was 'Don't Be Cruel', written by Otis Blackwell. Otis created the shuffle rhythm of 'All Shook Up' and Elvis also recorded 'Make Me Know It', 'Return To Sender', 'Paralyzed' and 'One Broken Heart For Sale'. He also wrote 'Fever', 'Handy Man', 'Great Balls Of Fire', 'Breathless' and a song Elvis should have recorded but didn't – 'Priscilla'.

With few exceptions, Colonel Parker did not like Elvis to meet his writers. On the face of it, this is nonsense. By meeting Elvis, the writers could have had a surer grasp of his preferences and his range and abilities, but Colonel Parker was against it. Why? I suspect he didn't want the writers to discuss the way they were being exploited, although Elvis certainly knew it was happening. When Elvis returned to Sun in December 1956 and was recorded at the informal Million Dollar Quartet session, he tells Carl Perkins and Jerry Lee Lewis, 'Faron Young wrote this song and sent it to me to record. He didn't want to give me any of it – he wanted it all.' Some compromise may have been reached, as Elvis recorded the song, 'Is It So Strange?', in January 1957.

Although they mightn't meet Elvis, the wily Colonel devised ground-rules for his client's material. The songs had to be in the first person so that the listener could identify with the King. Calling a girl 'darling' was out – far too adult – and 'baby' was more suitable. Elvis was such a prize that he was not allowed to have girls walking out on him in his songs. (This rule was reversed dramatically in the seventies.)

To make it easy for Elvis, you had to cut your demos in his key with singers who sounded as much like Elvis as possible. P. J. Proby, who did many of these demos, first met Elvis in Houston. 'Tommy Sands and I were regulars at the Hitching Post every Saturday and Elvis came there frequently. He was a regular on the Louisiana Hayride, which is the biggest country show besides Grand Ole Opry in the States. I met him there and he started going with my stepsister. They became engaged but he went off and became a huge star. I graduated from the Western Military Academy when I was seventeen and went straight to Hollywood and I got a job working as Elvis's demo man. I did the demos for his motion pictures. I got the work 'cause I could do them in one take. I knew how Elvis would treat it, so I was the favourite of the writers. While he was acting, I would cut the soundtracks and he would learn them from that. I would do them and I can sound very much like Elvis – almost any boy from the South can. Charlie Rich can sound like Elvis and so can Bob Luman and Conway Twitty – just listen to his first hit, "It's Only Make Believe".'

The material that Elvis recorded until he went into the army was almost uniformly great. My favourite is his revival of Lloyd Price's rhythm and blues hit 'Lawdy Miss Clawdy'. On paper, it's not much of a song – the lyrics hardly make sense – and yet it is a stunning performance, brimming with passion. This indicates that the words are only part of a record and it does not take lengthy lyrics to make a great song.

When Elvis returned from the army in 1960, he continued to record fine songs, and this is when Doc Pomus and Mort Shuman came into their own. Doc and Mort, two very different personalities, merged their talents to come up with 'A Mess Of Blues', 'Little Sister' and '(Marie's The Name) His Latest Flame'. They continued to write for Elvis well into his Hollywood years, generally injecting integrity into what he did.

Elvis always liked Mario Lanza. He knew the fans wouldn't buy straight recordings of operatic standards so he converted them to pop – 'O Sole Mio' became 'It's Now Or Never' and 'Torna A Sorrento' became 'Surrender'. His return to Sorrento was on a third-class ticket but 'It's Now Or Never' is a classic. The parallels with Mario Lanza can be seen throughout his career – both were on RCA, both loved the same arias, both ate to a phenomenal degree and became very bloated and overweight (Mario devoured seven chickens the night before his Royal Variety Performance), both took drugs excessively, and both died as a result of their habits at an early age. They were the original Super Mario Brothers.

G.I. Blues was an acceptable film although the scene in which Elvis's 'Blue Suede Shoes' is taken off the jukebox is somewhat symbolic. The film included 'Wooden Heart' and 'Big Boots', possibly the worst song he ever recorded, but there's also the underrated ballad 'Doin' The Best I Can', which could be a Number 1 country song for the likes of Randy Travis. *Blue Hawaii* is both the end of the golden period and the start of the decline. It contained both the magical 'Can't Help Fallin' In Love' and the dire 'Rock-A-Hula Baby', and its huge success led to a succession of cheapo-cheapo beach party movies with identical plots. Well, when I say cheapo-cheapo, Elvis didn't come cheap but nearly everything else did. He rarely had a comparable co-star because of the budgets involved.

The songs were still recorded with top-flight musicians but there was a lack of integrity. Anything went. No fan likes to think that his idol is not giving 100 per cent, but that is what happened. Elvis was immensely rich and he felt he had better things to do than listening to demos, attending recording sessions and planning his next tour. He wanted to have fun: he rode his motorbikes, drove his Cadillacs and had so many girlfriends that getting laid became a full-time occupation.

Once he saw that it worked on a few films, he kept it up. He would glide throughout his roles and make a fortune on the soundtrack albums. He could make them in his sleep – and he frequently did. And why not? It was a job like any other. How many people go into work purely for the money, just waiting for the end of the day?

And it is frequently said that Elvis's main aim in making a film was to pull the leading lady. He succeeded on several occasions but he was thrown into gloom when his advances were shunned, though Elvis usually got one of his henchmen to do the asking. A director who wanted an easy ride would have the good sense to find a leading lady who would be compatible with Elvis.

I also suspect that the King wanted to abdicate. He didn't relish being in direct competition with the Beatles: my God, that's hard work. He didn't have the inclination to try and top them, even if he could, and so he stayed in bottom gear. No wonder John Lennon, so disgusted with Elvis wasting his talent, dropped him from the cover of *Sgt Pepper's Lonely Hearts Club Band*. (A wise move for other reasons, as Colonel Parker would have charged royalties for the use of his picture.)

I have a bootleg album on RCA Victim, *Elvis' Greatest Shit!!*, which features 'the very best of the very worst'. The tracks include 'The Bullfighter Was A Lady', 'He's Your Uncle, Not Your Dad' and 'Old MacDonald Had A Farm'. There are twenty-two tracks but there could have been fifty. One of the most enduring things about Elvis is that he survived these terrible songs: most artists would have gone under. Some writers did nothing but give Elvis dire songs. Is Fred Burch proud of the fact that he wrote 'Sing, You Children', 'Yoga Is As Yoga Does' and 'The Love Machine' for Elvis? Did Sid Wayne realize that his 'Fun In Acapulco' was anything but fun? And how could Elvis keep on recording songs by Ben Weisman when he only managed three hits in over fifty songs?

Elvis wasn't totally somnambulistic. Occasionally he came out of the mire to record a gem, usually as a bonus track to one of his film soundtrack albums. He does a beautiful job on the ballads 'Love Letters' and 'It Hurts Me' and he sang a little-known Bob Dylan song, 'Tomorrow Is A Long Time'. Throughout it all, he always sang gospel music with conviction. Although he had developed his own interpretation of Christian behaviour, he loved singing gospel and the bookends from his Hollywood period are two excellent albums, *His Hand In Mine* (1960) and *How Great Thou Art* (1967), the latter giving him his first Grammy.

Of course, Elvis could have commissioned new songs from the likes of Gerry Goffin and Carole King, Burt Bacharach and Hal David, Jim Webb or even John Lennon and Paul McCartney. But he didn't bother. When both Ray Davies and Roy Wood gave him songs, he shrugged his shoulders and did something else. Elvis wanted inferior writers who were delighted to have a hotline to Elvis on the grounds that 50 per cent of something was better than 100 per cent of nothing. Many blame the Colonel, but I don't. If Elvis had said a few choice words to the press about his manager's tactics, Colonel Parker would have changed his ways. No, Elvis liked it that way. He couldn't care less if his fans got crap songs by crap songwriters. They'd buy them and he could still ride his motorbikes, drive his Cadillacs and screw his starlets. Hell, Elvis was so preoccupied that he couldn't even be bothered to write these awful songs himself and so amass himself more money.

Elvis was right. The fans did still go to the movies and buy the records – I even bought some myself. We knew Elvis didn't care but I have only recently realized how cynical he was. The sessions of Elvis recording 'A Dog's Life' have been released. From his comments, he knew he was singing rubbish and he couldn't care less. Where were his principles? Did he not realize that he once changed the world? Did he only do it for the mansion and the delights of the jungle room?

The psychedelic era did the trick. He hated it. Ironically, he hated the drug culture and he thought the country had gone to waste. Something in him stirred and he wanted to reclaim his throne. He made tentative moves with decent singles written by, and recorded with, guitarist Jerry Reed. There was 'Guitar Man' and 'U.S. Male' and a rewritten version of Chuck Berry's 'Too Much Monkey Business' with a reference to Vietnam.

Then came the TV special, the concert appearances and the wonderful sessions in Memphis. He added a touch of social conscience with Mac Davis's 'In The Ghetto' (a third-person song) and belted out 'Suspicious Minds', one of his greatest performances. The rubbish songs were discarded and Elvis's taste and craft had returned, at least for the next couple of years. Unfortunately, because of the problems over publishing rights, many songwriters didn't want to give him new songs and he often had to resort to cover versions such as 'You Don't Have To Say You Love Me' and 'Green Green Grass Of Home'.

He didn't always get it right, but 'American Trilogy' is regarded as one of his high spots. Mickey Newbury had the wonderful idea of combining three civil-war songs but I prefer Newbury's low-key rendition to Elvis Presley's no-holds-barred performance. Nevertheless, it has become an anthem of the South and is so popular in British country music clubs that cowboy-attired audiences stand to attention when it is played, firing their guns in the air at the end. 'God Save The Queen' would hardly have the same effect.

When Priscilla left him, Elvis wanted, for the first time in his life, to express his emotions in song. He wasn't able to write the songs so he chose ones that reflected how he felt – 'My Boy', 'Don't Cry Daddy', 'Always On My Mind' and 'You've Lost That Lovin' Feelin''. Songwriters were even asked to supply 'breaking-up-with-Priscilla' songs. His repertoire included maudlin country songs such as 'There Goes My Everything', 'You Gave Me A Mountain' and 'For The Good Times' and as the years went by country music became more and more important to him. He would joke about his old hits and send them up in ultra-fast versions on stage.

Elvis got into a rut in performing, always in America and usually in Las Vegas, just as he had been in a furrow when making films. He could do it without much thought and he was so confident on stage that he hardly needed to rehearse. Now he turned down film offers and it is mooted that he shunned the remake of *A Star Is Born* with Barbra Streisand although, being Elvis, he would have wanted Barbra's role.

Through sheer greed, Elvis had cut off his nose to spite his face. He needed good songs as much as they needed him. At every stage he should have been allowed to perform the best material possible, irrespective of publishing deals. Elvis was not alone in his actions – it is particularly common in country music – and it is always to the performer's artistic detriment.

Elvis could have gone through his career with the greatest songwriters of the century. They would have inspired each other. As it happened, few of his songwriters stayed for more than a few years: if they were any good, they realized that the rewards were greater elsewhere. Contrast Elvis with Frank Sinatra, who was not a songwriter either. In concert, Sinatra prefaced most songs with a credit for the songwriter: he cared who wrote the song. Elvis would have thought it a waste of time.

MORT SHUMAN
Writing for Elvis

For many people, the most important aspect of my songwriting career was the number of songs I wrote for Elvis (sixteen or twenty or anything in between, it all depends on who's counting and so much for my archives). It didn't matter that there were some other songs which were more important and of which I am somewhat prouder or that many of the Presley songs were illustriously unknown film fodder, and deservedly so. It didn't, and doesn't, matter that there are others who wrote at least twice as many for him as I did, people like Ben Weisman: perhaps it's because Ben never wrote a definitive Elvis song that his name is not mentioned along with Doc and Jerry and Mike and Otis and myself.

So, even though I never thought it was what my writing was about, when Elvis-time came to Tin Pan Alley, everyone was mobilized.

In the beginning, there was only one studio in New York for making demos – Associated on 7th and 49th on the fourth floor. Nat was the jovial, pipe-smoking boss who engineered, kept the books and swept floors: he then got Warren Schatz to sweep and engineer and, after that, Jerome Gaspar, who wound up as head of A&R at Epic. It was an old four-track machine and you listened on those metallic Ampex speakers. The room was nice and large so the conditions were comfortable. When the call came out, Associated was booked solid for two to three weeks, day and night. All of a sudden, people whom you never saw otherwise were congregating in front of the Turf Bar and Grill, which was on the ground floor of the Brill Building. On the other side of the entrance was Jack Dempsey's restaurant. Some of these people lived in the country and only came up at Elvis-time. So there they were, all with a song to write or to sell or to sing – and all the songs in a Presley mode. No other event got Broadway buzzing like an Elvis record or film.

Some of the writers (like myself) fancied themselves as singers and players. For the less multi-faceted, there was a pool of singers and musicians ready to out-Elvis Elvis in style and interpretation – singers like Jimmy Breedlove and Danny 'Run Joe' Taylor.

The little waiting-room at the studio was full of some of the greatest writing talent on the scene at the time, just coming out, waiting to get in, picking up dubs or just hangin' out.

You couldn't get more urban than Otis Blackwell, 'Daddy Rollin' Stone', and yet this man was one of the prime innovators of rockabilly, with songs like 'All Shook Up', 'Great Balls Of Fire' and 'Don't Be Cruel'. I met Otis when I was pitching my first song at Atlantic Records. Otis was like a father to Doc and me: he opened doors and helped us in many ways. There was a great solidarity then, due to the concentrated atmosphere of our professional lives. Otis might be talking to Aaron Schroeder, who was always in a hurry. Aaron was pure music business, wheelin' and dealin' all the time and writing with many. I'm sure he made a fortune and is now in unit trusts or farm machinery.

One of his partners was only that – J. Leslie McFarland, one of the greatest characters of rock 'n' roll and one of its most original talents. He was more than eccentric, he was mad, totally round the bend, yet no one ever writes or talks about him. He and Aaron Schroeder wrote 'Stuck On You', which was based on the shuffle Otis did for 'All Shook Up'. John Leslie and I wrote for a while when I was winding down with Doc. We never wrote for Presley together but we did do 'Little Children'. I always thought John wrote best by himself, even though his songs were not always accessible. Here is an example called 'Weeds':

> *The seeds of love were planted*
> *The first day that we met,*
> *I thought our love would blossom*
> *But much to my regret, there are*
> *Weeeeds, weeeeeeds, weeeeeeeds,*
> *Growing in the garden,*
> *The garden of love.*

Can you imagine Elvis recording that? John Leslie used to go to publishers with his arm in a sling and a patch over his eye, say that he had been beaten up and ask for an advance. They'd give it to him but he'd forget which arm he had in a sling and they'd see him the next day bandaged up in a different way. He made a couple of years of my life worthwhile.

The first song Doc and I wrote specifically for Elvis was 'A Mess Of

Blues'. 'A mess of blues' was a typical Doc Pomus expression: he loved the word 'mess' and he loved the blues, so 'Since you've gone, I've got a mess of blues' was perfect. It was only a B-side in the States but a lot of people picked up on it because they felt Elvis was returning to his roots.

We wrote 'Little Sister' in the Hotel Roosevelt in Hollywood. I had a guitar with me and I started fooling around with a riff which had nothing to do with the rhythm on Elvis's record. I had a very fast, driving guitar thing going and Elvis slowed it down by half. Doc came up with his inimitable R&B classic lyrics, which are really great. 'Little Sister' is among the Elvis records that I love best, and Ry Cooder did a cover version that was different again and I loved that too. It grooved and funked along and it worked just as well, so sexy too. I also love Dwight Yoakam's version of 'Little Sister', which was a big country hit. I went to see him at the Town and Country and thought he was a great country entertainer.

I can't deny it – I stole Bo Diddley's riff for 'His Latest Flame'. Everybody loves Bo Diddley. I don't know one blues or rock musician who doesn't love Bo Diddley. He is so special. I once saw Bo playing in the afternoon on some dinky fair, and yet the rhythm he was playing was one of the pillars of rock 'n' roll. It was his rhythm but there's no reason why someone shouldn't take it and do something else with it. After the Bo rhythm in 'His Latest Flame', we get to the middle eight where the song breaks and becomes something totally different. The record of 'Little Sister' and 'His Latest Flame' is pretty much my favourite Elvis 45, not because Doc and I wrote both sides but because they were two really strong songs, sung well, played well and produced well. In America, both sides went into the Top 10, which doesn't happen very often.

Doc and I never got to meet Elvis, but I didn't feel bad about it at the time. Now I realize that I would have at least liked to have shaken his hand and told him who I was. As it is, he gave strangers Cadillacs – and I never even got a Christmas card! For all the years that I submitted songs to Elvis, there was only one time when his people contacted me. They were trying to figure out a piano sound I had on the demo for 'His Latest Flame'. I had used some kind of echo on the middle eight but it was a fluke and I didn't know what I was doing. They couldn't fathom out what it was so they used straight triplets, which was also okay.

My greatest kick at the time was in writing the songs and in making those demos. 'Surrender' was never anything that I felt great about – we just did up an old song, 'Come Back To Sorrento', but there's a point in the demo of 'Surrender' where it breaks and we went from minor to major with me singing, 'Won't you please surrender to me?' Elvis did that exactly the way I did it, which made me feel good. It was nice to feel he was really listening to those demos.

RAMSEY CAMPBELL

I Went and Bought Myself a Ticket

The first time I saw Elvis was in a Liverpool cinema, the Essoldo, London Road, where the doorman warned one against venturing into the Gents in the stalls and the central heating seemed to stay unrepaired for years. Later the Essoldo would become a cinema club in which sex films were punctuated by strip artists, who reportedly performed their acts with all the swiftness of a silent film projected at the wrong speed so that they could shiver back into their clothes. My first sight of Elvis, however, was in 1961, when his debut feature *Love Me Tender* (1956) had reappeared as support for *The Fly*. The girls in the audience had a screaming contest when the unlucky scientist in the latter pulled the cloth off his new head, but as soon as Elvis came on the screen it was clear they had only been rehearsing. Come to think, the first close-up of Elvis in the trailer the previous week had produced the same response, and that must have been the first time I saw him.

Love Me Tender looks like someone's idea, or more likely a committee's idea, of a vehicle in which Elvis could ride onto the screen. It's an efficient colourless Western set at the end of the Civil War, in which Elvis has stayed home in the South and married Debra Paget under the misapprehension that his brother, who would have, has died in the war. It is directed by Robert D. Webb, and if I say that it is by far his best-known film you should have an idea of the problem. (Too often Elvis's films appear to have been directed by the cinematic equivalent of Colonel Parker.) Most of the second half consists of bunches of the cast riding around the same bit of landscape and missing one another. Twenty minutes of the film have passed before Elvis is even seen, by which time we've already heard the title theme more than once, and I'm not sure if delaying his appearance is a bit of canny foreplay by the director or evidence that the film isn't sure how to handle Elvis. Certainly his first break for song is shot largely from the waist up, though he does manage the odd on-screen pelvic jerk, one of them aimed at Clint's mother (Mildred Dunnock) to her shock and delight. Indeed, he sings the title

song half to her and half to his wife, and I'll leave it to other commentators
to decide whether all the older women in his films represent an attempt to
woo that audience or betray something more Oedipean. None of this, or
the weirdly inappropriate title, matters as much as Elvis, here at his most
southern and untamed. That first smouldering close-up in the trailer made
even the absurdly wide screen seem immaterial, and it's worth mentioning
that as an actor he more than held his own in such experienced company
as Neville Brand.

The following year's *Loving You* (a title presumably addressed to all the
girls in the audience) is less of a film. Elvis plays Deke Rivers, a hillbilly
who is delivering refreshments to a political rally when a clapped-out
bandleader (Wendell Corey) hustles him onstage to sing. Fame ensues.
He now tends to wear his guitar rather like a fig-leaf, and keeps breaking
strings – apparently by the power of his personality, since his hands rarely
stray anywhere near the instrument, which he flings off with what looks
suspiciously like relief whenever he finishes singing. It's one of those rock
musicals where the choreography consists of people clapping in the
background, several rotund matrons take a stand against the Devil's music
(though Lizabeth Scott, this film's older woman, reminds them that
Debussy and Stravinsky provoked the same reaction) but finally succumb
to jiving while remaining seated and the sub-plot dealing with the old
farts' on-off love affair is so dull that all we want is to get back to Elvis.
Eventually he finds someone more or less his own age and goes back to
the farm to sing the title song, while behind him a cow sits down to listen.
Towards the end the film cobbles together an identity crisis for him, which
is apparently resolved when Lizabeth Scott tells him (Freudians please
note), 'All your life you've been looking for someone called Momma.' The
real merit of *Loving You* is as a showcase for the kind of performance Elvis
must have been giving on stage at the time, with a generous helping of
good songs.

Now that Paramount had pretty well exhausted his autobiography, MGM
seem to have been unsure what to do with him, and *Jailhouse Rock* (1957)
looks like an attempt to make every kind of movie he might conceivably
fit into, not to mention a few of the opposite type. In the first twenty
minutes Elvis as Vince Everett (a better name for a disc jockey than for a
star) has killed a man, gone to jail for manslaughter, learned to play the
guitar, been strung up for a flogging (to the audible distress of the female

members of the audience when I first saw the film), left jail with an introduction to show business . . . You might think all this needed direction by somebody other than Richard Thorpe, who had recently made *The Student Prince*, and you'd be right. He makes perhaps understandably little of Vince Everett's struggle to fame, having his demo tape imitated by one Mickey Alba with eight golden discs to his name (by which time our hero has suffered a fit of artistic temperament at his first public appearance and smashed his guitar, leaving himself no protection). About halfway through, the director adds a commentary by the singer's partner, which certainly doesn't help, and nor does the attempt to contrive some love interest and class conflict between Elvis and the, er, otherwise little-known Judy Tyler. This relationship does yield one memorably hilarious scene, where Tyler takes him home and he walks out on her parents' guests for asking him about atonality and Dave Brubeck. When he shuts up her objections with a kiss and she protests, 'How dare you think such cheap tactics would work with me?', he responds, 'That ain't tactics, honey, that's just the beast in me.' Well, maybe that's the kind of thing you say when you're twenty-three years old, along with 'You look sexy tonight – you start the hammers pounding in my skull.' Soon Everett is snapped up by Climax Studios of Hollywood to play the businessman husband of an unsuitable leading lady, and the film begins to look unnervingly self-referential. The director's heart may be in the finale, when a punch up the bracket threatens to rob the singer of his voice. In true Hollywood style it returns, however, and Elvis very kindly sings to Judy Tyler, 'You're so young and beautiful.' That's my cue to mention that the film benefits from a fine score by Leiber and Stoller and a memorably bizarre bit of choreography for the title song, though I remember being disappointed that 'I Want To Be Free', an attractively stark number, wasn't heard in full as it was on the EP.

Nineteen fifty-eight brought him *King Creole*, a Harold Robbins tale of angst and gangsters in New Orleans, with a strong cast and a director with a reputation: Michael Curtiz, who once upon a time had made *Casablanca*. This announces itself as a musical, with a bit of ensemble singing along Bourbon Street at dawn, but most of the songs are solos with which Elvis punctuates the teenage suffering his character Danny Fisher carries about with him. If it's a decent enough performance, it does look as though Elvis is acting it out on behalf of his audience, with none of the true anguish of the, by then, late James Dean. At worst the songs feel as if they've been shoehorned into the plot – as if, for instance, someone involved in the production had the brainwave that as long as Danny Fisher has to distract the staff in a store while his cronies rob it, he might as well do so by singing. On the other hand, the scene in which gang boss Walter Matthau challenges him to sing and Elvis responds is worth the price of hiring the video. In this film, incidentally, his mother is dead, and he connives at the near-murder of his father, not that I'm suggesting that these details are in any way significant, you understand.

When he came out of the army in 1960 his best film as a film, *Flaming Star*, was waiting for him. Whereas *King Creole* was the last reasonably good film by a director once known for much better, *Flaming Star* was made by Don Siegel, who was seldom less than excellent. It divests itself of its songs in the opening five minutes, and after that it isn't a Presley vehicle but a film with Elvis in it. According to Siegel, it was based on a Nunnally Johnson script written with Brando in mind, but Elvis is entirely equal to the role of Pacer, an outsider who ultimately finds no home either with his white family or with the Kiowa tribe his mother came from. Siegel refused to take too much credit for Elvis's performance: 'Presley is a very fine actor, but he's given very little chance of being a fine actor . . . It's not a question of talent. He's in absolutely banal, stupid pictures endlessly, and he could make them for the rest of his life.'

Siegel said this in 1968, by which time it had been true for years. Even before *Flaming Star*, Elvis had made the dull if tuneful *G.I. Blues*, his or Colonel Parker's announcement that the army had domesticated him. For the rest of his movie career it is often difficult to remember more than the songs in the films, and sometimes even the songs. *Follow That Dream* is genial, *Kid Galahad* is unusually brutal for a demobbed Elvis film. *Viva Las Vegas* gives him a director as unabashedly vulgar as the setting and a lively co-star in Ann-Margret, and his return South in *Stay Away Joe* seems to have revived his boisterousness, but what else is there to say? Ironically, the year after Siegel's comments, Elvis made *Charro*, a Western without songs which looks like an attempt to rediscover what he learnt in *Flaming Star*, but it needed a better director than the man who made *The Unknown Terror*, a film in which people are turned into monsters that appear to have been dunked in Fairy Liquid. *Charro* resembles a spaghetti Western, not only because it provides Elvis with stubble like a penumbra to his sideburns and subjects him to the usual ignominies (branding, beating-up, abandonment in the desert) but also because the dialogue is so unspeakable, it sounds dubbed. Its British release was delayed for two years, and one can see why. Elvis made two more films in 1969, and then no more except for documentaries about him. After his death, one showed him bloated and sweating and forgetting the lines of 'Are You Lonesome Tonight?' onstage in Pershing, so that one might say he finally starred in his own horror film.

And yet, and yet . . . as time goes by, his later indistinguishable films seem to matter less and less. It was the early Elvis whom Peter Sellers did his best (alas, no longer very good) to imitate in his final film, and, far more to the point, David Lynch rounds off *Wild at Heart* by letting Nicolas Cage realize his ambition to sing 'Love Me Tender' in his best Elvis voice. While writing this brief reminiscence, I learnt that up in Jarrow a group of disabled musicians perform Elvis imitations in a local pub. At times towards the end Elvis became almost an Elvis-imitator himself.

The cinema has its own built-in nostalgia, and it romanticizes its heroes. Harrowing though Humphrey Bogart's last performance is, does anyone not think of *Casablanca* first when his name comes up? *The Green Berets* is unlikely to besmirch John Wayne's record for much longer, given all his good behaviour with John Ford and Howard Hawks, and Rod Steiger's wretched performance and worse wig in *The Kindred* can hardly destroy his Al Capone or his performance in *The Pawnbroker*. History is already in the process of preserving Elvis, and as time goes by he gets younger. There's nothing like the movies for keeping some people young.

HOWARD COCKBURN

The Shrimp, Petunia and Fort Lauderdale Chamber of Commerce: The Film Songs of Elvis Presley

To casual observers, it must be incomprehensible that the premier name in popular music, Elvis Presley, should suffer the indignity of appearing in such a motley assortment of films in the sixties. The quality of these films was, to be kind, mediocre.

Of course it was not always so! His Hollywood career began promisingly in the years 1956 to 1958 before the formula Presley films had been conceived.

By mid-1956 Elvis Aron Presley was the hottest singer in North America and his popularity was spreading throughout the world at a brisk pace and, as was common in those days, a shot at the big screen was obligatory. Tom Parker, Elvis's Svengali-like manager, was eager to explore all possible areas of exposure for his 'boy', and having conquered television, records and 'live' performances, the next logical step was Hollywood. The big question was, would Elvis appear solely through his acting skills or would music be his selling point. Paramount Pictures producer Hal Wallis was adamant that Elvis was hired for the musical side of his career and not his potential to be the new James Dean or Marlon Brando.

From the evidence of his first films, there was a genuine effort to give dramatic billing more than its fair share of emphasis. *Love Me Tender* could have survived without songs but there must have been great pressure to slot some in and cash in on Elvis's musical appeal. The film was made by Twentieth Century Fox, who made two further films with the focus again on drama but also featuring musical embellishments.

Although Hal Wallis signed Elvis to his first film contract (for Paramount), it was non-exclusive and Elvis was able to work for other companies during the Paramount period. Of the thirty-three films made by Elvis, fourteen were for MGM, nine for Paramount, four for United Artists, three for Fox and one each for Allied Artists, National General and Universal. These companies had a variety of policies when it came to Elvis and, consequently, the emphasis on drama and music varied considerably. Before Paramount exercised their option, Elvis first acted for Fox in 1956. The original story for *Love Me Tender* was *The Reno Brothers* by Maurice Geraghty, a cowboy yarn about the end of the Civil War. The title song became a single hit and the other three ('Let Me', 'Poor Boy', 'We're Gonna Move') are countryish items that are pleasant enough. Rock 'n' roll would have been somewhat out of place in 1865 so a toning-down was necessary. Fox's music supervisor Ken Darby wrote the four songs using his wife's name, Vera Matson. The politics of publishing came into play and all four songs have the name Presley on the credits. The politics and the financial wranglings associated with Elvis's songs were the root cause of the sixties slump in the quality of his music.

Fox's other two Elvis associations, *Flaming Star* and *Wild In The Country*, were essentially non-musicals and only featured a mandatory song or two. Apart from the title songs, *Star* had only one, *Country* only three and none of these took audience concentration away from the drama: both films could have survived without them. Only 'I Slipped, I Stumbled, I Fell' is of genuine importance and stands up in its own right. Fox did not pursue its association past 1961 and follow Elvis into the formula period.

Of Paramount's nine-film selection, the two pre-army offerings are both musical and dramatic stories about young singers. Extremely strong soundtracks were commissioned for both *Loving You* and *King Creole*. 'Teddy Bear', 'Loving You', 'Party', 'Mean Woman Blues' and 'Got a Lot O' Livin' to Do', all from *Loving You*, are high-order compositions that stand up in their own right. The songs used in *King Creole* achieve a similar standing and are also entirely suited to the film's New Orleans background. 'Trouble', 'King Creole', 'Dixieland Rock', 'Hard Headed Woman' and 'As Long As I Have You' remain favourites not only of Elvis fans but also of oldies radio shows. *Loving You* and *King Creole* both succeeded due to the quality of story, production, acting and the standard of the songs.

Elvis's first post-army film, *G.I. Blues*, was extremely successful at the box office and spawned an equally popular soundtrack album, setting the trend for the rest of the Paramount features through to 1966. Dramatically the film is lightweight, relying heavily on backdrops and longshots. The music is much more diluted and includes a German folk song 'Wooden Heart', a recut of 'Blue Suede Shoes', a lullaby, 'Big Boots', a singalong, 'Didja Ever', and some ballads and rockers of a less frenetic pace than of yore. All are entertaining but are from a different planet than the pre-army soundtracks. Paramount's follow-up was the even more successful *Blue Hawaii*, which is Elvis's biggest-grossing film ever. It contained a lot of Hawaiian music, a couple of pseudo-rockers in 'Rock-A-Hula Baby' and 'Slicin' Sand', plus a ballad that became a concert favourite, 'Can't Help Falling In Love'.

Blue Hawaii was where I entered the picture as it was the first Elvis film I saw, my youth preventing me from attending earlier features although I had been buying records since 1959. This situation may influence my viewpoint as I did not see the pre-army films until the mid-sixties, but the films from 1962 were seen chronologically. I say this because the decline in Elvis's films was not so apparent at the time as it now seems looking back. We are all more enlightened, much wiser and full of retrospective advice as to what should have been done back then.

Paramount's next feature, *Girls! Girls! Girls!*, brought our hero back to Hawaii for a second helping of sun, songs and girls. It gave us an Elvis classic in 'Return To Sender', from Otis Blackwell, the man who also wrote 'Don't Be Cruel' and 'All Shook Up'. However the remainder is average film-soundtrack fodder, ranging from an adequate rocker in 'I Don't Wanna Be Tied', a good ballad in 'Because Of Love' on down to a couple of shockers in 'Song Of The Shrimp' and 'The Walls Have Ears'. 'Thanks To The Rolling Sea' and 'We're Coming In Loaded', both written for the story, can now be seen as part of a deteriorating trend where the music was less important than the speed of production and quick return of capital.

Next stop was Acapulco, in Paramount's 1963 saga *Fun In Acapulco*. Complete with a Mexican feel, the soundtrack had little meat on the bone. 'Bossa Nova Baby' was a Jerry Leiber and Mike Stoller song from 1962 that provided the film's best musical moment, but 'The Bullfighter Was A Lady' and 'There's No Room To Rhumba In A Sports Car' should have triggered alarm bells in the Presley camp! How on earth could Elvis have agreed to sing such material? Was this the same man who recorded 'Good Rockin' Tonight' and 'Baby Let's Play House'?

Vernon, Gladys
and Elvis Presley,
1958. Note Gladys'
haunted look.

A family portrait
on Lisa Marie's third
birthday, 1971.

Elvis and his father
together on stage at
the final concert,
Market Square Arena,
Indianapolis, 1977.

ALWAYS ON MY MIND

Picture sleeve for
RCA reissue of
'Always On My Mind',
1985. The record
was pressed on
purple vinyl and
had a gold
'50th anniversary'
label.

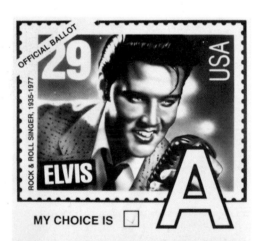

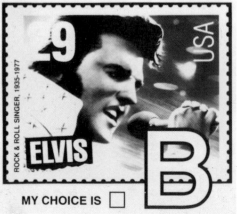

The voting card for the Elvis stamp, 1992.
Why didn't they issue both of them?

Above: Elvis and
his father with Governor
Wallace and his family,
1974. Governor Wallace
is in a wheelchair after
being shot while
campaigning.

Right: Colette Stevenson,
Michael Keating,
Martin Shaw (as Elvis)
and Paul Ridley in the
Liverpool Playhouse
production of Alan
Bleasdale's *Are You
Lonesome Tonight?*.
(Phil Cutts)

Songwriter Mort
Shuman, whose hits
include 'Little Sister',
'His Latest Flame' and
'A Mess Of Blues'.

Elvis leaving the
Astroworld Hotel,
1970. He had been
performing at the
Houston Astrodome
in between two halves
of a rodeo! Sonny West,
Elvis's chief of security,
smiles for the camera.
(*Maria Davies*)

Elvis on stage with a fan,
Elaine Coons, 1968.

Above: Contributor Tim Whitnall outside 'The cradle where it rocked' – Sun Records, Memphis, 1991. (*Nuala Munro*)

Right: Elvis on stage, 1956.

Below: Elvis performing the title song from *Jailhouse Rock*, 1957. (*MGM*)

Elvis with his shirt off, 1956. Colonel Parker charged $25,000 extra if Elvis was to take his shirt off in a film.

Unlike many of his songwriters, Mike Stoller (*left*) and Jerry Leiber knew Elvis. This picture was taken at MGM Studios, Culver City, California, 1957.

Elvis with the Jordanaires in 1964. From left to right: Neal Matthews, Gordon Stoker, Elvis, Hoyt Hawkins and Ray Walker. (*Gordon Stoker*)

Elvis with his arm
on C. Crumpacker's
shoulder, taken
backstage at Tommy
and Jimmy Dorsey's
'Stage Show', 1956.
(*C. Crumpacker*)

Part of the gatefold sleeve for
an EP, 'Elvis Sings Christmas Songs',
1958. This gatefold was unique for
an EP and RCA only printed
5,000 in this format.

Elvis with his parents,
Vernon and Gladys,
probably 1938.

Publicity shot for 'Love Me Tender',
1956.

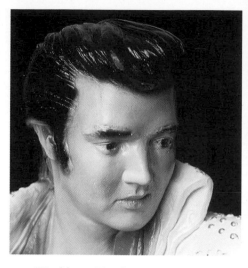

Would you like this in your home?
See Mike Evans' contribution.

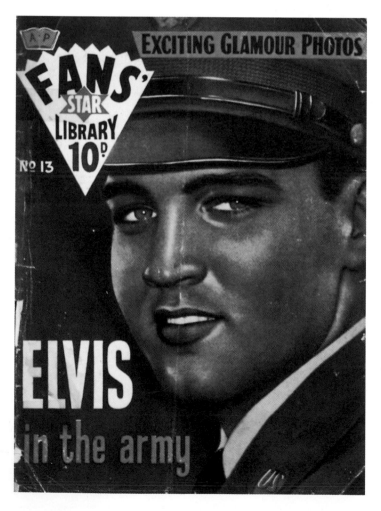

This fan magazine
cost less than 5p
at the time but
copies now fetch
around £20.

Elvis Presley by
Stuart Sutcliffe, 1957.
(*Pauline Sutcliffe*)

Elvis Presley 1 by Ray Johnson,
'the only painter in New York whose
drips mean anything'.
(*Private Collection*)

Peter Hatfield's print of Elvis
which formed part of an exhibition
accompanying Alan Bleasdale's play
Are You Lonesome Tonight?.

Elvis Lookalike
by Jock McFadyen, 1990.
(*Ferens Art Gallery, Hull City
Museums and Art Galleries*)

'Impersonators of the Elvis Impersonators', from the video/performance *Coiffure Carnival*,
Muriel Magenta, 1990.

The triptych *Elvis Victims Version* (*above*) and detail (*below*) by Simon Crump
(*Le Sou-Sol, Paris*)

An episode from Scott Saavedra's
three-part serialization *The King of Kings,*
Call Me Elvis and *A Doctor A Day*,
published in 1986 by Slave Labor
Graphics, California.

Everything Elvis: Joni Mabe's Travelling Panoramic Encyclopedia. (Joni Mabe)

Crucifixion, 1992
by Alexander Guy.
(*Glasgow Museums:*
Art Gallery
and Museum,
Kelvingrove)

At this time RCA executives may well have realized that ten or eleven mediocre film songs were not enough for an album, so extra tracks were added and these recordings came from regular RCA sessions. Ironically, they generally provided soundtracks with their better moments. *Fun In Acapulco* was the first of several albums to include 'bonus songs'.

After this Mexican jaunt, Paramount sent Elvis to the carnival for *Roustabout*. With a strong cast including Barbara Stanwyck, Leif Erickson and Pat Buttram, the storyline is merely a background for Elvis to wrap his vocal cords around another batch of second-rate outings. An old Leiber and Stoller song again becomes the highlight; this time it's the Coasters' hit 'Little Egypt'. Of the remainder, only a couple, the ballad 'Big Love, Big Heartache' and a moderate rocker, 'Wheels On My Heels', stand up in their own right. Elvis never sounded so bored as he does on the second side of *Roustabout*. 'It's Carnival Time', 'Carny Town' and 'It's A Wonderful World' are below-par performances and further evidence that Elvis was in agreement with the decision to use inferior songs. Elvis was the world's biggest star and it's unbelievable that the best writers would not be busting a gut to get their finest material to him. This opens up the debate on publishing and the intrigues that went on to persuade Elvis to record certain songs. The quality was to deteriorate even further in Paramount's next project, *Paradise Hawaiian Style*, which was an attempt to return to the success of *Blue Hawaii* four years earlier. This is the absolute nadir of Elvis soundtracks. There is an abundance of bad, a lot of mediocre and only a snatch of decent material. 'Queenie Wahine's Papaya', 'Scratch My Back', 'Datin'', 'A Dog's Life' and 'Drums Of The Island' offer no interest in terms either of substance or performance and even Elvis can do little to bring them to life.

Elvis's swan song for Paramount, *Easy Come, Easy Go*, had a superficial storyline about an ex-navy frogman and his search for sunken treasure. The sets are poor and the songs do little to enhance the scene. Elvis continues his descent into the abyss with 'The Love Machine', 'Yoga Is As Yoga Does', 'Sing You Children' and the title song. 'I'll Take Love' and 'You Gotta Stop' are more acceptable, but the thin backing detracts from the benefits of Elvis's vocals. I wonder what Elvis himself felt about the songs he had to record in these later Paramount films. Was he concerned? Could he have objected? Will we ever know?

Of the fourteen assignments for MGM, one was in 1957, eleven more between 1962 and 1968, indicating a certain swiftness in production considering the fact that films were being made for other companies at the time. The remaining films for MGM were the concert-documentaries, *That's The Way It Is* and *On Tour*, which I will not discuss here.

Jailhouse Rock, made in 1957, features a healthy mix of music and fine drama. Of the six songs presented, four were provided by Leiber and Stoller. 'Jailhouse Rock', 'Baby I Don't Care', 'I Want To Be Free' and 'Treat Me Nice' exude quality and are among Elvis's most memorable recordings, his regular studio work included.

Five years passed before Elvis presented himself to the MGM cameras again. *It Happened At The World's Fair* is family entertainment and has Elvis falling in love with a nurse, joining the space programme, fighting crooks and becoming an honorary uncle to a little girl, Sue-Lin. Oh, Elvis fits in ten songs too, the best of which is 'One Broken Heart For Sale', a single release at the start of 1963. The balance is made up of novelties, lullabies, ballads and mid-tempo beat items that hang together well but without being outstanding. The mix is much like *G.I. Blues* and, although not excellent, the set was a big chart item in the UK in mid-1963, rubbing shoulders with Cliff's *Summer Holiday*, the Beatles' *Please, Please Me* and Buddy Holly's *Reminiscing*. At the time I remember not only enjoying the film but also the album. Looking back I can see its true standing in celluloid decline, but it remains a personal favourite.

In the ensuing six years MGM rushed Elvis through movie after movie with scant attention to quality of either script or music. *Viva Las Vegas*, with its car-racing background, does have a quality co-star in Ann-Margret and an entertaining soundtrack with the usual mix of uptempo, ballad and novelty songs. The title song, 'C'mon Everybody', 'If You Think I Don't Need You', 'What'd I Say' and 'Today, Tomorrow and Forever' feature strong performances which compare favourably with the rest of his film work, both before and after. *Kissin' Cousins* followed in production although it was issued in the USA slightly before *Viva Las Vegas*. It was filmed in sixteen days and Elvis plays two roles in a mountain adventure with hillbillies on land required by the US Army. Along the way he fits in nine songs, including one fine ballad, 'Tender Feeling', a clutch of mid-tempo frolics in 'Kissin' Cousins', 'Catchin' On Fast' and 'Once Is Enough', leaving a patchy balance of mediocre performances and the ever-present novelty, represented by 'Barefoot Ballad'. The soundtrack album was filled with two bonus songs and another ballad that was cut from the film, the more acceptable 'Anyone'.

Girl Happy followed and contains the usual balance of good, bad and awful. From the last category comes 'Fort Lauderdale Chamber Of Commerce'. Can you believe it? Its lyrics include: 'Girls on the beaches commit a sin, If they don't show yards and yards of skin'. 'Do The Clam', released on a 1965 single, also plumbs the depths but 'Puppet On A String' has become a favourite, and the title song and 'The Meanest Girl In Town' both rock along pleasantly. The remaining refrains are inoffensive, but where is the sparkle that enlivened the early films? Excitement was far preferable to the mediocrity on offer in 1965.

MGM followed up with *Harum Scarum* (*Harem Holiday* in the UK) and the slope was getting more slippery. Only one song deserves repetition: 'So Close Yet So Far', which is a ballad that could have become great if worked upon. 'Shake That Tambourine', 'Hey Little Girl', 'Kismet' and 'Golden Coins' do not register among his finest moments.

Spinout (*California Holiday*) is another car-racing offering, this time with nine songs. Apart from 'Beach Shack' and 'Smorgasbord', the standard is generally higher, with Pomus and Shuman's 'Never Say Yes' leading the way for 'I'll Be Back', 'All That I Am', 'Am I Ready' and 'Stop, Look and Listen'. The soundtrack album was enhanced significantly by the inclusion of three studio recordings making a stronger than usual mix. By this time, 1966, the public had grown quite disenchanted with Elvis film soundtracks, which ceased to garner the sales that albums like *G.I. Blues* and *Blue Hawaii* had achieved earlier in the decade.

MGM's next Elvis product was *Double Trouble*, which featured eight numbers, including the direst version ever of 'Old MacDonald'. On the positive side there is 'Baby, If You'll Give Me All Your Love', 'Could I Fall In Love', 'City By Night' and 'There Is So Much World To See'. Another quickie, the film has little artistic merit but, as with other Elvis films of the period, it made money at the box office and as long as this situation continued, Elvis's management and MGM saw no reason to change.

Stay Away Joe was next for MGM and it provided an opportunity for Elvis to develop his ability to play comedy. This is essentially a non-musical: no soundtrack album could be issued as only three songs were available to RCA: 'Stay Away' is an uptempo 'Greensleeves' and 'All I

Needed Was The Rain' is a bluesy item sung with feeling by Elvis. Both songs are well above average and a return to former glories at a time when his studio work was also in the ascendant. Two other songs, 'Stay Away, Joe' and 'Dominic', were novelties, with the latter remaining unissued by RCA until their *Double Feature* series in 1994.

Speedway brought Elvis back to car-racing and a six-song soundtrack (actually seven, one is sung by Nancy Sinatra). 'Let Yourself Go' is strong as is his duet with Nancy, 'There Ain't Nothing Like A Song', but 'He's Your Uncle Not Your Dad' is best forgotten. Many soundtrack songs in the mid to late sixties were neither good nor bad but just very ordinary. Such songs are 'Speedway', 'Who Are You' and 'Your Time Hasn't Come Yet Baby', although the last mentioned made it to a single release in the middle of 1968. With only two more scripted films to complete for MGM, Elvis was no doubt looking forward. He made his TV Special in June 1968 for NBC and would only make four more acting films altogether.

Live A Little, Love A Little was a strange film for Elvis with, for the first time, sex rearing its head quite overtly. The film was disjointed and hard to keep in mind afterwards. It did not receive a cinema release in the UK although it was available for hire in the mid-seventies. Four songs were featured but not issued together. 'A Little Less Conversation' is a funky number, not identifiably film fare, but coupled with 'Almost In Love' for a single release it failed to make much impression of the charts, perhaps increasing evidence that film material was unpopular with the record-buying public of 1968.

The Trouble With Girls, MGM's final Elvis acting film, was more dramatic, with only three vocals released by RCA and one of those, a new version of 'Swing Low Sweet Chariot', not seeing a release during Elvis's lifetime. 'Clean Up Your Own Backyard' has a more modern country feel and 'Almost' is a superior ballad more reminiscent of his early-sixties Nashville work than a later soundtrack song. Three songs remain unreleased: 'The Whiffenpoof Song', 'Violet (Flower of NYU)' and 'Signs Of The Zodiac', a duet with Marilyn Mason. The first two form a short medley and the third is a rough-around-the-edges vaudeville number and not a typical Elvis product. Having said that, I could say the same about 'Wooden Heart'.

The remaining seven Elvis scripted films were fitted in between the product for MGM and Paramount. Four were released under the United

Artists banner, with two originating from the Mirisch Company, *Follow That Dream* and *Kid Galahad*. Filmed in 1961, both were different to the Paramount features made before and after them, with comedy, drama and music mixing well in both films. The songs in these two films are not focal points, but nor are they throwaways. The title song in *Follow That Dream* and 'I Got Lucky', 'King Of The Whole Wide World' and 'Home Is Where The Heart Is' in *Kid Galahad* are the strongest numbers, but even the remaining titles, like 'What A Wonderful Life', 'I'm Not The Marrying Kind' and 'This Is Living', are far superior to the poorer material on offer in some of the MGM and Paramount films discussed earlier.

Frankie And Johnny, made in 1965, was a full-quota musical, with twelve songs that run the gamut of appalling ('Petunia, The Gardener's Daughter') to a fine harmonica-led blues item in 'Hard Luck'. Along the way there is a selection of excellent ballads, 'What Every Woman Lives For', 'Please Don't Stop Loving Me' and 'Beginner's Luck', together with good-time numbers, 'Come Along' (over credits), 'Everybody Come Aboard' and 'Chesay'. The big production number is a workout of the old folk ballad used for the title of the picture. It is featured twice in the film, and Elvis recorded a second version for RCA record release.

The fourth United Artists release was *Clambake*, in 1967, and had a trading-places theme with a background of powerboat racing. Seven songs were featured, with a touch of excellence in 'The Girl I Never Loved' and a revival of the old country song 'You Don't Know Me'. Unfortunately the remaining numbers are very average, with 'Confidence' being a low moment, not only of the film but of Elvis's entire career. How did he come to record it? Also on a low level are 'Who Needs Money?' and 'Hey, Hey, Hey', but 'A House That Has Everything' manages to keep its head above water. The album, released in late 1967, is saved by the inclusion of five bonus songs taken from regular sessions. These songs included recent singles, 'Guitar Man' and 'Big Boss Man', so the standard of the album as a whole was much improved.

Allied Artists' *Tickle Me*, made in 1964, was a low-budget job with interior sets, backdrops and the use of old recordings from the period 1960 to 1963, but for this reason, the film ended up with the strongest selection of numbers of the mid-sixties films. A soundtrack album did not see release, except in South Africa, but two EPs were issued in the UK and an EP and two 45s in the USA. The classic recordings used included

'It Feels So Right', 'Dirty, Dirty Feeling', 'Long Lonely Highway' and 'Put The Blame On Me'.

Charro, made by National General (part of NBC) in 1968, featured only one song sung over the credits and is the only film in which Elvis does not sing during the course of the action.

The final film to be discussed and the final acting role undertaken by Elvis was *Change Of Habit*, in 1969. It is basically a straight drama, like the Fox films, but a smattering of songs was added as insurance. All four are above average, with the title song, 'Rubberneckin'', and 'Let Us Pray' being strong beat items not generally evident in his films from the same period. 'Have A Happy' is lighter but fits in with the scene in the film when Elvis sings to a child on a small carousel. However, the music in the film was not necessary and it could have survived very well without it.

Elvis featured over 230 songs in his thirty-one acting films; the numbers in each film ranging from one to fourteen and the standard being just as variable. *Jailhouse Rock* and *Paradise Hawaiian Style* are worlds apart. Their point of similarity is Elvis Presley and, true to the complex nature of his personality, the mystery of his movie career continues. We may speculate about managerial pressure and endless contracts for picture after picture, but where was Elvis's artistic integrity? It seems to have deserted him completely as he stumbled from picture to picture with tired scripts and lacklustre songs. He regained his integrity with his Nashville recordings in the late sixties and his Memphis sessions in 1969, by which time the movie contracts were almost completed and Elvis was free to return to his music.

As I see it, Elvis could never get the balance right between drama and musical, between soundtrack recordings and regular studio sessions for RCA. We know that Elvis's management was not at all interested in quality, only the balance sheet. The full reasons for Elvis's total submission to the will of his management and the film companies may never be explained.

The inconsistency of his writers is an apparent paradox. For example, Bill Giant, Bernie Baum and Florence Kaye supplied 'Queenie Wahine's Papaya', 'Beach Shack', 'El Toro', 'Scratch My Back' and 'Shake That Tambourine', but they also contributed 'Devil In Disguise', 'Edge Of Reality', 'City By Night', 'Power Of My Love' and 'The Sound Of Your

Cry' to the Elvis repertoire. This trio, together, supplied forty-one songs, both for soundtracks and regular studio sessions. As staff writers for the publishers Hill and Range, they had an open line to Elvis through the company manager, Freddie Bienstock, who was responsible for collecting material for Elvis to select. This is representative of the situation; a small coterie of writers all tied to Elvis's main publishers.

Need it have been like this? How much was the Colonel interested in quality? Never mind the quality, feel the paycheck.

And the films Elvis never made? *West Side Story*? Elvis could have sung convincing versions of 'Maria' and 'Somewhere' as neither was a million miles from 'It's Now Or Never'. P. J. Proby scored UK hits with both, and Proby, under his real name James Smith, recorded demos for some of Elvis's soundtrack work. *A Star Is Born* is the most quoted example of a film Elvis could have been involved in. Elvis is said to have been keen on the idea but thwarted by Colonel Tom. In reality, Elvis was way past contemplating a film of this type; his health, weight and physical status being just some of the problems, aside from any difficulties that would have arisen as a consequence of billing requirements. Would it have been an Elvis film or a Streisand film? A fine topic for discussion amongst Elvis fans, but probably more a passing thought than a genuine working idea.

And where does Elvis stand against other singer-actors? Frank Sinatra was always a better actor than singer, Bing Crosby was, for my money, on a level par and Cliff never made the grade as an actor. Sinatra and Crosby were both given genuine acting roles with Oscars ensuing: Crosby in *Going My Way* and Sinatra in *From Here To Eternity*. Elvis was never a serious contender for an Oscar: only those with extremely Elvis-coloured glasses would ever have considered this as a possibility. Elvis was promoted in his films as Elvis, and as a result his motion pictures were generally constructed to show his music rather than his dramatic flair.

Good songs, bad songs, good films, bad films; they are all part of the legend and its legacy. It's a testament to Elvis's talent and popularity that not only did he survive the poorer efforts, but they continue to be heard and seen without in any way diminishing his popularity.

BILL HARRY

His Latest Flame

Ginger Alden was the last of Elvis Presley's veritable army of girlfriends. The former Miss Traffic Safety and Miss Mid-South, nineteen years younger than her lover, found the man she alleged was about to marry her dead on the floor of his bathroom.

The bloated figure in a pair of blue pyjamas, his body pumped with enough pills to fill a pharmacist's prescription drawer, was a sad reflection of the man who once had the world at his feet.

Elvis was gifted with the looks of a Greek god and carefully retouched photographs of the star gave the appearance of his features being sculpted from butter. As the most famous singing idol in the world, a multi-millionaire, a box-office film star, he was the object of adoration for millions of women internationally.

Ginger was perhaps typical of an Elvis girlfriend. She was a lot younger than him and a former beauty queen.

Elvis loved glamorous women: film starlets, singers, showgirls, dancers, beauty queens. He also liked girls with virginal youth and innocence.

Compared to other figures in the public eye, Elvis's affairs were far from clandestine. Few stars can have had such a history of 'girlfriends'. Elvis was open about them, he posed for photographs with them, he lavished gifts on them and they have been thoroughly documented in magazines, books and television dramatizations.

On the surface it all seemed quite innocent: Elvis was attracted to a girl and he sent out one of his cohorts with an invitation to a 'date'. To the media in general, Elvis was just dating a girl – and he could be very generous, with gifts of cars and pets.

What received less publicity were the gifts of double beds he gave to some girlfriends, gifts which were probably too symbolic for the press to reveal – for despite the plethora of scandal magazines in the fifties and sixties, Elvis was so well loved by the public that his treatment in the media was unusually gentle.

His very first girlfriend was, reputedly, a little lass from East Tupelo

called Caroline Ballard, daughter of the Reverend James Ballard, pastor
of the First Assembly of God church in Tupelo. Elvis was nine years old
at the time!

By the age of fifteen, he'd learnt how to balance two sweethearts at the
same time. He was dating a skinny little neighbour called Betty McMann
and when she wasn't teaching him to dance, he was slipping off to
serenade thirteen-year-old Billie Wardlow.

In February 1954, while at the Rainbow Rollerdrome, he was spotted
by a fifteen-year-old girl who'd noticed him at the local church. Her name
was Dixie Locke and she became Elvis's steady – and one of the first of
the girls he discussed marriage with. However, Dixie became disenchanted with the fact that Elvis was absent with his group so often and
broke off the relationship – she later became President of the first Elvis
Presley Fan Club.

Another high-school sweetheart was Barbara Hearn, who was later to
appear in a bit part in the film *Loving You*.

In 1955, when Elvis began his life on the road, he dated receptionist
June Juanico, country singers Anita Carter and Wanda Jackson, with
whom he was touring, and Barbara Pittman, one of the minor artists signed
to Sun Records.

The following year saw the beginning of his fascination with Las Vegas
showgirls. He dated two of the showgirls who worked at the hotel he was
appearing in, Kathy Gabriel and Sandy Preston. He also dated singer
Kitty Dolan, whom he met in Vegas that year, and other romantic interests
of the period were Kate Wheeler and Sharon Whiley.

In 1957 he met Arlene Bradley, who claimed that their romance lasted
until 1963, and during the same year he dated Las Vegas dancer Dorothy
Harmony and had a week-long romance with stripper Tempest Storm.
During the same year, in Hollywood, he stepped out with Joan Bradshaw.

Around this time, Elvis also enjoyed the regular company of three
fourteen-year-old girls, Gloria Mowel, Heidi Heissen and Frances Forbes.
The Memphis teenagers were Elvis's constant companions for a time,
although he didn't have sexual relations with them. It's indicative of how
Elvis felt comfortable in the company of girls in their early teens (Lolitas?)
and is perhaps a hint at his forthcoming fascination with Priscilla.

1957 was also the year in which he met another girl he wanted to
marry, Anita Wood. The nineteen-year-old had all the qualifications which

appealed to Elvis – she was a small-town southern girl and she was also outlandishly glamorous, with blonde hair, a dazzling smile and a 35–23–35 figure. She'd won a number of talent contests.

Their first date was arranged by intermediaries, a typical Elvis move. Once they began dating seriously, Elvis was said to have discussed marriage: in his eyes she was a 'good girl'.

Anita was the marrying kind, but marriage with Elvis didn't happen. It was suggested that Colonel Tom Parker vetoed it, advising Elvis that he must wait several years before he considered getting married. Anita, whom Elvis called 'Little Beadie', later got hitched to a football player, Johnny Brewer.

With Hollywood beckoning, Elvis found a new category of girlfriend – the actress, usually a starlet or a minor actress. He developed a crush on Debra Paget, the actress in his first film, *Love Me Tender*, but she didn't return the affection. He said, 'I sent her flowers, I was nuts about her, but she wouldn't even give me the time of day.'

As it turned out, the first actress Elvis dated was Natalie Wood. She starred in his favourite film *Rebel Without A Cause* and he cited her as one of his favourite actresses. The romance became serious and Elvis took her home to stay with him and his parents in Memphis. It's said that they'd decided to elope to Las Vegas, but Colonel Tom Parker intervened and, together with Gladys Presley, talked him out of it.

Elvis also dated actresses Rita Moreno and Dolores Hart. Dolores appeared with Elvis in *Loving You* and *King Creole*. He often gave nicknames to the girls he liked and he called Dolores 'Whistle Britches'. She later entered a convent as a nun, which gave rise to speculation that she did it because of her unrequited love for Elvis.

Immediately before he left for Europe, he had several girlfriends, including the Las Vegas showgirl Dotty Harmony, who accompanied Elvis when he arrived at the Kennedy Veterans' Hospital in Memphis for his army examination. After the physical he took her to the airport and put her on a plane to Los Angeles. Other girlfriends included June Wilbank, Yvonne Lime, Jana Lund and Venetia Stevenson.

When Elvis was drafted and stationed in Germany in 1958, his appetite for beautiful young girls was unaffected. He was soon seen with a teenage Russian actress, Vera Tschechowa, nightclub dancer Anjelika Zehetbauer and a sixteen-year-old girl, Margit Buergin, whom he called his 'little puppy'.

The most important relationship in Germany was forged when he met a fourteen-year-old American girl, Priscilla Ann Beaulieu. The romance between the star and a girl who was merely a child would seem to be somewhat bizarre. When she was introduced to Elvis, the child, whom he was to call 'Cilla', was wearing a blue and white sailor-suit dress with white socks. Her stepfather (her father had died when she was six months old) allowed them to date on condition they were chaperoned, and they continued dating throughout his tour of Germany. Elvis invited her to Graceland and then asked her stepfather's permission for her to live at Graceland permanently, with Elvis as her guardian. With an assurance that she would be enrolled at school and would be chaperoned by Elvis's father and stepmother, Joseph Beaulieu agreed. Priscilla was being groomed to become Elvis's wife and the couple were eventually married in May 1967. All indications were that it was Colonel Tom Parker who insisted that Elvis marry Priscilla, who had just turned twenty-one.

In the meantime, Elvis had embarked on a Hollywood career in earnest and his attention returned to romances with actresses. He dated Nancy Sharp, a wardrobe mistress, when he was filming *Flaming Star*. In 1961 he was often spotted with actress Connie Stevens and by 1963 was dating actress Sharon Hugueny. Other actresses his name was linked to included Peggy Lipton and Cybill Shepherd. Cybill was later to come to prominence following her appearance in *The Last Picture Show* and found fame in the television series *Moonlighting*. She was seventeen and a former Miss Teenage Memphis when the thirty-one-year-old Elvis began dating her in 1966.

The actress most associated with Elvis is Ann-Margret, who was called 'the female Presley'. She co-starred with him in one of his most popular movies, *Viva Las Vegas*. Stunningly beautiful, intelligent and a talented singer, dancer and actress, she completely charmed Elvis and the two began a serious relationship which lasted after the filming had ended. It came to an abrupt end, however, without any explanation. Elvis, at one moment completely besotted by the vivacious star, suddenly became uninvolved. Rumours abounded that the split came after Ann-Margret had committed the unforgivable – she'd discussed their romance with the press. While in London Ann-Margret mentioned that Elvis had given her a huge, pink double bed and that the couple were considering marriage. However, the other theory is that Ann-Margret had a career of her own, while Elvis wanted his wife to be the little woman who waited for him at home. He realized that a relationship between two career-minded people wouldn't work.

During the mid-sixties Elvis also dated singers and went out with Jackie de Shannon for six months. He also went on dates with Bobbie Gentry. Kathy Westmoreland, a member of the Sweet Inspirations, Elvis's backing singers, claimed that the two of them had slept together, although they didn't have any sexual relations. The details of their affair were outlined in her book, *Elvis and Kathy*.

Some of his girlfriends went on to marry celebrities. Venetia Stevenson married Don Everly in 1962; Judy Powell, whom he dated in 1958, married millionaire Adolph Spreckles, and Sandy Ferra, a girlfriend in 1960, was to marry Wink Martindale of 'Deck of Cards' fame.

When his marriage to Priscilla was breaking down, Elvis began dating Vicki Peters and, in 1971, after he and Cilla separated, he began dating Las Vegas showgirl Sandra Zancan, beauty queen Diana Goodman and a young girl from Memphis called Cathy Jo Brown Lee.

His major romance of the early seventies was with another beauty queen, Linda Thompson, and they lived together in Graceland from 1972 to 1976, although in 1975 he was also dating a *Playboy* Playmate, Sheila Ryan, who was later to marry actor James Caan.

Thompson was a former Miss Liberty Bowl and Miss Memphis and the story of her four-and-a-half-year live-in romance with Elvis was filmed as *Elvis and the Beauty Queen* in 1981. The working title of the movie had been *Elvis and Me*, which actually became the title of another television movie – about the romance between Elvis and Priscilla Beaulieu Presley, in 1988.

When Elvis split with Linda he began stepping out with a succession of girls, including Malessa Blackwood, an eighteen-year-old girl from Memphis, and glamour girls Mindy Miller and Ann Pennington.

Elvis's last major romance was with another live-in-lover, Ginger Alden. At the time of Elvis's death, Ginger, who found his body, claimed that he had proposed to her on 26 January 1977 and that they had intended getting married the following Christmas. Ginger later said that she was able to contact Elvis via psychic dreams.

With so many girlfriends out in the open, it would seen uncharacteristic for Elvis to have had secret love affairs – but since his death that has been the claim of numerous women. A bizarre element is the number of claims from women who said that they had been either married to Elvis or involved in lengthy secret affairs. In several cases the women revealed their marriage secrets in publications such as the *National Inquirer* – but, in most cases confessed that their marriage certificates and other evidence of their wedlock to the King had been lost.

Barbara Young claimed she began a two-year romance with Elvis in 1954 and gave birth to his daughter, Deborah Presley, in March 1956. Strikingly similar is the claim by Barbara Jean Lewis, who said that she met Elvis in North Carolina in 1954 and gave birth to a daughter, Deborah Presley, in 1955. Terri Taylor claimed she met Elvis in 1955 when she was a fifteen-year-old singer. She alleged that she became pregnant with his child, Candy Jo, who was born in December 1957. A Hollywood waitress, Patricia Ann Parker, took out a paternity suit in August 1970, claiming Elvis was the father of her child, Jason, but the case was dropped when blood tests proved negative. Jane Clarke, a dancer, claimed to have been Elvis's secret lover since they first met in 1959. Virginia Sullivan alleged that she'd been Elvis's secret lover for fourteen years, from 1963 until his death. Deborah Watts claimed to have been his secret lover between the years 1972 and 1977. Zelda Harris alleged that she and Elvis were married in Mobile, Alabama. Ann Farrell said that she married Elvis soon after they met in 1957. Billie Jo Newton said she was Elvis's first wife and bore him three children. She claimed that he married her when she was fourteen and divorced her in 1956. Lucy De Barbin claimed that she and Elvis carried on a twenty-four-year relationship and that she bore him a daughter, Desiree Presley, in August 1968. Her claims were detailed in her book *Are You Lonesome Tonight?*

Elvis's preferences veered from the angelic to the temptress, from the tender young innocent to the overtly sexual. There seems to be no middle ground. Such a firm pattern lends itself readily to analysis and no doubt a psychological profile would provide some insight.

Elvis had a stillborn twin brother, Jesse Garon. Gladys insisted that she had been carrying identical twins and impressed upon Elvis a belief that the personality of his stillborn brother had been transferred to him. Possibly Elvis felt he had two people inside his head.

There was also the influence of his mother, Gladys. He adored her – and any future wife and mother of his children would also be placed on a pedestal. His future wife would therefore be chaste . . . while he, on the other hand, could continue to sow his wild oats!

While Priscilla had been living at Graceland and studying at local schools, Elvis had moulded her into the image of his various fantasies, encouraging her to dye her hair black because he liked the colour of Debra Paget's hair. Yet the decision to marry Priscilla was the Colonel's. The man who had prevented Elvis marrying other *amours* literally ordered him to propose – and then took control of the wedding arrangements and resulting publicity. Exactly nine months after the marriage, Elvis's only child, his daughter Lisa Marie Presley, was born. The marriage didn't even survive five years and the couple split in 1972 when Cilla became romantically involved with a karate teacher, Mike Stone. Elvis divorced her the same year.

Priscilla then sought a career in show business, although she turned down the role of Tiffany Welles in *Charlie's Angels* before appearing as Jenna Wade in the *Dallas* series. In recent years she has appeared as the romantic foil of Leslie Neilson in the *Naked Gun* comedy movies. Through the years she has also been involved in affairs with a number of men, including actor Michael Edwards, hairdresser Ellie Ezerzer and writer Marco Garibaldi. She gave birth to Garibaldi's child, Navarone, in 1987.

Priscilla Presley who, at first, appeared to be a little girl, easily manipulated, developed into a strong, mature businesswoman with a mind of her own.

The fact that his own wife would reject him for another man shattered Elvis's confidence. For the King to be cuckolded was humiliation enough, but many of his friends felt he began to go downhill after such a blow and began to lose himself in drug dependency. Women would still flock round him, he could still take his pick of beautiful, teenage girls – and continued to do so – but something within Elvis had died when Priscilla turned out to be a Delilah.

TONY BARROW

The Night the Beatles
Met Elvis Presley

Elvis Presley was still waving goodbye from the steps outside his front door as we climbed back into the Beatles' limousine. When we pulled away, John Lennon was the first to speak, 'That wasn't Elvis, it was just a feller.'

It was early on the morning of Saturday 28 August 1965 and we were leaving the Presley Californian home in Bel Air, high above the Los Angeles plain, to drive back to 2850 Benedict Canyon where the Beatles had rented a luxurious hillside bungalow during their summer concert tour of North America. About three hours earlier, at around eleven o'clock the previous evening, our small and élite party, only a handful of closest associates and aides from the group's travelling entourage, plus the four Beatles themselves, had arrived at Presley's place full of great expectations. I for one left somewhat disillusioned with the man if not his music.

I suppose relatively few outsiders beyond Presley's innermost circle of managers, minders and playmates used to spend long in his company. Our little group was with him for three hours, not in any stressful backstage situation but on his own domestic territory, in the comfort, intimacy and privacy of the man's own house, where he was surrounded by familiar faces and should have been at his most relaxed and contented. But, to be truthful, although I found Elvis superficially friendly, I thought he was generally boring.

John Lennon or Paul McCartney, I forget which, actually introduced me to Elvis, saying something like 'Tony's from Liverpool like us, he's our press agent, he does all our publicity.' Presley responded prematurely with a nod of the head and an 'uh huh' each time the Beatle paused for breath. Then he pumped my hand up and down very firmly and smiled a thoroughly rehearsed smile, 'Liverpool, huh, Liverpool.'

For most of their time together that night, The Beatles and Elvis Presley communicated musically and that was fine fun. Musically, the five guys were fluent in the same language and they could converse naturally and prolifically. On guitars and a piano, they exchanged a host of thoughts, opinions, ideas, jokes and anecdotes to the accompaniment of a jukebox that played Presley's own hit singles non-stop. Ringo recalled recently that he heard a Cilla Black record on the Presley Jukebox that night, but my memory is that we listened to nothing but Elvis.

At one point, during a lull in the instrumental conversation, while the Beatles were having their glasses recharged with booze, Elvis paused by my side and we chatted in a stiff and stilted fashion. He opened with, 'OK, so are you getting everything you need? Another bourbon?' I said yes thank you, everything was OK. He went on, 'You go on tour with your boys?' The answer seemed obvious from the fact that I was there and we were all there and it was the middle of this Beatles' tour. So I did an Elvis and drawled, 'Uh huh.'

While we talked, he grinned a great deal and looked directly into my face, not my eyes but somewhere in the centre of my forehead. 'So you're from Liverpool, huh?' I surely was.

Then Elvis asked me the question I still get today from every fan of the Beatles I encounter, but it was unexpected from him, 'Which one of the boys do you like best?' I have never answered that one within earshot of a Beatle.

Finally Elvis asked me, 'Do the boys smoke at all, Tony?' Did they?! Only a couple of days earlier at the Benedict Canyon bungalow during a private screening of the movie *What's New Pussycat?*, I had been fascinated to watch George Harrison roll up and pass round one of the fattest joints I ever saw. Whether Presley was on the point of handing out grass to his guests I never found out because he was whisked out of my presence by a minder who thrust a fresh bourbon and Seven in my hand and said, 'Excuse us.'

Apart from being at the awe-inspiring Beatles/Presley Bel Air summit meeting, I subsequently saw Presley perform in a vast cabaret showroom in Las Vegas, and the two facets of the same person struck me as being poles apart. There, the King was still lean, youthful-looking and comparatively undamaged by drug abuse, and he looked magnificent in his rhinestone-studded stage outfits. In a show setting, Elvis displayed a powerful personality that was thrice as large as life. He was totally in control of his audience of 2000 people, extraordinarily eloquent when he sang, professionally competent when he spoke to the crowd, physically impressive when he strutted to and fro across his wide stage, a different fellow altogether from the one we met in Bel Air.

What was fundamentally wrong with the Bel Air get-together may have been the way it was set up. The meeting of the superstars was the idea of a *New Musical Express* journalist, Chris Hutchins, who claimed a great closeness with Presley's personal manager, Colonel Tom Parker. At first, the fact that someone from the press was involved put the Beatles off. George put into words what the others were thinking, 'If this is going to be another dirty big press party, let's forget it. We want to meet Elvis but not with a gang of photographers and radio DJs hassling us.'

The deal with Hutchins was that there would be no pictures, no taping, no leaking of details in advance. Keeping the time and place confidential was in his interests because Hutchins would have the story exclusively to himself.

The Beatles' manager, Brian Epstein, was nervous about a leak and warned me, 'The boys will pull out if the rest of the press find out.' Keeping it from them was not easy since we had invited a dozen or more international journalists and radio presenters to travel round America with us as part of the Beatles' entourage.

The next hurdle was to agree on where the meeting should be held. Such famous folk dared not drop in on one another unannounced. The very formality of debating the venue made the Beatles uncomfortable. Paul asked, 'Has Parker laid it down that we have to go to Elvis? Why can't he come over to Benedict Canyon?' Some of the Byrds and the Beach Boys had been over to sit by the pool, so had actress Eleanor Bron.

John told me in private, 'If we do go to Elvis, I'd prefer it to be just the five of us, not even Brian, not even you. If both sides start lining up teams of supporters it will be like a contest to see who can field the most players.'

Inevitably, power politics came into play. Parker would be present, so Epstein had to be. Chris Hutchins was invited, and if a journalist had to be involved, the Beatles wanted to bring me. Presley would have his army of minders and road managers on hand, so the Beatles' roadies, Neil Aspinall and Mal Evans, made it onto the list. John was adamant that there shouldn't be anyone else, 'Let's stop there or it'll get out of control.'

The Beatles agreed unanimously that they didn't like the idea of an outsider such as Chris Hutchins acting as the go-between. They told

'Eppy' that he should call the Colonel personally and organize the whole thing on a one-to-one basis.

'I don't have Parker's direct number,' admitted Eppy limply, but I got hold of it for him a little later from a local newsman. The Beatles' usually flamboyant personal manager seemed to be subdued by the sheer enormity of the meeting that was being planned. Without much of a fight he bowed to Parker's emphatic wish that John, Paul, George and Ringo should make the short trip over to Bel Air rather than Elvis visiting them in Benedict Canyon.

Friday 27 August was not the first choice of date. Elvis was not sure when he would be at home, and the Beatles had concert commitments. It had to be between Portland on the 23rd and San Diego on the 28th, but it couldn't be on the 24th because Capitol Records were hosting an almighty party in honour of the Fab Four with a guest list that included Jane Fonda, Groucho Marx, James Stewart and Rock Hudson. Keen as they were to meet their hero and fellow megastar, John, Paul, George and Ringo became increasingly unhappy about the complexities of the arrangements.

The only person among us unaffected by the various responsibilities and routine of negotiation with the Presley camp was the group's genial roadie Mal Evans, a gentle giant of an easily starstruck gofer who was infatuated with the mere idea of being in the same room as the King. Mal couldn't hide his immense glee when told the summit was certainly on. From that moment on he spoke of little else and wore a permanent grin. The rest of us were also looking forward to the occasion, but we tried hard to show a professionally blasé indifference to what was going to be one of the most memorable experiences of a lifetime.

By the time we drove off from Benedict Canyon on the 27th, it was clear that the four boys had mixed feelings about the whole affair. John asked, 'Do you think the Colonel's bothered to tell Elvis we're coming?' Mal said, 'I hope they'll let us in.' Paul said, 'Did anyone remember the guitars?' Relieving the tense atmosphere a little, Ringo added quietly, cryptically and with a straight face, 'I always remember the guitars.' For the rest of the journey all of us remained silent, each making our mental pictures of the big meeting. Most of the tension was caused by genuine last-minute nervousness, which would disappear when they walked into Presley's home just as it did when the Beatles walked onto a stage, the adrenalin drowning the butterflies.

A bunch of heavies guarded the gate outside the Presley property but they had been primed to let the Beatles' limousine sweep through without challenge. They must have passed word of our approach to the house because there was Elvis himself standing alone on the doorstep as we drove up. He was dressed immaculately but casually in a colourful tightly tailored red shirt and pale grey trousers.

There was a flurry of mutual greetings and accompanying small talk as we were led into an enormous circular room bathed in red and blue lights and on into the equally vast main lounge. More than twenty people faced us from the far side of the room, Colonel Tom Parker flanked by about ten or twelve minders posing as road managers, plus their wives and other women. Suddenly, as our group stood in line opposite Presley's assembled people, a weird silence fell upon us all. For seconds that felt like hours, the English team surveyed the scene, waiting for someone to make a move, physical or verbal.

Almost simultaneously, John launched into babbling conversation with Elvis while Colonel Parker put a plump arm round Brian Epstein's shoulder and asked how the tour was going. This was the signal Presley's henchmen had waited for. Burly minders, some with an identifiable Memphis Mafia look about them, began to move among us, introducing themselves, shaking hands, offering drinks.

Of the four Beatles, clearly John was enjoying himself most from the start, blurting out questions and scarcely waiting for Presley's answers: 'Why do you do all these soft-centred ballads nowdays? What happened to the good old rock 'n' roll? When are you doing the next film? How long is it since you were in Memphis?'

Paul wanted to know how long it took Elvis to make one of his movies and the King replied, 'No more than a month if we're lucky.' That was even faster than the Beatles!

George Harrison, never a good flyer, told Elvis how an engine on the Beatles' chartered aircraft, a Lockheed Elektra, had caught fire on the flight into Portland the previous Sunday afternoon: 'We were flying through a sort of narrow canyon, rocks on either side of us, when Paul noticed the flames. It's OK to laugh about it afterwards but I was really convinced we were going to crash.' Elvis recalled a similar mid-air drama when one of his aircraft engines failed over Atlanta.

They swapped tales of touring, compared notes on their fans, talked about inadequate sound systems provided by concert promoters and venue managers. Then, quite suddenly, all five artists seemed to run out of conversation at the same time. At once Elvis changed the direction of the proceedings by calling for some guitars. A whole range of instruments was produced from behind a couple of sofas. Someone had taken the trouble to provide replicas of some guitars used by the Beatles, but their source was a little out of date. Elvis handed out the guitars, turned down the sound on the television and started the jukebox. It was laden with his own recordings. I remember thinking that if the summit had been held at Benedict Canyon, we wouldn't have been playing the Beatles' records.

With the end of his guitar, Elvis prodded the buttons at the front of the television set to change channels until he found a silent picture that seemed to suit him. He changed channels quite frequently over the next hour or so, usually for no obvious reason, probably a nervous habit. As I watched, a minder confided, 'He also does that a lot when we're trying to watch programmes.'

When the Beatles and Elvis began playing along to his records, the evening took on a much less formal air. Paul moved between guitar and piano, the others waged minor battles among themselves, a bit like jazzmen improvising simple tunes and trying to outdo one another in creative but primitive musical combat. Without a set of drums, Ringo Starr felt left out of this jam session. For a while he beat out the rhythms with his fingers on the edge of an occasional table. Then he left the instrumentalists and joined a bunch of roadies who were playing pool.

Parker and Epstein also withdrew from the musical circle and went into the other room where they sat together in a quiet corner for the rest of the evening. Who knows what matters of great consequence to the world's entertainment industry the two management moguls thrashed out between them that night – or maybe they just made smalltalk. Epstein never revealed any details of their long and apparently intense discussion.

While the Beatles and Elvis played for one another, a perfectly formed clone of Cleopatra moved elegantly amongst us, a slender and stunning black-haired beauty with a silky-soft southern accent and a sparkly tiara in her long swept-up hair. This was the lovely Priscilla in the days before she went blonde or became a soap star. At this stage she was Elvis's personal and most attractive ornament, an incredibly sexy lady who recognized the precise nature of her role and played it brilliantly.

I can't remember what triggered our eventual departure or if our host dropped any hints or made any signals to hasten the end of the visit. By then I had swallowed far too many stiff bourbons to appreciate the passage of time or notice if the King felt we were outstaying our welcome. In any event, the key players appeared to have drained one another of worthwhile conversation, musical and verbal, and to have stayed longer would have pleased nobody except Mal Evans.

Towards the end, the five musicians had abandoned their instruments on the floor in front of the still-flickering colour television screen and moved on to play games with Ringo and the minders, some at the pool table, others at arcade-style amusement machines.

Just before we left, the Colonel dished out sets of Elvis Presley albums to everybody as a souvenir of the occasion. I didn't ask Elvis to sign mine, I wanted to but it would have been professionally incorrect.

At the front door, Elvis said, 'Don't forget to come and see us again in Memphis if you're ever in Tennessee.' The Beatles never did take up that invitation.

Most of us fell asleep on the journey back to Benedict Canyon. One of the Beatles said afterwards that he'd had more fun meeting Engelbert Humperdinck. Another, having engaged Elvis briefly in chatter concerning songwriting, wondered aloud how the King managed to bluff his way through with musicians and tunesmiths, adding bitchily, 'I reckon he knows as much about composing as your average six-year-old.'

There was certainly something missing about the evening but I do know that Ringo enjoyed his game of pool.

TODD SLAUGHTER
A Date with Elvis

In the summer of 1968, Elvis Presley recorded his first full-length television special for NBC. It was broadcast on 3 December, and it spearheaded Elvis's return to live entertainment: Presley's first concerts for eight years would be presented at the newly constructed Las Vegas International Hotel, later renamed the Las Vegas Hilton.

Many fans were disappointed at Las Vegas being chosen as the venue. Many remember Elvis's 'failure' in 1956 when he appeared at the New Frontier Hotel, but this time it was going to be different. The showroom, at the time the biggest Las Vegas had seen, would accommodate an audience of 2000 – and, on occasion, stretched to 2500 – and would offer the plushest surroundings, sound and seating the resort could offer.

The whole world was made aware of Elvis's return to live musical entertainment and there was great expectation that Elvis would start appearances outside the USA. In the fifties Elvis had appeared in Canada, but this turned out to be his only sortie outside the USA apart from his army service in Germany, where he never entertained anyone, except possibly those with whom he was billeted.

In 1972 we organized the first trip to the USA for members of the Official Elvis Presley Fan Club of Great Britain. The club had previously taken groups by coach to fan club events in Belgium, Luxembourg and France, but this was the first time we had chartered a plane. It was a World Airways DC-10 with room for 193 passengers: our flight left with just seven empty seats. For the majority of passengers – tour guides included – it was their first trip to the USA. In previous years, most fans' hopes of visiting America hung on being successful in a competition printed on packages of Kellogg's corn flakes.

In the sixties, *Elvis Monthly* editor Albert Hand had tried to take readers to the States in the hope that travellers would catch Elvis in Memphis or on a Hollywood film set. The V-form currency restrictions imposed by the Labour government meant that travel to the States was a nightmare, putting paid to any possibility of group travel that wasn't for business purposes. By 1972 the economy was stronger, but even then it wasn't too easy to find a planeload of devotees with enough cash to make it. In August 1972, we were taking fans to Nashville, Memphis, Tupelo, Las Vegas and Los Angeles. It was a fourteen-day package for £175 – all flights, all coaches and, unusually for American holidays, all food included. We had to impose an £8 surcharge, which shocked some people rigid.

For many years I had been in correspondence with Colonel Parker, but I never expected to meet Elvis's manager. However, within hours of reaching Las Vegas, the Colonel had called my hotel room. Off I went to the Las Vegas Hilton with Tony Prince from Radio Luxembourg, Ian Bailey, who helped run the fan club operations, and David Wade, our tour operator. None of us asked the Colonel to meet Elvis, but he said that we would, though he didn't know when. Tony Prince asked if he could interview Elvis for Radio Luxembourg, and the Colonel replied that, providing he didn't see a tape recorder, he would not mind. With this in mind, he asked his sidekick, Tom Diskin, to remind him *not* to wear his glasses.

No one outside the hotel could have missed the fact that Elvis Presley was in town. Las Vegas was awash with Elvis. Taxi cabs, billboards, radio stations and supermarkets all screamed out 'Elvis'. Within the walls of the Hilton, Elvis's name, likeness and image were everywhere. Souvenir stands were in prime positions within the casino area, and buntings and banners covered every wall space.

The Colonel was everything we expected him to be: everyone was at his beck and call. He took over the Las Vegas Hilton, and, although he was just responsible for his act, he ran the whole show. Dealers, waiters and top management were all subservient to his demands. When the Colonel spoke, everyone listened. When he shouted, everyone came running. When he screamed, everyone ran away. The Colonel was boss.

On our last night in Las Vegas, the Colonel came to our showroom booth and asked me to select a dozen fans to meet Elvis. What an awful thing to do – to select twelve from nearly 200, although admittedly some of them had already met Elvis through the Colonel.

We went backstage and were ushered into one of the Hilton's guest reception rooms – and in walked Elvis Presley.

I had met many British pop acts, including the Beatles, Cliff Richard,

Tom Jones and the Rolling Stones, but none of these previous encounters had prepared me for meeting Elvis. The biggest surprise was that, although Elvis was larger than life, he was not 'show business' in his approach. Far from it. He was quiet, reserved, ultra-polite and taken aback by his overseas following. Indeed, whenever Elvis was on stage, he would greet his British audiences.

That night Elvis accepted all the gifts which the fans brought him. He rewarded the men with a handshake and a happy-snap opportunity and all the girls with a scarf and a kiss. One of the Swedish girls in our party later commented that 'his kiss was okay, but he didn't go for my tongue'.

So, what do you say to a 'god'? I was in the fortunate position of simply introducing Elvis to our gathering and presenting him with yet another *New Musical Express* award. Everyone else said the usual silly things. Tony Prince took the Colonel at his word and hid both the tape recorder and its microphone on his person, which gave rise to a very fuzzy interview for 208, but at least he got something.

The following year we also took fans to Las Vegas, but our ticket allocation, previously agreed with the hotel, was withdrawn. It was awful. The showroom management stated that our people would not get seats owing to the fact that huge groups of junket players were in town and they had to receive priority – they were there to play the tables – our people got about as far as the five-cent slot machines. This was one game I managed to win, but I was told that the Hoover dam was not far away. This year Tony Prince did put a microphone directly up to Elvis's mouth, but less than a minute of recording time was available.

I met Elvis again in 1974, and then again just before his very last concert in Indianapolis on 26 June 1977 – six weeks later he was dead. With hindsight, I would have handled each meeting differently, but, of course, I treasure my memories and my photographs.

We did discuss with the Colonel the possibility of Elvis appearing in the UK. The Colonel said there were not enough big venues here and Elvis didn't want to appear in the open. Elvis himself said he wanted to appear in Europe, and in the mid-seventies some of his men came to the UK to see what might be available, but this might have been only a sweetener.

However, I can correct the view that Elvis did not travel outside the USA because Colonel Parker was an illegal immigrant who might not be allowed back in. Prior to managing Elvis, he had ridden a horse to a London hotel as publicity for his 'cowboy' star, Eddy Arnold. In 1991 he discussed the various shipping lines between Rotterdam and the UK with me, and he also went to Australia and Japan during Elvis's career. The Colonel never hid his Dutch origins and when we took parties to America he would talk with Dutch fans in their language.

I am sure that had Elvis had been dedicated to overseas travel, then he would have travelled, if only as a visitor. He never did, and I can only assume that he didn't have any wanderlust. The Colonel's argument about the lack of large venues has some validity, but this hasn't prevented Frank Sinatra making regular appearances here.

Would an event like Live Aid have changed the situation? Had there been a Live Aid during Elvis's lifetime, I doubt if he would have appeared, but then few other major artists would have appeared on stage alongside other managers' acts. Apart from an *NME* pollwinners' concert early in their career, the Beatles didn't share the bill with the Rolling Stones. These multi-starred events didn't start until the eighties, but if Elvis had survived to Live Aid, I like to think he would have agreed.

MARIA DAVIES

Can't Help Falling in Love

The news that Elvis was to appear in Las Vegas in August 1969 for four weeks hit me like a punch from Muhammad Ali. With my sister Gladys, I had made contingency plans for Elvis coming to England; the cash for fares and tickets was always at the ready, together with sleeping bags for the all-night vigils – but getting to see him in Las Vegas had not been part of our agenda. I was on good terms with Colonel Parker's office, and they told me they were not handling the tickets – these would have to be obtained from the International Hotel in Las Vegas – but if we got there, we were invited to contact the Colonel, an invitation I was not about to pass up. The summer was spent making phone calls to the States and buying what I considered suitable frocks for the event. I enjoyed sending the sales girls into a state of shock when, after enquiring for what occasion did I require the dresses, I replied 'to see Elvis Presley in Las Vegas'. It was only seventeen days before the start of our trip that we received confirmation that the shows we had asked for had been reserved.

We were lucky that, on our first day in Vegas, our fan club badges served as an introduction to some fans from Salt Lake City who explained the system of booking for the shows. Your reservation allowed you into the room: where you sat depended on the number of greenbacks you were prepared to give the waiter, 'and you must see at least one show from the front row'. They suggested a $10 tip and we could increase it if we did not get the seats we wanted. Gladys and I decided we would worry about food after we left Las Vegas and we would give $20 to save time and hopefully to get front row seats. At 5 p.m. we came down to the Showroom for the 8 p.m. show. There were 50 people ahead of us in the line; a passing American looked at us in amazement and said 'I would not stand in line for the President of the United States.' 'Neither would I,' I told him. Our gamble paid off and at six-fifteen we were seated front row just to the right of centre stage. The waiting was interminable, the dinner taken away uneaten, and I felt I was going to pass out. I spent the time practising the deep-breathing exercises taught to guardsmen to prevent them fainting at the Trooping of the Colour.

At long last the Sweet Inspirations and the comedian Sammy Shore finished their acts and the gold curtains were raised to reveal Elvis's rhythm group playing a rock 'n' roll riff. The audience was shrieking in anticipation, but the artist did not appear and guitarist James Burton kept looking to his left. Suddenly a leg stretched out from behind the curtain in the manner of a burlesque dancer, sending the audience into a greater state of hysteria. Then in the most casual manner E.P. strolled out on stage, with a Mona Lisa smile and his hooded eyes flickering over the audience. We were told he weighed 140lbs this engagement, and he looked like a boy of twenty-two. My eyes were riveted on those broad shoulders, that long back, and those even longer legs. When he reached the centre of the stage he seized hold of the guitar and whipped the strap over his head. He then took up his stance at the mike, right leg slightly in front of left, left knee snapping in time to the music, head held up, eyes slightly closed; he loved to hear the audience, but it made him nervous to see them, hence the closed eyes. Elvis blasted into 'Blue Suede Shoes' followed by 'I Got A Woman' and 'All Shook Up'. At the end of these songs, he took off the guitar and grabbed the mike like a bullwhip, saying, 'Good evening ladies and gentlemen, welcome to the big funky International Hotel.' The décor of the room was not to his liking: Louis XIV and Marie Antoinette murals on the walls and the fattest angels I have ever seen. Elvis never lost an opportunity to joke about the decoration: 'Those little weirdo dolls on the walls and those little funky angels on the ceiling – man, you ain't seen nothing until you've seen a funky angel. Before the evening's out, I am sure I will have made a complete and utter fool of myself, but I hope you get a kick out of watching. During the show you will see I drink a lot of water. This is because the desert air is very dry and it affects my throat. I have here some Gatoraid. (This pale yellow liquid is advertised on TV as quenching thirst twelve times faster than water.) It looks as if it has been used before, but it aids my gator.'

He then sang 'Love Me Tender' and walking along the edge of the stage, he bent down to kiss the girl sitting there and then worked his way along the front row, kissing all the women and shaking hands with the men. Everyone started jumping up and standing on their chairs. I jumped on mine and when Elvis looked in my direction, I stretched out my arms and beckoned him over. I nearly died when he walked over to me. I flung my arms around him and said, 'Elvis, you are simply great. We have come from England to see you – you are just marvellous.' He kissed me and Gladys and while I was hugging him Gladys ran her fingers through his hair and she said it was soft as silk. We were mortified later to find out he couldn't stand anyone to touch his hair, not even his family.

After this he said, 'I would like to do for you some of my big records, actually they were no bigger than this,' and he indicated the size of a 45rpm. He then sang 'Mystery Train,' 'Jailhouse Rock', 'Heartbreak Hotel' and 'Don't be Cruel'. He crouched down, left leg bent under him, right leg stretched out to the side, guitar slung out like a tommy-gun. He held this pose for five minutes while he fooled around with the following dialogue – 'So I looked her square in the eye because all she had was one square eye, and there we were like this, see, both with our guitars bumpin' and she said to me, "Is that your pick, man?" and I said "Yep, that's about the size of it!" She said, "Funny lookin' pick, man," and I said, "Well, don't look at it then," so there we were watchin' my sweat dropping on the floor' (and Elvis's sweat was dropping on the floor) 'and I said to her, "Baby, Baby," and she said "Deeper, deeper," so I said, "Baby, Baby," (in a deeper voice) so she got disgusted and got up and left, so I was left there like this, and I said . . .' He then roared into 'Hound Dog' with the strobe lights flashing and his hair flying all over the place.

After this Charlie Hodge brought over a stool and handed him an electric guitar. Elvis sat down and said, 'I would like to talk to you a little bit about how I came to get started in this business, a lot has been written about it but never from my side. In 1954 I made a record and it got to be played on radio and got pretty big in my home town. I started playing in little clubs and little football fields. In those days you didn't see people with long hair and sideburns and people said, "Who is he? what is he? he is squirrelly, man, he's just out of the trees, get him." You didn't see people moving around on stage too much, they were getting it in the back rooms, you know, but you didn't see it out front. Then I met Colonel Sanders, no I mean Colonel Parker, and then I got to be on television, I did *The Milton Berle Show*, *The Steve Allen Show*, and *The Ed Sullivan Show*. On *The Ed Sullivan Show* they dressed me in a tuxedo and filmed me from the waist up. They had me singing to a dog, you know "You ain't nuttin' but a hound dog" and the dog's on heat and I don't know it, and there I am singing "You ain't nuttin' but a hound dog" and the dog's going (Elvis imitates a dog panting), so they take the dog and lock it away, don't know if it was to protect me from it or it from me. Ed Sullivan is sitting there saying "son of a bitch", and I'm saying, "Thank you, Sir," 'cause I don't know what it means. So then I go to Hollywood, that's what happens to you in this business, you have a hit record, go on television and then you go to Hollywood, and I'm not ready for it, and it's not ready for me. I made *Love Me Tender, Loving You, Loving Her, Loving Anyone I Can Get My Hands On At The Time, Jailhouse Rock* and I am getting used to the life, you know, driving around in a Cadillac with my feet up and dark glasses on, saying, "I'm a movie star", eating hamburgers and drinking Pepsi, and I made *King Creole* then I got drafted and shafted and it was all over for me. The guys in the army were watching me to see what I would do, and when they saw I was doing just like they were, everything was all right. The guys in the service must get awful lonely because they call one another "Mother" – that's only the half of it. Well, you know, I picked this up but wasn't very popular when I got back to Hollywood – I would see some big producer and say, "Hello, Mother" then I made *G.I. Blues, Blue Hawaii, Viva Las Vegas, Girls! Girls! Girls!*, but the point of telling you all this is to say I got into a rut and I really missed contact with the live audience, that's why I am here tonight.' This brought loud applause and Elvis started to tune up the guitar and said 'Contrary to what most people think, I can really play this thing.' He said, 'Is that a G? Man, if your G-string is wrong it's terrible.' He then played the guitar while singing 'Baby What You Want Me To Do' and 'Are you Lonesome Tonight?'. He hummed a few notes of 'It's Now Or Never', and every time he did, the audience applauded, but he'd say, 'I'm not going to sing that thing.' He then sang 'my version' of 'Yesterday', singing, 'I'm not half the stud I used to be.' Then he started to sing 'Hey Jude' and worked his way across the front row. He had been presented with a gold 'Lonsdale' belt by the Hotel in recognition of the number of people attending his shows. I wanted to know what was written on the main buckle. I decided I would ask him this when he came to me. During the excitement of the show, my contact lens had shot out of my left eye. When Elvis stood before me and bent down to give me a kiss, I held on to the scarf to keep his head down and asked him to tell us what the inscription was. I was told later he would have been too modest to tell me, but he didn't understand what I had asked and said, 'Huh?' I repeated my question and then the most mischievous smile came over his face. He put his thumbs into the top of the belt and thrust his hips into my face. With only one good eye it took me some time to make out the inscription, which was 'World Championship Attendance Holder Las Vegas, Nevada' and 'ELVIS' in diamonds, with the International Hotel's logo and stars in diamonds down each side of the inscription. While I was scanning this, Elvis said, 'You sure have a lotta nerve, baby.' The Showroom erupted with laughter and my sister, who could not imagine what I was asking him, tried to haul me back into my seat. After the show many people stopped to ask what I had said. They had only heard Elvis's answer. 'You have no idea how funny it looked,' I was told. Elvis's family told us later he just loved to embarrass people and would have really enjoyed the situation. We were also told that Elvis's father, Vernon, had spotted us in the coffee shop and was telling everyone that he was so proud that we had come all the way from England to see his son. Elvis continued the show with 'Memories', 'Suspicious Minds', and closed with 'Can't Help Falling In Love'. The gold curtain came down slowly and he was gone – no encores. If you wanted to see him again, you would have to come to the next show. He was never on stage for less than one hour. The hotel told him, 'You are killing yourself to entertain these people, we don't expect this from you.' With good reason, while his shows were on, the takings from the gambling were well down.

A couple of nights later, while we were watching Colonel Parker play roulette, he turned to us and said, 'Has Tom Diskin told you what we are trying to arrange for tomorrow night?' 'No,' I said. 'Well,' he replied, 'we are trying to get you backstage to Elvis.' He made this sound as if it was Elvis's decision but we knew this was up to the Colonel. 'Don't leave the hotel tomorrow,' he said. We sat in our room all day and then got ready for the show – we were going to the midnight one – and went down and stood outside the showroom from 5.30p.m. At 9.45p.m. the first show finished and, as the crowds streamed out I thought we would be swamped, but then I heard a voice saying, 'Follow me.' Tom Diskin then led us to the backstage area. A woman latched on to us saying, 'Can I come too?' but Tom replied, 'No.' 'Well, you cannot stop me walking with you,' she said. 'But you will not be allowed down,' he retorted. We eventually reached a flight of stairs with an armed security guard standing at the top. Tom said to the woman who had walked with us, 'You stay here.' We went down the stairs and entered a small room which only contained a bed covered with a brown blanket and a white coffee table with a lamp on it, the only light in the room. Ahead of us were six fans from Canada, who had won a contest organized by RCA. Colonel Parker was standing behind Elvis and, as we came through the door, he patted Elvis on the shoulder and said, 'These are the two fans from England.' The people ahead of us gave us the time to have a really good look at Elvis. He was wearing black pin-striped trousers, black silk shirt, pink scarf around his neck and an Indian silver belt around his hips and he looked so elegant and handsome. The atmosphere was almost monastic. It was so quiet and peaceful and such a contrast to what went on upstairs. We had bought a present for his daughter, Lisa, a gold ring set with a cabochon garnet which had been displayed at an antique dealers' fair in London as an example of Victorian jewellery for children. When Elvis gave anyone jewellery, he always said 'It's gold, you know' so we had included a letter giving the history of the ring, 'It's gold, you know'. When our turn came to stand with Elvis I put the gift on the table and told him how much we were enjoying the shows. He asked me to spell my name Maria Luisa, and he signed a souvenir book of pictures. When Gladys gave him her name he smiled – it was the same name as his mother – and as he was signing Gladys's book, a bimbo came rushing in from another door, gazed up at him and said, 'Elvis, do you remember me?' 'Sure I do, honey, you're Joanne.' However, he had the wrong name, and the bimbo said her real name and pouted.

At that moment Tom Diskin said, 'Can you find your own way back?' and we knew this was their way of saying it was time to go. When Elvis came on stage at the midnight show he walked over to where we were sitting, raised his hand in greeting and smiled at us, saying, 'Thank you', which we knew was an acknowledgement of the gift. Everyone around us was twittering why should he do that. We had been told not to tell anyone we had been backstage, so we just sat there like two kittens with a bowl of cream.

At every show Elvis introduced an amazing number of stars from Hollywood and television: Diana Ross, Jim Webb, Roy Orbison, Bill Cosby, Nancy Sinatra, Paul Anka, Wayne Newton, James Coburn, Neil Diamond. I asked Tom Diskin why all these stars came to see him and he replied, 'They come to see what makes him tick, and when they go home, they'll still not know. If you think the reception here has been good, wait until you see him in the South among his own people.' We were lucky to be at the Astrodome in Houston, Texas, when 43,000 people greeted him, many giving the Rebel warcry of the Deep South. We were told it was the most emotional welcome of Elvis's career and it is such a pity that it was not officially recorded.

Elvis was a master showman: his concerts were the most memorable and exciting anyone could hope to see. He was able to control the audience in the nicest way. He performed with such grace and elegance and was always in control of all those with him on stage. He was truly a child of destiny.

BARNEY HOSKYNS

Memphis Blues Again: Elvis '69

Elvis Presley must have sensed that his credibility was on the line when he made the decision, in early January 1969, to cancel a Nashville recording date and book instead what were to be his first Memphis sessions in fourteen years. Fresh from the lean, mean triumph of the NBC-TV 'Comeback' special aired in December, he knew he had to capitalize on the excitement which that performance had generated.

Among the people urging him on was Marty Lacker, a prominent member of Presley's 'Memphis Mafia' who just happened to be vice-president of a company called American Group Productions. Over dinner at Graceland one night, Lacker persuaded Elvis that he should switch his forthcoming session from Nashville to AGP's studio at 827 Thomas Street, Memphis. It was hardly a difficult pitch, given that American was at that point perhaps the hottest studio in America. Indeed, Neil Diamond was in the process of wrapping up the sessions which were to produce the Top 10 hits 'Sweet Caroline' and 'Holly Holy'. Other acts to have benefited from the studio's glory run included B. J. Thomas, Dionne Warwick, and Dusty Springfield, the latter in the *Billboard* Top 20 that very week with the sultry 'Son Of A Preacher Man'.

American was the brainchild of Lincoln 'Chips' Moman, a key figure in the germination of the post-Sun Memphis music scene. Chips had been in on the beginning of Stax, had co-written and produced James Carr's classic soul ballad 'Dark End Of The Street' and even played on Atlantic sessions for Jerry Wexler in Muscle Shoals, Alabama. (It's his telling guitar fill you can hear on Aretha's 'I Never Loved A Man'.) Having built the Thomas Street studio with the proceeds of a $3000 settlement from Stax in 1964, Chips had gone on to assemble a crack session team from the bands of Bill Black and Ace Cannon: guitarist Reggie Young, bassists Tommy Cogbill and Mike Leech, keyboard maestros Bobby Wood and Bobby Emmons, and drummer Gene Chrisman.

Moman had a knack for juggling black acts such as Bobby Womack and James and Bobby Purify with white ones such as the Gentrys and pop-country chanteuse Sandy Posey, eventually chalking up a string of hits unparalleled even by nearby Stax. Indeed, so used to success were the American sessionmen by 1969 that even Elvis Presley seemed to them 'just another date'. 'We'd been doing Neil Diamond just before Elvis came in, and he was a big deal to us,' recalled trumpeter Wayne Jackson. 'We were thrilled about Elvis, but it wasn't like doing Neil Diamond.'

If this strikes one as unduly blasé, it's worth bearing in mind that to these guys Elvis was just a fellow Southerner, and a Memphian to boot. Like him, they had broken through their own racist conditioning to embrace the blues, R&B, and gospel of southern blacks. What did they care about *Girl Happy* or *Paradise Hawaiian Style*? Consider also that, the TV special notwithstanding, Presley's commercial standing was hardly at its highest in January 1969. As Peter Guralnick put it, 'It's difficult to recall just how far removed Elvis was, not simply from the pop mainstream, but from any degree of critical respect or even social recognition at that time.' Much of this was due to the mismanagement of Colonel Tom Parker, whose understanding of the pop market bordered on the farcical. Thanks to Parker, Elvis had lost sight of what had made him great in the first place. But for the vision of NBC producer Steve Binder, the second wind that was the comeback special might never have happened.

The Colonel Tom problem initially threatened to undo the whole point of the American Studio sessions. 'At first I thought it wasn't gonna work,' Chips Moman admitted to me in 1985. 'They were bringing in exactly the same kinda songs he'd been doing for years, whereas the only way it was gonna work was if there was a change of repertoire.' It was Marty Lacker who finally prevailed upon Presley to see that Parker's greed in taking huge cuts of publishing royalties meant that he was missing out on countless good songs. The result was that, in addition to the new Mac Davis and Dallas Frazier songs gathered by A&R man Felton Jarvis, Elvis wound up cutting a whole slew of vintage R&B and country songs – from Percy Mayfield's 'Stranger In My Own Home Town' to Eddy Arnold's 'I'll Hold You In My Heart (Till I Can Hold You In My Arms)' – and even trying his hand at such '60s soul numbers as Chuck Jackson's 'Any Day Now' and Jerry Butler's 'Only The Strong Survive'.

Moman and the 827 Thomas Street Band had a mere four days to prepare for the sessions, which commenced on Monday 13 January. By a neat coincidence, cutting tracks in the next-door studio at American was the great R&B balladeer Roy Hamilton, whose fusion of gospel and pseudo-operatic sobbing had exerted a decisive vocal influence on the young Presley. 'He talked a lot about Hamilton being his idol and about how he'd copied him,' Chips recalled, and the two men even sat in on each other's sessions. Elvis must have loved Hamilton's delirious version of Conway Twitty's 'It's Only Make Believe' (AGP 125), one of the man's last sides before his death from a stroke six months later.

Presley's own sessions usually kicked off in mid-afternoon, with Elvis himself fooling around on the ivories and warbling his favourite inspirational songs. (Note that his last proper studio album had been 1967's *How Great Thou Art*.) The gospel leanings infused most of the tracks recorded that week, what with the massed backing singers and Elvis's own evident sense of vocal liberation. 'Elvis wasn't the world's greatest singer,' said Chips, 'but he had a sound and that's all that's important.' If Chips often had to pick Elvis up on his pitching – 'his whole entourage would nearly faint,' the producer remembered – the results he got by pushing for improvement spoke for themselves. Elvis would never be the elastic, ecstatic singer he was in 1955, but Moman knew the man could do better than the hammy pub-singer pastiche of *bel canto* he'd been getting away with for too long. In his book *Lost Highway*, Peter Guralnick compared the sessions to the TV special: 'There continues to be that same sense of tension, the atmosphere remains nervous and almost self-effacing, and there is that strange anxiety to please and constriction in the voice which seems a million years away from the perfect self-assurance of the nineteen-year-old "natural" who first recorded for Sun so very long ago.'

A perfect case in point is 'I'll Hold You In My Heart', a country and western hit for Eddy Arnold back in 1947. With a false start intro as contrived as the one which had kicked off 'Milkcow Blues Boogie' all those years before, Elvis's version quickly turns into a prime piece of the kind of country-soul Moman and the band had cut a hundred times, with a rock-solid rhythm section and the telltale Telecaster fills of Reggie Young. Accompanying himself somewhat falteringly on the piano, Elvis really goes for it, pushing Arnold's staid original to wild heights of improvised gospel abandon. The song ends up like something from Dylan and the Band's *Basement Tapes*, a raggedy reworking bringing an old country chestnut back to life.

Like *The Basement Tapes*, too, the Memphis sessions served as a kind of 'grab-bag' – in this case for the multiple musical personae Presley had adopted throughout his career, from the raucous blues belter of 'Power Of My Love' to the cod-gospel penitent of 'Who Am I?', from the uptempo pop swaggerer of 'Wearin' That Loved-On Look' to the schmaltzy balladeer of 'Don't Cry Daddy'. Elvis the Soul Man may leave something to be desired next to Jerry Butler, but one has to applaud the fact that he attempted 'Only The Strong Survive' in the first place. Moreover, the backing of the Thomas Street Band actually improves on the original. Chips Moman might not have created a 'sound' as distinct as that of Stax or Hi (or Fame in Muscle Shoals), but his variation on the sound Jerry Wexler had patented at Atlantic, with its 'live' drums and punchy Jerry Jermott-style bass figures, was always exciting. Wexler himself was hardly blind to this: despite professing disappointment at Chips's decision to cut a distribution deal with Larry Utall's Bell label rather than with Atlantic, he nonetheless brought acts like King Curtis and the Sweet Inspirations to record at American. Dusty Springfield's great *Dusty In Memphis* and Herbie Mann's *Memphis Underground* were just two of the Atlantic albums cut in the studio.

The twelve songs which eventually made it onto the *From Elvis In Memphis* album that summer were fairly evenly weighted between contemporary pop and older country and R&B material. Of the 'retro' numbers, 'Long Black Limousine' was almost as good as 'I'll Hold You In My Heart'. A typical small-town sermonette, the song concerns a girl who splits for the big city vowing to return in a 'big fancy car'. She keeps her promise, except that the 'long black limousine' in question turns out to be a hearse. 'Elvis was no fool,' wrote Greil Marcus; 'he knew the song was about him, the country boy lost to the city if there ever was one, but he sang as if he liked that fact and loathed it all at once.' As with 'I'll Hold You In My Heart', Presley turned a sombre, low-key country tune into a full-on vocal blowout.

The new pop material – including the Glen Campbell hit 'Gentle On My Mind' and Dallas Frazier's 'True Love Travels On A Gravel Road' – was some of Presley's strongest in years. Elvis himself was uneasy about recording 'In The Ghetto', given that so-called 'message songs' were not exactly his forte. But Mac Davis's schlocky sketch of inner-city deprivation gave the King his biggest hit in four years. An even bigger hit was held back from the album, and came close to not being recorded at all. Mark James's 'Suspicious Minds' was published by Chips Moman's own Press Music company, and Presley's publishers Hill and Range wanted a big chunk of it. Incensed by their greed, Chips apparently told their representatives Freddy Bienstock and Tom Diskin to get the hell out of his studio. Eventually they backed down, making it possible for Elvis to cut what has come to be regarded as a classic pop single. It's one of those over-the-top three-and-a-half-minute melodramas of the 'Everlasting Love' variety, a record which keeps lifting to another irresistible emotional peak. As Dave Marsh remarked, 'Here's the final piece of evidence that what happened at Sun was no fluke.' Elvis never sang so powerfully again.

Further hits followed with the shameless Mac Davis weepie 'Don't Cry Daddy' and with future country-pop star Eddie Rabbitt's 'Kentucky Rain', one of a speight of 'rain' songs from the early seventies. (Another of them, Dan Penn's haunting 'Raining In Memphis', would have suited Presley perfectly. All in all, the fourteen days Elvis spent at American in January and February of 1969 resulted in four Top 20 singles and two gold albums. (The remaining Memphis material wound up as the second half of the double album *From Memphis To Vegas/From Vegas To Memphis.*)

Presley briefly seemed galvanized by the Memphis sessions, going on to record the compelling concept album *Elvis Country*, as well as songs by southern writers such as Dennis Linde ('Burning Love') and Tony Joe White ('Polk Salad Annie'). But it wasn't long before the King had slumped back into barbiturated pap like *Aloha From Hawaii Via Satellite*, and not a lot longer before he was scarcely in a fit state to record at all. As for Chips Moman and American, when the Memphis boom came to an end in 1972 he wound up in Nashville, bastion of all the mainstream country values he despised. Happily, however, he got cosy with the burgeoning Outlaw contingent and wound up producing Waylon Jennings' *Ol' Waylon*, the first platinum album ever to come out of Nashville. And when Johnny Cash, Jerry Lee Lewis, Roy Orbison and Carl Perkins congregated for a 'Memphis Rock 'n' Roll Homecoming' in September 1985, it was Chips Moman who got the job of producing the resulting album. When you cast your eyes down the credits of *Class Of '55* the same old names popped up from the past: Gene Chrisman, Mike Leech, Bobby Emmons, Bobby Wood, Reggie Young, Wayne Jackson, Dan Penn.

'When shadows fall in the valley/To that precious memory we cling,' sang Johnny Cash on the album's 'We Remember The King', one of many artifacts that implicitly equate Presley with Jesus Christ. If cling we must, let it at least be to the memory of Elvis in 1969, 'thin as a rake and more handsome than ten movie stars', singing his heart out at 827 Thomas Street.

ALAN BLEASDALE

'Are You Lonesome Tonight?'
(An outtake)

A scene that never saw the light of day . . .

[*Elvis is alone. Almost alone . . . He is talking, as he was known to talk in 'real life' behind closed doors to his still-born twin brother, Jesse.*

At this stage in his life, sensing death, and knowing that disgrace is just around the corner when his former friends tell tales and make headlines, Elvis believes that his still-born twin brother is the only person left in the world whom he can trust . . .

Elvis is sitting down, facing an empty chair which is the size and shape of a throne.]

PRESLEY: . . . Poor Jesse, could have been me . . . gone even before he came – still born, still dead gone but not forgotten, not by my mama . . . and now not by me . . . always a place at the table for you, Jesse boy, know that? My mama – your mama – laid a place for you every day of her life. And you never showed up once – what kind of a son are you . . . ?

[*He turns away. Turns back. Smiles. Shakes his head.*]

. . . I wanna ask you one question, Jesse. I wanna ask you this – who is the most famous person in the world? Right – it's either me or Muhammad Ali – well, maybe it might be him – he's a nice guy an' I like him – *but* he cheated – no man, he did – the bastard's got the Third World in his pocket – all that Muslin mumbo-jumbo stuff – religion comes free but y' need money in yah pockets to buy my records, and the Third World ain't got no money – so I don't care if they never heard of me – so all right, take away the starvin' – an' I know that sounds cruel, Jesse – but take them away anyway – an' what're you left with – y' left with me! I am the most famous person in the world. I'm not boastin', brother – that's a fact.

[*Grabs some loose tablets from a nearby table. Swallows them.*]

. . . But what did I do wrong? . . . that's what I wanna know.

[*Presley picks his guitar up, plays the opening chords of 'I'm So Lonesome I Could Cry'.*]

. . . I wanna tell you somethin', Jesse – 's all right, I'll be leavin' you soon – gettin' late – but listen to this – an' you better be fuckin' listenin' – I'm Elvis Presley [*Grins easily at the empty throne.*] – but you know all this . . . I mean my money and my boys and my many women and all my fame . . . all this . . . sharecroppers' dream . . . [*Sings.*] 'Poor boy, I'm just a poor boy . . .' those dreams my mama an' daddy made me dream, not that they *made* me dream them dreams, but . . . their fuckin' lives made me kinda – you get up in the mornin' [*Smiles, sings the spiritual briefly.*] . . . but then, hey man, it's all downhill. Best part of the day is the dreams you have at night [*Shakes his head.*] – before those dreams become nightmares . . . but I mean, man, there I was just off the titty, on a knee, being sung to, hallelujah and poverty, a wooden shack my daddy built, an' then he's taken off to prison for changin' a fourteen-dollar food cheque to forty-four dollars – three years' hard labour for a lousy thirty bucks . . . man, my mama an' me [*He points.*] – an' Jesse makes three . . . God knows my mama . . . no wonder she . . . but that's all that a poor boy's got – I ain't got one picture of me wearin' a shirt the right size . . . an' a boy does wish, Jesse, I'm tellin' you – he lusts an' wishes an' dreams it all, for the boy, for him, yeah, but for all the good old boys an' for his mama an' daddy, for his dead brother who never lived, for his eventual wife an' children, his family an' friends an' fuckin' fools an' stooges, for the niggahs in the field – those boys in the back of the bus – for total strangers even [*He laughs mockingly.*] – for his every friend . . . his friends . . . who plan to publish books . . . done it all, man. I am Elvis Presley. An' I done the lot. An' what've I got? What do I end up doin'? Talkin' to a fuckin' chair in an empty room . . . at three in the mornin'.

[*He stands up.*]

Move!

[*He waits a while then looks away from the chair as if Jesse has stood up. He sits on Jesse's 'throne'. He points to his own 'throne'.*]

Sit there.

[*He stands up, goes to and stands above 'Jesse'.*]

Open your mouth wide and say 'Ahhhhhhhhhh'. [*Shakes his head.*] Lucky to be alive, young man.

[*His laughter fades on him. He returns to and sits on Jesse's 'throne'. Looks back.*]

Come on, you bastard – perform. Come back with me, Jesse Presley. [*Sings.*] 'Oh why, oh why can't my dreams come true? . . .' Let me see you, I can see most everythin' I wanna see – wanna see you now – right at the very start, boy – you can do it, Jesse, cos you'd have had the one thing I never had . . . guess I never . . . never had the ability to . . . control my life. Wish I'd have been . . . cleverer. I just ain't . . . clever. Like that. Me – I could fail a blood test. But you an' me together, Jesse; my talent, my good looks, my sex appeal, my left leg . . . [*Laughs warmly.*] Ain't too much left for you. 'Cept for one thing. You would have won. *You would have won!* . . . You would have – an' I ain't complete without you, man. I done everythin' – 'cept win. Come on, you bitch of a fuckin' boy, square the circle, Jesse . . . COME ON!

[*Presley stares hard in the hope of a miracle, sighs and turns away.*]

. . . Nah, you ain't comin' back, are you? . . . just like all the others . . . least you got a good excuse, boy . . .

[*He picks up the guitar and begins to sing, with a plaintive beauty, 'I'm So Lonesome I Could Cry'.*]

ADRIAN HENRI

Memphis Sunset

You forgot to remember to forget
how the Sun came up at 78 rpm,
a battered panel truck
parked in the studio back lot
until the blue moon set over Kentucky.

All around the world
every boy and girl heard the news
there was good rockin' in Memphis,
put on their rockin' shoes.

But this time they made you a mountain,
a mountain you really couldn't climb.
Impossible. Its rhinestone slopes,
Lone Star peaks, impassable.
Impassive avalanches of applause,
snowblind in the spotlights.

An echoing voice
says you have now left the stadium,
scuffed blue suede shoes
forgotten in the dressing room.

Outside,
the black stretch limo waits.

MARK HODKINSON

Of Not Kicking with the Crowd

It had to involve a football match, everything always did back then. They didn't have to be classic games, far from it, but they still acted like Blu-Tack for the memory, so that profound incidents from life were inextricably affixed to football, bloody football.

We'd drawn the first round of the cup at home against Halifax. Alan Tarbuck, in tribute to his comedian namesake, had bundled the ball over the goal line in the last minute with his nose. Unorthodox for sure, but it secured us a replay over the Pennines in West Yorkshire.

The Shay, Halifax's ground, is a hole in the ground surrounded by cinder, or at least it was back in 1977. The hills gathered on all sides, still grumbling about last year's winter. A speedway track, now redundant, encircled the pitch, so a microphone was needed to shout abuse at the craggy left back your side had signed on a free transfer from Southport.

One side of the ground banked up high and majestic like a classic piece of Roman architecture, except the effect was spoiled by the sparseness of the crowd, a few dozen fanatics clutching meat pies and hoping to catch the last bus home.

It was mid-August, the season in its youth. The pitch was verdant and the air sweetly scented by cut grass. I was twelve years old and this was glamour. And I was with my dad.

We won two–one. Bob Mountford headed home the winner, I think. He usually did. He had the wickedest, flyest afro in the Football League, and he wasn't even black. He was deadly from corners, launching himself at the ball, confident that if his forehead didn't make it, his hair would.

All the way home we talked about the victory, Dad and me. We should have scored four. They were still hay making in the fields. The ref was a disgrace. The road skirted reservoirs and woods. Who will we get in the next round? The sun dissolved into a petrol-blue lake above us.

Football fans know that there is not only the victory itself to savour, but also its promulgation. The television was switched on, we needed to see the result, hear the newscaster say the words, just five words: 'Halifax Town one, Rochdale two.'

A piece of paper was suddenly handed to the newscaster. It broke his concentration, there was a slight pause; there is always this nervous pause before any cataclysmic late news item.

'We have just been informed that Elvis Presley, known to millions as the King of Rock 'n' Roll, has died. We will bring you more news on this as soon as we have it.'

Elvis dead. He couldn't be, he was my dad's hero, as omnipresent in the house as an older brother. I looked at him, not sure of how he would react. He shrugged.

'I've still got his records.'

I expected more, something melodramatic at least. After all, he played the records, watched the films, read the books, he even looked like Elvis Presley. His dark hair was pushed back and flattened at the sides, while the strands on top were shaped into a quiff. He wore jeans one size too large, left empty Brylcreem tubs in the bathroom and his record collection was hardly varied. It went: Elvis Presley, Elvis Presley, Elvis Presley, the Platters, Elvis Presley, Elvis Presley, Del Shannon, Elvis Presley, Elvis Presley.

He didn't look after his records very well. Did anyone then? In the sixties and seventies it seems, they were played and handled until they disintegrated, unlike today when they are too often a lifestyle instead of a lifeblood. The machinery of music, the records and record player, was also shown no respect – the singer and the song were everything. He'd mix up the covers. Most records were without their inner sleeves. He'd yank at the record player's arm and crash down the needle on a track he wanted to hear. The collection was housed in a long wire device which resembled a toast rack. And, even then, I knew that the scraping noise as he took them out would mean another scratch, another crackle through 'Jailhouse Rock'. As long as he could hear the beat and discern the backing track, he could fill in the rest himself anyway.

I was indoctrinated, my brain washed and hung out to dry on the refrains of Elvis Presley, all the Elvis Presleys: the scruffy hillbilly with a lop-sided quiff; the crew-cut, clean-cut army boy; the wooden actor who always got to get the girl and the schmaltzy songs; the leather-wrapped troubadour at the comeback show; and, finally, the besuited torch singer in sideburns and sunglasses. He loved them all, and he loved his son enough to instil this love in him.

After tea I was often summoned from the child's twilight world between washbasin and bed. It was another request to do my Elvis. Strangely, my forte was not a profuse rendition of uptempo songs like 'Blue Suede Shoes' or 'Hound Dog', but the ballads, the luscious, sentimental tones of 'The Wonder Of You' and 'Suspicious Minds'. Dad pulled out one of the RCA Victors from the toast rack and conducted me proudly into the mime. The collar of my pyjama top was turned up and I performed with hysterical histrionics. In conclusion ('Ladies and gentlemen, you've been a great audience'), I would close with a tearful rendition of 'Mama Liked The Roses'. Elvis Presley has now left the building, and gone to bed.

Birthdays were no problem. Every year Dad would receive a new Elvis record, a double set if my younger sister contributed her pocket money. Once, I daringly altered routine and bought him an Elvis mirror that put the 'T' in both 'Tacky' and 'Tasteless' with room to spare.

A few years later, when I was fourteen, I went serious with my first girlfriend. This meant we kissed a few times after collecting wood for bonfire night, had a day trip to Blackpool and talked about people at school whom we both hated. I sneaked her into the house while my parents were out. She saw the Elvis mirror and laughed. She still mentions it when we meet and jokes of a time when we knew nothing of kitsch. I've never mentioned that at least children aren't supercilious.

Christmas for other children was dull and predictable compared to mine. It involved, like their's, presents, a tree, a break from school, an advent calendar, rain (never snow), re-runs of *Jason and the Argonauts* and more food than Oliver Twist could eat, but I also had something extra, something which became more synonymous with Christmas than the nativity – the Elvis Christmas album. It was like a vintage wine from which the family could take only a few sips once a year. The wonderful record would appear just a few days before Christmas Day, usually on the afternoon when my parents finished work and arrived home weighed down with carrier bags of food. Elvis, wearing his best-ever smile, was flung on to the floor by Dad. Christmas was here, official.

Unfortunately, my father's loyalty to Elvis blurred his capacity to unravel the brilliant from the banal. As the record covers became increasingly gaudy through the seventies and rock 'n' roll was superseded by nursery rhymes ('Old Macdonald Had A Farm', for Heaven's sake), I realized my own taste in music was significantly different from his own. There might also have been a latent air of rebellion, because from thirteen years old I no longer sought out Elvis records and, indeed, went to my room when he played them. I'd moved on to heroes of my own like Gary Glitter, who was regularly on *Top of the Pops* and, more poignantly, whom my dad couldn't stand.

I became obsessional about music, condemned to a life spent thumbing through record racks, always on the lookout for anything new, fresh, different; something no one else had heard of, never mind actually heard. I carried around my record collection like a carbuncle, packed it in boxes, logged it in books. And all the time it grew and needed feeding with more of itself. Limited edition, free sew-on patch, programme of the tour, twelve-inch re-mix, I had the lot and some more.

Record collecting, like train-spotting and bird-watching, has its own circle of acquaintances. We meet and swap stories about the lesser-spotted, gate-folded first edition of *Diamond Dogs*. We scrutinize *Record Collector* magazine and spend too many hours in musty church halls picking our way through over-tightly packed records (why do they do that, are they sick?) as they wobble on trestle tables.

In my early twenties I met another addict, ten years older with a collection mirroring the fact. He kindly allowed me to rifle through and tape the songs I liked. I had spent hours listening to every obscure garage band America had ever produced. Maybe it just felt like hours, but I had barely used up one side of a C90. Dad was on the landing outside my bedroom and knocked on the door. He'd heard the music.

'What are you up to?'

I told him.

'You can tape some of my Elvis stuff if you want,' he said matter of factly.

I didn't want to hurt the old boy's feelings, he meant well. I faked some lukewarm enthusiasm and he returned with a plastic bag full of records, still in the wrong sleeves and some with telephone numbers scribbled on the back.

It had been almost a decade since I had last listened properly to Elvis. It sounded different, it had a new clarity. I heard songs that had clearly influenced bands I exalted – the Smiths even covered '(Marie's The Name) His Latest Flame' at their concerts. One side of the tape was filled immediately. I wasn't sure whether I'd ever play it, so I put on the other side an album by a suitably obscure band called the Homosexuals; any friends finding it would see the Elvis side as an aberration and my image as champion of the modern and esoteric would remain intact.

The Homosexuals were played just once, and that was too much, but the Elvis side was hammered. 'Suspicious Minds', (Marie's The Name) His Latest Flame' (I love the fastidiousness of those brackets), 'Blue Suede Shoes', 'Wooden Heart', 'In The Ghetto' – dripping with tunes, passion, charisma, atmosphere. And Dad, never one for showy emotion, welcomed back the prodigal son. Elvis Presley is back in the building.

Lamentably, Elvis is not held in such esteem by others of my generation. To them he is a doughy mess in a lurid white suit flopped down dead in his Graceland bathroom. The cupboard door is open. The pills are teeming out. He's somewhere between the toilet and the sink. The dimples and celebrated upper lip are still.

He died in grisly, ignominious circumstances and this has become the lasting memory for those too young to remember the other version, the one which was thin and cheerful and handsome and humorous. They mock his death, as if it equalled the life that preceded it. He has become a cartoon and a parable, a badge for overindulgence, vanity and weakness of character.

Within a year of his death I recall a news story claiming he had an unusually small penis; no indignity was too great with which to affront his memory. The Las Vegas cummerbund was tugged from him until he stood naked before us, left without decorum and mystery.

Jimi Hendrix and Jim Morrison had similar deaths but they became cultural icons. Perhaps it was because they died younger, before the comeback tours, but nonetheless their squalor is perversely glamorous: they died for their art, Elvis died because he was stupid. It's not true, of course. Each exited stage left through his own recklessness and negligence, it's just that *revering* Hendrix and Morrison equals rebellion (albeit a fuzzy and inarticulate rendering), in the same way as *ridiculing* Elvis does.

Elvis, you see, is for dads, the generation we're supposed to be kicking against. But I can't kick with the crowd, it's too much like denying my antecedents; how I got to be where I am. And, I got to be here because of two—one victories at the Shay, nil—nil draws at Gigg Lane and Elvis mirrors.

ALAN CLAYSON

The Thistledown Flash:
A Fictional Piece

Normally, I couldn't care less what Reg got up to after we'd finished as long as he could pile in if there was trouble over money or outface a gauntlet of hard cases when we were loading up. His knockout punch was one of our biggest assets.

He was also good at dressing while running – because he liked to have the evening's sex life sorted out by the intermission. Sometimes we'd have to fill in with an instrumental at the start of the second half until he panted on, either zipping up his flies or wiping sticky hands on his star-spangled, bat-winged bolero.

In the beginning, Reg had kitted himself out in a shiny Elvis-pink nylon suit, made by a tailor in Farnham. Like everyone else, he'd been 'gone' on Elvis since 'Heartbreak Hotel'. Unlike everyone else, however, he'd never regarded it as just an adolescent folly and that he'd grow out of it on attaining man's estate. Four years after 'Heartbreak Hotel', he was still living the part; even wearing stage clothes merely to mooch down to the corner shop with hunched shoulders, hands rammed in pockets and chewing gum in a half-sneer.

Lately, he'd added seedy-flash accessories of leopard-skin cuffs and lapels to go with the bolero, the black-and-white winkle-pickers and the Gene Vincent medallion. An experiment with dye on mousey hair had divided his precarious, grease-glistening pompadour with a three-inch turquoise stripe. As the Fireball McTavish in Fireball McTavish and the Sunstrokes, Reg reckoned that the 'fans' expected him to look 'sort of far-out, wild'.

The rest of us kept our given names – which in my case is Roger Skinner – though I was to be Reinhardt (after Django) Skinner later. We Sunstrokes skulked in our chief show-off's shadow in identical drainpipes, nondescript shirts, slim-jim ties – which, like Reg's fluorescent socks, had musical notes on them – and silver-grey waistcoats cut from the

French-window curtains that Adrian's married sister had been about to give to a Townswomen's Guild jumble sale.

Adrian – who hacked subordinate rhythm beneath my lead – thought it unfair that a slob like Reg could take his pick of the sillier girls who clustered below the central microphone. With his tooth brace, dandruff, mottled skin and Buddy Holly glasses, Adrian would move in on horsey-looking ones on the 'intellectual' ticket. As a serious musician, his line always included a put-down of Reg. Any fool could roll about on stage as if he had a wasp in his pants, Adrian would whisper seductively. Into the bargain, Reg 'couldn't sing' – not 'real singing', like Elvis when he did hymns. Be it 'Hound Dog' or 'Peace In The Valley', Reg just growled whatever was put in front of him.

Whatever Adrian's opinion of him, I'd been not so much Reg's friend as his disciple. True enough, he was no genius musician. He'd been less than a genius anything when at Aldershot's Holy Name Secondary Modern. During his last year there, he'd been ignored by the more timorous teachers. Just short of openly defying school rules, he'd customized his charcoal-coloured flannels to Presley standards, slouching into the playground on legs that seemed as if they'd been dipped in ink. With his knees up to his chin behind a tiny desk at the back, he'd survey the class with a mixture of scorn, pity and contempt.

The only master to warm to Reg had been the head of music, who'd seen skiffle and rock 'n' roll not as an evil but as a more effective means of getting his pimpled charges interested in his subject than could be achieved through Beethoven and all that. Once it had been associated with dago heel-clattering but now the guitar was what Elvis played. Nevertheless, Reg couldn't quite get to grips with learning the instrument because he had, he said, funny finger joints. These made *barre* chords unbearably painful. Adorning his digits with brass rings illicitly procured from the metalwork room didn't help either, but, theorized Reg, if you had the same amount of weight on your hands as Fats Domino with his jewellery you could pound piano like him. Reg pounded one like Reg.

Similarly, the sodding sticks were why he couldn't keep time on a music-room snare drum. Nevertheless, through a natural rowdiness, red-fisted strength and ingrained bossiness, Reg had a walkover in the power struggle for leadership of the Holy Name Skiffle Combo. This continued after his expulsion – something to do with imprisoning an epileptic prefect in a gym horse – and the Combo's subsequent mutation, via wary amplification, into Fireball McTavish and the Sunstrokes – after Sun Records who started it all.

Leading by example, Reg had some kind of vice-like grip on Trev – another cast out for the gym-horse affair – and a stunted, rat-faced creature he addressed as 'Dids'. He could persuade both to do almost anything. Before Trev could be a Sunstroke, he had to hold down half a bottle of Polish vodka – and it had been Reg's wish too that Dids asked a particularly crabby tobacconist for 'twenty Player's Vagina, please'. None of the three worked to keep alive, but what times they had baiting lone squaddies from the Parachute Regiment; potting the prizes rather than the ducks when lunaticking round amusement arcade shooting galleries; underage drinking in the Heroes of Lucknow, where they picked up a prostitute between them – and, of course, Reg's inspired heist of the Shakeouts' AC30 amplifier.

This had been the Crime of the Century to me – even though I'd considered myself a most frightful desperado, having just been chucked out of school too. It could have been far worse. Like every self-respecting seat of learning near the home of the British army, Thistledown Grammar had an army cadet force. It was grim beyond belief – and it was no use comforting yourself with the thought of Private E. A. Presley then squarebashing in Germany.

You could only be excused it if your father sent a note stating that he was a conscientious objector. Mine wouldn't – so rather than waste every Friday on the parade ground in an itchy dung-brown uniform, me and a pair of twins called Nello and Gral took to sloping off via a changing-room window to Aldershot. Apart from hatred of cadets, I hadn't much in common with them. Nello thought Elvis was a nancy boy, and Gral had once turned nasty over my ignorance about his favourite first division team. They were from an army family, always on the move, and they spoke with adenoidal Liverpool accents which in those days sounded both alien and 'common' to me. Neither were they very bright, slacking as they were among boys a year their junior.

Our Fridays in Aldershot usually began in Macari's with a transparent cup of frothy coffee and either Woodbines or the more sophisticated cigarettes I'd taken from my father's walnut case. After the usual revel in our wickedness, I'd grow tired of Gral's endless details of Everton's near-relegation and Nello's lies about what he got up to with a girl named Mary Hunt, a haughty Irish-Catholic lass who'd never give him a second glance. In turn, Gral and Nello would get sick of my noncommittal nods and polite guffaws. Around mid-morning, talk would peter out and, after staring into space for a bit, someone would suggest a spot of shoplifting.

We came to specialize in junk shops. The idea was to pinch something from one to sell to another. Some of the buyers guessed what we'd been up to and took advantage, but we were happy enough to finish up back at Macari's with a bit left over after a packet of fags each to see us through the weekend. Once, we got five pound ten for a pocket-sized picture frame with a sepia photo of four Victorian children standing in an attitude of sullen defiance. It certainly beat half-killing yourself on a paper round.

Around noon one summer's day, we tried an ambitious pile of 78 rpm records in Maud's Bargains. The place reeked of dirty old Maud's cats, over which she was cooing as I distracted her by pretending I was thinking about buying a china mug inscribed with 'A Present For A Good Girl From Fishguard'. She was remarking that there was nothing she loved more than nice warm sunshine as my stiff-armed accomplices sneaked out.

Then came the clunk of a chair falling over and a yell of 'Wur!' A bald-headed cove with braces and a mouthful of food suddenly reared from behind the blistered door that had been slightly ajar behind the counter. He'd been spying on us over his lunch. In juvenile court a few weeks later, Nello and Gral would learn that he was Mr Woolley, Maud's son-in-law.

The brothers got probation but I'd been lucky. From beneath their blazers, the 78s had clacked onto Maud's doorstep in black shards as her door pinged and we fled. Immediately round the corner was a shoe shop into which I dodged a second before Woolley lumbered into view. By the time he caught up with the other two, a Hattie Jacques type was prising a sensible brown bombhead onto my foot and wondering why I kept twisting round to gaze outside.

Naturally, the twins spread the blame by implicating me after Woolley, assisted by a bus conductor who'd joined the chase, had marched them to the police station. Naturally too, I blustered that, yes, I should have been at school but I was led astray by rough boys. I didn't know they were going to pinch anything. I ran off because they did. I couldn't say why. I was sixteen and liable to do anything.

The law was convinced, and my good name remained unblemished by a criminal record – but parental protests that I was halfway through A-levels had no effect upon my pious old hypocrite of a headmaster. A heavy smoker himself, he remembered me as one of a whole gang he'd caned for smoking in the toilets, and had me down as Trouble. Nello and Gral gauged that if a Lower Sixth-former like me was going to be slung out, they certainly would be. A fortnight after our farewell sermon in the head's study, Gral saw me in the street and turned the air blue with abuse. He was pedalling a tradesman's bike, delivering meat.

As my Mum and Dad wouldn't hear of me entering the world of work before I'd completed my 'education', I went along with whatever I thought might shut them up after my disgrace. With hardly a murmur, I started two years of business studies at Thistledown Tech in autumn 1959. The reasoning behind this was that, though it wasn't university – their original goal for me – if I stuck at office organization, accountancy and so forth, I'd get a job with a suit rather than overalls.

On the same course was Adrian Hilton – and some found it hard to grasp why we became friends. With hands supporting chin, my eyes glazed over unblinking in the drone of convertible debentures and compound interest in pounds, shillings and pence. Adrian, however, was always interested and alert. What drew us together was guitars.

I'd conned my Dad into buying me one on the understanding that I was going to start school-sponsored classical guitar classes. At one of the two I attended, the tutor showed us how *not* to play by smashing out a fast twelve-bar blues shuffle. When my parents next went out, I swapped the gut strings for steel and Sellotaped a tape recorder mike over its hole. Through a classmate's accident – he'd been technically dead when the ambulance arrived – I'd become aware that electric guitars weren't plugged directly into the mains so I sent mine through a Dansette record player.

At first, I didn't actually play it much. Instead, I'd place 'All Shook Up' on the Dansette turntable, and get into position in front of the wardrobe mirror. From the opening bars to the final chord, I'd curl my lip, hip-shake and pretend to slash chords and pick solos with negligent ease. I'd mouth the lyrics, yeah-ing and uh-huh-ing to imaginary thousands of ecstatic girls. Some only too real girls – some of my sister's schoolfriends – once burst in. Gaping at the stunned faces in the doorway, I felt no end of a fool.

This shaming incident goaded me, I suppose, to take the trouble to learn properly. Over the following weeks, I plucked and strummed along to the few other records I'd dared to buy, and some borrowed from my cousin Rick who lived a few streets away. He swore by Carl Perkins and had acquired what appeared to me a stunning expertise on his less expensive guitar with its f-holes and movable bridge. He'd realized that certain basic chord cycles recurred *ad nauseam*. It never occurred to me that I might be cleverer at anything than Rick, who'd been offered a place at Leicester University and – as my aunt enjoyed telling Mum – had only to pass with two Bs to become the first in the family to benefit from such exalted learning.

In a different way, Adrian's pushy mother was like Aunt Jean. Mrs Hilton – who'd done a year at RADA – tended to enter her son's activities with a zest that other mums would consider excessive, particularly when she could tease from him more glamorous aspirations than leaving Holy Name to do business studies. After he saw Lonnie Donegan at Guildford's Civic Hall, she noticed that he'd traced guitar shapes in the vapour of the kitchen window. Therefore, at the foot of his bed that Christmas was a semi-acoustic Futurama 'cutaway' and a copy of Bert Weedon's *Play in a Day*.

Adrian then made the depressing discovery that he was no natural musician. Nevertheless, even to the detriment of homework, he'd position yet uncalloused fingertips on the tortuously wound strings, and pore over 'When the Saints Go Marching In', 'Simple Blues for Guitar' and other exercises prescribed by Bert. After much effort, he moved on to the more advanced manual that I glimpsed sticking out of his briefcase one morning when my attention wandered during economic geography. With some amazement, I asked him about it in the corridor afterwards. Until then, we'd exchanged hardly a sentence.

Swot he might have been, but the breathtaking fascination of stock warranty and the irrigation of Latvia's inner waterways did not keep Adrian from dwelling on the fast flashes of knicker when girls jived in gingham during students' union dances. His hard-won proficiency on the

Futurama had combined with the rising sap of puberty, and he was looking for an opening in a pop group. Boys were spotty, girls untouchable, but being in a group might provide him readier access to female flesh than most of the other blokes who'd paid half a crown to shuffle about in the gloom past the burning footlights.

Adrian and I both came to realize that there was an occasional price that musicians had to pay for this privilege. Cow-eyed attempts by front-row girls to grab onstage attention sometimes led to jealous vendettas – especially in a palais frequented by common soldiers who were obliged to wear their hair planed halfway up the skull, which added to a built-in sense of defeat when pursing romance. Slit-eyed with frustration and beer, they'd seek more brutal sensual pleasure.

At the Central ballroom one night, a horde of squaddies hurled chairs towards the cocky endeavours of Dickie Pride – one of many innocuous British 'answers' to Elvis. With a wave and a ghastly grin, he quit the stage, the building and the town within ten minutes. His backing outfit, the Shakeouts, were left to face the music.

We were hanging around outside when, assuming they had to fend for themselves, the group was hurriedly loading the van via a fire door from behind the stage down some steps when it happened. From hostile shadows emerged a sauntering phalanx of squaddies, shining with malicious glee. They shaped up *Gunfight at the OK Corral*-style, legs apart, thumbs hooked in belts, narrow-eyed heads slightly to one side. Seconds slithered by as, immobile and lynx-like, they watched the Shakeouts. There was nothing yet to justify a fight. Weighing things up, they focused on the weedy-looking drummer as the others looked as if they might be able to take care of themselves.

His throat constricting, his skin crawling and his heart pounding like that of a hunted beast – which he was – the victim forced a shaky smile in the teeth of the tight-lipped stares. Then he said it – 'Good evening' to a gruff 'Ullo'. This was the thrill divine – and there wasn't a moment to be lost. For being such a toffee-nosed git, he was brought down by a knee in the balls. To amused jeers, he collapsed onto the asphalt, gasping. That, however, wasn't good enough. It was going to carry on until it stopped being fun.

Beneath the sole back-porch light, bestial faces watched the drummer writhe around in a forest of kicking feet. He was yelling in panic and blood was cascading from his face.

Generally, I like to have my fill of unofficial spectator sport like this before creeping off – but Adrian was one of these dangerous, upright prigs who, if I hadn't restrained him, would have waded in to even the odds for the Shakeouts. However, sidling up beside us, a barrel-shaped lout with sideboards like scimitars and half a head taller than me contented himself with swearing under his breath before charging forward – presumably to join battle. He did, indeed, land a few punches before police arrived and the hated squaddies scattered. He vanished too – and it was discovered later that one of the group's AC30 amps was missing.

Thus ended my first encounter with Reginald Douglas McTavish, to whom I was formally introduced about a fortnight later by Adrian, who'd been on the periphery of the Holy Name Skiffle Combo.

'I'm sure this'll be a big hit soon. It's Vince Taylor's "Jet Black Machine"' was Reg's distorted announcement in All Hallows' Young People's Club as we each handed over a tanner admission to a 'with-it' curate in a cardigan. Known behind his back as 'Pontifical Paul', he was sitting next to a youth nursing a nosebleed.

We were privileged to be witnessing the public debut of Fireball McTavish and the Sunstrokes. In the playing area, a solitary white bulb served as illumination as they pitched into 'Jet Black Machine'. I noticed that their three guitars and Reg's microphone were all – via two shared jacks – plugged perilously into one AC30 on which the embossed legend 'Shakeouts' was discernible beneath a cursory lick of paint. A new-fangled electric bass was fed through an amplifier that someone had soldered together from a kit I'd seen advertised ('with a ten-watt punch') in *Melody Maker*.

Blue smoke started curling from it after a stomach-churning quarter-hour or so of clashing slam-chords, flurries of bum notes, meandering tempos and long pauses between items which included 'Be-Bop-A-Lula' (twice), 'Blue Moon Of Kentucky' in Z minor and a 'Jailhouse Rock' in which Reg forgot the words. At the abrupt silence of the bass during 'Rip It Up', the heedless drummer – Dids – continued to thrash his cheap 'Gigster' kit with sticks sawn off from a fishing rod. The guitarists glanced at each other, shrugged shoulders and carried on too.

When it shuddered to a halt to a desultory spatter of clapping, there was some fidgeting and Reg mumbled something with 'bloody' in it. This sparked off nervous giggles from a prattle of girls, and a few malicious squints in the direction of Pontifical Paul, who'd ceased snapping his fingers and was staring hard at the stage. He looked as if he was about to do something. Appalled delight greeted a leering Dids, who'd suddenly produced a pair of knickers which he stretched between his index fingers. With shocked dignity, the curate strode into the light.

'I won't have it!' he began in a brogue that betrayed an upright Irishman and an even more upright Catholic. 'Is no corruption beneath you? The only reason I let you lot in in the first place was because this good-for-nothing' – indicating an official on the club committee – 'convinced me that your racket would bring more customers in tonight – and into Mass on Sunday!' – he was nearly shouting – 'Instead, we've had the carrion of the streets pushing in without paying while Gerald was on the door. Into the bargain, I've had nothing but complaints about noise from this Teddy Boys gala. I want no more of you and your filth! You'll shove off right now and take this electrical junk with you!'

If it had been a non-sectarian place, the outcome might have been more interesting but, rather than the punch-up some might have hoped for, Paul was protected by his dog collar. For all their brashness, Reg and most of the others were Roman Catholics to the bone, with superstitious terror of the eternal punishment of sin. Into the bargain, half of Presley's recent *Christmas Album* had been 'religious' in content, and it was whispered that he had a private chapel in Graceland and was prone to loud bouts of piety. Though it was suspected that the deity Elvis worshipped was not so much God as 'The Lord' – a sort of divine pimp with an amused tolerance of human frailty but enough self-discipline to seldom indulge Himself – He probably drew the line at wrecking Church youth clubs and snarling with laughter as someone like Pontifical Paul pleaded ineffectually.

There were a few low mutterings, but the puny gear was gathered and Fireball McTavish, his Sunstrokes and their entourage – which, I noticed, included Nello (who ignored me) – meekly shuffled out of All Hallows' Young People's Club.

It was flattery of a kind, I suppose, that Adrian and I looked sufficiently disreputable to be worth a 'Comin' then?' from the bass player as he pushed past with his instrument under an arm and the damaged amp in a shabby school satchel. He turned out to be Trev, remembered by Adrian as a tractable Holy Name pupil who'd worn a sports coat and cavalry twills outside the school. Now in imitation leather jacket with upturned collar, and sunglasses unnecessary in the twilight, he was recognizable only by his broad Hampshire burr.

An electrician's son, Trev was from Crondall, a village beyond Farnham, and had been looked down upon as a bumpkin by Reg, Adrian and other Holy Name town boys. Nevertheless, as steady as he was dull, any musical or social failings Trev had were balanced by an inherited mechanical turn that ensured that overloaded amps with naked wires were made less lethal and less likely to cut out midway through a number. The incident at All Hallows' was an isolated exception.

With nothing else to do till bedtime, Trev, Adrian and I joined the rest in the playground opposite where we could smoke and utter 'bloody' and even 'bugger' unreproached. For something to say, I asked Dids where he got the knickers from – probably his sister – but I never found out because no one was capable of having a sensible conversation with him. 'What they got you on then?' he retorted. 'Indian rope trick?'

As if trying to regain his reputation as a hard case, Reg was marinating the air with denunciations of the Young People's Club as kid's stuff with its ping pong, slide shows and that constipated old shitbag, Pontifical Paul. He also bragged about his performance and, with a penetrating gaze at Nello, of groping the famous Mary Hunt. Having talked himself into the mood, Reg then started sniffing round Lena, an obliging sort who was seated next to him on the seesaw. The rest of us waited, speechlessly. Ten minutes dragged by.

Because you only brought 'good blokes' to meet Reg, there was a querulous note to Adrian's 'Reg, this here's Roger'. Without looking away from Lena, the arrogant bastard outstretched his brass-ringed funny fingers over a shoulder for me to shake. Turning away, I let slip a remark that changed everything.

'Go chase yourself' was an expression I'd heard my Dad use. I'd only meant Adrian to hear, and felt instantly stupid – and scared – when it came out louder. Not as engrossed with Lena as he seemed, Reg froze and, without looking round, gritted in an unexpectedly soft, freezing husk, 'You said something just then, mate. What was it?' Then, with John Wayne deliberation, he swung a leg over the seesaw and rose slowly. He dropped his cigarette and ground it with a toe. Everyone watched him.

Nothing would stop Reg if he was the type who beat you up to impress girls. 'Why don't you hit me now,' I asked, 'and get it over with?' He glared fathomlessly. I couldn't stand it, and looked away. Then he lit a Woodbine, exhaled with a sigh and his features pinched in thought. He lowered himself back onto his seat. Very suddenly, he started speaking: ' "Go chase yourself . . ." Only one other bugger's ever said what you just said – and that was Vince Taylor . . .' He didn't stop talking for about twenty minutes. Everyone listened.

Reg particularly admired – no, worshipped – Taylor, another sub-Elvis who was, nevertheless, England's ultimate rocker, all chains and biker leathers. He'd been scheduled to appear with his group, the Playboys, at the Agincourt in Thistledown not quite eighteen months ago. Reg had taken the entire day off school to prepare, spending most of it squeezing out blackheads and whorling his hair into a glacier of brilliantine. That morning, his adoring mother had collected the Elvis-pink suit that – though perfectly clean – he'd given to the laundry with an attached note he'd made her write that hinted at legal proceedings or worse if it wasn't ready on time.

Alone for once, and in all his finery plus a comb jutting out of his top pocket ready for a quick adjustment, he'd bused over to Thistledown in the rush hour. During the journey, he'd thought of the name 'Fireball McTavish'. After the fuggy warmth of the jolting number 16D, the winter evening's cold struck like a hammer but, rather than stumble into a cafe, he'd hovered round the double door that opened directly backstage at the Agincourt. An hour later, he'd sunk onto the concrete step in a languid daze induced by the fixity of staring at the entrance to the service car park.

Beneath early evening street lamps, the Playboys' exhausted van bumped from the high street onto the gravel. As the barman who answered their banging had assumed he was a Playboy too, Reg, in paradise, braked his usual exuberance to help lug the group's careworn equipment into the darkened hall with its chilly after-hours essence of disinfectant and a flat echo of yesterday's booze and tobacco intake.

'I'll smoke it later please if you don't mind,' he'd said in an unconscious parody of politeness after one of the guitarists had flashed a ten-pack of Senior Service. To keep his comb company, he tucked in the cigarette, along with an amber plectrum he'd had the presence of mind to swipe. Both would be guarded as relics for as long as he remained alive.

The Playboys went out for fish and chips, but Reg, too excited to be hungry, took up a post outside the frowzy dressing room that Vince – surely the greatest man (after Elvis, of course) ever to have walked the planet – must surely use. Rehearsing mentally what he was going to say and the cool way he'd say it, he felt infinitely patient and found a vague enchantment in imagining that his vigil was to be endless.

Even in torpor, Reg sensed the moment and was automatically brought up sharp when, flanked by retainers, Taylor, in uncharacteristic overcoat and unseasonable sunshades, was shepherded through those cavorting on a dance floor that by about half past eight was already full. Unobtrusive, yards from safety, he was confronted by a burly youth who smiled as if his mouth was full of salts.

'Hi . . . man! They call me Fireball McTavish,' spluttered Reg, 'I sing with a group!'

It was all coming out wrong. Vince walked on by but Reg persisted. 'I'm gonna go solo,' he bawled. 'It'll be me with the other buggers backing me – just like it is with you, Vince . . .!'

Not even a fist in the belly from one of Taylor's bodyguards deflected his unfocused purpose. Someone swept ahead to fling open the dressing room door as Reg's arm shoved through the wall of security to seize the belt of Vince's overcoat and pull with despairing triumph. As the startled star's protectors pitched in, the sunglasses toppled from his nose and, as stripped of cool as Reg, Taylor swivelled round, let fly a wild punch and met Reg's eyes. In the emergency of the situation, however, he did not advise, say 'Get your fucking paws off me!' but 'Go chase yourself!'

The scuffle finished when the Agincourt's bouncers raised Reg aloft and pitched him down the foyer steps. Even as he lay bruised on the cold pavement, Reg lapped up his idol's behaviour and its humiliating sequel as the prerogative of glamour. 'Hit me again, Vince,' he groaned. 'Go chase yourself!'

This tale seemed more believable than the one about Mary Hunt. On the seesaw, Reg's voice trailed off. Then, with a lopsided grin that could have meant anything, he looked me up and down as if for the first time. He laughed loudly and clearly like you do at a funny joke. We all joined in. No one knew why.

Reg heaved himself up and everything hushed again. 'I need to piss,' he said importantly as if it wasn't a thing he did every day. He ambled towards the rhododendron bushes that lined the railings, and I thought that I'd never been more overwhelmed by anyone in my whole life.

CHAS 'DR ROCK' WHITE

First in Line

' The way it all started – I made a record for my mother, just made it, not for any particular occasion. I worked five days a week, and on Saturday, I called up this recording company and asked them if I could make a record. The record I made was "My Happiness", one of the Inkspots' numbers. I made it to surprise her and give her pleasure. At the time I never did sing much. The only time I ever sung was on these little variety shows at school.'

So, a truckdriver called Elvis Presley became the twentieth century's musical equivalent of splitting the atom. By walking into the Sun Recording Service in Memphis, he changed the course of musical history and produced powerful images of mammoth and messianic extremes. Yet there was nothing extraordinary about his background. He was born in Tupelo, Mississippi, on 8 January 1935 to a poor southern family and they moved after his father, Vernon, had been caught forging a cheque. On arrival in Memphis, Vernon got a job in a paint factory and Gladys, Elvis's beloved mother, worked at a local hospital as a nurses' aide. Elvis himself attended L. C. Humes High School and, like many other school kids, he mowed lawns, delivered goods and got an evening job as a cinema usher.

Memphis musician Marcus Van Story, who shared the same federal housing apartment block and who knew Elvis before he shot to fame, remembers Elvis as a shy boy who sometimes did the laundry for his mother, who had health problems. 'Sometimes I'd see him with his guitar, pickin' away in the laundry room. My daughter and he walked to school together for a few years. Elvis would give blood for money. He overdid it one day and I remember the health people warning the family not to let it happen again.'

While still in his teens, Elvis listened to black music, mainly on radio station WDIA. He also frequented Beale Street, where he absorbed the black R&B music. He loved gospel quartets such as the Golden Gate and Blackwood Quartets. He also loved singers like Clyde McPhatter and

Jackie Wilson: later, he would describe and imitate Wilson's imitation of himself.

He also listened to the popular middle-of-the-road favourites of the day: Dean Martin, Perry Como, Frank Sinatra and Bing Crosby. Many youngsters were doing the same, so what made Elvis the greatest star the world has ever known?

Sam Phillips, the head of Sun Records, was given the tape of Elvis's recording of 'My Happiness' by his secretary, Marion Keisker, and said, 'I think I could do something with that voice.' Sam asked Elvis to work out a style with Bill Black and Scotty Moore, who both did regular studio work for him. The role of Marion Keisker – and also of Scotty and Bill – has always been overshadowed by that of Sam Phillips. Yet Elvis said of her, 'I'll always be in her debt.'

Sam said, 'If I can find a white boy who could sing like a Negro, I could make a billion dollars.' He had also run his own recording business successfully before discovering Elvis and he was to go on and discover some of the greatest names in the history of American music: Carl Perkins, Charlie Rich, Johnny Cash, Jerry Lee Lewis, Sonny Burgess, Roy Orbison, Billy Lee Riley, Jack Clement – the list goes on and on.

On 5 July 1954, whilst in Sun and recording 'I Love You Because', they had a break and Elvis, Scotty and Bill burst spontaneously into an uptempo version of Arthur Crudup's 'That's All Right, Mama'. Sam Phillips, as usual, had left the tapes running. At last he had got his magic formula. The fusion of musical styles that occurred at this session was described as 'white hillbilly, Negro blues' and one of Elvis's first nicknames was the Hillbilly Cat.

There is a misconception that it was all Elvis and only Elvis, but Scotty and Bill helped to mould this moment too. After all, they had been working with Elvis on a sound for six months. But Sam's role goes beyond his own perception of Elvis. When 'That's All Right, Mama' and 'Blue Moon Of Kentucky' were released on Sun 209, music was to undergo a metamorphosis that is still going on and will continue for as long as this planet exists.

The intense public popularity Elvis created was like a tidal wave; he broke down barriers and created controversy. His image shocked the conservative Americans of the fifties. In the words of Jerry Lee Lewis, cultural- and Establishment-basher supreme, 'He looked dangerous'. He looked like a threat to the Establishment with his greasy hair and sideburns alone, but the physical movement when he sang really caused a stir.

Elvis took the world by storm when he first came to the public's attention, as the media, the Establishment, the church and the pillars of society could not cope with his image. Early interviews portrayed him as nothing more than a passing fluke.

The dominant mood of the media was condescending ridicule. They could not perceive what Elvis Presley was all about. 'Rock 'n' roll is the most important cultural revolution for 200 years,' says Professor Charles Hamm, and Elvis Presley was the major figure.

In 1956 the *New York Times* said, 'Presley has no discernible singing ability, his speciality is rhythm songs that he renders inane and indistinguishable, while his phrasing, if it can be called that, consists of stereotype variations that go with a beginner's aria in a bathtub. For the ear, he is an unutterable bore.' *Time*, also in 1956, accepted that he was the hero of the new generation but poured scorn upon 'his poor diction, over-sexy movements and sinister appearance'. This was the tip of the iceberg. Preachers, teachers and politicians accused him of vulgarity, profanity and obscenity, while some southern Bible-bashers proclaimed the Antichrist. Throughout it all, Elvis remained a quiet, well-mannered southern gentleman. When interviewed, he called the interviewer 'Sir' and thanked him graciously. He spoke with wit and humour.

'What kind of girls do you like, Elvis?'

'Female, sir.'

Admittedly, it sounds feeble now, but it was original then. And his hip-swinging movements led to his nickname of Elvis the Pelvis.

'Why do you shake your hips when you sing?'

'Well, some people clap their hands while they sing, others tap their feet. I just move around a little.'

Maybe Elvis did not give interviews in later life because the media in 1956 seemed hellbent on destroying him. No matter how ill-informed or biased the interviewer was, Elvis remained polite and charming.

'I hear in Ottawa that there's a situation you've probably experienced elsewhere on your travels across the continent. The school board unanimously passed a motion in which they were going to encourage the parents and the teachers to stay away from your show because they thought your singing was vulgar. No doubt you've run across these situations before. What is your answer?'

'Well, yes, I've run across them before. I just wish people would stop judging a tree by its bark, something they've heard or something they've read. They should come out to the show and judge it for themselves. If they still think it, well, just let them think it because that's all I can do, you know. I certainly don't mean to be vulgar or suggestive, and I don't think I am.'

'That's all part of your performance, your technique.'

'It's just my way of expressing songs. You have to put on a show for people. You can't stand there like a statue.'

'Your feeling is that your show is entertainment, and you go on to give them a show.'

'That's true, I mean, there are people that like you, there are people that don't like you. Regardless of what field you're in, regardless of what you do, there's gonna be people who don't like you, I mean even if you are perfect. I'm not saying I'm perfect because no man is perfect. There was only one perfect man and that was Jesus Christ and people didn't like him, you know. They killed him and he couldn't understand why. I mean, if everybody liked the same thing, we'd all be driving the same car and married to the same woman. It wouldn't work out.'

So Elvis was the perfect southern polite-mannered boy and the media did not know how to handle him. They were uncertain: winds of insecurity were blowing across the USA, and Elvis was the tornado.

'Speaking of rock 'n' roll, what's your opinion of this phase which is going through the country just now?'

'Rock 'n' roll has been in for about five years. I'm not gonna sit here and say that it's gonna last. It might change, like when years ago the Charleston was real popular, the vaudeville acts, stuff like that: you could have told those people it was gonna die out and they wouldn't have believed you. Four or five years from now, well, rock 'n' roll may be dead.'

'But as far as rock 'n' roll goes, you really like it?'

'Yes, as far as rock 'n' roll goes, I really like it, I enjoy doing it. The people think it's great and it just makes me want to keep giving them something they enjoy.'

'Say something about your unique style. Where did you get the idea for this?'

'I'm a pretty close follower of religious quartets and they do a lot of rock 'n' roll and spirituals and so that's where I got the idea from. Really, just quartets.'

The projected image of American society was epitomized in the *National Geographic* (magazine) by a family in their white convertible with their white suits, their gleaming white teeth, their whitish blond hair, their squeaky clean society. However, this was far from reality. Racial tension was brewing up, so too was youth culture, with Marlon Brando and James Dean spearheading the new attitude in such films as *The Wild One*. When Marlon Brando is asked, 'What are you rebelling against?' he replies, 'What ya got?'

There was also the sexual revolution, and Elvis combined all these threats into one. He sang like a Negro and oozed indestructible sexuality. It's amazing that the FBI did not 'find' Elvis in bed with a young Negro girl or some such 'destroy-a-career' tactic.

Sam Phillips says now, 'I think rock 'n' roll has had a very favourable impact on the understanding among races. The young are not as prejudiced as the old, and if I've done something to stop the prejudice growing up, then I think I've done something.'

And what did Colonel Tom Parker do? First of all, he is not a real colonel, but an honorary colonel, which is quite common in the southern states: if you had enough empty cornflake boxes, you could get one. In actuality, the Colonel was a fairground hustler who saw rich pickings in Elvis.

In 1956, Elvis product alone made $22m. The Colonel had no intention of stopping the money flow. Whilst amassing millions of dollars from record sales, he was even selling photos of Elvis at his concerts for ten cents apiece. Yes! You've gathered, the Colonel loves money. Throughout Elvis's career, the Colonel gave me the impression that he was there to exploit Elvis totally, and at all times, for himself.

The Colonel is often portrayed as a moneymaking machine but he was an excellent businessman and he looked after Elvis's fortune very well indeed. When he negotiated with Little Richard's manager, Robert 'Bumps' Blackwell, he was generous in his dealings. Bumps told me, 'The Colonel gave me an extra $10,000 and let me keep my rights to "Good Golly Miss Molly". That $10,000 saved my daughter's life as she needed to have heart surgery.'

The Elvis phenomenon was more than just a good-looking guy making rock 'n' roll records: it was the spearhead of an artistic and cultural revolution that went far beyond chart success.

Elvis said of his success, 'I like it. I enjoy rock 'n' roll. A lot of people like it and a lot of people don't, but as long as it lasts and as long as it sells, I'll continue doing it. If it dies out, I'll try to do something else and if that doesn't work, then I'll just say, "Well, I've had my day."'

In Europe, television's popularity was only starting so Elvis was first seen on cinema screens by the vast movie-going public. Elvis attracted Hollywood because he was so huge on record and on American television.

Hollywood wanted to mould Elvis into a quick moneyspinner. They saw him as a passing trend and wanted to exploit him as quickly as possible. His first movie was *Love Me Tender*, a second-rate cowboy effort in which Elvis was cast as a country boy, singing on the porch of a hillbilly shack. If Elvis had read the back of the cereal packet, he would have attracted as much attention.

Hollywood had rejected Elvis's rock 'n' roll band as a bunch of hillbilly pickers and brought in some sterile screen music. The next two movies, *Loving You* and *Jailhouse Rock*, got as near to capturing the genius of his musical talent as the movies ever did.

My first experience of hearing Elvis was on the radio as a young boy in the west of Ireland: 'That's All Right, Mama', 'I Want You, I Need You, I Love You', 'Heartbreak Hotel', 'Hound Dog' and 'Don't Be Cruel' poured joyfully through the radio via Radio Luxembourg, AFN, RTE and, occasionally, the BBC. The local cinema, the Royal, played 'Hound Dog' and 'Don't Be Cruel' a dozen times before the Sunday matinée. It was a new cinema with new speakers and CinemaScope had just arrived. We went early to hear the music and all senses were enhanced by this superb sound. We had seen pictures of him but knew little of the controversy. I remember him singing 'Poor Boy' in *Love Me Tender* and thinking, 'Great stuff, but what's all the fuss about?' The lad was shaking and wiggling but he was only reacting to his own natural rhythm – big deal. But it was high energy sexual suggestiveness. Elvis was going to seduce every female in the world. Incidentally, Jayne Mansfield offered him her voluptuous body for a night of lustful passion if he would play opposite her in *The Girl Can't Help It*. Elvis, with commendable restraint, declined.

King Creole, the final movie before he joined the army, had fire and spirit but was too tainted by the way the movie industry saw Elvis. The movies after this are so awful that they serve as the ultimate monument to those who waste supreme talent. It was like training a thoroughbred racehorse to perfection and then getting it to pull a rag-and-bone cart. It was dreadful material from greedy song publishers who wanted their rights, their monies and a share of the action. They are the ones who should bow their heads in shame, not Elvis Presley.

So by the mid-sixties, the greatest performer of the twentieth century was making moronic movies and recording trashy soundtracks. Some songs were so bad that he broke into hysterical laughter in the middle of recording them.

How did such a handsome, charming and great artist decline into a self-destructive drug addict? John Lennon said, 'Elvis died when he went into the army.' Not strictly true – Elvis made many great recordings after his army service – but it was here that Elvis encountered his first experience of what would become his downfall: drugs. It started when the sergeant on duty during night manoeuvres for Presley's tank regiment suggested that Elvis should take some pep pills to keep alert at night.

Elvis was always concerned about his public image and even his loyal fans have no idea how controlled his life was by drug addiction. Most fans boasted that Elvis did not drink or take drugs. Elvis was made an FBI narcotics agent by the then-President of the United States, Richard Nixon.

The first mortal blow for Elvis came when his mother died. The next was when he was separated from his wife, Priscilla, and his beloved daughter, Lisa Marie, in February 1972. This incident, more than any other, set Elvis on the road to fatal drug addiction. Many blame Dr George Nichopolous, Elvis's doctor, for not protecting him and weaning him off drugs, but those who lived with Elvis say he demanded drugs and could get them at will because of his power and influence. Dr Nick has faced medical boards for overprescribing drugs. He also gave drugs to Jerry Lee Lewis, who is reputed to have taken several times the amount that Elvis consumed. His role has led to highly volatile arguments amongst Elvis's followers.

From his army days when he first took amphetamines – which led to Dexedrine pills, Desputal and Escotrol Placidyl, to the most lethal drugs available – Elvis became a devotee of drugs. Red West, Elvis's old school friend and bodyguard, said, 'He takes pills to go to sleep. He takes pills to get up. He takes pills to go to the john. There have been times when he was so hyper on uppers that he had trouble breathing and on one occasion he thought he was going to die.'

Why did those close to Elvis allow him to die? The doctor, the Memphis Mafia and, above all, the Colonel. Those close to Elvis were fully aware of his intense addiction. They were also in awe of his knowledge of drugs. At first they thought he knew what he was doing, but in the early 1970s they must have known that the end was near. How could they stand by and let the man who had given so much to the world die? The answer lies in Elvis's own background and behaviour.

He was a shy southern boy with a limited education and a far from intellectual command of any subject. He felt insecure and surrounded himself with his own hometown friends.

Barney Kessel, the jazz guitarist who was a session musician and arranger on many of Elvis's movies and, incidentally, hated rock 'n' roll, says, 'Elvis seemed like a very nice young man, he really did. Seemed like he had learnt his manners very nice, very nice. He seemed unsure of where he was, always had a problem of relating to people outside his own circle. That's why he always kept this entourage from Memphis.'

Elvis's chums were mainly old pals from Memphis to whom he gave good salaries and the passport to a glamorous lifestyle in Hollywood and Las Vegas. In return Elvis demanded total loyalty and expected them to act as bodyguards and lackeys and to join in whatever sport or entertainment interested him. The Memphis Mafia experienced the extremes of Elvis's lifestyle. His generosity was mammoth, not only to them but to many others.

He would buy expensive cars for his boys at a whim and often buy them horses, watches and jewellery. When he read in the Memphis press that a poor black lady was desperate for a wheelchair, he bought her the most expensive model available. While driving through Memphis in disguise one evening, he spotted a young couple gazing into a car showroom and pointing at a sports car. Elvis hopped out of his limo and said to the young couple, 'You want that car?' They replied, 'We'd love it but we can't afford it, we've just got engaged.' Elvis said, 'It's yours.' He went into the showroom, bought the car and gave it to the couple.

That he gave so much to those less fortunate is a fact that has been sadly neglected in favour of the vile imagery pursued by the gutter press. The Memphis Mafia continued to indulge Elvis's whims, which always seemed extreme. His obsession with guns became lunatic. He had a huge arsenal of weapons in his home, Graceland, which were all over the house. A new maid at Graceland had to serve Elvis breakfast in bed at five o'clock one afternoon. He sat up, turned on his huge wide-screen TV, saw Robert Goulet – a singer he despised – rolled a Magnum pistol from under his pillow and blasted the TV. 'That's enough of that shit,' he growled. The maid fled back to the kitchen. She was assured that this was normal behaviour for Elvis: he frequently blasted TV screens.

During the writing of this piece I journeyed to Memphis and toured Graceland. The Elvis trophy room has a section devoted to Elvis's arms, his official police badges, his sheriff badges and his FBI drug enforcement badge, which was personally presented by President Nixon. If he had been arrested himself when presented with this badge, he might well be living today. Clearly, he had a boyhood desire to become a sheriff.

All this meant that Elvis lived more and more in his own world, doing exactly as he wanted. He was his own boss, and Colonel Parker looked after his business. 'Taking care of business' was an Elvis motto. The Colonel managed Elvis's business, but why did he not try to save Elvis from destruction? He was as close to Elvis as anyone, but he stuck rigidly to his rule of not interfering in Elvis's personal life. The only known incident of the Colonel's involvement in Presley's private life was when he encouraged him to marry Priscilla, whom he had kept at Graceland since she was a teenage schoolgirl. In 1991, at his Palm Springs home, the Colonel stated that 'Elvis knew what he was doing with drugs and told me not to interfere'. So the Colonel, who has always been subjected to fierce criticism for not protecting Elvis, has justified his role in handling only Presley's business affairs. When Elvis had reached crisis point with drug addiction, he had worn the Memphis boys down to their lowest psychological level. Their influence was zero. Elvis was strung out. He really blew a fuse in Las Vegas: 'I've just returned from New York where I attended a meeting of the International Federation of Narcotic Agents and I've been awarded honorary membership, ladies and gentlemen.' Applause. 'I don't pay any attention to movie magazines or newspapers because in my case they make the stories up. When I hear rumours flying around, I get sick. In this day and age, you can't even get sick. They said I was strung out on heroin and I've never been strung out on anything but music.' Applause. 'If I ever find out who started that I'll knock their goddamn head off, the son of a bitch. That is dangerous to me, my family, my friends and my little girl. If I find out who started this, maids or room clerks or freaks that carry your luggage up, I'll rip their tongues out by the roots!' Applause. 'Now I'll sing "Blue Hawaii" from the movie.'

This was not the charming young Elvis Presley, this was a great star in the final throes of self-destruction, yet no one tried to save him.

Rick Stanley, stepbrother to Elvis, described the awesome sexuality of Elvis: 'He would pick up dozens of girls. He had more women than any man who lived.' By all accounts, Elvis attracted millions of women of all types, ages, colours and creeds. They threw themselves at him and, by all accounts, he obliged. He was as sexy as a million panthers on heat. Priscilla's tolerance was amazing in retrospect, but she eventually left him on 23 February 1972.

The inevitable happened on 16 August 1977: Elvis died, and then the show really began. His record sales zoomed to a billion. Boxed sets of his albums, unreleased movies like *Elvis in Concert* and the Warner Bros production *This is Elvis*, plus all the better-known recording outputs of Elvis were revamped, repackaged and released. There have been hundreds of albums released featuring Elvis recordings from professional studio productions to nauseous cheapo/cheapo releases, often recorded by enthusiastic fans on inferior cassette recorders, given to fellow fans in affectionate generosity and exploited by ruthless bootleggers. Take *Elvis at Pittsburg 31.12.76*. Sure, you can just about confirm that it is Elvis, and you certainly can hear the clapping and screaming delight of the audience. The only piece of interest is when a voice shouts from the audience, 'God save the King,' and Elvis replies, 'Why, thank you.' *The King Speaks* on Redwood Records even apologizes for its bad sound quality and blames Elvis for banging the microphone! These recordings are only for chronic Elvis fans.

On the other hand, the RCA/BMG series *The Essential Elvis* features excellent studio outtakes and previously unreleased tracks which give a great insight into Elvis Presley's musical genius. He takes a song like 'Love Me Tender', a slow ballad, but does it at a different tempo, even rocking it up. An alternative 'Treat Me Nice' is with a Latin flair. On the second volume, he shows his full control over the material at hand – it is clear that he needs no producer and is totally at one with the musicians and the musical content of 'It Is No Secret', a gospel song, the music that

Elvis loves passionately. He stops the recording instinctively, 'No! No! It does not break in there.' If that occurred at a recording session today, the producer, the backing singers, the engineers, in fact the whole studio staff, would walk out. Elvis had the respect of the musicians and the Jordanaires because he knew exactly what he was doing.

Steve Sholes, a recording manager and producer with RCA, says, 'Presley used to hold the guitar close to his mouth, so it was hard to record him vocally. We got him to use a flat pick so the guitar didn't come through so strongly. One day he dropped the pick but went on banging the guitar with his fingers. When he was done, his fingers were bleeding. I asked him why he didn't quit and the son-of-a-gun said, "It was going so good I didn't want to break it up." He'd work till he dropped to get it right.'

They had rehearsed, and the music was a major part of their lives. Today's recording sessions are an exercise in clinical commercialism: the drum machines, the synthesizers, the computerized pre-recorded soulless and spiritless sounds of plastic microchip emptiness are far removed from the joyous, vitally energetic music of Elvis Presley.

The furore caused by Elvis's initial impact on society did not cause hypocritical outbursts from the Establishment alone, as the musical fraternity was also very snobbish about him. None more so than country music people, when all but shunned Elvis during his lifetime. Country music magazines and encyclopaedias virtually ignored Elvis until after his death. Then, he became a 'Country Star'. At first, Elvis's brand of rock 'n' roll had been regarded so far from country's image that country fans could not absorb it. However, Presley's personality infiltrated country music after his death and the country fans accepted him. I maintain that country music would have died if it were not for Elvis and rock 'n' roll.

In 1981 *Elvis*, a biography by Albert Goldman, shook the world with its horrifically degrading portrayal of Elvis's life. It is the most cowardly, back-stabbing piece of work ever conceived. This major biography on Elvis was written by no less than the professor of English and Comparative Literature at Columbia University, New York City. His major biographies on Lenny Bruce, Elvis Presley and John Lennon have been structured to destroy the character and image of these personalities. He is an excellent writer, but in the case of Elvis, the towering battlements of his intellectual capabilities were smothered by his own prejudices.

Elvis admirers were so enraged when it was first published that there were threats to Goldman's life and he went into hiding. His biography relied on an earlier book by Elvis's bodyguards, Red West, Sonny West and Dave Hebler, *Elvis – What Happened?*, published just before his death. Goldman embellished his biography with the North/South conflict, i.e. subconsciously lacing the tapestry of the book with the bigotry of the American Civil War. He attacked Elvis's sexuality, 'He saw his beauty disfigured by an ugly hillbilly pecker.' This is naked, contemptuous jealousy. If you put a balding, bespectacled and middle-aged college professor and Elvis in a room with a dozen beautiful women, the professor would be as significant as a decaying lizard in some distant desert.

Whilst running a college course on the development of rock 'n' roll, I asked thirty students to read Goldman's book, *Elvis*. All concluded that it was a cheap, vulgar attempt to destroy Elvis's image and to make quick money out of gutter sensationalism. What a shame that Goldman chose the biography to destroy Elvis, which in retrospect did taint Elvis, but Goldman really degraded himself by airing the putrid pathogenicity of his own mind.

More trite books followed. *We Love You Elvis* by Dee Presley, Elvis's stepmother, and her boys Rick and David Stanley. Just call it, *We Exploit You Elvis With Insincerity*, and you've got another excursion into the cheap and nasty. Richard Davis was one of Elvis's closest friends. He worked as a stand-in in Elvis's movies and as his wardrobe manager and bodyguard. He says of the books that have been written about Elvis: 'I don't agree with the books, there has never been a book written about Elvis yet that's totally truthful. There is some truth in all of them, but not 100 per cent truth in any of them. There are a lot of lies in them and a lot of fabrication. I don't agree with them because they're only written to make money at Elvis's expense, and he's not here to defend himself. George Klein (Elvis's best man) and myself want to write a book and collaborate with a couple of other guys who were true friends of Elvis, who have never written a book but have nothing but love in their heart for Elvis. We have beautiful memories which we would like to share with the fans. We want to show the fun side of Elvis – tell about all the good things he did for people – all the funny, crazy, dumb, stupid things we did in our lives, all the practical jokes we pulled. He had a heart of gold. He loved people. He truly cared for all people, all humanity, regardless of their race, creed or colour. He had the most fantastic sense of humour of anybody I have ever met in my entire life. Our life together was full of practical jokes. And to quote Alan Bleasdale: 'The interesting thing about Elvis Presley, and it's something that people don't often comment on, was the fact that he was an extremely witty and humorous man.'

And how would the 'witty and humorous' Presley view the bizarre news stories of later years, the Elvis sightings, the concept of Elvis still being alive? And which hapless Elvis imitator had been placed in his coffin?

In 1988 Gail Brewer-Giorgio, cashing in on the tabloid rumours that Elvis was still alive, published *Is Elvis Alive?* with a tape which was supposed to have Elvis talking from his current hideaway. A tidal wave of media hysteria followed. A phone line was set up so that people could listen to the tape. This netted thousands of dollars. Gail Brewer-Georgio had learnt the basic rule of making a quick buck, that is, 'no one ever went broke by underestimating the poor taste of the public'.

Whilst in Memphis during 1992, I heard a waitress giving instructions to some tourists: 'Ya take a right onto Elvis Presley Boulevard, you know, the one who is still alive.' Everybody in the restaurant burst out laughing. A meeting with Dawn Massey of the Memphis Tourist Board conveyed the uncertainty that the city fathers have in Graceland, the city's biggest attraction. Because of the writings of Brewer-Giorgio, the *National Enquirer, et al.* – the *al* being Albert Goldman – there remains an insecure feeling about the great and supreme artistic musical genius of Elvis Presley and they appear torn between promoting Graceland or a new downtown building, The Pyramid, a huge complex containing sports facilities, entertainments, shopping and concert arenas. This, too, has the stain of scandal as a case of fraud hangs over its construction.

I assured Dawn that Graceland would outshine anything that exists in Memphis. Elvis Presley, America's singular cultural icon, will continue in popularity.

In 1991 nearly a million people visited Graceland and brought over $150 million into the city's coffers. It is one of America's greatest attractions, and will remain so. No matter how much is written about Elvis, it is his music and his unique voice that will stand the test of time. In centuries to come, when people listen to 'It's Now Or Never', 'Hound Dog', 'Don't Be Cruel', 'All Shook Up', 'Jailhouse Rock', or any of Elvis's classic recordings, they will hear the joy and spirit of twentieth-century music. They will hear Elvis Presley, the greatest star the world has ever known.

I know the pen is mightier than the sword but, in the case of Elvis Presley, the music and the voice conquer all. Just listen to *The Sun Sessions*, *The All-Time Greatest Hits*, *Essential Elvis* or *Reconsider Baby*. Man, if that don't move you, you will never be real, real gone.

FRED DELLAR

I Remember Danny Mirror

I don't know who Fitting and Rockingham were but they really started something. At least, I think they did. Thing is, back in 1956 they penned a song called 'My Boy Elvis', which eventually got handed on to Janis Martin, a rock 'n' rollin' country singer. A member of Jim Reeves's show, she turned up on Dave Garroway's *Today* show one day in '57, sang 'My Boy Elvis' and was promptly signed to play the Grand Ole Opry. Even then, a mention of Elvis in a song could prove the key to a performer's dreams. Things haven't changed much in the interim. When singer/songwriter Marc Cohn moved into New York's Quad Recording Studios to cut his 1991 debut album for Atlantic Records, he recorded a track called 'Walking In Memphis' that related how he saw 'the ghost of Elvis on Union Street' and followed the spectre up to the gates of Graceland. Released as a single, 'Walking In Memphis' became a worldwide hit and sparked Cohn's career in instant fashion. Thanks again, Elvis.

Other contemporary frontrunners such as U2 ('Elvis Presley And America'), Billy Joel ('Elvis Presley Boulevard'), Was Not Was ('Elvis' Rolls Royce') have fashioned namecheck material, along with Paul Simon, another who's tipped his hat in the direction of the one-time Memphis Flash. An Elvis fan all his life ('My favourite record of all time is "Mystery Train" by Elvis Presley,' Simon once revealed), he used El's Memphis home as a symbol of a kind of promised land when fashioning his 1986 album *Graceland*. Again, Simon was well rewarded for his pains. Come Grammy time, *Graceland* was adjudged Album Of The Year. And the royalties couldn't have been half bad. The album remained in the US charts for fifty-three weeks, spawning a hit single or two.

Simon didn't really need the Elvis connection. Had his album been called *White House* in honour of Rockin' Ronnie Reagan, it would doubtless have sold just as well. But his was a genuine tribute. How many times, though, has Elvis been the victim of a blatant cash-in, the use of his name becoming a ploy to prise mucho moolah from those who have helped purchase 150 million or so Presley records? Sometimes it's hard to tell.

Not every recording artist has had quite the gall of the guy who released 'Spelling On The Stone' on LS/Curb Records in 1988. The single, which bore no artist's name on the label, featured an Elvis soundalike warbling a lyric about the spelling on the Presley gravestone (Elvis's middle name is spelt Aron on his birth certificate but Aaron on the headstone), the suggestion being that Elvis wasn't really dead but had turned up at their studios to provide recorded proof that he was still around! The record probably sold to the same people who fled when Orson Welles revealed that the Martians had landed. Certainly, the Elvis-is-alive rumour was handled with more humour by Kirsty MacColl on 'There's A Guy Works Down The Chip Shop Swears He's Elvis'. Never was the audience left in doubt about the authenticity of the phantom pan-handler: 'He's a liar — and so are you,' sang Kirsty. Quite right too.

I suppose the real cash-in began the day Elvis popped his clogs, 'clogs' being the operative word. The 'Elvis Is Dead' headlines had barely dried before Dutch singer Danny Mirror had a record in the charts proclaiming 'I Remember Elvis Presley (The King Is Dead)'. And there were many others, like Ral Donner's 'The Day The Beat Stopped', Bobby Freeman's 'Elvis Goodbye', Jack Hickox's 'We're Sure Gonna Miss You Old Friend', Leigh Grady's 'Blue Christmas (Without Elvis)', Johnny Farago's 'The King Is Gone' and Shilo's 'God Brought The Curtain Down'. If tears were beers, the whole sham world of pop music would have been blotto in the wake of Elvis's demise. Some 'tributes' came in clear vinyl, some were pressed up in coloured plastic. None came with flashing dollar signs on their labels or a stick-on instruction to 'BUY ME'. Which would have been more honest in most instances. Thing is that these are the very records that are sought after today. Elvis collectors, having bought every Sun, RCA and bootleg item that cheque books would allow, have often moved on to acquiring any other record that contains an Elvis reference.

It's all part of keeping the legend alive. While someone sings his praises or even employs his name in ridicule (did I hear someone mention Pinkard and Bowden's 'Elvis Was A Narc'?), Elvis breathes, Elvis sighs, and 16 August 1977 didn't really happen. So, maybe there is a place on record shelves for the likes of Fireman Sam's 'Elvis Cooks The Lunch', The Stingrays' 'Elvis, Gladys And The Guru', Wall Of Voodoo's 'Elvis Bought Dora A Cadillac', Peter Singh's 'Elvis, I'm On The Phone' and Underneath What's 'Elvis Presley's Doctor'. But not on mine.

PATRICK HUMPHRIES
Never Loved Elvis

N*ever Loved Elvis* is the title of the Wonder Stuff's 1991 album. 'Elvis Is Dead' gloated Peter & The Test Tube Babies and Living Color. 'Elvis Should Play Ska' advised the pre-Tears For Fears Graduate. I was sad that Peter (The Screaming Pakistani) Singh's album *Turbans Over Memphis* never made it onto vinyl; his single did, though, with the unforgettable chorus: 'I don't take drugs, I don't drink bourbon/All I wanna do is shake my turban.' Elvis was one of the targets Public Enemy lashed on 'Fight The Power'. On '1977', The Clash sang: 'No more Elvis, Beatles or Stones in 1977', and Johnny Rotten reacted to Presley's death in his usual good-humoured way: 'Fuckin' good riddance to bad rubbish. I don't give a fuckin' shit, and nobody else does either. It's just fun to fake sympathy, that's all they're doin.' When Elvis died, the punks were snarling at the gates of the city, and one D. P. MacManus got plenty of mileage out of his new moniker, Elvis Costello – pairing his great grandmother's maiden name with the best-known Christian name in history.

If you were a new band, you had to strut your street stuff by hating Elvis, as he represented everything that was rotten in the state of rock – and why not chuck in a 'glad they got John Lennon too . . .' to emphasize your cred. Punk taught you to hate everything that came before, no one influenced you, nothing pre-'77 mattered. But it all changed in the eighties, and now people are falling all over each other to cite their influences, and you can hear chastened iconoclasts muttering, 'Yeah, well, I always really liked Led Zeppelin . . .'. This led to the extraordinary sight of those great pop ironists, the Pet Shop Boys, crooning through 'Always On My Mind' – and keeping the Pogues from their deserved Number 1 at Christmas 1987.

But for everyone who sneered whenever Elvis's name was mentioned, there were real villains to be fingered, the ones who *really* never loved Elvis: academics like Albert Goldman, who used Elvis as a corpulent symbol of everything he hated in popular culture, because he knew books on Elvis always sold, and because he knew the dead can't sue . . . that's where the real hate is.

Because of the enormity – metaphorical rather than physical – of Elvis, he is an industry: as with Princess Di, a book about Elvis will sell, a book that lifts the lid on Elvis (just tick the list: incest; drugs; suicide; murder; never really died . . .) will sell even more. If you knew him, demons will nag you as you write: if you really dish the dirt, you'll ship more copies. It's a late twentieth-century phenomenon: assassination after death. I have no doubt that Elvis was neither sinner nor saint; 'He was some kind of a man', Marlene Dietrich's epitaph for Orson Welles in *Touch Of Evil* still stands. Lionized in life, rubbished and deified in death, Elvis still spellbinds, maybe because we are fascinated by just how it all went so horribly wrong.

If you grew up in the sixties, Elvis may not have been dead, but he was dead boring. You only ever got one crack at growing up, but you knew that the soundtrack to your adolescence deserved to be better than *Blue Hawaii*. A whole generation grew up associating Elvis with those dreadful sixties movies – the lukewarm charm of *Follow That Dream*; the reheated futility of *Kid Galahad*; the hollow promise of *Girls! Girls! Girls!* While the rock world was taking its first significant step after Elvis with the Beatles, the man responsible for the revolution was under sentence for *It Happened At The World's Fair*, *Kissin' Cousins* and *Roustabout*.

Times had moved on, but Elvis had ossified. New groups that sprung up around that time looked over their shoulders towards the Elvis that inspired them in the fifties, but had little favourable to say about the sleek sixties model. Back then, the troublesome nasal truths spilling from Bob Dylan's mouth spoke for a generation, not 'Do The Clam'. The Beatles, the Rolling Stones, the Who, the Kinks and the Animals clutched the keys to the kingdom, not the King who had discarded them half a decade before. Marooned in Hollywood, with advice only from sycophantic courtiers, unaware that the Beatles were tilting the world in the same way he had done a decade before, Elvis had lost the plot. More than that, it was the fate facing every pop idol: Elvis had become your parents.

And on it went, and on and on. While RCA and the Colonel pumped out substandard albums and recycled Elvis hits, Elvis became a Pharaoh, buried in a pyramid of unnecessary vinyl that did nothing to enhance his reputation. It was only when real fans – like *NME*'s doggedly determined

Roy Carr – got access to the mainframe with his lovingly compiled 1975 album *The Sun Collection* that a new generation began to appreciate the impact Elvis had made over twenty years before. 'Every generation throws a hero up the pop charts,' sang Paul Simon in 1986 and he undoubtedly had Elvis in mind for the fifties (no coincidence that his most successful solo album took its name from his idol's home), but for the sixties it was the Beatles and Bob Dylan; the seventies David Bowie and Bruce Springsteen; the eighties Prince and Madonna, and the nineties . . .?

Elvis's imprint on the staid 1950s was so massive, so seismic that it is literally inconceivable from the vantage point of the nineties ('you mean there wasn't even Radio 1? Only *two* TV channels . . . in black and white?'). Not everyone was convinced during the distant fifties. While the fans screamed and squealed, while the sociologists tried to comprehend the threat that Elvis, Marlon Brando and James Dean posed to the established order, the first critics were licking their lips:

'Is it a sausage? It is certainly smooth and damp looking, but whoever heard of a 172lb sausage six foot tall? Is it a Walt Disney goldfish? It has the same sort of big, soft, beautiful eyes and long curly lashes, but whoever heard of a goldfish with sideburns? Is it a corpse? The fact is it just hangs there, limp and white with its little drop-seat mouth, rather like Lord Byron in the wax museum' (*Time* magazine on Elvis in *Love Me Tender* circa 1956).

'Elvis Presley is unspeakably untalented and vulgar, just short of true obscenity' (John Crosby, *New York Herald Tribune*).

'There was nothing morally reprehensible about Elvis's performance. It was merely awful' (*New York Times* on his 1960 comeback TV show with Frank Sinatra).

'A whirling dervish of sex' (Reverend Graff, St John's Episcopal Church, Greenwich Village).

'I wouldn't have Presley on my show at any time' (Ed Sullivan).

'Presley and his voodoo of frustration and defiance have become symbols in our country and we are sorry to come upon Ed Sullivan in the role of promoter' (Reverend Shannon, *Catholic Sun*, 1956).

'He can't last. I tell you flatly, he can't last' (Jackie Gleason).

'I want to count Elvis's hound dogs twenty years from now. Only time will tell if Elvis is collecting Cadillacs in 1976' (Spike Jones, 1956).

'I wouldn't let my daughter walk across the street to see Elvis Presley perform' (Billy Graham).

So, Elvis sucked, what else is new? That which cannot be understood is criticized; that which cannot be tamed is destroyed. Elvis threatened by being the living, breathing, hip-shaking embodiment of rebellion and nonconformity at a time when deeply entrenched, ordinary domestic values were cherished.

Elvis on the Dorsey Brothers' TV Show was an act of rebellion: it may not have compared with Castro's storming of Havana, but its impact was as forceful. Even then, Elvis annoyed by being a polite, well-mannered southern boy who called every lady 'ma'am' and every man older than himself 'sir'.

He later upset by not coming out against the Vietnam War; he caused disbelief when he was seen shaking hands with President Nixon and siding with his crusade against youth culture. Elvis betrayed the promise by becoming sucked into the vacuous universe of 'showbiz celebrity', his formative musical roots buried under layers of brassy elevator music. Elvis became an embalmed Las Vegas marionette, strutting his still-potent stuff to legions of blue-rinsed matrons and plump rednecks, catering to the fans for whom he could do no wrong simply because he was Elvis.

For those fans, there could be no criticism of his dreary sixties movies (they gave you a chance to see Elvis), nor of his low-parody Vegas shows (they gave you a chance to see Elvis). There was little criticism either of his production-line albums (they gave you a chance to hear Elvis) and his frequently deplorable choice of songs (they gave you a chance to hear Elvis). These were the fans that the Sex Pistols railed against: 'Blind acceptance is a sign/of stupid fools who stand in line.' Not just Elvis fans though, but fans of Dylan or Springsteen or the Beatles or Barry Manilow or George Michael – any fans who worship their heroes uncritically. But yes, Elvis fans most of all, because they worshipped the longest; they worshipped the loudest; they worshipped the most fervently; they worshipped the most uncritically; they worshipped the most blindly.

The focus of all that worship, all that love and obsessive devotion, was, musically, a spent force by 1960. OK, we've heard all the arguments over and over that it's a fallacy that Elvis lost it before he joined the army, that he *did* make some great records after he came out of the army; but it's not really true. You're snatching at straws if you honestly think that 'My Boy' is as good as 'I'm Left, You're Right, She's Gone'; that 'Way Down' can hold a candle to 'Mystery Train'.

Of course, Elvis was still capable of making good records – occasionally *great* records – 'Suspicious Minds' stands alongside the best of his fifties work; but all the stuff on Sun, all the early RCA sides weren't just great records, they were a clarion call to arms, they were the trumpets that felled the walls of Jericho, they were rock 'n' roll; they were records the like of which nobody had ever heard before, and which nobody would ever hear in the same way again, because you can never recapture that first excitement.

It all began on 5 July 1954, some time late in the afternoon, in Sam Phillips' cramped Sun Studios in Memphis. Between takes, Elvis Presley goofed off on Arthur Crudup's 'That's All Right, Mama', and set something seismic off. 'That's All Right, Mama' wasn't the first rock 'n' roll song (Ike Turner's 1951 'Rocket 88' has that distinction); it wasn't the first white rock 'n' roll song (Bill Haley recorded '(We're Gonna) Rock Around The Clock' in April 1954 – the same month his 'Shake, Rattle And Roll' was a hit – but it didn't make its worldwide impact until it was used on the soundtrack of *Blackboard Jungle* in 1955). Elvis didn't even invent the phrase 'rock 'n' roll' (a tip of the hat to DJ Alan Freed). No, what the Hillbilly Cat did was fuse it all together, was to be young and sexy, to swivel his hips when avuncular old Bill Haley could only flick his kiss curl.

What Elvis did in the sweaty confines of Sun's studios was unique, and what he accomplished in his sixteen-month Sun stint changed everything. What he (and Scotty and Bill and Sam Phillips) accomplished and achieved dwarfed everything that had gone before and overshadowed everything that came after. So that even if you hate Elvis for being a racist, a fat slob, a genius who sold out, a sad travesty, a living myth . . . what you can never deny him is the genius that fused together black rhythm and blues and white country and western into something that we call rock 'n' roll.

Sure, there may have been half a hundred hillbilly cats strutting their stuff around the deep South in the long evening of the Eisenhower Presidency who *could* have done it. But it was nineteen-year-old Elvis Aron Presley that did it, and the world never forgot.

It was that early triumph which eclipsed everything that followed and makes the subsequent shoddy movies and substandard recordings such a betrayal.

Forty years on from the swinging spontaneity of those Sun days (such was its magic that during 1988, when they were the biggest band on the planet, U2 went to 706 Union Street to record and try to capture some of its magic), time has not buried Elvis Presley. He was vilified then and has been damned since his death: he never said anything worth recording in any dictionary of quotations, yet more has been written about him than any other figure apart from Jesus Christ and Adolf Hitler.

The hate Elvis inspires is as puzzling as the devotion, so deep is the sense of betrayal because so much was promised and, in the end, so little delivered. It is hard to reconcile the sultry, hostile beauty of the young Elvis, the world stretching out before him, cocking a snook at society and standards, with the bloated, caped crusader conversing with Nixon in the Oval Office or strutting his porcine stuff during one of those revivalist meetings that passed for concerts during the seventies.

Unknowingly and unwittingly, something fused in Elvis Presley during that hot July afternoon in 1954. Like a lightning conductor he was struck by the sudden possibility of change, of upheaval; the moment was instinctive and highly charged, and from that sweltering, spontaneous session Presley raced on to produce some of the most exhilarating and influential popular art of the twentieth century. You may hate what he became, but you cannot help but love what he was at the very beginning, before the world went mad. Just listen to the way Elvis talks through 'I Love You Because', the very first song he recorded at that first studio session, hear the clumsy sincerity, the naïve delight, hear him talk of the future that stretches bright ahead. Then listen again and hear the *promise*.

The Goldman Factor

Elvis Presley was the unknowing centre of controversy in his quite short life: only being screened from the waist upwards on TV so that his suggestive pelvic thrusts would not corrupt the young was just one example of the hand fate dealt him, but even greater controversy has dogged him beyond the grave – unless, of course, he really is working in a supermarket in the American heartland. No controversy about that, it's just an extreme example of his magnetism, and it's more than likely that he was selected as a subject by the late Albert Goldman due to that very magnetism, rather than for any aesthetic or musical qualities.

Goldman's credentials for writing *Elvis*, his first huge-selling book on Presley, were minimal: a book about Lenny Bruce which few, if any, of my acquaintance have read, music critic for *Life* and *Esquire* (both mainstream publications which often use critics who are not necessarily very devoted to their subject matter but are more interested in earning money by writing) and *The New Leader* (eh?), contributions to a lot of faintly highbrow-sounding American mags like *The Nation*, and, so the brief biog on the dust wrapper of that myth-shattering book (published by Allen Lane – a Penguin by any other name – in 1981) suggests, the *Sunday Times*, *Vogue*, *Cosmopolitan* and – wait for this – *High Times*, the dope mag. It also says he 'taught for twenty-three years in New York City, at Columbia University, where he was a Professor of English and Comparative Literature'. Is that passage in quotes capable of more than one meaning? Was the sentence chopped off before it was complete and did it actually have a long list of other posts he also held in New York apart from the stint at Columbia?

What is most damaging to those of us who broke a lifelong rule by buying the hardback edition (price £9.95 then, equivalent to maybe £25 or more today) is that Goldman had clearly never liked Elvis Presley's music very much, and, more to the point, probably hadn't heard very much of it. If you look at the imprint page of the book, the copyright notice attributes the book's ownership to Goldman himself, Kevin Eggers and Lamar Fike, although Goldman is the only name mentioned as author. In the acknowledgements, he thanks 'Kevin Eggers, who first conceived this project, Lamar Fike, who was my guide to the Presley circle and who conducted a number of valuable interviews'. Now, whether there is any significance in the name Kevin Eggers, who knows? Is he the Kevin Eggers who has recently resurrected a record label called Tomato, significant because it was the first label to record Robert Cray, and which also owns most of the album catalogue of Texan singer/songwriter Townes Van Zandt? Lamar Fike, if my memory serves, was one of the more obsequious members of the Memphis Mafia, the band of mainly gold-diggers who were employed by Elvis to be his friends. One Presley book notes: 'Lamar became a trusted employee who stayed until the very end, working at Hill & Range in Nashville. Because of his ballooning weight and good humour, Fike became the court jester of the "Memphis Mafia" over the years.' Now that sounds like a man with a potential grudge against the world in general and Elvis in particular. Having been the object of Elvis's doubtless desperately dumb and, more importantly, degrading and wounding 'jokes' for many years – Fike was supposedly an early fan from Texas and so may have been around Elvis for close on twenty years – he had missed his chance to get in with Red and Sonny West and their co-author, Dave Hebler, who wasn't in Elvis's employ for long but who apparently helped the Wests write *Elvis – What Happened?*, which can surely be said to have been the 'prequel' (not that such a stupid word had been coined fifteen years ago) to the Goldman book.

What happened to Lamar Fike after Elvis died? How about this for a possible scenario: Fike meets Eggers and says that he knows 'the truth' about Elvis, Eggers smells a potential fortune but has to find a writer who will not be concerned about assassinating the King (who is, after all, already applying for a job in a supermarket, having proved his immortality by rising from the dead), and who has enough resources to undertake such a mammoth project. The story goes – and please note that this is not stated as fact, but as a factoid, something which has been repeated so often that it is regarded as the truth and, as such, is rarely doubted – that Goldman was lecturing a class of would-be cub reporters as part of his job as a teacher, and conceived the brilliant idea of giving them hands-on experience of journalism by assigning them practical projects which involved taping interviews with many of the minor players in the Presley story. The two pages of acknowledgements in *Elvis* include well over a hundred names, some of which may well belong to those journalism students, and if that's true, Goldman's task was more one of coordination than of first-hand research.

Whether or not the assumptions which may easily be made about the above are correct, let us not stint with our praise for Goldman's achievement in bringing this project to fruition. It is a *chef-d'oeuvre*, a monstrous work which deservedly sold zillions of copies, and which may very well be the biggest-selling 'rock book' of all time. For that, Goldman deserves some credit, but it must also be said that *Elvis* is one of the more mean spirited books of this century, from the awful cover painting (described as 'a spiritual portrait of the young Elvis') to the innumerable damning revelations about Presley's human failings, which may have been true but were hardly of paramount importance to those of us who hoped to learn more about the greatest hero of popular music. Goldman could see little point in wasting words on the music and the early, relatively positive, aspects of Elvis's career – that had already been done by Jerry Hopkins and many lesser writers – when there was the very good chance of a scandalous epic which could be the equivalent of the 'disclosure' that Rocky Marciano might have been a transvestite (which there is no reason at all to suspect may be true). Elvis was an icon, and icons make wonderful copy – ask the British Royal Family! The more scurrilous the revelations the better, of course, which would be no problem for Lamar Fike – did Elvis call him 'Fatty' Fike or the American equivalent of the Michelin Man? He's not likely ever to admit it, so we may never know for certain, but the theory seems to fit the known facts and might make interesting reading . . .

As a kid of twelve who first heard Elvis in 1956, and who thought 'Heartbreak Hotel' was pretty amazing compared to Ruby Murray, having one of my early heroes ridiculed was distasteful – but it was hard to put the book down, and no doubt others can echo my personal memory of reading it, all 600-ish pages, in two or three days at most. Riveting stuff, and hard to put down, especially because the strong feeling was that Goldman would surely not have dared to use some of the stories had he been unable to defend them in court – which, it now transpires after some thinking, could have been another condition which he made part of his deal with Fike. By this time, the Memphis Mafia had virtually dispersed –

Priscilla didn't want them around, and even poor old Vernon was probably bored with them sponging off him and living around Graceland when the only reason for their presence there had gone to meet his Maker. They might not agree to being interviewed without a sweetener of some sort, plus a promise that Goldman wouldn't apportion any of the blame for Presley's self-indulgence and bad habits to them, and a nice fat wad of dollars would come in very useful for a bunch of people who had been used to living high on the hog but were now virtually unemployable. Fike knew them all, and he would even conduct some of the interviews, which would give the project credibility. Without making any accusations of any sort, one wonders about the possibility of some key interviews being supposedly private chats which were taped without the knowledge of the interviewee, which might explain why so many erstwhile 'friends' of the King were apparently so willing to unburden themselves of secrets about Elvis having to wear nappies in bed because he was so out of it that he might shit himself in his sleep, Elvis firing loaded guns at televisions because people he didn't like were on the screen, and Elvis behaving like a complete wanker most of the time. The worst one, or so it seemed to me, was Elvis playing Scrabble, and having seven tiles himself but only letting his opponents in the game have five, so as to ensure that he didn't – couldn't – lose very often.

Becoming unimaginably wealthy and the first and still the biggest heart-throb of rock 'n' roll was not necessarily as wonderful as the immature may think it sounds. After all, Elvis wasn't too smart, but he lucked onto what became a phenomenon – rock 'n' roll music existed before Presley, and it took Bill Haley to spread it nationally, then internationally, after which Elvis hung onto the chief Comet's slipstream for a few months, then selected second gear and consigned Haley to oblivion. Maybe Sam Phillips' much quoted desire to discover a white singer that sounded black, and the input of Scotty Moore and Bill Black have been undervalued – whatever, Elvis got very famous very quickly: he didn't ascend gradually into superstardom, he got there during a slot on television in which his vocals seemed incomprehensible and he wiggled his hips like a male stripper. He had no idea what was happening, but he was treated like Frank Sinatra, and he could get more nookie than anyone could even imagine. He liked this new life, but he got bored with the money and the fame and the paternity-suit potential, and that was when he started recruiting the Memphis Mafia – schoolfriends and their relatives and others who could keep Elvis amused all the time he was awake, and would obey his every command, for which they would be paid handsomely and live in the lap of luxury. They would also travel a lot and get a lot of nookie from the boilers Elvis didn't want. This was on the rarely fulfilled promise that the females concerned would be introduced to Elvis at some unspecified future time (or even on the premise that they were 'road-testers' for Elvis and had been assigned the onerous task of making a verbal report to Elvis on the capabilities – 'best blow-job ever' – and possibilities of whomever they had managed to entice into sex). The Memphis Mafia did not argue with Elvis most of the time, because it was, after all, more than their job was worth. Elvis can never have been much more than a mental cripple during his whole forty-two years, which is actually a tragedy, and there were two groups of people who became righteously indignant when the Goldman book emerged in 1981: the dedicated fans, whose sanity seemed suspect to the general public, inevitably hit the roof and wrote those complaining letters to papers in the hope that their defences of their hero would be published, but those less biased correctly condemned the book on quality grounds because it was like becoming obscenely rich through kicking a cripple.

The book was a huge seller, but not due to its execution, although anyone who accused Goldman of being a poor writer in terms of vocabulary or use of language would be vengeful rather than accurate. People bought it because it was scandalous, for the same reason so many of us bought *Lady Chatterley's Lover* when it came out for 3/6d in 1960. Anyone remember who published *Lady C*? The answer is Penguin, whose head at the time was Sir Allen Lane, and those who have been reading this essay diligently may recall that the hardback publishing house responsible for *Elvis* was Allen Lane . . . Some would enjoy the 'revelations' in *Elvis* because, for whatever reason, they resented its subject, who provoked jealousy in many males because he was a fantasy lover to numerous females. 'See? He was a pervert junkie who shat himself and overdosed on cheeseburgers and pills.' There is little reason to suppose that what Goldman wrote about Elvis was inaccurate – Goldman seems practised in the art of introducing topics very skilfully and in a low-key manner before the next Shock! Horror! revelation. Was Goldman resentful of Elvis because some girlfriend had compared him unfavourably to the hunk? On the basis that he cannot possibly have felt any shame about what he was doing, Albert Goldman must have been doing it for the money.

One can only arrive at an identical conclusion in the case of Goldman's 1991 follow-up, a considerably less gripping 190-ish-page paperback with no less than eighteen chapters, *Elvis: The Last 24 Hours* (Pan). This is a huge cash-in, and Goldman's is the only name listed in the copyright information. One might hope he was forced to write it in order to be able to afford the legal defence costs of the threats (of disclosure?) resulting from the earlier book, but, sadly, that probably wasn't his motivation at all. The story goes that Albert Goldman, like Presley himself, died in a lavatory. The record producer Phil Spector, writing in *Rolling Stone*, said: 'As a creature on this planet, Goldman was a vulture, which explains why he would wait until people were dead to pick their bones. My dearly beloved friend John Lennon once paraphrased an old proverb that I believe to be very apropos to the death of John Lennon: "Time wounds all heels."'

It is, however, unfortunate that Albert couldn't have survived a few more months. I would have enjoyed his views on Lisa Marie's marriage to Michael Jackson. Meanwhile, *Elvis* remains an incredible book – borrow it from a public library.

BRYAN BIGGS

Kitsch Elvis has Surely Come:
Elvis in Art

Elvis Presley is rock 'n' roll's most iconic figure. Familiar representations – from the hip-swivelling, lip-curling rebel to the rhinestone-jumpsuited spectacle of the Las Vegas concerts – have been recycled to such a degree that any potency these images might once have held has become dissipated, lost amidst the myths and clichés that now envelop the King of Rock 'n' Roll.

In pop culture, visual images as much as recorded sound – previously unreleased tracks or interviews, for instance – meet the demand of fans hungry for more material that might bring them closer to their idols. In Elvis's lifetime this function was well served by the publication of copious photographs and, of course, on celluloid through his own movies, filmed concerts, television interviews and newsreel footage. A large reservoir of visual imagery is therefore available to fuel the Elvis industry, which has witnessed since his death an increase in the volume of souvenirs and memorabilia on the market. On posters, postcards, greetings cards, tee-shirts, album covers, mugs, rugs and towels, in magazine illustrations, limited edition prints and original works of art, there is a constant circulation of images, each with a different visual interpretation of Elvis.

The continuing fascination that Elvis holds for artists is demonstrated in publications such as *Elvis in Art* (compiled by Roger C. Taylor, Elm Tree Books, 1987), a book which essentially offers a selection of portraits, many of them intended for reproduction on posters or in some of the other commercial forms mentioned above. Also included are paintings by Warhol, Blake and Oxtoby, representing a different tradition, one rooted in fine art, but one that has, as we shall see, been able to cross over – through its subject matter – into the wider arena of popular culture.

In looking at a necessarily selective collection of paintings, drawings, prints, cartoons, photographs and other artworks – stretching back almost four decades – which have focused on the phenomenon of Elvis, several aspects of art's relationship to popular music become evident.

Muriel Magenta, whose *Impersonators of Elvis Impersonators* is discussed later, is one artist who successfully brought a live element to her work through the use of performance art and video. Yet most art about Elvis has tended to be in the more traditional forms of painting and sculpture, neither of which are particularly suited to convey the excitement, movement, sound and energy of a live performance. These limitations are seen most clearly in the various Elvis statues erected in his memory. In common with countless bronzes of the Beatles, a naturalistic approach invariably yields unconvincing results. Jon Douglas's 1981 statue, for instance, suffers in this respect. Installed at the Elvisly Yours Centre in London, it has however become something of a shrine for Elvis fans, and has a particularly colourful history of its own, having survived a road accident whilst in transit to its unveiling ceremony, and having almost been arrested outside Buckingham Palace during a publicity stunt! (The full story of the statue is told by Sid Shaw in *Rare Elvis Volume One*, published by Elvisly Yours, 1990.)

In work of this nature, made in homage or as a memorial to Elvis, symbolic value often outweighs artistic merit. It is also rare to find an artist – David Oxtoby being an obvious exception – able to sustain the production of a large body of work concerned with pop music without it lapsing into mannerism, cliché, or the purely illustrational. In contrast, an expressly critical approach to the subject of Elvis has produced the most effective and enduring results though such work is rarely approved of, or even known, by the fans.

In 'Where Were You When Elvis Died?' (*Village Voice* 29 August 1977), rock-writer Lester Bangs saw Elvis as 'more like the Pentagon, a giant armored institution nobody knows anything about except that its power is legendary'. Particularly since Elvis's death, in visual art as in writing, the focus has been on dismantling that power, not simply to demythologize Elvis, rather to examine what this symbol has come to represent: e.g. the paradox of personal failure within public success, the embodiment of kitsch, a self-destructive revenge on an image out of control, a metaphor for the American psyche. For several artists discussed here it is the declining, disintegrating image of Elvis that is of interest, the figure of self-parody who lives on in endless impersonation in pub and club entertainment, in lookalike contests, in television comedy sketches. For others it is the youthful promise, sexuality and sense of danger that Elvis exuded before he was effectively tamed by mediocre film roles and military service that appeals. This response manifested itself in the occasional appearance of Elvis and other rockers in the canvases of art school students in the late 1950s and early 1960s – an indication of the collision of the worlds of pop music and art that was beginning to take place, particularly in Britain, where the 'art school connection' became such an important factor in shaping the style and direction of youth music, from beat to punk. Interestingly, in a sketchbook of one such student this interrelationship finds expression in a small study entitled 'Elvis Presley'. It is by Stuart Sutcliffe, completed in 1957 during his time at Liverpool College of Art where he first met John Lennon. As so vividly portrayed in the film *Backbeat*, Sutcliffe's obvious talent as a painter and his ambition to succeed as a serious artist compensated for his musical shortcomings as the 'fifth Beatle'. His passion for both worlds however is demonstrated in this modest yet telling sketchbook painting. Compositionally it pastiches the modern masters – Mondrian, Léger and Picasso – that Sutcliffe would have been studying as part of his course. Yet the inclusion of Elvis, rendered in Cubist style, surrounded by guitars, jiving figures and the titles of some of his hits, pays equal homage to rock 'n' roll. At Sutcliffe's old college, now Liverpool John Moores University, his life and work are being commemorated by the establishment of a student fellowship which will specifically support the creation of work that combines visual art and music or sound – further evidence of the reciprocation that still exists between these two spheres of contemporary culture. How though did Elvis first come to attract the attention of artists less closely connected to pop music than Sutcliffe?

Whilst the post-war period witnessed the increasing dominance of American abstract painting focused on a New York that had superseded Paris as the centre of the international art market, by the mid-1950s young artists on both sides of the Atlantic were beginning to articulate new responses to the developing consumer culture that surrounded them. In this context the style and philosophical approach of the Abstract Expressionists, like Jackson Pollock and Mark Rothko, proved inappropriate (except perhaps in their use of scale). Instead, the starting point for this new movement, which would come to be labelled Pop Art, was the raw material of everyday experience: images from advertising, pulp fiction and comics, mass-produced consumer goods and packaging, stars from the worlds of film and popular music. As the first hero of rock 'n' roll, it was natural that the image of Elvis Presley should be drawn into the repertoire of these young artists.

Preceding the more familiar Pop Art paintings by Warhol and Blake, it was the American Ray Johnson who in 1955 was arguably the first professional artist to depict Elvis. Taking published photographs of the singer, he altered them through cutting and the addition of collage and paint, to render the new rock 'n' roll sensation a somewhat sad, vulnerable figure. Johnson applied similar graphic techniques to photographs of Shirley Temple, James Dean and others, and though it has been suggested that the results do no more than mock modern heroes, the effect of these small pictures is to achieve an intimacy and a poignancy, qualities absent in Pop Art's later, more characteristically brash treatment of contemporary icons. Johnson referred to one of the Elvis series, *Elvis Presley No. 1*, in which red paint seeps from the eyes, as *Oedipus*. Working at a time when the dominant style was for highly expressive, splashy, abstract painting, he said, 'I'm the only painter in New York whose drips mean anything' (quoted in Lucy Lippard's *Pop Art*, Thames & Hudson, 1966).

By the early 1960s Pop Art as a movement was beginning to have a tremendous impact on the art world, particularly in London and New York. During this period it was in the paintings of Andy Warhol – who would himself attain the celebrity status of those he chose to portray – that the image of Elvis was most dynamically reworked. In Warhol's treatment of Elvis, as with his other portrait subjects like Marilyn Monroe, Jackie Kennedy, James Dean and Elizabeth Taylor, the star becomes as much a product to be consumed as Coca-Cola or Campbell's Soup. Glamour is reduced to the level of the banal, the images of these popular icons rendered with the same apparent detachment that Warholl displayed elsewhere in paintings of dollar bills, packaged food or taboo subjects such as suicides, car crashes or the electric chair.

A fan magazine provided the source for Warhol's first Elvis painting, *Red Elvis*, in which a brooding, somewhat sultry close-up photograph is repeated thirty-six times in black ink, silkscreened on a deep red background. Through repetition the image becomes emptied of meaning and, far from offering us a personal response to Elvis's character, Warhol comments instead on the nature of fame itself: the more the star's image multiplies and the more familiar we become with it, so his remoteness from us increases. Warhol even employs a commercial technique of mechanical reproduction, silkscreen printing, to parallel the processes through which images of our contemporary heroes are perpetuated in the mass media to the point of saturation.

Warholl exploited this method further in a series of paintings using a second image of Elvis, this time a full-length pose from a publicity still for the Western movie *Flaming Star*. Aiming directly at the viewer, a gun-toting Elvis adopts a threatening cowboy stance. Warhol printed this image larger than life-size onto uncut rolls of canvas which had been sprayed with aluminium automobile paint, this silver background a reference to the silver screen from which the image was derived. When first shown in Los Angeles in 1963, the entire exhibition comprised this identical image – Warhol's intention had been to create a 'continuous surround' – presented singly or in multiple overlapping variations. In *Triple Elvis*, by the time the third print had been pulled, the ink had begun to thin (Warhol made no attempt to correct such technical imperfections), leaving a fading imprint of an evaporating Elvis.

A similar effect is achieved in a print by Peter Hatfield, one of a series he showed alongside lengths of printed fabrics in an exhibition staged at the Liverpool Playhouse to coincide with Alan Bleasdale's play *Are You Lonesome Tonight?* in 1985. The fabrics were initiated as small-scale collages which were then developed into semi-abstract biographical images. Hatfield's interest lay in 'the demise of Elvis as a musician and a human being, from the beginning of his comeback tour, after his release from the army, to his last tacky, repetitive, bloated Las Vegas performance in 1976', a theme running through much of the recent art produced on Elvis.

There were marked differences between British and American Pop Art produced in the early 1960s. By and large, the American paintings were immediate, confident and full of verve, easily able to adopt the conventions of commercial art practice and new printing techniques from the mass media – a direct response, in fact, to the brashness of the consumer culture dominating modern life. In contrast, many of the paintings emanating from London at this time tended to be smaller in scale, fussier in both composition and execution, and more reliant on traditional modes of painting. Nowhere is this restraint peculiar to British Pop Art seen more clearly than in the work of Peter Blake.

It was Blake more than any of his contemporaries who incorporated pop iconography into his art, Elvis appearing in paintings, collages and drawings from the late 1950s and early 1960s. In addition to the overt Elvis representations, there are more discreet references, such as the Elvis/heart tattoo on the leg of the circus entertainer *Siriol, She-Devil of Naked Madness*, an 'I love Elvis' badge worn by the young girl in *On the Balcony*, and an actual cardboard cutout figure of Elvis displayed alongside other rock 'n' roll ephemera, toys and adolescent amusements in the window of *Toy Shop*. *Girls with their Hero* was Blake's first and most ambitious attempt at capturing the allure of Elvis, whose image appears repeatedly in the composition as a mishmash of fan photographs. Though continuing to collect further images to be incorporated into the painting, Blake never completed it, having stopped work after three years, a decision apparently made partly in response to Elvis's failure to visit Britain during his military service in Europe. Despite remaining unfinished, the painting is one of Blake's most intriguing. Its central figures, a group of female fans, are principally derived, like the fragmentary images of their hero, from photographs in the mass media. And just as the sketchy pin-ups of Elvis offer us tantalizingly little, so too the fans remain without identity, as intangible as the object of their worship.

Elvis's relationship with his fans is the subject of several other works completed by Blake during the period in which he was working on *Girls with their Hero*. Less complex and more dynamic in composition, *Got a Girl* and *El* are barely paintings at all in the traditional sense, being comprised almost entirely of collage elements, including photographs of Elvis instead of painted portraits. A photograph pasted into the corner of *El* was gleaned from a fan's scrapbook (complete with traces of a lipstick kiss). In *Got a Girl*, fan pictures of fifties pop stars Fabian, Frankie Avalon, Ricky Nelson, Bobby Rydell and Elvis (twice) are ranged above a bold enamel zigzag tricolour. The inclusion of a record, a 1960 chart single by the Four Preps, provides the title and key to the picture: the song deals with the frustration of a boy whose girlfriend's thoughts are occupied with her pop heroes rather than with him.

In *Self Portrait with Badges*, Blake reveals his obsession with American

culture and a nostalgia for his own childhood: adorned with a Fred Perry
shirt, bumper boots and denim suit, festooned with badges, including a
prominent Elvis one and others from Blake's childhood, and clutching an
Elvis fanzine, the artist has the appearance of an overgrown schoolboy.
The portrait, set in what appears to be a suburban garden with broken
fencing, seems to sum up British Pop Art's limited ability to articulate an
authentic response to the new pop culture emanating from America. As
John Walker has noted in *Cross-Overs: Art into Pop/Pop into Art* (Comedia,
1987): 'The contrast between the static, prim self-portrait rendered in a
fussy academic style and the energy of one of Presley's live performances
could not be more striking.'

Reflecting on these paintings, Blake has said, 'I hoped that if I painted
a picture of Elvis Presley, Elvis fans would enjoy the picture. But they
didn't go to the galleries, they didn't look at the magazines, they didn't
even see the picture' (quoted in David Bailey's *Goodbye Baby and Amen*,
Condé Nast, 1969). One fan, however, had in 1962 taken notice of the
Elvis fanzine in *Self Portrait with Badges*; Albert Hand wrote in *Elvis
Monthly*, 'Serious footnote. This portrait is a fine work of art, and on
behalf of all Elvis fans everywhere, I would like to extend my sincere
congratulations to Peter Blake, for his success with this work.' This
encouragement aside, Blake's hopes for broadening the audience for his
art came via another route altogether, in his designs for record sleeves,
most notably *Sgt Pepper*. Here, Elvis is curiously absent from the crowd
of modern icons, though he does turn up in Cal Schenkel's brilliant parody
of the Beatles' sleeve, created for the Mothers of Invention's 1967 album
We're Only In It For The Money.

In contrast to Pop Art's often ironic detachment from its subject matter,
David Oxtoby's work reflects an intense passion and knowledge of the
music with which his art has become synonymous. A contemporary of
David Hockney at art school in Bradford, Oxtoby's career did not quite
parallel that of the sixties Pop Artists, major success coming to him the
following decade. In 1977, the exhibition *Oxtoby's Rockers*, held at
London's Redfern Gallery and which subsequently toured, was enormously
popular, and the publication (by Phaidon Press) the following year of a
book of the same name was instrumental in introducing his work to an
even wider public. Though a large proportion of the paintings that brought
him to prominence were later destroyed in Denmark when a gang,

apparently enraged at not finding a more easily disposable haul, set fire to the truck carrying them to an exhibition, Oxtoby's images from this period remain widely known.

He continues to celebrate a range of icons from pop history, concentrating in depth on rock 'n' roll figures from the 1950s, charting the music's black roots in blues and R&B artists like Howlin' Wolf, Willie Mae Thornton and Ray Charles, through to its more commercial expression via the predominantly white singers who reaped considerable, if in some cases short-lived, success. All the major stars, as well as other more obscure performers, are treated with equal affection, Elvis being the most commonly represented. Though photographs provide Oxtoby with essential source material, he works intuitively, developing his images in unexpected directions. From small etchings and notebook drawings to large paintings on canvas, he has explored various technical means to convey both the raw energy of Elvis in performance and, crucially, his own emotional response to his subject.

He confronts in various ways the problems of trying to represent sound and movement two-dimensionally. In *The King – Fairground Sounds*, for instance, the border and lettering that frame two portraits of Elvis echo the brightly coloured, hand-painted decorations seen at fairgrounds, one of the few places in England in the 1950s where rock 'n' roll records could be experienced at a suitably loud level. The painting contrasts the raucous, unbridled Elvis of 1957 with a glossy, almost crooning, 1975 model, the contrast serving to heighten Oxtoby's evocation of an atmosphere from a now distant period.

The bleaching out of features seen in the Las Vegas image of Elvis in this picture is extended in *Sunspot*, one of a series in which Oxtoby explores the effects of light and movement. In an almost abstract composition of dramatic light and shadow, Elvis is rendered featureless by the intensity of the spotlight that catches him, yet he remains instantly recognizable through his characteristic pose.

Oxtoby's perspective is that of the eternal fan, his unpretentious approach expressing a sheer enjoyment of both the activity of painting and the music that has inspired it. If his depictions of Elvis and other rockers have been dismissed for being nostalgic, it is worth noting Fenella Crichton's observation (in the catalogue to Oxtoby's 1977 Chester Arts Centre exhibition) that 'Oxtoby gives it [nostalgia] back to its original two-edged meaning: a need to romanticize the past with a mixture of tenderness and cynicism'.

Even before his death, Elvis's deification was the subject of ironic comment in the work of Belgian artist Guy Peellaert. *Rock Dreams*, published in 1974 by Pan Books, is a collection of illustrations exploring the myths and excesses of the pop era, executed in a slightly awkward, airbrushed photocollage style. In it, in a parody of *The Last Supper*, Elvis presides Christ-like over a table spread with cheeseburgers, bottles of Coke and tomato ketchup, surrounded by his twelve disciples, who include Eddie Cochran, Ritchie Valens and Fabian, alongside British rockers Tommy Steele, Billy Fury, Terry Dene and Cliff Richard. The picture is captioned by Nik Cohn: 'Elvis Presley is the King. We were at his crowning.'

From the mid-seventies onwards, and particularly since his death, Elvis has been subject to increasingly ironic interpretation by artists. Charles Stuart, for instance, entitled his 1979 exhibition at the Midland Group in Nottingham, *King Elvis has surely come*. Though the paintings and prints incorporated classic fifties imagery, the reference is more metaphorical, as suggested by Stuart in the exhibition brochure: Elvis, the failure of an imported American Dream – 'If you'd come to us by airmail instead of on the airwaves we could have made you whole, but now I see your image in all of the faces of all the boys queuing on the corner for their dole'; Elvis, the product of a mass media 'that has drawn a curtain over the world that no X-Ray Spex can see through'; Elvis, a reminder of the fallibility and uncertainty of the modern age.

A decade after Peellaert's celebration of a rock world which appeared to be, at the same time, both glamorous and sinister, idealistic and superficial, Elvis had come to epitomize for some artists the sham, manipulative, even grotesque aspects of the pop process. His musical career was of little interest compared with the potential offered by the tragic facts of his demise, the quasi-religious devotion of his fans, or the continuing simulation after death through the phenomenon of impersonators. In other words, the emphasis shifted away from iconic representations of the King of Rock 'n' Roll to an examination of the ways in which images of Elvis continue to have currency and continue to exercise a hold over people's lives.

Jock McFadyen's modest portrait *Elvis Lookalike* (in the collection of the Ferens Art Gallery, Hull), painted in 1990, profiles what appears to be an ageing Ted, whom we might assume to be a club comedian were it not for the painting's title. The tacky background suggests a sleazy pub environment – it is in fact the artist's local, situated near his studio in London's East End, and the occasion is one of the pub's 'Elvis Nights'. A major feature of McFadyen's work is an interest in low-life subjects drawn from this urban environment, and though his characteristic social commentary is less to the fore here, the painting does point to the singer's affinity with a bygone era, of which, for him, Elvis still remains a symbol.

Whilst McFadyen's lookalike resembles only his hero in his sideburns and obesity, Muriel Magenta has drawn inspiration from the devotees whose ambition is to assume Elvis's appearance completely, to take on the mantle of his gaudy splendour: the Elvis impersonators. An American multi-media artist using video, sculptural installation, computer painting and performance, Magenta began in the early 1980s to make work concerned with hair as a cultural signifier. In her video trilogy – *In Defense of a Hairdo*, *Salon Doo* and *Coiffure Carnival* – the final part includes scenarios focusing on the hairstyles of famous historical and mythical figures such as Lady Godiva, Louis XIV, Samson and Medusa. Magenta's fascination with contemporary icons from popular culture 'who project their individuality through hairstyle' not surprisingly drew in Elvis, whose distinctive quiff and sideburns came to symbolize sexual power and the promise of eternal youth. Magenta parodies such idealizations through exaggeration, and presents Elvis impersonators mimicking other Elvis impersonators: in one vignette, four entertainers, wearing outrageously over-the-top wig sculptures and equally flamboyant costumes, perform against a set dominated by a ten-foot-high sculpture *The Comb for the Ultimate Doo*. Though the Elvis reference is but one element of Magenta's enterprise, it does illustrate how forms of expression from popular culture can be successfully appropriated, an important strategy for artists seeking an engagement with broader cultural issues and a point of access for a wider audience.

Elvis as a wholly artificial creation is apparent in *Home*, a 1991 colour photograph by the Rotterdam artist Henk Tas. Appropriating existing images and objects – often trivia associated with adolescence such as a pair of Beatle Boots, a photo of the Ronettes, plastic toys – Tas arranges these in contrived settings which he then rephotographs. Elvis has the appearance here of a plastic dummy or waxwork that is either weeping or melting under the theatrical turquoise light that bathes him, whilst the blue moon (of Kentucky?) glows from a distant TV screen.

Sheffield-based artist Simon Crump admits to a perverse fascination with Elvis. He is particularly interested in how, despite the excesses, corruption, tackiness and ultimate failure of Elvis's life, he still exerts a considerable psychological hold over individuals. In extreme psychiatric cases, this type of fixation manifests itself in the patient believing himself actually to be the object of his obsession: he becomes an 'Elvis Victim'. Crump has produced complex photoworks on this theme. The triptych *Elvis Victims Version* comprises three full-length photographs of a naked figure (the artist), bound with ropes to suggest some form of ritualistic torture. The composition is reminiscent of crucifixion scenes painted on mediaeval altar pieces. Framing each figure is a geometric pattern of superimposed photographic motifs – photocopied dollar bills, photo-booth portraits and a set of Elvis playing cards: the victim is literally trapped by the illusory and tragic nature of his condition. The work's religious connotations, with their suggestion of martyrdom and sacrifice, reflect Crump's interest in the parallels between Roman Catholicism and the adoration of Elvis, each with its attendant liturgical paraphernalia and kitsch souvenirs.

In a further photowork, a diptych entitled *Bob and Geraldine* (in the collection of the National Museum of Photography, Film and Television, Bradford), the references to mortality and Catholicism are again evident, this time in the quilted pattern of crucifixes, scapulars and clocks that make up the bedspread covering a sleeping figure – the Elvis of his dreams is represented by a frame of playing cards that surrounds him, whilst in the accompanying panel his female companion dreams of another male stereotype, the muscle man. Fantasy and reality come together in another aspect of Crump's work dealing with Elvis: a developing body of as yet unpublished experimental writing, in which bizarre fictional episodes are intertwined with equally strange yet factual accounts from Elvis's life, with no indication of which is which.

In the genre of Comic Art, several artists, particularly in the USA, have used Elvis themes in their strips. It is interesting to note that, as a child, Elvis was an avid comic reader and, as Elaine Dundy has revealed in *Elvis and Gladys* (Weidenfeld & Nicolson, 1985) modelled himself on

Captain Marvel Junior, the 1940s comic character created by Mac Raboy. Details like the cape and lightning-bolt emblem were adopted later, but initially Elvis was drawn to his hero's distinctive hairstyle and authoritative, mildly sexual stance. It is appropriate, then, that Elvis should himself become the subject of comic stories, though these more recent strips are a considerable distance away from the moral tone that Elvis found in the Captain Marvel books.

In Gary Panter's *Invasion of the Elvis Zombies* (Raw Books, 1984), a crazed, somnambulist, blood-lusting, alien Elvis monster terrorizes a B-movie neighbourhood till he's tracked down, exorcised and mutilated: 'Girls from all over the world come to take a bite out of Elvis. Happy ever after, they shower him with laughter. He exploded with recognition. Wordlessly they tiptoed back. He waits with vinyl lips and mascara to repay them.' Panter's expressive, undiluted punk style, formal ingenuity and enigmatic narration, combine to present a complex and disturbing, yet highly entertaining, vision – one whose graphic inventiveness conveys more of rock 'n' roll's raw energy than perhaps any of the other artists discussed here.

Similarly uncompromising are the deranged acid-tripping Elvis impersonators who stalk the supermarket aisles in Roy Tompkins' self-published comics. And, in *Now Act*, a finely drawn strip by Ted McKeever, the main character, Eddy Current, seeks refuge from the rainy night in a run-down bar, only to find himself the sole customer and audience for the evening's entertainer, Elvis Frith, whose rendition of 'Are You Lonesome Tonight?' has an unexpectedly dramatic climax. Another Elvis impersonator encounters an alien species, the Elvi, in Scott Saavedra's three-part serialization *The King of Kings*, *Call Me Elvis* and *À Doctor à Day* in the comic *It's Science with Dr Radium*. Travelling back to the twentieth century in search of their king, pursued by the inept scientist Dr Radium, the cute Elvi creatures mistakenly believe they have found Elvis. Taken away and lauded by the aliens, the impersonator achieves the recognition he was denied on Earth, till things start to go hilariously wrong.

In Britain, Steve Bell, creator of the *Guardian* newspaper strip *If*, illustrated his spoof Queen's Christmas Message with snaps from the family photo album showing Her Majesty's secret trip to Graceland. The photographs were montaged with drawn caricatures of 'The King' and the Queen, who leaves behind a heart-shaped wreath as a tribute – with a message from E.R. to E.P. Elvis has received more sustained treatment from Ray Lowry, whose incisive cartoons about the pretensions and cynicism of the rock industry and pop culture are well known through publication in the *New Musical Express* and elsewhere. In his cartoons Elvis appears in several improbable situations and guises: as 'Godzilla the Pelvis', as an illiterate Sicilian grape-treader, and as the central figure in Michelangelo's rock 'n' roll ceiling for the Sistine Chapel. Lowry has also produced several cartoons concentrating on the 'Frankly Fat Years'. In one, the ghost of Elvis returns to haunt a couple's refrigerator, in another he prepares to go on stage donning the 'Elvis Presley utility belt', containing 'cheeseburgers, popsicles, soda-pops, uppers, downers, a couple of lines of coke and a supply of candy bars . . .' In *King of Rock 'n' Roll!*, Shakey Kane caricatures Elvis giving his last interview, in which he expresses his fears about going to sleep on his back, having just seen the film *The Elephant Man*.

Fantasy, which the comic and cartoon genre allows, at least provides an equivalent context to the unreal existence that Elvis led. Few of the artists discussed here have been able to – or indeed set out to – sidestep the myths and offer an insight, through visual means, into Elvis as an individual, a real person. In any case, such an enterprise could be considered futile in a world of mediated truths, where the authentic becomes increasingly difficult to locate. As has been demonstrated, artists employing devices such as repetition, simulation or exaggeration in their work have perhaps come closest to revealing a clearer understanding of the Elvis phenomenon.

No other pop icons, save perhaps the Beatles or, more specifically, John Lennon, have attracted the same level of interest from gallery curators and artists in terms of the construction of entire exhibitions around them. From her base in Athens, Georgia, artist Joni Mabe has created the remarkable *Travelling Panoramic Encyclopedia of Everything Elvis*, a sort of mobile shrine obsessively packed with artworks, ephemera and relics, including a toenail reputedly gleaned by Mabe from Graceland. A visit to Elvis's Memphis home also inspired Scottish artist Alexander Guy to produce a memorable series of paintings, several of which are now in the collection of Glasgow City Art Gallery. The central motif of each is a sequinned jumpsuit, empty of Elvis's body, yet, like the Invisible Man, adopting various poses. Walking on water, suffering crucifixion, or

'What's the matter with you guys, have you never heard of Godzilla the Pelvis?!!'

'Believe me, this kid would have been bloody enormous if he hadn't been born to a family of illiterate grape-treaders in a remote Sicilian village.'

Two cartoons by the irreverent Ray Lowry

ascending to heaven, Elvis becomes here a modern-day martyr and miracle-worker, a contemporary Christ – a parallel confirmed by Guy's notes to the paintings: 'Jesus died for our sins, Elvis died for our twentieth-century sins. If Jesus is alive today, then so is Elvis. The fact is that they are equally both dead and alive . . .'

Mail Art – the international network of artists using the post (and increasingly fax and computer links) to distribute and exchange their work – has also witnessed several projects on an Elvis theme, resulting in exhibitions like the one in England in 1990 at Darlington Arts Centre, compiled by Ade Barradell. Even the Elvis stamp has already found its way into the work of several artists: Newcastle-upon-Tyne-based artist Paul Stone, for instance, incorporated a sheet of the stamps in his 1993 set of Cibachrome prints entitled *I want you I need you I love you.*

Despite the suggestion at the start of this piece that images of Elvis have been rendered impotent through endless circulation and familiarity, it is undeniable that, as a symbol, he has proved remarkably resilient. A reminder of his continuing currency for visual artists was provided by two quite different exhibitions seen recently in Britain. The Barbican's *The Sixties*, a survey of the London art scene during that era, brought to light further references to Elvis in little-known works by Pop Artist Pauline Boty (a painting entitled *It's a Man's World*) and abstract painter William Green (a photostatic print of Elvis's face in negative). *Trojan*, a painting completed some thirty years later and distinguished by an empty speech bubble emanating from an obese Elvis, was one of Jason Brooks's works featured in another exhibition, the 1993 *BT New Contemporaries*, a showcase of new talent from Britain's art schools. What other popular entertainer, alive or dead, can share Elvis's claim to have entered the visual vocabulary of artists of different generations so deeply?

STEPHEN BARNARD
Oh What a Circus

Your first glimpse of Elvis at London's Rock Circus comes while waiting for a photo call with Tina Turner's waxwork (prints available in the shop in forty minutes). There he stands in Las Vegas mode circa 1971, atop a circular tableau, with Stevie Wonder and Little Richard beneath. If seen in the window of Tower Records on the other side of Piccadilly Circus, the effect might be impressive; here, the indifferent likenesses of most of the models and the shopping mall atmosphere remind one not so much of a rock-centred Madame Tussaud's (whose showpiece this is) as a dummy-thick branch of Miss Selfridge. But worse is to come – an animatronic show of rock stars, presided over, bizarrely, by a working model of Tim Rice, in which Elvis (with computer-programmed lip curl, according to the brochure) reappears moving to 'Jailhouse Rock' in silhouette and then in gold lamé gear miming to 'Love Me Tender'. His spot is mercifully brief – shorter than the tasteless appearance of an animatronic Janis Joplin, whisky bottle in hand, pontificating on life as a 'rock victim', and that of an unrecognizable Madonna twitching a leg to 'Like a Virgin'. When the show closes to the Beatles in *Sgt Pepper* costumes, there's noticeably no applause or murmur of approval, just an embarrassed silence as the crowd shuffles off to the really important business of negotiating the souvenir shop on the way out.

Like the worst Presley tracks, and indeed the worst rock music, Rock Circus is technically efficient and totally soulless. The smug, knowing commentary by Paul Gambaccini – heard on headphones as you pass from exhibit to exhibit – chronologizes the story of rock glibly and seamlessly and communicates no real sense of the music's dramas, energies, contradictions, idiocies and obsessions. Though the whole air of Rock Circus is celebratory, it misses the mythic qualities of rock by failing to locate the music's great personalities – particularly the pioneer rock 'n' rollers like Presley and Jerry Lee Lewis – within the mythology they created for themselves. There's no attempt to present Elvis or anyone else as anything other than a xerox of his much-photographed public self, no attempt to dig at the inner demons in the way that Guy Peellaert and Nik Cohn managed in their book of illustrations, *Rock Dreams*, published in 1974. Peellaert's depiction of Elvis giving his blessing Last Supper-style to twelve copycat rock 'n' roll stars (Tommy Steele, Cliff, Ricky Nelson *et al.*) was unforgettable – nothing in Rock Circus matches the wit, imagination and truth of that one picture. For all the apparent attention to physical detail, Rock Circus is a face-value affair that diminishes the artists concerned by failing to represent in any way their simple special-ness. It reduces rock stars to a physically human level, yet the effect is ultimately dehumanizing. That's why any dutiful father who takes his children along hoping to inspire love and respect for the great figures – like those Edwardian parents who dragged their offspring to Tussaud's to see the kings and queens of England – is likely to end up agreeing with my own son's summation that it was 'worse than *Thunderbirds*'. Rock Circus is puppetry without the poetry.

Its unequivocal success is a tribute to 1980s target marketing: Rock Circus is first and foremost a tourist enterprise, the first stop on the 'doing London' trail for young foreign visitors, particularly from mainland Europe and Japan. Not for nothing is the Circus located close to Tower Records, to the Rock Tour of London bus terminus, and barely a mile from the Hard Rock Café (the ambience of which the Circus's own Rock Island Diner seeks to emulate). Like Tussaud's itself, it belongs partly in the entertainment world, partly in the world of 'heritage', in the name of which the Brontë Parsonage gets redecorated in Laura Ashley wallpaper and families pay good money to share the Blitz 'experience' at the Imperial War Museum. It's tempting to describe the Rock Circus version of rock history as Disney-like, but then Disney had a sense of fun that is palpably lacking here. Rock Circus is simply a tourist-board equivalent of wall-to-wall golden-oldie radio – not so much 'yesterday once more' as a stylized, carefully sanitized and curiously joyless version of it.

In the end, Rock Circus preserves neither memory nor myth, and in the case of Elvis it leaves one longing for the honest tack of Graceland itself or the Presley memorabilia collection housed on Blackpool sea front a couple of years back. Even the worst Presley impersonator could be relied upon to give a better sense of what the man meant to teenagers in the 1950s and continues to mean to many. Yet one of the paradoxes of Rock Circus is that while it seeks to present rock as a unified culture with a clear sense of its past, the evidence of its customers is that the unity is an illusion and Elvis and his fellow rockers in particular are no more than sideshows from history. Far from confirming to me Presley's lasting cultural impact as the supreme iconic figure in rock, the visitors to Rock Circus had me wondering whether Elvis lives on as no more than a rock 'n' roll Glenn Miller, a period piece: they glance at Elvis the visual cliché and disconcertingly move on to take snaps of Eric Clapton and Michael Jackson. It's as if the concept of rock as a continuing tradition stretching from Bill Haley to Madonna is itself wearing very thin – and when did you last hear an Elvis track on Radio 1? Even the appreciation of Elvis in Gambaccini's commentary and the accompanying brochure belittles his impact (and his artistry) by revering him as a catalyst for what came next. Is that all Elvis was important for – for making Cliff Richard, Rick Nelson and Tom Jones possible?

It doesn't help that Elvis's musical legacy is rooted mainly in some pretty shallow rock 'n' roll, though it is possible to see the very shallowness of Elvis's attitude and musical approach – what Greil Marcus in *Mystery Train* calls 'that distance, that refusal to really commit himself, in his best music and his worst' – as a positive virtue. If much of Elvis's music sounds superficial, the argument goes, at least it's gloriously superficial, celebratory, frivolous – rock 'n' roll at its most limited yet liberating. As Marcus points out, when Elvis treated his material with respect and deference, as he did his country and gospel songs, his vitality, charm and arrogance were stifled by the proceedings. I agree with all this, but I'm no longer sure it's really the stuff of greatness: the lack of fulfilment still depresses.

Maybe, being British, I'm jaundiced. UK fans suffered incredibly badly at the hands of Elvis's management, who cynically played on the man's remoteness and were never ever seriously interested in bringing him to Britain. Those contemporaries who did visit the UK (Gene Vincent, Buddy Holly, Eddie Cochran) proved far more influential figures in the UK in a musical sense, and, for what it's worth, all spawned tougher tributes (Ian Dury's 'Sweet Gene Vincent', Mike Berry's 'Tribute to Buddy Holly', even Heinz's 'Just Like Eddie') than the limp I-remember-Elvis songs written after his death. His aloofness at first added to the mystique but, after his late 1960s comeback, became simply tiresome: when a UK fan-club convention was presented with Elvis's bicycle in lieu of the man in the early 1970s, even the most loyal fans made no secret of their embarrassment.

And if he *had* come to Britain, would there ever have been the need for a Rock Circus? Surely the whole story of rock would have been different if he had toured here around 'Heartbreak Hotel' time: perhaps he would have inspired *real* riots and removed at a stroke any need for the country's rock 'n' roll copycats; perhaps Cliff would have stayed on pushing invoices at Atlas Bulbs after all. Certainly skiffle would have died the death long before Lonnie Donegan sang 'My Old Man's a Dustman', and where would that have left the beat-group revolution of the 1960s? Maybe Elvis would have remained such a dominant figure that rock would never have progressed into 'artistic' territory at all.

The Rock Circus Elvis is a cartoon Elvis, and my children can't be alone in looking upon it in total puzzlement. A few, though, might see the connection with that wonderful kids'-TV character Elvis Cridlington, the dumb but kind-hearted Pontypandy fireman in *Fireman Sam*. This is a programme obviously created by real fans: their Elvis has bushy sideburns, a DA haircut, a Teddy-Boy demeanour and, no doubt, obsessive rock 'n' roll-loving parents from the kind of Welsh mining valley that produced any number of would-be Elvises, including the most convincing of all home-made Presleys, Tom Jones. The touring show of *Fireman Sam* even has the cast singing a rock 'n' roll pastiche, 'When Elvis Burns the Lunch'. The character of Elvis Cridlington is difficult to beat for warmth, good humour and, yes, integrity. And *that* is how to keep a memory alive.

MIKE EVANS

From Heartbreak Hotel to
Hamburger Hill

The most remarkable – and depressing – aspect of Elvis Presley's enduring image is that the least attractive version of that image seems to have endured the most.

Contemplating a kitscher-than-kitsch plaster bust of the King which a friend recently brought back from Toronto for my fiftieth birthday, it struck me that the white-jumpsuited safe-as-milk Las Vegas Elvis has been preserved in media posterity rather than the brooding, sexy and ultimately threatening Elvis who turned the heads and ears of a generation back in 1956.

Just like the rather sad Elvis impersonators who unwittingly conspire to undermine everything worthwhile their hero ever stood for, the bust manages to combine the slicked-back fifties hairstyle with seventies rhinestone collar and blue sweat scarf, while still looking nothing like him at all.

There's a dread inevitability about American showbiz that sees genuinely revolutionary performers, artists like Louis Armstrong, Frank Sinatra and Ray Charles, artists who literally turned popular music on its head, becoming ultra-respectable – the toast of suburbia, Las Vegas and even the White House. This is usually characterized by numbing lapses in taste – think of 'What A Wonderful World' or 'My Way' – and it is not altogether surprising in an America where tastelessness is part and parcel of the cultural status quo.

But who would have predicted that this fate would befall Elvis when he stood astride the world, legs apart and guitar slung low, challenging all that had gone before with a sullen shrug, curl of the lip and knowing gesture of the hips?

In his *Unsung Heroes of Rock 'n' Roll*, in an introduction that argues that rock 'n' roll was virtually finished by 1955 (the year of its official birth), Nick Tosches makes the claim that when Elvis introduced 'Milkcow Blues Boogie', his third record, made in December 1954: '. . . raw power had already turned to schmaltz. You can hear it in that well-rehearsed false start, followed by that voice foreshadowing bad beatnik movies to come: "Hold it, fellas. That don't move. Let's get real, real gone." He didn't have far to go from there to "Bossa Nova Baby".'

Extreme stuff, but Tosches, with tongue placed somewhere cheekwards, articulates a latent suspicion that the emasculation of El began as soon as Sam Phillips flogged his Sun contract to RCA.

Certainly, the RCA sides were what shook the world – it was 'Heartbreak Hotel' not 'Baby Let's Play House' that kicked pop music up the arse, and it was on the back of those hits of '56 that his image was launched on an unsuspecting planet.

Looking back, the strangest thing at the time was that here in the UK we had very little to go on. The open-mouthed legs-apart picture on the debut *Rock 'n' Roll* LP was the received image, and in truth it looked little like Elvis. Funnily enough, it looked a bit like Johnnie Ray.

Johnnie Ray was the link between the crooners – Sinatra, Perry Como, English big-band idols like Dickie Valentine – and Elvis. He was a swooner, like his fans. He wept and broke down on stage, much as the females in his audience did. He was labelled by the press the 'Cry Guy', 'Nabob of Sob' and 'Prince of Wails' and sobbing singles like 'Cry' and 'The Little White Cloud That Cried' had him bawling all the way to the bank. Visually, he paved the way for the extrovert (some would say exhibitionist) excesses of the rock 'n' rollers, and of Elvis Presley in particular.

Country singer Bob Luman described the nineteen-year-old Elvis's appearance at a concert at Kilgore, Texas: 'This cat came out in red pants and a green coat and pink shirt and socks, and he had this sneer on his face and he stood behind the mike for five minutes, I'll bet, before he made a move.'

The big image-maker then, of course, was still the movies, and it was there that elements of Elvis's style were already established. The flecked jackets, peg-bottom pants, suede sneakers were pure *Rebel Without A Cause* James Dean, while the sneer, the smouldering eyes came straight from Marlon Brando in *The Wild One*. (Although both these pieces of seminal cinema came just before the outbreak of rock 'n' roll, the soundtrack and incidental music from on-screen jukeboxes and car radios was big band jazz.)

While in America Elvis was soon getting saturation coverage on coast-to-coast TV shows, in Britain he was initially perceived by description as much as illustration. He was immediately dubbed 'The Pelvis' by an hysterical American press, and while we read all about his gyrations and the outcry that ensued, there was only a smattering of fan photos to relate it all to. Anticipation, then, was at fever pitch when his first film, *Love Me Tender*, was about to be released.

Although the film was a disappointment in terms of Elvis's by now legendary stage act – there was little evidence of it in the movie, basically a straight Western drama – at least we saw what he really looked like. (The part, it has to be added, was originally intended for James Dean, who subsequently visited Elvis several times during the shooting.)

But from there on in, the image was everywhere. Before his second movie, *Loving You*, was even released, he had almost singlehandedly stereotyped the rock 'n' roll singer as a visual as well as a musical icon. And icon it truly was; in addition to his photograph in every newspaper or magazine you opened, the proliferation of his image on merchandised goods – from bedclothes to bubblegum – was unprecedented.

It was the peak of the King's commercial success, with eight consecutive US chart-toppers in 1956/7, and his image reflected this perfectly. Although he quickly acquired the trappings of a star, the wall-to-wall suits, innumerable pairs of shoes and flash cars, it was still an audacious, outrageous flaunting of his new-found wealth.

'He [Elvis] showed me a gold horseshoe ring studded with eleven big diamonds he was wearing. "Look at all the things I got," he said, "I got forty suits and twenty-seven pairs of shoes," and I asked him how he knew it was exactly twenty-seven pairs and he said, "When you ain't got nothing, like me, you keep count when you get things."' (*Daily Mirror*, 30 April 1956)

He was the local boy made good, the truck driver who struck it rich. The shoes were blue suede (courtesy of Carl Perkins) or black and white sneakers, the Cadillacs pink and the suits culminated in the gold lamé creation on the sleeve of *Elvis' Golden Records* by Nude's of Hollywood, normally tailors to the country and western fraternity.

This was *the* image of Elvis, the rock 'n' roll rebel who 'made it', for teenagers all over the world. Although it was just big business for an established record company like RCA, the vision transcended all that; parents still loathed him, girls wet themselves at the thought of him, boys simply wanted to be him; and Elvis just grinned as he launched into 'Don't Be Cruel' on nationwide TV.

But with every hit and every TV appearance – not to mention every award and accolade – Squaresville loomed ever nearer as cool credibility began to disappear over the hip horizon.

The biggest boost Colonel Tom could possibly have had in regularizing the erstwhile 'teen rebel' Elvis came courtesy of Uncle Sam, when the singer's draft papers landed on the Graceland mat one morning early in '58. Parker's instinct for the populist approach knew no bounds as the whole world saw the sideburns shaved, the hair cut and the cool clothes swapped for army fatigues – all in patriotic service to flag, country and President. A long way from the Hillbilly Cat who prowled Lonely Street in search of Heartbreak Hotel. There was even an EP, *Elvis Sails*, recorded at the dockside as the now All-American Hero left for the G.I. Blues in Germany.

The death knell of his apparently irrevocable reputation as an icon of youth began to toll when he was demobbed in the spring of 1960, with an 'I'm really a family entertainer' appearance on primetime TV as a guest on *The Frank Sinatra Show*, duetting with 'the Governor'.

The sure slide into musical mediocrity which came with the interminable candy-floss movies during the sixties has been well documented, and epics like *Fun In Acapulco*, *Tickle Me* and *Paradise Hawaiian Style* had an equally sanitizing effect on El's visual image. While the rest of rock reflected the good vibrations of the revolution, these technicolour travelogues were pure sportswear-and-casuals Frankie Avalon, as though the beach party would never end.

Then, in 1968, with the comeback TV special, things looked good again. The tough, no-nonsense musical approach, back-to-the-roots rock 'n' roll with Scotty Moore and D. J. Fontana was reflected in a black-leather image that put Elvis back on the pedestal as the epitome of what rock was all about. And this at a time when the excesses of flower power were becoming more and more distanced from the raunchy essentials of the music.

But, ironically, the success of this return to live performance and the initial concert dates that followed, was to lead to the latter-day image of Elvis – the one encapsulated most clearly in the public mind – of the corpulent cabaret star churning out his old hits in true showbiz fashion, in outfits that suggested a parody of their wearer's former self.

Exaggerating elements of fifties style which he had popularized in the first place – the upturned collar, tight pants, greased-back hair and sideburns, which were *de rigueur* with British 'teds' through the late fifties – Elvis managed to incorporate the flared trouser bottoms and medallion-man machismo of the early seventies to achieve a kitsch caricature which all the plaster busts in the world could only imitate, never rival.

The main culprit in this descent into the dross of dress – given that Elvis *chose* to look this way – was designer Bill Belew, who created most of the numbers that helped the King look like rock's answer to Liberace. Surprisingly, it was Belew who had come up with the comeback leather gear, but the way his imagination was moving was clear when the initial Presley stage shows had the star sporting a four-inch-wide belt with a proportionately overstated buckle.

The early 'revival' appearances (apart from the belt!) still saw El, as at his 1969 debut at the Las Vegas International Hotel, in relatively cool clobber – black suede, leather, at least nothing you could joke about.

But soon the ubiquitous jumpsuits made their mark, usually Bill Belew creations with fancy names – like 'Concho', the silver outfit he wore on his second Vegas season and US tour in 1970.

By the time he played Madison Square Garden in '72, Elvis's clothes were well into Dolly Parton country, complete with rhinestones. That was the debut appearance of Belew's 'Shooting Star' stage suit, the white one-piece outfit with gold-lined matching cape.

While Belew's influence could be seen elsewhere – he designed the Osmonds' stage suits, in which the Brothers Grin toured Europe in 1975, and the Elvis-imitator industry was beginning to take off a couple of years before their model was in the mortuary – Elvis even designed some of his later outfits himself.

One such self-created jumpsuit, which he wore towards the end of his life when the Great had become the Grotesque, was described later in a sale of such memorabilia as having 'silk kick pleats, elaborate turquoise embroidery, jewel work, and zip front with custom plastic collar stay'.

Presley's personal problems were increasing – his marriage floundered as he returned to a life on the road – and with them his waistline, as the now legendary diet of pills 'n' cheeseburgers took its toll on the once sleek symbol of rock 'n' roll.

The style – or lack of it – went with him to the grave. Even Dead Elvis, the overfed chicken-in-a-casket lying in state at Graceland, was wearing a white high-collar number. While plaster-bust factories all over the world braced themselves for the arrival of the gravy train, the mystery train long gone into the Memphis Sun-down.

BRYAN BIGGS

Return to Sender: The Elvis Stamp

> *Unbind your mind*
> *There is no time*
> *To lick your stamps*
> *And paste them in*
> *DISCORPORATE*
> *And we will begin . . .*

(from *Absolutely Free*, Mothers of Invention, 1967)

In the history of popular music, the letter has been the subject of countless songs. As a means of communication between distant lovers, delivering words of reconciliation or heartbreak, the handwritten message has endured, like its spoken equivalent the telephone call, in a variety of titles. The Delta blues singer Son House received chilling news in 'Death Letter Blues', whilst James Brown sent a package metaphorically containing his heart in 'Signed, Sealed and Delivered', a similar title and idea also being used by Stevie Wonder. Billy Fury's letter was full of tears, Brian Hyland's was sealed with a kiss, the Marvelettes and the Beatles implored the postman to deliver theirs 'the sooner the better'. The Singing Postman, attired in GPO uniform, remained, however, too much of a Norfolk novelty to make any impact on the charts in Britain, let alone elsewhere. In contrast, Elvis Presley scored massively with 'Love Letters' and 'Return to Sender', a song which some thirty years after first topping the charts took on a new resonance.

When Anthony M. Frank, the appropriately named sixty-sixth US Postmaster General, declared, 'I think an Elvis stamp would be fun', he surely couldn't have envisaged the ruse that would be played on his Department when the stamp was finally issued in 1993. Due to Elvis fans sending letters bearing the stamp to fictitious American addresses, the US Mail recorded a tenfold increase in the number of letters it was obliged to return, duly marked 'Return to Sender – Address unknown'.

Instantly popular, the 29-cent Elvis stamp was issued, it appears, not so much as an enlightened decision by the US Postal Service to celebrate American popular music – though a series of stamps featuring other singers did follow – but more as a result of an intensive campaign led by fan Pat Geiger over a nine-year period – initially as a one-woman crusade. Her enthusiasm for the idea of an Elvis stamp quickly spread through the network of fan clubs in the US and elsewhere. Petitions and thousands of individual letters were sent to the Postmaster General, the Citizens' Stamp Advisory Committee, and to US Senators and Representatives. The official response to Geiger's first request was that, US Presidents excepted, a person had to be dead for at least ten years before he or she could be considered for commemoration on a stamp. (There are those of course who argue that Elvis is still alive and therefore ineligible!) Optimistically, then, an Elvis stamp might appear in 1987, thought Geiger; however, she was unaware of the complicated internal workings of the US Postal Service and its rules and regulations governing proposed subjects for new stamps. Neither did she foresee the controversy the proposal would cause.

Once the media had picked up on the campaign, following Mr Frank's suggestion that an Elvis stamp was a distinct possibility, the whole debate about Elvis's suitability to be celebrated in this way began. 'The day the US Postal Department puts a drug addict on a stamp is when we had better throw in the towel,' was typical of the response of the opposition, whose declaration that it would never lick Elvis's backside found sympathy with the Citizens' Stamp Advisory Committee. Essentially the selection body for new stamps, this group's opposition was overruled by the Postmaster General.

Despite moral majority protestations, the objection that Elvis was an unsavoury role model for the youth of America was becoming less of an issue as his accommodation into the Establishment increased. By the start of the 1990s his portrait hung in the National Portrait Gallery and Graceland was included in the National Register of Historical Places. Economically and patriotically, he was proving good for business. As Lt. Col. James P. Verney reminded the troops at a Graceland ceremony in 1991, Elvis never shirked his military obligations, thus sending 'a powerful message to our young people – freedom isn't free and we must all share in the responsibility of keeping America strong'. As long as this wholesome image of Elvis predominated, his later lifestyle of drug dependency and over-indulgence could be forgiven. Pro-Elvis campaigners could also point to the example of novelist Ernest Hemingway, whose alcoholic suicide had not prevented his philatelic commemoration in 1989.

As media interest in the stamp grew, the main contention focused on its design: how would this most deified of pop heroes be depicted? Already rock's most universally familiar icon, how could the countless representations of his image be distilled into a single portrait? The US Postal Service shortlisted two designs and took the unprecedented step of conducting an Elvis poll, circulating ten million ballot cards featuring the portraits. The people would decide! Over a three-week period in April 1992 the debate raged over which image would eventually be used: a 1950s version, designed by Mark Stutzman, or a 1970s one, by John E. Berkey.

Derided by fans of the younger Elvis for what they regarded as the embarrassment of the Las Vegas years, the latter version – dubbed the 'old, fat Elvis' – was in fact based on an image from the 1973 TV special *Aloha from Hawaii via Satellite*. It has, though, all the hallmarks of Elvis's terminal decline: ridiculously high star-studded collar, bejewelled fingers clutching microphone, face going through the emotional motions, the lyrics clearly not meaning anything any more. His classical features are relatively intact but, with an expression bordering on perplexity and not a bead of sweat in sight, the face is unreal, a mask worn to conceal the mess into which the singer's body, and indeed life, were rapidly disintegrating.

The portrait does, however, suggest a live performance, Elvis in action. In comparison, the earlier portrait has all the static appearance of a publicity still. Elvis's trademark quiff and the 1950s period microphone serve to signify rock 'n' roll's first rebellious rush, yet the composition fails to convey any of the danger and excitement of Elvis's first electrifying performances. A full-length pose – clearly a nonstarter for a 4×3 cm horizontal-format stamp – would at least have allowed for a hint of pelvic gyration, but instead Stutzman concentrates on the head and shoulders. Recognizably vintage fifties Elvis, the result, on closer inspection, is less convincing. The awkwardly held microphone might just as well be a cheeseburger about to be devoured, so absent is any suggestion of singing, of the voice that was to shake popular music to its foundations. Neither do we get a sense of Elvis's compelling physiognomy, his sultry looks forsaken for a faintly jocular expression that fails to fix us: gazing elsewhere, his glazed blue eyes focus on the middle distance, on nothing in particular. Technically the drawing style resembles Guy Peellaert's somewhat sickly, airbrushed representations of pop heroes in the book *Rock Dreams* (Pan, 1974). Unlike the Belgian artist's homage to rock 'n' roll, however, irony is absent in Stutzman's portrait, which, though a competent illustration, remains no more than an approximation of Elvis, superficial and lifeless.

Sufficient numbers of Americans were, however, convinced by the 1950s image, giving it a stomping victory by 851,000 votes to 277,723. This represented just over ten per cent of the total ballot cards distributed. Available at post offices as well as inserted into *People* magazine, many of the remaining millions have doubtless found their way into collections of Elvis memorabilia worldwide. A disappointed John E. Berkley concluded: 'I painted the King. That other guy is the Prince. The fanatical fans like the older one.' Older fans who had grown up with Elvis's music, amongst them Pat Geiger who cast thirty-five votes herself, may well have preferred the mature version. Arguably though, the US Postal Service would have found it difficult to justify its use of an Elvis image more associated in the public's mind with his years of drug abuse and self-destruction. Besides, Elvis's musical achievements had been, by and large, in the 1950s, the increasingly self-parodic 1970s proving creatively bankrupt, inspiring nothing but an industry of impersonators.

Issued on 8 January 1993 (on what would have been Elvis's fifty-eighth birthday), the stamp was launched at a special ceremony at Graceland, where Elvis's daughter Lisa Marie accepted the first cancelled stamp. Replying to a reporter's question about what she thought of her departed pop, she replied, without apparent irony, 'He was just an enormous being.' In Amarillo a supermarket had mistakenly sold sixty stamps before the issue date and, thus postmarked, these became an instant rarity. Elsewhere, on the correct day, fans queued up at post offices and other outlets across the States to purchase the first of the stamps. In Hollywood, Mexican Elvis impersonator 'El Vez' was first in line, affixing his stamps to a letter addressed to President-elect Bill Clinton, to whom he wrote, 'You are presidente, but he will always be the King. If enough people buy and collect the stamp, he could help you pay off the deficit in two shakes of a chihuahua's tail' (reported in the *Los Angeles Times*, 9 January 1993). Certainly, the US Postal Service stood to make a considerable profit, not only from 'stamp retention' – stamps bought by fans but never used – but also from related merchandising and licensing fees. With 500 million stamps produced, three times the normal print run for a commemorative stamp, the issue has little investment value to the collector, but the accompanying first-day covers and other limited edition 'collectables' have provided the necessary rarities. Manufacturers found a ready market for such tasty items as the 'Elvis Presley Stamp Clock' or the equally desirable 'Elvis Presley Museum Stained Glass Tableau', advertised thus: 'standing tall in its hand-rubbed walnut base, the luminous brass-trimmed image of the Elvis Presley Stamp is a full eight inches by ten inches! This is authentic individually painted and kiln-fired stained glass. By window, lamp or candlelight, it comes to life and is guaranteed never to fade.'

Mark Stutzman supplemented the standard $3000 fee for his design with earnings from a limited edition lithograph of the stamp which the Postal Service had allowed him to produce. The Service also commissioned him to design three further stamps in the Legends of American Music series dedicated to rock 'n' roll and rhythm and blues – Bill Haley, Buddy Holly and Richie Valens. All three share a similar fate to Elvis at Stutzman's hands, their iridescent flesh unnaturally aglow, their expressions offering varying degrees of inanity: Haley appears to be laughing hysterically, Valens resembles a woozy pub entertainer, Holly a squeaky-clean ventriloquist's dummy. The images reveal the artist's continuing difficulty in rendering hands and hair convincingly. In contrast, the three black legends that complete the series are altogether more successfully depicted: a soulful Otis Redding, an awesome Dinah Washington and a coolly confident Clyde McPhatter. Further commemorative stamps in the Legends of American Music series include Hank Williams, whose eligibility was ensured when he overdosed on the way to his final gig. Appearing on both a single stamp and in the booklet of country and western stars, he is depicted full torso, the concentration on guitar and cowboy hat at the expense of facial detail working to good effect.

The US Postal Service's choice of subjects raises interesting questions about whom it deems worthy to be thus commemorated and, by extension, how America itself wishes to celebrate its musical heritage both domestically and internationally. The USA has long valued the role its cultural exports play in the economic and ideological global stakes, and whilst a postage stamp is hardly comparable to Hollywood or the giant communications corporations in this respect, it nevertheless sends – literally – a message, reinforcing a particular national self-image. It is an image that is exclusive and ultimately conservative: as rappers Public Enemy observe in 'Fight the Power', Elvis may have been a hero to most, but 'most of my heroes don't appear on no stamp'. We may speculate that Richie Valens's inclusion was intended to reflect his popularity with America's Mexican and Puerto Rican communities. Arguably he is no less ephemeral in pop history terms than, say, fellow air-crash victim the Big Bopper. Equally we might question Clyde McPhatter's significance over Sam Cooke's. We may safely bet, though, that America's most controversial and frequently also its most innovative musical icons will not find their way onto future stamps. A psychedelic category for example, featuring the likes of counter-culture casualties Jimi Hendrix, Janis Joplin and Jim Morrison, is as unimaginable as one devoted to Frank Zappa (who has more chance of receiving such official recognition in Czechoslovakia, for whom he acted as Cultural Liaison Offier with the West). This one-time leader of the Mothers of Invention said in his wry introduction to the song quoted at the start of this essay, 'Discorporate means to leave your body.' All the American musical legends discussed above did just that – in a mortal sense – in order to qualify for commemoration by the US Postal Service. Elvis has the distinction of being the first to be celebrated in this way: he is also surely the only one whom we steadfastly refuse to let rest in peace.

SIMON FRITH

Wise Men Say

I don't think El will ever rate with the more serious students of popular song – his syrupy crooning with vibrato went out with Rudy Valee.
Arthur Jackson 'Light Side', *Audio and Record*, August 1962

The academy never had much interest in Elvis Presley anyway. There are already many more theoretical articles about Madonna than about the King; indeed, there are, by now, more solemn studies of Elvis fans and impersonators than of the man himself. Greil Marcus tells me that there is an Institute of Elvis Presley Studies, in Toronto, but my immediate professional response is that it can't be serious. Bob Dylan Studies, yes; Jimi Hendrix Studies, maybe; but an Elvis Presley Institute seems, by definition, loopy, the musicological equivalent of Edinburgh's Arthur Koestler chair in Psychic Studies.

Now, in one respect there's no reason why the academy should have any interest in Presley – it has never been much interested in any aspect of popular culture. And, in academic cultural terms, Elvis (unlike Dylan) has no redeeming features whatsoever. Everything he did was trashy and I doubt if he'd even heard of T. S. Eliot or Charles Ives. Given that one of the academic's self-proclaimed tasks is to defend great art from the barbarians, Presley was clearly more barbaric than most. Henry Pleasants writes:

> A phenomenon common to all the most original and the most influential of the great American popular singers has been the animosity they have aroused. It is not quite the right word. Loathing probably comes closer, or contempt.[1]

1. Henry Pleasants: *The Great American Popular Singers*, London: Victor Gollancz, 1974, p. 269. For the earliest and still most entertaining account of such contempt (which, in the end, the author shares) see Alan Levy: *Operation Elvis*, London: Andre Deutsch, 1960.

In this respect, Albert Goldman, though a fourth-rate scholar, is, alas, a university type.

What concerns me here more than the posturing of high academics, though, is Presley's place in popular music studies. In the last seventeen years, since his death, these have become respectable. There are now scholarly journals (*Popular Music, Popular Music And Society*), a scholarly organization (the International Association for the Study of Popular Music) and scholarly centres (such as the Institute of Popular Music at Liverpool University); there is a growing scholarly literature, and pop and rock have a developing place on school, college and university curricula. Where, amidst all this activity, is Elvis Presley?

In constructing 'popular music' as an object of study, academics have created their own rock canon, their own account of musical history and value. Elvis has a voice in this but an oddly muted one. Paul Taylor's 1985 guide to popular music literature lists ninety books on Presley, of which two might be described as academic (Jac L. Tharpe's collection, *Elvis: Images and Fancies*, and Neal and Janice Gregory's *When Elvis Died*); I know of only one subsequent academic study, Patsy G. Hammontree's *Elvis Presley: A Bio-Biography*.[2] In its first decade, *Popular Music* has not published a single article on Presley; in their five international conferences so far, IASPM members have not heard a single Presley paper.

One reason for this apparent lack of interest is that the scholars feel that they already know Elvis's place in the scheme of things. This becomes obvious when we turn to the basic academic books. John Shepherd's *Music as Social Text* has just two Presley references, one referring to his mix of 'parent culture' (country) and 'marginal' sounds (R&B), one suggesting that Presley's singing, like Buddy Holly's, 'reveals a marked innuendo of virile and individualistic masculine sexuality eminently successful in flouting the propriety of middle class sensibilities.'[3]

2. Paul Taylor: *Popular Music Since 1955: A Critical Guide to the Literature*, London: Mansell, 1985. And see, for confirmation, Mark W. Booth: *American Popular Music: A Reference Guide*, Westport, Connecticut: Greenwood Press, 1983. Patsy G. Hammontree: *Elvis Presley: A Bio-Biography*, London: Aldwych Press, 1985. This is essentially a reference book, complete with bibliography, filmography and discography, as well as a guide to Elvis interviews. It tells Presley's story by reference to the best primary sources, but makes no attempt to theorize or analyse.
3. John Shepherd: *Music as Social Text*, Cambridge: Polity, 1991, p. 146.

These two sorts of argument – musical and sociological – are developed by other scholars. Peter Wicke's *Rock Music: Culture, Aesthetics and Sociology* characteristically confines Presley's significance to the brief moment of rock 'n' roll's origins. Presley 'embodied the uncertain and consuming desire of American high school teenagers in the fifties, the desire somehow to escape the oppressive ordinariness which surrounded them without having to pay the bitter price of conformity'.[4] Iain Chambers's *Urban Rhythms: Pop Music and Popular Culture* situates Presley in the same moment, but focuses on what his 'Americanness' meant to Britons, with its 'suggestive combination of Latin good looks, country speech and manners, Negro sartorial taste and performance, and their musical equivalent in ballads, country music and R&B'. The 'force of Presley's voice and performance' meshed all this together in 'a new musical and cultural code'. Like Shepherd (if with a rather better sense of detail), Chambers sees Presley's importance as putting the 'black' into white popular music: 'What emerges from Presley and rock 'n' roll is the Atlantis of a previously largely unknown musical continent.'[5]

What we have here is popular music studies orthodoxy. On the one hand, Presley is heard as the boy who first and most powerfully put together black and white sounds to 'recode' mass music; on the other hand, he is recognized as the star who first and most powerfully caught the post-war mood of American (and then European) youth, who 'recoded' the teenager. His phenomenal success was an effect of his integration of these musical and social forces, but, from an academic point of view, what really matters is what Presley led to, and his own subsequent career is of no interest whatsoever. This argument is, perhaps, most obvious in the two most general academic texts, Charles Hamm's musicological *Yesterdays: Popular Song in America* and my own sociological *Sound Effects: Youth Leisure and the Politics of Rock and Roll*. We both refer to Presley with respect; we both acknowledge his historical importance; but for both of us he is, for the most part,

4. Peter Wicke: *Rock Music: Culture, Aesthetics and Sociology*, Cambridge: Cambridge University Press, 1990, p. 42.
5. Iain Chambers: *Urban Rhythms: Pop Music and Popular Culture*, London: Macmillan, 1985, pp. 36–37.

just a name to attach to an underlying logic of rock 'n' roll and youth culture.[6]

Two things are striking about this position. The first is that it is almost certainly misleading, misunderstanding both Presley's musical and sociological place and misreading popular music history. I haven't got the space to go into this further here, just to make the point that these academic Presley references depend not on scholarly research but simply on a rewriting of pop convention. The second point, which I do want to explore, is that, in these accounts, Elvis himself – as an artist, as a star – is not really the issue. He is treated rather as a symptom, a randomly chosen medium through which musical and social currents passed. 'If it hadn't been him,' we are constantly told, 'it would have been someone else.' But it *was* him, and the unanswered academic question is what difference that made – to the history of music, to the history of culture.

THE MUSICOLOGICAL ELVIS

In his wonderfully angry review of Goldman's Presley biography in the *Journal of the American Musicological Society* ('the first time that rock 'n' roll and Elvis Presley had been mentioned in that venerated journal in any context' – and, to my knowledge, the last), Charles Hamm makes the point that Goldman's high cultural dismissal of Presley's musical abilities reflected his own musical ignorance. Goldman, true to his debased form of academic orthodoxy, assumed, first, that Presley's success could have nothing to do with his sound (for Goldman, the Presley problem was precisely 'the incongruity between his limited talents and his limitless fame') and, second, that his sound was, anyway, too crude, naïve and sentimental to represent anything but a throwback to nineteenth-century ignorance and southern rural idiocy. Hamm concludes:

> This may be Goldman's story but it is not the story of early rock 'n' roll.
> The book is a disgrace. The publisher should withdraw it, and libraries

6. See Charles Hamm: *Yesterdays: Popular Song in America*, New York: Norton, 1979, pp. 403–8, and Simon Frith: *Sound Effects: Youth Leisure and the Politics of Rock and Roll*, New York: Pantheon, 1981, *passim*.

should reclassify it as fiction. Neither of these is likely to happen, though, so we musicologists should take matters into our own hands by beginning to produce responsible, disciplined studies of the music of our own time, against which such a book as *Elvis* could be measured, and by subjecting the literature on popular and vernacular music to the same critical scrutiny we lavish on other books.[7]

For all Hamm's earnest plea, though, few musicologists have since turned their attention to Elvis Presley himself. There are a couple of reasons for this, I think. The first problem is generic. The best studies of American vernacular music focus on specific musical forms – country, gospel, blues; Elvis seems marginal (if not a threat) to their concerns. Thus, in his exhaustive *Country Music USA*, Bill C. Malone devoted just two pages (out of 422) to Presley's career, and later admitted, 'I felt that Presley was a disrupter and that, as evidenced by the response given to him, the future of country music was dim.'[8] Similarly, Tony Heilbut's *The Gospel Sound* refers only to Presley's attendance at East Trigg Baptist Church, even though, as Charles Wolfe points out, both the history of white gospel music itself and a proper account of Presley's own musical aesthetic, need to take as much account of Presley the gospel singer as of Presley the country or blues singer: 'Some day, when the full story of modern southern gospel music has been told and placed in perspective, we can make some serious judgements about the origins of a singing style that changed the face of American popular music.'[9]

For country and gospel musicologists, then, the problem is that Presley's approach was hybrid while their primary concern is the 'purity' of a tradition and a style. For academic writers on blues and rhythm and blues, meanwhile, Presley is plainly derivative (this is the argument on which Goldman draws so relentlessly), therefore either not worth consider-

7. Charles Hamm: review of Albert Goldman's *Elvis* in the *Journal of the American Musicological Society*, 1982, p. 340.
8. Bill C. Malone: 'Elvis, Country Music and the South' in Jac L. Tharpe (ed.): *Elvis: Images and Fancies*, London: Star Books, 1983 (originally published in 1979 as a special issue of *The Southern Quarterly*), p. 124. And see Bill C. Malone: *Country Music USA*, Austin and London: University of Texas Press, 1968.
9. Charles Wolfe: 'Presley and the Gospel Tradition' in Tharpe, pp. 153–4. And see Tony Heilbut: *The Gospel Sound*, New York: Simon and Schuster, 1971.

ation at all (as in most blues studies) or only as an example of what Chapple and Garofalo call 'black roots, white fruits' – sociologically but not musically significant.[10]

The question of Presley's 'originality' leads to a second analytical problem. Academic musicology is a discipline rooted in the study of the composer and the score (rather than of the performer and the performance). Popular musicology, equally, focuses on composers, whether singer/songwriters (such as the Beatles and Dylan) or innovative instrumentalists (such as Jimi Hendrix). Presley neither wrote his own songs nor (it is assumed) arranged (or even chose) his own material; he was not an innovative instrumentalist. There is nothing here for a musicologist to study.

This is, again, to accept the popular myth of Elvis as primitive or puppet, and to ignore the obvious point that he was a profoundly creative musician – as a singer. (Musicologists have always had problems with the voice.) As Henry Pleasants puts it in his admirable study of Presley in *The Great American Popular Singers*, 'He has a voice. He has an art. He has always had them. No singer survives for nearly twenty years without them.'[11]

The most interesting musicological work on Presley is, therefore, focused on this voice and on how Presley, as an artist, used it. Pleasants himself gives a technical account of the unique 'confidence and inventiveness' (Charlie Gillett's terms) that rock fans and critics and historians have heard in Presley's early records, describing Elvis's 'extraordinary compass' and 'very wide range of vocal colour'.

> The voice covers about two octaves and a third, from the baritone's low G to the tenor's high B, with an upward extension in falsetto to at least a D flat. His best octave is in the middle, from about D flat to D flat, granting an extra full step either up or down. In this area, when he bears down with his breath on the cords, the voice has a fine, big, dark baritone quality. When he eases off, as he often does in ballads, he achieves a light mellow, seductive sound reminiscent of Bing Crosby, if rather breathier, with a wide

10. Steve Chapple and Reebee Garofalo: *Rock 'n' Roll Is Here To Pay*, Chicago: Nelson-Hall, 1977, pp. 242–6.
11. Pleasants, p. 274.

vibrato that he may have got from Billy Eckstine. Elvis' vibrato, however, is faster and less conspicuous. Call him a high baritone.

The voice has always been weak at the bottom, variable and unpredictable. At the top it is brilliant . . .[12]

To take Presley seriously as a singer in these terms is to take him seriously as a musician. To begin with, he clearly did 'arrange' his own material – it is dominated by his vocal style – and, in the only musical way that matters, 'wrote' it too. In Pleasants's words:

It is not merely a matter of timbre, of the quality, color or size of the voice as it is heard on any single pitch, or even as it might be heard in a vocal exercise. The sound becomes fully alive and distinctive only in the articulation of the musical phrase as shaped by the text and by the singer's identification with language. Elvis Presley's enunciation has not always been immaculate, although it can be as distinct as anybody's when he wants it to be. But he has never sung a phrase whose contours were not derived from his own native Southern American speech.[13]

Musically, then, Presley did know what he wanted: 'while deferring to Colonel Parker in promotional matters, he has been in charge of his own music-making.' Pleasants's insight here has been followed up most illuminatingly by Richard Middleton, in his study of Presley's use of 'romantic lyricism' and 'boogification'. In giving Presley's singing a close musical analysis, Middleton makes three significant points. First, Presley was a self-conscious technician – the choice of vocal attack, the making of musical decisions, the playing of genre games, can be heard in the songs themselves; this is not a matter of 'instinct'. Second, Presley was well aware that pop songs are implicitly about their own performance – and

12. Pleasants, pp. 274–5. One of the values of Pleasants's approach is that he places Presley in the history of American popular singers, and not just in terms of country/blues influences or as a teen rebellion against the mainstream. As Chris Spedding has more recently pointed out in *Musician*, Presley's early ambition to sound like Dean Martin should be taken seriously – in a comparison of Martin's 'Memories Are Made of This' and Presley's 'Don't Be Cruel', for example. See Michael Jarrett: 'Concerning the Progress of Rock & Roll', *South Atlantic Quarterly* 90(4), 1991, pp. 813–14.
13. Pleasants, p. 264.

their own performers; his 'narcissism' as a singer always had an ironic inflection, and the force and effect of that inflection – the rhetorical devices of embarrassment and seduction, sincerity and flippancy – were a key aspect of his appeal. Third, and perhaps most importantly, Presley's musical gifts were not momentary or accidental, something he 'had' in the Sun or early RCA days and then lost (or had stolen from him). He was always a vocal artist, a vocal technician, a vocal craftsman, even if he often had (at all times in his career) shoddy material on which to work (in this respect, Elvis Presley's art resembled more that of, say, Billie Holiday than that of a Chuck Berry or Hank Williams). As Middleton concludes (subtly varying the usual academic line), 'Elvis's originality, then, lay not so much in the cultural mix which he helped to bring into being – that was in the air and would have happened anyway – as in what he did with it'.[14]

THE SOCIOLOGICAL ELVIS

The sociological Elvis doesn't really exist. That is to say, sociologists have accepted the broad strokes of the comic-book Elvis story without ever investigating them. His relationship with Sam Phillips and Colonel Parker, the move from Sun to RCA, the years of bad movies, the return to public performance, the Las Vegas era – in as far as sociologists interested in 'the production of culture' refer to Elvis at all they refer to the facts gathered by Jerry Hopkins; they don't then measure them against more sophisticated accounts of how the music industry worked and changed between the 1950s and the 1970s. It is difficult on Hopkins's evidence, for example, to know whether Parker was a good or bad manager or, indeed, what these terms might mean, but it is noteworthy that Presley survived as a star more lucratively than any other white pop singer of his generation and that, in terms of, say, international marketing, the Hollywood strategy was far more effective than endless world touring. Just as musicologists have too often accepted the picture of Presley as musically

14. Richard Middleton: 'All Shook Up? Innovation and Continuity in Elvis Presley's Vocal Style' in Tharpe, p. 163. For Middleton's further thoughts on Presley, see his excellent *Studying Popular Music*, Milton Keynes: Open University Press, 1990, *passim*.

primitive, sociologists, too, have often treated Parker as economically primitive. This may or may not be the case; a proper analysis of Elvis Presley's career moves has yet to be made.

I find similar problems with the sociological tendency to treat Presley as uncomplicatedly a 'product' of his time or circumstances. Again this has become a sociological truism, but begs questions – questions, in fact, about his time and circumstances, questions not addressed by vague references to the South, to youth, to 'the 1950s' – and it takes a non-academic, Dave Marsh, to place Presley more precisely in history, to relate Presley's experience of school and work and family to specific effects of the New Deal.[15] The problem, as Marsh suggests, is that to treat Presley as a social symptom is to fall into the same condescending trap as the musicologists who treat him as a musical symptom: this denies Presley any agency, any character, any moral force.[16]

There is no rigorous sociological study, then, either of Elvis as commodity (the details of his various deals remain hidden in RCA's archives) or of Elvis as working-class hero (no one has even gone through the mass of memorabilia to analyse what a boy like Elvis – at that time, in that place – could have known or thought or felt). Rigorous sociological study has been concentrated, rather, on a different issue: the media Elvis. And what both Stephen Tucker's study of Presley's 1956 to 1965 magazine appearances and the Gregorys's exhaustive trawl through the coverage of Presley's death reveal is not just the gap between Elvis's image and reality but also, more importantly, the fact that the contours of Presley's life, the lineaments of his fame, were determined not by anything he said or did, but by the ideological needs and anxieties of the media themselves.[17]

This is to move into a different area of Presley scholarship, American studies, an area dominated by Greil Marcus who is not techically an academic but whose extraordinary 'Presliad' in *Mystery Train* is undoubt-

15. See Dave Marsh: 'Elvis: the New Deal Origins of Rock 'n' Roll' in *Musician*.
16. One of the few scholarly studies which manages a grand reading of Presley (as 'a radical romantic') without losing sight of the specificities of his experience is Van K. Brock: 'Images of Elvis, the South and America' in Tharpe.
17. See Stephen R. Tucker: 'Visions of Elvis: Changing Perceptions in National Magazines, 1956–1965' in Tharpe, and Neal and Janice Gregory: *When Elvis Died*, Washington, DC: Communications Press, 1980.

edly the most cited piece of Presley literature (and whose *Dead Elvis* greatly extends our understanding of the USA if not of Presley himself). And what most strikes me about the scholars who have followed in Marcus's footsteps is that, unlike his, their arguments seem less derived from what they hear, the records, than from what they've read about the records (which may define the academic approach). Thus, whether Elvis is dissected as an example of southern identity (as in Linda Ray Pratt's interesting account of his sentimentality) or placed in American literary tradition (as in Joan Kirkby's elegant account of his innocence and vulgarity), what seems to be at issue is less his music than his image.[18] The question that immediately arises is what, aesthetically, is being asserted: is Elvis the author or a character in such readings? And, if the latter, as seems to be the case, *who wrote him?*

THE CULTURAL STUDIES ELVIS

Contemporary cultural studies, the newest branch of academe to take a Presley interest, has a simple answer: his fans. In the early days of cultural studies this was merely a matter of reading Presley's meaning in his fan appeal. So, as Paul Willis explained:

> The assertive masculinity of the motor-bike boys also found an answering structure in their preferred music. Elvis Presley's records were full of aggression . . . his whole presence demanded that he should be given respect.[19]

But as subcultural theory has moved from a study of the 'homologies' between cultural forms and consumers' values to a more aggressive account of the culture created in the moment of consumption itself, so academics have begun to devote more time to the ethnography of fandom,

18. See Linda Ray Pratt: 'Elvis, or the Ironies of a Southern Identity', and Joan Kirkby: 'Memphis Faun: a View from Australia', both in Tharpe. I assume there is a considerable body of such work in American studies journals by now, but this is not a field I know much about.
19. Paul Willis: *Profane Culture*, London: Routledge, 1978, p. 71. For a feminist critique of this approach to Elvis through male fan fantasies, see Sue Wise: 'Sexing Elvis' in Simon Frith and Andrew Goodwin: *On Record*, New York: Pantheon, 1990.

more attention to the process of adoration. Thus, Lynn Spigel describes the dead Elvis as 'a semiotic system of preservation'. The most besotted Elvis fans, she argues, are not just engaged in a form of storytelling, but also in a politics of memory:

> Impersonation thus becomes a kind of interpretation, a reading strategy through which the performer revives a memory for a community of fans – a memory which they consider more authentic than scandal, hype and rumour.[20]

The impersonated Elvis is thus more true to life than the historical Elvis, more true, that is, to the Elvis experience: Elvis fans 'know' Presley in a way that gets beneath the encrustation of fame and fable.

If one problem of this sort of analysis is that Elvis Presley himself exists in it only as a figment – or series of figments – of some very odd imaginations, another is that the academic also begins to float free from the material, to lose any sense of reason. One Elvis story becomes as good as any other. 'Elvis is alive,' a prominent cultural studies academic tells Greil Marcus earnestly on a radio talk show. 'Not just in people's heads, but really, with a new face and a new life, courtesy of the FBI, the DEA . . .'

In February 1992, the *London Review of Books*, a quasi-academic journal, published a review of Greil Marcus's *Dead Elvis* which succinctly expressed the familiar academic attitude. Presley's career was reduced to cliché: 'His first year of stardom may have been subversive, but thereafter he settled in to become one of the most conservative, least adventurous of all pop singers.' The reviewer, Graham Coster, expressed the British snob's contempt for the craftsman:

> Elvis never said no to anything . . . He could be a rock 'n' roll singer, a gospel singer, a Christmas carol singer (frequently), a balladeer, a crooner – but he wasn't any of them. He was brilliant at turning his hand . . .

20. Lynn Spigel: 'Communicating With the Dead: Elvis as Medium', *Camera Obscura* 23, 1990, p. 184.

And the high cultural disdain for popularity: 'what looks like democracy is really only meretriciousness . . . People like Elvis because he gave them nothing to fear . . .'

> Presley's great skill, and great shallowness, was that he could make you forget what he was singing about. Death – as in 'Long Black Limousine'; poverty – as in 'In the Ghetto': he sang them into mawkish sentiment, song by song.[21]

The argument slips easily down. No, of course Elvis wasn't worth much in the great cultural scheme of things. No, of course he wasn't a real artist – 'there is no consistent, cumulative, considered body of work bequeathed to us'. How can we take this man seriously? But then I listen to the music again, and wonder at the layers of assumption through which Coster must hear things. I go back to those academics who are prepared to let Presley reach them directly.

> Elvis' is, in a word, an extraordinary voice – or many voices. In classical singers a multiplicty of voices is commonly the result of a singer's failure to achieve a uniform sound as the voice moves up and down the scale and through the register breaks. It is counted a fault unless the variety of color is related to characterization.
>
> In Elvis' early records, the multiplicity of voices is often clearly faulty, especially in ballads . . . in later years the vocal multiplicity has been rather a matter of idiom, with Elvis producing a sound for country, a sound for gospel, a sound for ballads, and a sound for rhythm-and-blues. He would seem always to have been a naturally assimilative musician, with an acute sense of style.[22]

The same basic description as Coster's but in a different tone, a tone blessedly free of the mannerisms of high-culture-looks-at-low-culture-and-sniffs.

21. Graham Coster: 'Uncle Vester's Nephew', *London Review of Books* 14(4), 1992, p. 22.
22. Pleasants, pp. 275–6.

Or Middleton: Elvis, he agrees, 'is all things to all men *throughout* his career', and he documents Presley's mastery of various song-types:

> The unifying factor is Elvis himself – or more precisely, Elvis constructed
> as a particular category: 'Elvis as romantic hero.' He turns all his songs
> into celebrations of his own power, exercises in self-presentation.[23]

Again, the same point as Coster's but spun to take account of what is in the songs (and not what Coster supposes to be in the heads of the listeners).

My conclusion is that the only academic studies of Presley that make any sense at all are those that begin with love and affection and bring all their scholarly skills to bear on its sources: the right academic question is: why does Elvis do this *to me*? The wrong question – leading to an equally mindless contempt for Elvis himself and/or admiration of his fans – is: why does he do it to other people? Coster quotes *Dead Elvis'* last sentence:

> The story shrinks then, down to the size of your favourite song, whatever it
> is – down to the size of whatever mystery *it* contains, whatever it was that
> made you like it then, and like it now.

He then dismisses it as the banal comfort of a late night DJ. The point, though, is that anyone who doesn't *hear* the mystery in Presley's music (or in any other art) should not be writing about it.

23. Middleton in Tharpe, pp. 164–5.

ALAN CLAYSON
Selective Bibliography

Such is the volume of literary spin-offs both before and after his death that someone ought to write a book about books about Elvis. Even while the corpse was still warm, publishers were liaising with authors and, within weeks, a dam burst on a river of Presley-centred manuscripts ranging from scurrilous trash to well-researched, scholarly works that any historical figure of his stature would warrant. There surfaced, too, countless volumes containing raw information that only the most crazed devotee would not find too insignificant to be interesting.

Therefore, rather than attempt a long – and probably incomplete – list of dry titles for further reading, it makes more sense to compile a selection with brief commentary of prototypical accounts of particular aspects of Elvis Presley's life and artistic output.

Elvis Presley: His Complete Life Story in words and Illustrated with more than One Hundred Pictures (London Illustrated Publications, 1956). Neither a triumph of linguistic ability nor a penetrating insight into the human condition of Elvis, this advisedly anonymous assignment was, nevertheless, the first of more Presley biographies than anyone in 1956 could ever have comprehended.

Hopkins, Jerry: *Elvis: The Final Years* (W. H. Allen, 1980). This brings up to date 1972's *Elvis: A Biography*, written by Hopkins and Hunter Davies – and is still accepted by most as the standard work.

Goldman, Albert: *Elvis* (Allen Lane, 1981).
Intricately-researched muckraking, this must be read with the understanding that the good doctor disliked both Elvis and pop, and that he did it for the money.

Brewer-Giorgio, Gail: *Is Elvis Alive?* (1988).
Self-deception, genuine belief and seemingly irrefutable evidence mingle in this fantasy that Elvis is alive and well and living in Michigan.

Tobler, John, and Bates, Graham: *The A–Z of Elvis* (Mason's Music, 1982).
A most comprehensive reference work that lists and provides basic facts about the films, song titles, people and places in Presley's life.

Wertheimer, Alfred: *Elvis '56: In the Beginning* (Cassell, 1980).
A first-hand – and first-rate – photographic essay with detailed text of 'the last moments before the man became a legend'.

Stanley, David: *Life with Elvis* (Marc Europe, 1986).
One of the more compassionate 'insider' efforts, this is a stepbrother's weighing of experience and recounting of many unfamiliar anecdotes.

Stern, Jane and Michael: *Elvis World* (Bloomsbury, 1987).
Supplemented by high-quality illustrations, a most balanced and entertaining overview not only of the music and the films but also of the fans and the kitsch.

Rijff, Ger: *Long Lonely Highway* (Pierian, 1988).
An intriguing compilation of press cuttings and media snippets that go part way to recreating the feeling of being there during Presley's climb to fame.

Slaughter, Todd: *Elvis Presley* (Wyndham, 1977).
Half-finished by the time of Presley's death, this concise biography by the long-time organizer of the King's official fan club is recommended for both beginners and experts.

Marsh, Dave: *Elvis* (Elm Tree Books, 1982).
While not definitive, this coffee-table tome, instigated by *Rolling Stone* magazine, is essential to those who want to know how it all began and how it kept going.

Hawkins, Martin, and Escott, Colin: *Elvis Presley – The Illustrated Discography* (Omnibus, 1981).
A straightforward guide to the fellow's recording career with session details, UK and US release dates, catalogue numbers and album and EP track listings – all riven with a potted year-by-year biography.

Harper, Betty: *Suddenly and Gently: Visions of Elvis through the Art of Betty Harper* (Sidgwick and Jackson, 1987).

The title says it all about this visual hagiography aimed at those for whom Elvis sits at the right hand of God – though, as a representational artist, Betty is no Raphael.

Farren, Mick, and Marchbank, Pearce (ed.): *In his own Words* (Omnibus, 1977).
This selection of categorized quotes is as near to an autobiography as you'll ever find.

Cotten, Lee, and De Witt, Howard A.: *Jailhouse Rock: The Bootleg Records of Elvis Presley* (Pierian, 1983).
If rather humourless, this exhaustive and alphabetical annotation of illicit releases represents awesome dedication on the part of the authors – who also include counterfeits (and how to distinguish them from official recordings) and videos.

Henderson, William McCranor: *Stark Raving Elvis* (W. H. Allen, 1985).
An amusing novel in which a factory assembly-line nobody and part-time Elvis impersonator believes that the King has nominated him as heir apparent.

Marcus, Greil: *Dead Elvis* (Viking, 1992).
The author of *Mystery Train* and *Lipstick Traces* explores beyond-the-grave Presley phenomena in an anthology of post-1977 writings, both light-hearted and deadly serious.

Doll, Susan (ed.): *Elvis: A Tribute to his Life* (Omnibus, 1990).
An expensive but lavishly produced photo/text eulogy that his fans loved – and very much the sort of book that Elvis himself might have approved.

Rijff, Ger: *Return to Sender* (Pierian, 1988).
A complete discography of Presley tribute discs – soundalikes, novelties, narratives *et al.* – from 1956 to 1986, containing photographs of the more unusual merchandise.

Tharpe, Jac L. (ed.): *Elvis: Images and Fancies* (Star, 1983).
Though it might help to have a dictionary close to hand, there is much food for thought in the essays – with titles like 'Innovation and Continuity in Elvis' Vocal Style' – by staff and students from the University of Southern Mississippi.

PETER DOGGETT

Complete Discography of Official
Elvis Presley Recordings 1953—1977

In July 1953, a nervous eighteen-year-old ventured into the offices of the Memphis Recording Service to cut a private acetate. Twenty-four years later, a sick, bloated forty-two-year-old was taped for his final, chilling in-concert TV special.

Listed below is what happened in between – a complete chronicle of Elvis Presley's recording career. Besides his studio sessions and the concert appearances that were officially taped and mastered by RCA, the discography below also includes private tapes and acetates that have been made available to RCA since Elvis's death in August 1977.

The single, EP, LP or CD on which each track first appeared is also detailed, based on the original American release schedule rather than the revamped albums that often appeared outside the USA.

JULY 1953
'My Happiness' – *Great Performances* CD
'That's When Your Heartaches Begin' – *The Complete 50s Masters* box set

JANUARY 1954
'I'll Never Stand In Your Way' – unissued
'Casual Love Affair' – unissued

5 JULY 1954
'I Love You Because' (master) – *Elvis Presley* LP
'I Love You Because' (take 1) – *The Complete Sun Sessions* LP
'I Love You Because' (take 2) – *A Legendary Performer Vol. 1* LP
'I Love You Because' (take 3) – *The Complete Sun Sessions* LP
'I Love You Because' (take 4) – *The Complete Sun Sessions* LP
'I Love You Because' (take 5) – *The Complete Sun Sessions* LP
'Harbour Lights' – *A Legendary Performer Vol. 2* LP

'Harbour Lights' – *The Complete Sun Sessions* LP
'That's All Right, Mama' – single A-side
'That's All Right, Mama' – *The Complete Sun Sessions* LP

6 JULY 1954
'Blue Moon Of Kentucky' – single B-side
'Blue Moon Of Kentucky' – *A Golden Celebration* box set

19 AUGUST 1954
'Blue Moon' – *The Complete 50s Masters* box set
'Blue Moon' – *Elvis Presley* LP

10 SEPTEMBER 1954
'Tomorrow Night' – *Reconsider Baby* LP
'Tomorrow Night' (overdubbed) – *Elvis for Everyone* LP
'I'll Never Let You Go' – *Elvis Presley* LP
'I'll Never Let You Go' – *The Complete Sun Sessions* LP
'Just Because' – *Elvis Presley* LP
'Satisfied' – unissued
'I Don't Care If The Sun Don't Shine' – single B-side
'I Don't Care If the Sun Don't Shine' – *The Complete Sun Sessions* LP
'Good Rockin' Tonight' – single A-side

16 OCTOBER 1954
'That's All Right, Mama' (live) – *Elvis: The Hillbilly Cat* LP
'Blue Moon Of Kentucky' (live) – *Elvis: The Hillbilly Cat* LP

10 DECEMBER 1954
'Milkcow Blues Boogie' – single A-side
'You're A Heartbreaker' – single B-side
'My Baby's Gone' (take 7) – *The Complete Sun Sessions* LP
'My Baby's Gone' (take 8) – *The Complete Sun Sessions* LP
'My Baby's Gone' (take 9) – *The Complete Sun Sessions* LP
'My Baby's Gone' (take 10) – *The Complete Sun Sessions* LP
'My Baby's Gone' (take 11) – *The Complete Sun Sessions* LP
'My Baby's Gone' (take 12) – *The Complete Sun Sessions* LP
'My Baby's Gone' (take 13) – *The Complete Sun Sessions* LP
'I'm Left, You're Right, She's Gone' – single B-side

18 DECEMBER 1954
'Tweedle Dee' (live) – *The First Live Recordings* LP

5 FEBRUARY 1955
'Baby Let's Play House' – single A-side
'I Got A Woman' – unissued
'Trying To Get To You' – unissued

circa MARCH 1955
'Fool, Fool, Fool' – *The Complete 50s Masters* box set
'Shake, Rattle & Roll' – *The Complete 50s Masters* box set

MARCH 1955
'Good Rockin' Tonight' (live) – *The First Years* LP
'Baby Let's Play House' (live) – *The First Years* LP
'Blue Moon Of Kentucky' (live) – *The First Years* LP
'I Got A Woman' (live) – *The First Years* LP
'That's All Right, Mama' (live) – *The First Years* LP

11 JULY 1955
'I Forgot To Remember To Forget' – single B-side
'Mystery Train' – single A-side
'Trying To Get To You' – *Elvis Presley* LP

AUGUST 1955
'Baby Let's Play House' (live) – *The First Live Recordings* LP
'Maybelline' (live) – *The First Live Recordings* LP
'That's All Right, Mama' (live) – *The First Live Recordings* LP

SEPTEMBER 1955
'When It Rains, It Really Pours' – *A Legendary Performer Vol. 4* LP

10 JANUARY 1956
'I Got A Woman' – *Elvis Presley* LP
'Heartbreak Hotel' – single A-side
'Money Honey' – *Elvis Presley* LP

11 JANUARY 1956
'I'm Counting On You' – *Elvis Presley* LP
'I Was The One' – single B-side

28 JANUARY 1956
'Shake, Rattle & Roll'/'Flip Flop & Fly' (live) – *This Is Elvis* LP
'I Got A Woman' (live) – *A Golden Celebration* box set

30 JANUARY 1956
'Blue Suede Shoes' – *Elvis Presley* LP
'My Baby Left Me' – single B-side
'One-Sided Love Affair' – *Elvis Presley* LP
'So Glad You're Mine' – *Elvis* LP

31 JANUARY 1956
'I'm Gonna Sit Right Down And Cry Over You' – *Elvis Presley* LP
'Tutti Frutti' – *Elvis Presley* LP

3 FEBRUARY 1956
'Lawdy Miss Clawdy' – single B-side
'Shake, Rattle & Roll' – single A-side
'Lawdy Miss Clawdy' – *The Complete 50s Masters* box set
'Shake, Rattle & Roll' – *The Complete 50s Masters* box set

4 FEBRUARY 1956
'Baby Let's Play House' (live) – *A Golden Celebration* box set
'Tutti Frutti' (live) – *A Golden Celebration* box set

11 FEBRUARY 1956
'Blue Suede Shoes' (live) – *A Golden Celebration* box set
'Heartbreak Hotel' (live) – *A Golden Celebration* box set

18 FEBRUARY 1956
'Tutti Frutti' (live) – *A Golden Celebration* box set
'I Was the One' (live) – *A Golden Celebration* box set

17 MARCH 1956
'Blue Suede Shoes' (live) – *A Golden Celebration* box set
'Heartbreak Hotel' (live) – *This Is Elvis* LP

24 MARCH 1956
'Money Honey' (live) – *A Golden Celebration* box set
'Heartbreak Hotel' (live) – *A Golden Celebration* box set

3 APRIL 1956
'Shake, Rattle & Roll' (live) – *A Golden Celebration* box set
'Heartbreak Hotel' (live) – *A Golden Celebration* box set
'Blue Suede Shoes' (live) – *A Golden Celebration* box set

11 APRIL 1956
'I Want You, I Need You, I Love You' – single A-side
'I Want You, I Need You, I Love You' – *A Legendary Performer Vol. 2* LP
'I Want You, I Need You, I Love You' – *The Complete 50s Masters* box set

6 MAY 1956
'Heartbreak Hotel' (live) – *Elvis Aron Presley* box set
'Long Tall Sally' (live) – *Elvis Aron Presley* box set
'Blue Suede Shoes' (live) – *Elvis Aron Presley* box set
'Money Honey' (live) – *Elvis Aron Presley* box set

5 JUNE 1956
'Hound Dog' (live) – *This Is Elvis* LP
'I Want You, I Need You, I Love You' (live) – *A Golden Celebration* box set

1 JULY 1956
'I Want You, I Need You, I Love You' (live) – *A Golden Celebration* box set
'Hound Dog' (live) – *A Golden Celebration* box set

2 JULY 1956
'Hound Dog' – single B-side
'Don't Be Cruel' – single A-side
'Any Way You Want Me' – single B-side

2 AUGUST 1956
'Love Me Tender' – single A-side
'Poor Boy' – *Love Me Tender* EP
'We're Gonna Move' – *Love Me Tender* EP
'We're Gonna Move' (take 4) – *The Complete 50s Masters* box set
'Let Me' – *Love Me Tender* EP
'Love Me Tender' – *Essential Elvis* CD

1 SEPTEMBER 1956
'Playing for Keeps' – single B-side
'Love Me' – *Elvis* LP
'How Do You Think I Feel' – *Elvis* LP
'How's The World Treating You' – *Elvis* LP

2 SEPTEMBER 1956
'Paralyzed' – *Elvis* LP
'When My Blue Moon Turns To Gold Again' – *Elvis* LP
'Long Tall Sally' – *Elvis* LP
'Old Shep' – *Elvis* LP
'Old Shep' – *Elvis* LP (UK only)
'Old Shep' – *The Complete 50s Masters* box set
'Too Much' – single A-side

3 SEPTEMBER 1956
'Anyplace Is Paradise' – *Elvis* LP
'Ready Teddy' – *Elvis* LP
'First In Line' – *Elvis* LP
'Rip It Up' – *Elvis* LP

9 SEPTEMBER 1956
'Don't Be Cruel' (live) – *A Golden Celebration* box set
'Love Me Tender' (live) – *A Golden Celebration* box set
'Ready Teddy' (live) – *A Golden Celebration* box set
'Hound Dog' (live) – *A Golden Celebration* box set

26 SEPTEMBER 1956
'Heartbreak Hotel' (live) – *A Golden Celebration* box set

'Long Tall Sally' (live) – *A Golden Celebration* box set
'I Was the One' (live) – *A Golden Celebration* box set
'I Want You, I Need You, I Love You' (live) – *A Golden Celebration* box set
'I Got A Woman' (live) – *A Golden Celebration* box set
'Don't Be Cruel' (live) – *A Golden Celebration* box set
'Ready Teddy' (live) – *A Golden Celebration* box set
'Love Me Tender' (live) – *A Golden Celebration* box set
'Hound Dog' (live) – *A Golden Celebration* box set
'Love Me Tender' (live) – *A Golden Celebration* box set
'I Was The One' (live) – *A Golden Celebration* box set
'I Got A Woman' (live) – *A Golden Celebration* box set
'Don't Be Cruel' (live) – *A Golden Celebration* box set
'Blue Suede Shoes' (live) – *A Golden Celebration* box set
'Baby Let's Play House' (live) – *A Golden Celebration* box set
'Hound Dog' (live) – *A Golden Celebration* box set

28 OCTOBER 1956
'Don't Be Cruel' (live) – *A Golden Celebration* box set
'Love Me Tender' (live) – *A Golden Celebration* box set
'Love Me' (live) – *A Golden Celebration* box set
'Hound Dog' (live) – *A Golden Celebration* box set

4 DECEMBER 1956
'Million Dollar Quartet' jam session – *The Million Dollar Quartet* LP

16 DECEMBER 1956
'I Was The One' (live) – unissued
'Love Me Tender' (live) – unissued
'Hound Dog' (live) – *The First Live Recordings* LP

6 JANUARY 1957
'Hound Dog' (live) – *A Golden Celebration* box set
'Love Me Tender' (live) – *A Golden Celebration* box set
'Heartbreak Hotel' (live) – *A Golden Celebration* box set
'Don't Be Cruel' (live) – *This Is Elvis* LP
'Too Much' (live) – *A Golden Celebration* box set

'When My Blue Moon Turns To Gold Again' (live) – *A Golden Celebration* box set

'Peace In The Valley' (live) – *A Golden Celebration* box set

12 JANUARY 1957

'I Believe' – *Peace In The Valley* EP

'Tell Me Why' – single A-side

'Got A Lot O' Livin' To Do' – *Loving You* LP

'All Shook Up' – single A-side

13 JANUARY 1957

'Mean Woman Blues' – *Loving You* LP

'Mean Woman Blues' – *Essential Elvis Vol. 2* LP

'Peace In The Valley' – *Peace In The Valley* EP

'Peace In The Valley' – *Essential Elvis Vol. 2* LP

'Peace In The Valley' – *Essential Elvis Vol. 2* LP

'I Beg Of You' (take 1) – *Essential Elvis Vol. 2* LP

'I Beg Of You' (take 6) – *Essential Elvis Vol. 2* LP

'I Beg Of You' (take 8) – *Essential Elvis Vol. 2* LP

'I Beg Of You' (take 12) – *Essential Elvis Vol. 2* LP

'That's When Your Heartaches Begin' – single B-side

'That's When Your Heartaches Begin' (take 4) – *Essential Elvis Vol. 2* LP

'That's When Your Heartaches Begin' (take 5) – *Essential Elvis Vol. 2* LP

'That's When Your Heartaches Begin' (take 6) – *Essential Elvis Vol. 2* LP

'Take My Hand, Precious Lord' – *Peace In The Valley* EP

15–18 JANUARY, 14 FEBRUARY 1957

'Lonesome Cowboy' – *Loving You* LP

'Party' – *Loving You* LP

'Party' – *Essential Elvis* LP

'Hot Dog' – *Loving You* LP

'Got A Lot O' Livin' To Do' – *Essential Elvis* LP

'Mean Woman Blues' – *This Is Elvis* LP

'Loving You' (fast, take 1) – *Essential Elvis* LP

'Loving You' (fast, take 8) – *Essential Elvis* CD

'Loving You' (fast, takes 20/21) – *Essential Elvis* LP

'Loving You' (slow, take 10) – *Essential Elvis* LP
'Loving You' (slow, take 14) – *The Complete 50s Masters* box set

19 JANUARY 1957
'It Is No Secret' – *Peace In The Valley* EP
'It Is No Secret' (take 1) – *Essential Elvis Vol. 2* LP
'It Is No Secret' (take 2) – *Essential Elvis Vol. 2* LP
'It Is No Secret' (take 3) – *Essential Elvis Vol. 2* LP
'Blueberry Hill' – *Just For You* EP
'Blueberry Hill' – *Essential Elvis Vol. 2* LP
'Blueberry Hill' – *Essential Elvis Vol. 2* LP
'Have I Told You Lately That I Love You' – *Just For You* EP
'Have I Told You Lately That I Love You' (take 2) – *Essential Elvis Vol. 2* LP
'Have I Told You Lately That I Love You' (take 6) – *Essential Elvis Vol. 2* LP
'Have I Told You Lately That I Love You' (take 12) – *Essential Elvis Vol. 2* LP
'Have I Told You Lately That I Love You' (take 13) – *Essential Elvis Vol. 2* LP
'Is It So Strange' – *Just For You* EP
'Is It So Strange' (take 1) – *Essential Elvis Vol. 2* LP
'Is It So Strange' (take 7) – *Essential Elvis Vol. 2* LP
'Is It So Strange' (take 11) – *Essential Elvis Vol. 2* LP

24 JANUARY 1957
'Teddy Bear' – single A-side
'One Night' – *A Legendary Performer Vol. 4* LP

23 FEBRUARY 1957
'Don't Leave Me Now' – *Loving You* LP
'I Beg Of You' – single A-side
'One Night' – single A-side
'True Love' – *Loving You* LP
'I Need You So' – *Just For You* EP

24 FEBRUARY 1957
'Loving You' – single A-side
'When It Rains, It Really Pours' – *Elvis For Everyone* LP

30 APRIL 1957
'Jailhouse Rock' – single A-side
'Jailhouse Rock' – *Essential Elvis* LP
'Jailhouse Rock' – *Essential Elvis* LP
'Young And Beautiful' – *Jailhouse Rock* EP
'Young and Beautiful' – *Essential Elvis* LP
'Treat Me Nice' – *Essential Elvis* LP
'I Want To Be Free' – *Jailhouse Rock* EP
'Don't Leave Me Now' – *Jailhouse Rock* EP
'Baby I Don't Care' – *Jailhouse Rock* EP
'Baby I Don't Care' – *Essential Elvis* LP

5 SEPTEMBER 1957
'Treat Me Nice' – single B-side
'Blue Christmas' – *Elvis' Christmas Album* LP

6 SEPTEMBER 1957
'My Wish Came True' – single B-side
'White Christmas' – *Elvis' Christmas Album* LP
'Here Comes Santa Claus' – *Elvis' Christmas Album* LP
'Silent Night' – *Elvis' Christmas Album* LP
'Don't' – single A-side

7 SEPTEMBER 1957
'O Little Town Of Bethlehem' – *Elvis' Christmas Album* LP
'Santa Bring My Baby Back To Me' – *Elvis' Christmas Album* LP
'Santa Claus Is Back In Town' – *Elvis' Christmas Album* LP
'I'll Be Home For Christmas' – *Elvis' Christmas Album* LP

15 JANUARY 1958
'Hard Headed Woman' – single A-side
'Trouble' – *King Creole* LP
'New Orleans' – *King Creole* LP
'King Creole' – *Essential Elvis Vol. 3* LP
'King Creole' – *Essential Elvis Vol. 3* LP
'Crawfish' – *King Creole* LP
'Crawfish' – *Essential Elvis Vol. 3* LP

16 JANUARY 1958
'Dixieland Rock' – *King Creole* LP
'Lover Doll' – *King Creole* LP
'Don't Ask Me Why' – Single B-side
'As Long As I Have You' – *King Creole* LP
'Steadfast, Loyal and True' – *King Creole* LP
'As Long As I Have You' – *Essential Elvis Vol. 3* LP
'As Long As I Have You' – *Essential Elvis Vol. 3* CD
'Steadfast, Loyal and True' – *Essential Elvis Vol. 3* LP

23 JANUARY 1958
'King Creole' – *King Creole* LP
'Young Dreams' – *King Creole* LP
'Danny' – *A Legendary Performer Vol. 3* LP
'My Wish Came True' – unissued
'Doncha' Think It's Time' – unissued

1 FEBRUARY 1958
'My Wish Came True' – unissued
'Doncha' Think It's Time' (take 47) – *Essential Elvis Vol. 3* CD
'Doncha' Think It's Time' (take 48) – *Essential Elvis Vol. 3* CD
'Doncha' Think It's Time' – single B-side
'Doncha' Think It's Time' – *50,000,000 Elvis Fans Can't Be Wrong* LP
'Your Cheatin' Heart' – *The EP Collection Vol. 2* box set
'Your Cheatin' Heart' – *Elvis For Everyone* LP
'Wear My Ring Around Your Neck' – single A-side

10 JUNE 1958
'I Need Your Love Tonight' (take 2) – *Essential Elvis Vol. 3* LP
'I Need Your Love Tonight' (take 5) – *Essential Elvis Vol. 3* LP
'I Need Your Love Tonight' (take 10) – *Essential Elvis Vol. 3* LP
'I Need Your Love Tonight' – single B-side
'A Big Hunk O' Love' – *Essential Elvis Vol. 3* LP
'A Big Hunk O' Love' – single A-side
'Ain't That Loving You Baby' (take 1) – *Essential Elvis Vol. 3* LP
'Ain't That Loving You Baby' (take 5) – *Essential Elvis Vol. 3* LP
'Ain't That Loving You Baby' (take 11) – *Essential Elvis Vol. 3* LP

'Ain't That Loving You Baby' – single A-side
'A Fool Such As I' – single A-side
'A Fool Such As I' – *Essential Elvis Vol. 3* LP

11 JUNE 1958
'I Got Stung' (take 1) – *Essential Elvis Vol. 3* LP
'I Got Stung' (take 12) – *Essential Elvis Vol. 3* CD
'I Got Stung' (take 13) – *Essential Elvis Vol. 3* LP
'I Got Stung' (take 14) – *Essential Elvis Vol. 3* LP
'I Got Stung' – single B-side

circa. 1959
'Danny Boy' – *A Golden Celebration* box set
'Soldier Boy' – *A Golden Celebration* box set
'The Fool' – *A Golden Celebration* box set
'Earth Angel' – *A Golden Celebration* box set
'He's Only A Prayer Away' – *A Golden Celebration* box set

1960s (undated recordings)
'Dark Moon' – *A Golden Celebration* box set
'My Heart Cries For Me' – *A Golden Celebration* box set
'Write To Me From Naples' – *A Golden Celebration* box set
'Suppose' – *A Golden Celebration* box set

20 MARCH 1960
'Make Me Know It' – *Elvis Is Back* LP
'Soldier Boy' – *Elvis Is Back* LP

21 MARCH 1960
'Stuck On You' – single A-side
'Fame And Fortune' – single B-side
'Fame And Fortune' – *A Legendary Performer Vol. 3* LP
'A Mess Of Blues' – single B-side
'It Feels So Right' – *Elvis Is Back* LP

26 MARCH 1960
'Fame and Fortune' (live) – unissued

'Stuck On You' (live) – unissued
'Witchcraft'/'Love Me Tender' (live) – *From Nashville To Memphis* box set

3 APRIL 1960
'Fever' – *Elvis Is Back* LP
'Like A Baby' – *Elvis Is Back* LP
'Like A Baby' – *Collectors Gold* box set
'It's Now Or Never' – single A-side
'It's Now Or Never' – *From Nashville To Memphis* box set

4 APRIL 1960
'The Girl Of My Best Friend' – *Elvis Is Back* LP
'Dirty, Dirty Feeling' – *Elvis Is Back* LP
'The Thrill Of Your Love' – *Elvis Is Back* LP
'I Gotta Know' – single B-side
'Such A Night' – *Elvis Is Back* LP
'Such A Night' – *A Legendary Performer Vol. 2* LP
'Are You Lonesome Tonight' – single A-side
'Girl Next Door Went A-Walkin'' – *Elvis Is Back* LP
'I Will Be Home Again' – *Elvis Is Back* LP
'Reconsider Baby' – *Elvis Is Back* LP

27 APRIL 1960
'Shoppin' Around' – *Elvis Aron Presley* box set
'Didja' Ever' – *G.I. Blues* LP
'Doin' The Best I Can' – *G.I. Blues* LP
'Doin' The Best I Can' – *The EP Collection Vol. 2* box set
'G.I. Blues' – *G.I. Blues* LP
'G.I. Blues' – *The EP Collection Vol. 2* box set
'G.I. Blues' – *Collectors Gold* box set
'Frankfort Special' – *A Legendary Performer Vol. 3* LP

28 APRIL 1960
'Tonight Is So Right For Love' – *G.I. Blues* LP
'What's She Really Like' – *G.I. Blues* LP
'What's She Really Like' – *The EP Collection Vol. 2* box set
'Big Boots' – *Elvis Sings For Children & For Grownups Too* LP

'Big Boots' – unissued
'Pocketful of Rainbows' – *The EP Collection Vol. 2* box set
'Pocketful of Rainbows' – *Collectors Gold* box set
'Blue Suede Shoes' – *G.I. Blues* LP
'Wooden Heart' – *G.I. Blues* LP
'Wooden Heart' – *A Legendary Performer Vol. 4* LP

6 MAY 1960
'Big Boots' – *G.I. Blues* LP
'Shoppin' Around' – *G.I. Blues* LP
'Pocketful of Rainbows' – *G.I. Blues* LP
'Frankfort Special' – *G.I. Blues* LP
'Tonight's All Right For Love' – *A Legendary Performer Vol. 1* LP
'Tonight's All Right For Love' – *Elvis Aron Presley* box set
'Big Boots' – *G.I. Blues* LP
'Big Boots' – *Collectors Gold* box set

8 AUGUST 1960
'Summer Kisses, Winter Tears' – *Elvis By Request: Flaming Star* EP
'Summer Kisses, Winter Tears' – *Collectors Gold* box set
'Flaming Star' – *Elvis By Request: Flaming Star* EP
'A Cane And A High Starched Collar' – *A Legendary Performer Vol. 2* LP
'Britches' – *A Legendary Performer Vol. 3* LP
'Black Star' – *Collectors Gold* box set

30 OCTOBER 1960
'Milky White Way' – *His Hand In Mine* LP
'His Hand In Mine' – *His Hand In Mine* LP
'I Believe In The Man In The Sky' – *His Hand In Mine* LP
'He Knows Just What I Need' – *His Hand In Mine* LP
'Surrender' – single A-side
'Surrender' – *From Nashville to Memphis* box set
'Mansion Over the Hilltop' – *His Hand In Mine* LP

31 OCTOBER 1960
'In My Father's House' – *His Hand In Mine* LP
'Joshua Fit The Battle' – *His Hand In Mine* LP

'Swing Down Sweet Chariot' – *His Hand In Mine* LP
'I'm Gonna Walk Dem Golden Stairs' – *His Hand In Mine* LP
'If We Never Meet Again' – *His Hand In Mine* LP
'Known Only To Him' – *His Hand In Mine* LP
'Crying In The Chapel' – single A-side
'Working On A Building' – *His Hand In Mine* LP

7 NOVEMBER 1960
'Lonely Man' – single B-side
'Lonely Man' – *Collectors Gold* box set
'In My Way' – *Elvis For Everyone* LP
'Wild In The Country' – Single B-side
'Wild In The Country' – *Elvis Aron Presley* box set
'Forget Me Never' – *Elvis For Everyone* LP

8 NOVEMBER 1960
'I Slipped, I Stumbled, I Fell' – *Something For Everybody* LP
'I Slipped, I Stumbled, I Fell' – *Collectors Gold* box set

12 MARCH 1961
'I'm Comin' Home' – *Something For Everybody* LP
'Gently' – *Something For Everybody* LP
'Gently' – *Collectors Gold* box set
'In Your Arms' – *Something For Everybody* LP
'Give Me The Right' – *Something For Everybody* LP
'Give Me The Right' – *Collectors Gold* box set
'I Feel So Bad' – single A-side
'It's A Sin' – *Something For Everybody* LP
'I Want You With Me' – *Something For Everybody* LP
'I Want You With Me' – *Collectors Gold* box set
'There's Always Me' – *Something For Everybody* LP
'There's Always Me' – *Collectors Gold* box set

13 MARCH 1961
'Starting Today' – *Something For Everybody* LP
'Sentimental Me' – *Something For Everybody* LP
'Judy' – *Something For Everybody* LP

'Judy' – *The EP Collection Vol. 2* box set
'Put The Blame On Me' – *Something For Everybody* LP

21 MARCH 1961
'Hawaiian Sunset' – *Blue Hawaii* LP
'Aloha Oe' – *Blue Hawaii* LP
'Ku-u-i-po' – *Blue Hawaii* LP
'No More' – *Blue Hawaii* LP
'Slicin' Sand' – *Blue Hawaii* LP

22 MARCH 1961
'Blue Hawaii' – *Blue Hawaii* LP
'Ito Eats' – *Blue Hawaii* LP
'Hawaiian Wedding Song' – *Blue Hawaii* LP –
'Island Of Love' – *Blue Hawaii* LP
'Steppin' Out Of Line' – unissued
'Steppin' Out Of Line' – *Pot Luck* LP
'Almost Always True' – *Blue Hawaii* LP
'Moonlight Swim – *Blue Hawaii* LP

23 MARCH 1961
'Can't Help Falling In Love' – *Blue Hawaii* LP
'Can't Help Falling In Love' – *Elvis Aron Presley* box set
'Can't Help Falling In Love' – unissued
'Beach Boy Blues' – *Blue Hawaii* LP
'Rock-a-Hula Baby' – *Blue Hawaii* LP

25 MARCH 1961
'Heartbreak Hotel' (live) – *Elvis Aron Presley* box set
'All Shook Up' (live) – *Elvis Aron Presley* box set
'A Fool Such As I' (live) – *Elvis Aron Presley* box set
'I Got A Woman' (live) – *Elvis Aron Presley* box set
'Love Me' (live) – *Elvis Aron Presley* box set
'Such A Night' (live) – *Elvis Aron Presley* box set
'Reconsider Baby' (live) – *Elvis Aron Presley* box set
'I Need Your Love Tonight' (live) – *Elvis Aron Presley* box set
'That's All Right, Mama' (live) – *Elvis Aron Presley* box set

'Don't Be Cruel' (live) – *Elvis Aron Presley* box set
'One Night' (live) – *Elvis Aron Presley* box set
'Are You Lonesome Tonight' (live) – *Elvis Aron Presley* box set
'It's Now Or Never' (live) – *Elvis Aron Presley* box set
'Swing Down Sweet Chariot' (live) – *Elvis Aron Presley* box set
'Hound Dog' (live) – *Elvis Aron Presley* box set

25 JUNE 1961
'Kiss Me Quick' – *Pot Luck* LP
'That's Someone You Never Forget' – *Pot Luck* LP

26 JUNE 1961
'I'm Yours' – *Pot Luck* LP
'I'm Yours' – *From Nashville To Memphis* box set
'His Latest Flame' – single A-side
'His Latest Flame' – *The EP Collection Vol. 2* box set
'His Latest Flame' – *From Nashville To Memphis* box set
'Little Sister' – single B-side
'Little Sister' – *The EP Collection Vol. 2* box set

5 JULY 1961
'Angel' – *Follow That Dream* EP
'Follow That Dream' – *Follow That Dream* EP
'Follow That Dream' – *Elvis Aron Presley* box set
'What A Wonderful Life' – *Follow That Dream* EP
'What A Wonderful Life' – *Collectors Gold* box set
'I'm Not The Marrying Kind' – *Follow That Dream* EP
'A Whistling Tune' – *Collectors Gold* box set
'Sound Advice' – *Elvis For Everyone* LP

15 OCTOBER 1961
'For the Millionth And Last Time' – *Elvis For Everyone* LP
'Good Luck Charm' – single A-side
'Good Luck Charm' – *The EP Collection Vol. 2* box set
'Anything That's Part Of You' – single B-side

16 OCTOBER 1961
'I Met Her Today' – *Elvis For Everyone* LP
'I Met Her Today' – *Collectors Gold* box set
'Night Rider' – *Collectors Gold* box set

26 OCTOBER 1961
'King Of The Whole Wide World' – unissued
'A Whistling Tune' – *Kid Galahad* EP
'Home Is Where The Heart Is' – *Kid Galahad* EP
'Riding The Rainbow' – *Kid Galahad* EP

27 OCTOBER 1961
'I Got Lucky' – *Kid Galahad* EP
'This Is Living' – *Kid Galahad* EP
'King Of The Whole Wide World' – *Kid Galahad* EP

18 MARCH 1962
'Something Blue' – *Pot Luck* LP
'Gonna Get Back Home Somehow' – *Pot Luck* LP
'Easy Question' – *Pot Luck* LP
'Fountain Of Love' – *Pot Luck* LP
'Just For Old Time Sake' – *Pot Luck* LP
'Night Rider' – *Pot Luck* LP
'You'll Be Gone' – single B-side

19 MARCH 1962
'I Feel That I've Known You Forever' – *Pot Luck* LP
'Just Tell Her Jim Said Hello' – single B-side
'Just Tell Her Jim Said Hello' – *Collectors Gold* box set
'Suspicion' – *Pot Luck* LP
'She's Not You' – single A-side

MARCH 1962
'I Don't Want To' – *Girls! Girls! Girls!* LP
'We're Comin' In Loaded' – *Girls! Girls! Girls!* LP
'Thanks To The Rolling Sea' – *Girls! Girls! Girls!* LP
'Thanks To The Rolling Sea' – *Elvis Aron Presley* box set

'Where Do You Come From' – single B-side
'Girls! Girls! Girls!' – *Girls! Girls! Girls!* LP
'Return To Sender' – single A-side
'Because Of Love' – *Girls! Girls! Girls!* LP
'The Walls Have Ears' – *Girls! Girls! Girls!* LP
'Song Of The Shrimp' – *Girls! Girls! Girls!* LP
'A Boy Like Me, A Girl Like You' – *Girls! Girls! Girls!* LP
'Mama' – *Let's Be Friends* LP
'Earth Boy' – *Girls! Girls! Girls!* LP
'Dainty Little Moonbeams' – *Kid Galahad/Girls! Girls! Girls!* CD
'Girls! Girls! Girls!' – *Kid Galahad/Girls! Girls! Girls!* CD
'I Don't Want To Be Tied' – *Girls! Girls! Girls!* LP
'Plantation Rock' – *A Legendary Performer Vol. 4* LP
'Plantation Rock' – unissued
'We'll Be Together' – *Girls! Girls! Girls!* LP

SEPTEMBER 1962
'Happy Ending' – *It Happened At The World's Fair* LP
'Take Me To The Fair' – *It Happened At The World's Fair* LP
'I'm Falling In Love Tonight' – *It Happened At The World's Fair* LP
'I'm Falling In Love Tonight' – *Elvis Aron Presley* box set
'Cotton Candy Land' – *It Happened At The World's Fair* LP
'A World Of Our Own' – *It Happened At The World's Fair* LP
'How Would You Like To Be' – *It Happened At The World's Fair* LP
'Beyond The Bend' – *It Happened At The World's Fair* LP
'Beyond The Bend' – *Collectors Gold* box set
'One Broken Heart For Sale' – single A-side
'One Broken Heart For Sale' – *Collector's Gold* box set
'They Remind Me Too Much Of You' – single B-side
'They Remind Me Too Much Of You' – *Elvis Aron Presley* box set
'Relax' – *It Happened At The World's Fair* LP

22 JANUARY 1963
'Bossa Nova Baby' – single A-side
'I Think I'm Gonna Like It Here' – *Fun In Acapulco* LP
'Mexico' – *Fun In Acapulco* LP
'The Bullfighter Was A Lady' – *Fun In Acapulco* LP

'Marguerita' – *Fun In Acapulco* LP
'Vino, Dinera Y Amor' – *Fun In Acapulco* LP

23 JANUARY 1963

'Fun In Acapulco' – *Fun In Acapulco* LP
'There's No Room To Rhumba In A Sports Car' – *Fun In Acapulco* LP
'El Toro' – *Fun In Acapulco* LP
'Guadalajara' – *Fun In Acapulco* LP
'Guadalajara' – *A Legendary Performer Vol. 3* LP
'You Can't Say No In Acapulco' – *Fun In Acapulco* LP

26 MAY 1963

'Echoes Of Love' – *Kissin' Cousins* LP
'Please Don't Drag That String Around' – single B-side
'Devil In Disguise' – single A-side
'Never Ending' – single B-side
'What Now, What Next, Where To' – *Double Trouble* LP
'Witchcraft' – single B-side
'Witchcraft' – *Collectors Gold* box set
'Finders Keepers, Losers Weepers' – *Elvis For Everyone* LP
'Love Me Tonight' – *Fun In Acapulco* LP
'Love Me Tonight' – *Collectors Gold* box set

27 MAY 1963

'Memphis Tennessee' – *Collectors Gold* box set
'Memphis Tennessee' – *From Nashville To Memphis* box set
'Long Lonely Highway' – *Kissin' Cousins* LP
'Long Lonely Highway' – single B-side
'Ask Me' – *Collectors Gold* box set
'Western Union' – *Speedway* LP
'Slowly But Surely' – *Fun In Acapulco* LP
'Blue River' – single B-side

JULY 1963

'Night Life' – *Flaming Star* LP
'C'mon Everybody' – *Viva Las Vegas* EP
'C'mon Everybody' – unissued

'If You Think I Don't Need You' – unissued
'Viva Las Vegas' – single A-side
'I Need Somebody To Lean On' – *Viva Las Vegas* EP
'What'd I Say' – single B-side
'Santa Lucia' – *Elvis For Everyone* LP
'Yellow Rose Of Texas'/'The Eyes Of Texas' – *Fun In Acapulco* LP
'Do The Vega' – *Fun In Acapulco* LP
'The Lady Loves Me' – *A Legendary Performer Vol. 4* LP
'You're The Boss' – *Collectors Gold* box set
'Today, Tomorrow And Forever' – *Viva Las Vegas* EP
'Today, Tomorrow And Forever' – unissued
'Today, Tomorrow And Forever' – unissued

OCTOBER 1963
'Kissin' Cousins' – single A-side
'Kissin' Cousins' – *Kissin' Cousins* LP
'Catchin' On Fast' – *Kissin' Cousins* LP
'Once Is Enough' – *Kissin' Cousins* LP
'One Boy, Two Little Girls' – *Kissin' Cousins* LP
'Smokey Mountain Boy' – *Kissin' Cousins* LP
'Tender Feeling' – *Kissin' Cousins* LP
'There's Gold In The Mountains' – *Kissin' Cousins* LP
'Barefoot Ballad' – *Kissin' Cousins* LP
'Anyone' – *Kissin' Cousins* LP

12 JANUARY 1964
'Memphis Tennessee' – *Elvis For Everyone* LP
'Ask Me' – single A-side
'It Hurts Me' – single B-side

FEBRUARY/MARCH 1964
'Big Love, Big Heartache' – *Roustabout* LP
'Carny Town' – *Roustabout* LP
'Hard Knocks' – *Roustabout* LP
'It's A Wonderful World' – *Roustabout* LP
'It's Carnival Time' – *Roustabout* LP
'Little Egypt' – *Roustabout* LP

'One Track Heart' – *Roustabout* LP
'Poison Ivy League' – *Roustabout* LP
'Roustabout' – *Roustabout* LP
'Roustabout' – *Collectors Gold* box set
'There's A Brand New Day On The Horizon' – *Roustabout* LP
'Wheels On My Heels' – *Roustabout* LP

JUNE/JULY 1964
'Cross My Heart And Hope To Die' – *Girl Happy* LP
'Girl Happy' – *Girl Happy* LP
'Girl Happy' – *Collectors Gold* box set
'The Meanest Girl In Town' – *Girl Happy* LP
'Puppet On A String' – *Girl Happy* LP
'Do Not Disturb' – *Girl Happy* LP
'I've Got To Find My Baby' – *Girl Happy* LP
'Fort Lauderdale Chamber Of Commerce' – *Girl Happy* LP
'Startin' Tonight' – *Girl Happy* LP
'Do The Clam' – single A-side
'Wolf Call' – *Girl Happy* LP
'Spring Fever' – *Girl Happy* LP

FEBRUARY 1965
'Go East, Young Man' – *Harum Scarum* LP
'Shake That Tambourine' – *Harum Scarum* LP
'Golden Coins' – *Harum Scarum* LP
'So Close, Yet So Far' – *Harum Scarum* LP
'So Close, Yet So Far' – *Collectors Gold* box set
'Holiday' – *Harum Scarum* LP
'Mirage' – *Harum Scarum* LP
'Animal Instinct' – *Harum Scarum* LP
'Kismet' – *Harum Scarum* LP
'Hey Little Girl' – *Harum Scarum* LP
'Wisdom Of The Ages' – *Harum Scarum* LP
'My Desert Serenade' – *Harum Scarum* LP

MAY 1965
'Come Along' – *Frankie And Johnny* LP

'Petunia, The Gardener's Daughter' – *Frankie And Johnny* LP
'Chesay' – *Frankie And Johnny* LP
'What Every Woman Lives For' – *Frankie And Johnny* LP
'Frankie And Johnny' – single A-side
'Look Out Broadway' – *Frankie And Johnny* LP
'Beginner's Luck' – *Frankie And Johnny* LP
'Down By The Riverside'/'When The Saints Go Marching In' – *Frankie And
    Johnny* LP
'Shout It Out' – *Frankie And Johnny* LP
'Hard Luck' – *Frankie And Johnny* LP
'Please Don't Stop Loving Me' – single B-side
'Everybody Come Aboard' – *Frankie And Johnny* LP
'Frankie and Johnny' – unissued

2 AUGUST 1965
'Drums Of The Islands' – *Paradise Hawaiian Style* LP
'This Is My Heaven' – *Paradise Hawaiian Style* LP
'Sand Castles' – *Paradise Hawaiian Style* LP

3 AUGUST 1965
'Scratch My Back' – *Paradise Hawaiian Style* LP
'Stop Where You Are' – *Paradise Hawaiian Style* LP

4 AUGUST 1965
'Datin''' – *Paradise Hawaiian Style* LP
'Datin''' – *Elvis Aron Presley* box set
'A Dog's Life' – *Paradise Hawaiian Style* LP
'A Dog's Life' – *Elvis Aron Presley* box set
'Paradise Hawaiian Style' – *Paradise Hawaiian Style* LP
'Queenie Wahine's Papaya' – *Paradise Hawaiian Style* LP

FEBRUARY 1966
'Stop, Look & Listen' – *Spinout* LP
'Stop, Look & Listen' – *Collectors Gold* box set
'Adam And Evil' – *Spinout* LP
'All That I Am' – single B-side
'Never Say Yes' – *Spinout* LP

'Am I Ready' – *Spinout* LP
'Am I Ready' – *Collectors Gold* box set
'Beach Shack' – *Spinout* LP
'Spinout' – single A-side
'Smorgasbord' – *Spinout* LP
'I'll Be Back' – *Spinout* LP

25 MAY 1966
'Run On' – *How Great Thou Art* LP
'How Great Thou Art' – *How Great Thou Art* LP

26 MAY 1966
'Stand By Me' – *How Great Thou Art* LP
'Where No-One Stands Alone' – *How Great Thou Art* LP
'Down In The Alley' – *Spinout* LP
'Down In The Alley' – *From Nashville to Memphis* box set
'Tomorrow Is A Long Time' – *Spinout* LP
'Love Letters' – single A-side
'Love Letters' – *Collectors Gold* box set

27 MAY 1966
'So High' – *How Great Thou Art* LP
'Farther Along' – *How Great Thou Art* LP
'By And By' – *How Great Thou Art* LP
'In The Garden' – *How Great Thou Art* LP
'Beyond The Reef' – *Elvis Aron Presley* box set
'Somebody Bigger Than You And I' – *How Great Thou Art* LP
'Without Him' – *How Great Thou Art* LP

28 MAY 1966
'If The Lord Wasn't Walking By My Side' – *How Great Thou Art* LP
'Where Could I Go But To The Lord' – *How Great Thou Art* LP
'Come What May' – single B-side
'Come What May' – *Collectors Gold* box set
'Fools Fall In Love' – single B-side

10 JUNE 1966

'Indescribably Blue' – single A-side
'I'll Remember You' – *Spinout* LP
'If Every Day Was Like Christmas' – *Memories Of Christmas* LP
'If Every Day Was Like Christmas' – single A-side

JUNE 1966

'Double Trouble' – *Double Trouble* LP
'Baby If You'll Give Me All Of Your Love' – *Double Trouble* LP
'Could I Fall In Love' – *Double Trouble* LP
'Long Legged Girl' – single A-side
'City By Night' – *Double Trouble* LP
'Old Macdonald' – *Double Trouble* LP
'I Love Only One Girl' – *Double Trouble* LP
'There's So Much World To See' – *Double Trouble* LP
'It Won't Be Long' – *Double Trouble* LP

SEPTEMBER 1966

'Easy Come, Easy Go' – *Easy Come, Easy Go* EP
'The Love Machine' – *Easy Come, Easy Go* EP
'Yoga Is As Yoga Does' – *Easy Come, Easy Go* EP
'You Gotta Stop' – *Easy Come, Easy Go* EP
'Sing You Children' – *Easy Come, Easy Go* EP
'I'll Take Love' – *Easy Come, Easy Go* EP
'Leave My Woman Alone' – unissued
'She's A Machine' – *Flaming Star* LP

FEBRUARY 1967

'Clambake' – *Clambake* LP
'Who Needs Money' – *Clambake* LP
'A House That Has Everything' – *Clambake* LP
'Hey, Hey, Hey' – *Clambake* LP
'The Girl I Never Loved' – *Clambake* LP
'How Can You Lose What You Never Had' – *Clambake* LP
'How Can You Lose What You Never Had' – *Collectors Gold* box set
'You Don't Know Me' – *Double Feature* CD

'Confidence' – *Clambake* LP
'Confidence' – unissued

20 MARCH 1967
'Suppose' – unissued

JUNE 1967
'There Ain't Nothing Like A Song' – *Speedway* LP
'Your Time Hasn't Come Yet Baby' – single B-side
'Five Sleepy Heads' – *Speedway* LP
'Who Are You' – *Speedway* LP
'Speedway' – *Speedway* LP
'Suppose' – *Speedway* LP
'Let Yourself Go' – single A-side
'He's Your Uncle, Not Your Dad' – *Speedway* LP

10 SEPTEMBER 1967
'Guitar Man' – *Clambake* LP
'Big Boss Man' – single A-side
'Big Boss Man' – *From Nashville To Memphis* box set

11 SEPTEMBER 1967
'Mine' – *Speedway* LP
'Singing Tree' – unissued
'Just Call Me Lonesome' – *Clambake* LP
'Just Call Me Lonesome' – *Guitar Man* LP
'High Heel Sneakers' – single B-side
'You Don't Know Me' – single B-side
'We Call On Him' – single B-side
'You'll Never Walk Alone' – single A-side

12 SEPTEMBER 1967
'Singing Tree' – *Clambake* LP

JANUARY 1968
'Too Much Monkey Business' – *Flaming Star* LP
'Going Home' – *Speedway* LP

'Going Home' – *Collectors Gold* box set
'Stay Away' – single B-side
'All I Needed Was The Rain' – *Flaming Star* LP
'Dominic' – *Double Feature* CD
'Stay Away, Joe' – *Let's Be Friends* LP
'Stay Away, Joe' – *Almost In Love* LP
'U.S. Male' – single A-side

7 MARCH 1968
'Almost In Love' – single B-side
'A Little Less Conversation' – single A-side
'A Little Less Conversation' – *Almost In Love* LP
'Wonderful World' – *Flaming Star* LP
'Edge Of Reality' – single B-side

JUNE 1968
'Nothingville' – *Elvis! NBC TV Special* LP
'Let Yourself Go' – *A Legendary Performer Vol. 3* LP
'Big Boss Man' – *Elvis! NBC TV Special* LP
'It Hurts Me' – *A Legendary Performer Vol. 3* LP
'Where Could I Go But To The Lord' – *Elvis! NBC TV Special* LP
'Up Above My Head' – *Elvis! NBC TV Special* LP
'Saved' – *Elvis! NBC TV Special* LP
'Little Egypt' – *Elvis! NBC TV Special* LP
'Guitar Man' – *Elvis! NBC TV Special* LP
'Trouble' – *Elvis! NBC TV Special* LP
'If I Can Dream' – *He Walks Beside Me* LP
'If I Can Dream' – single A-side
'Memories' – *Elvis! NBC TV Special* LP
'A Little Less Conversation' – unissued
'Motherless Child' – unissued

27 JUNE 1968
'That's All Right, Mama' – *A Legendary Performer Vol. 4* LP
'Heartbreak Hotel' – unissued
'Love Me' – *A Legendary Performer Vol. 1* LP

'Baby What You Want Me To Do' – *Elvis! NBC TV Special* LP
'Blue Suede Shoes' – *This Is Elvis* LP
'Lawdy Miss Clawdy' – *Elvis! NBC TV Special* LP
'Are You Lonesome Tonight' – *A Legendary Performer Vol. 1* LP
'When My Blue Moon Turns To Gold Again' – *unissued*
'Blue Christmas' – *Elvis! NBC TV Special* LP
'Trying To Get To You' – *A Legendary Performer Vol. 1* LP
'One Night' – *Elvis! NBC TV Special* LP
'Baby What You Want Me To Do' – *A Legendary Performer Vol. 2* LP
'Memories' – unissued
'Santa Claus Is Back In Town' – unissued
'Tiger Man' – *Flaming Star* LP
'Blue Suede Shoes' – *A Legendary Performer Vol. 2* LP
'If I Can Dream' – unissued

29 JUNE 1968
'Heartbreak Hotel' – *Elvis! NBC TV Special*, LP
'One Night' – unissued
'Hound Dog' – *Elvis! NBC TV Special* LP
'All Shook Up' – *Elvis! NBC TV Special* LP
'Can't Help Falling In Love' – *Elvis! NBC TV Special* LP
'Jailhouse Rock' – *Elvis! NBC TV Special* LP
'Don't Be Cruel' – unissued
'Blue Suede Shoes' – *This Is Elvis* LP
'Love Me Tender' – *Elvis! NBC TV Special* LP
'Trouble'/'Guitar Man' – unissued
'Baby What You Want Me To Do' – unissued
'If I Can Dream' – unissued

23 AUGUST 1968
'Clean Up Your Own Backyard' – single A-side
'Swing Down Sweet Chariot' – *A Legendary Performer Vol. 4* LP
'Signs of the Zodiac' – unissued
'Almost' – *Let's Be Friends* LP
'The Whiffenpoof Song' – unissued

15 OCTOBER 1968
'Charro' – single B-side
'Let's Forget About The Stars' – *Let's Be Friends* LP

13 JANUARY 1969
'Long Black Limousine' – *From Elvis In Memphis* LP
'This Is The Story' – *From Memphis To Vegas* LP

14 JANUARY 1969
'You'll Think Of Me' – single B-side
'A Little Bit Of Green' – *From Memphis To Vegas* LP
'Wearin' That Loved On Look' – *From Elvis In Memphis* LP

15 JANUARY 1969
'Don't Cry Daddy' – single A-side
'Gentle On My Mind' – *From Elvis In Memphis* LP
'I'm Movin' On' – *From Elvis In Memphis* LP
'I'm Movin' On' – *Guitar Man* LP

16 JANUARY 1969
'My Little Friend' – single B-side
'Inherit The Wind' – *From Memphis To Vegas* LP
'Mama Liked The Roses' – single B-side

20 JANUARY 1969
'Rubberneckin'' – single B-side
'In The Ghetto' – *From Nashville To Memphis* box set

21 JANUARY 1969
'From A Jack To A King' – *From Memphis To Vegas* LP
'In The Ghetto' – single A-side

22 JANUARY 1969
'Hey Jude' – *Elvis Now* LP
'Suspicious Minds' – *From Nashville To Memphis* box set

23 JANUARY 1969
'Without Love' – *From Memphis To Vegas* LP
'I'll Hold You In My Heart' – *From Elvis In Memphis* LP
'I'll Be There' – *Let's Be Friends* LP
'Suspicious Minds' – single A-side

17 FEBRUARY 1969
'True Love Travels On A Gravel Road' – *From Elvis In Memphis* LP
'Stranger In My Own Home Town' – *From Memphis To Vegas* LP
'This Time'/'I Can't Stop Loving You' – *From Nashville To Memphis* box set

18 FEBRUARY 1969
'Power Of My Love' – *From Elvis In Memphis* LP
'After Loving You' – *From Elvis In Memphis* LP
'After Loving You' – *Guitar Man* LP
'And The Grass Won't Pay No Mind' – *From Memphis To Vegas* LP

19 FEBRUARY 1969
'Kentucky Rain' – single A-side
'Kentucky Rain' – *From Nashville To Memphis* box set
'Do You Know Who I Am' – *From Memphis To Vegas* LP

20 FEBRUARY 1969
'It Keeps Right On A-Hurtin''' – *From Elvis In Memphis* LP
'Only The Strong Survive' – *From Elvis In Memphis* LP

21 FEBRUARY 1969
'The Fair's Moving On' – single B-side
'Any Day Now' – single B-side
'If I'm A Fool' – *Let's Be Friends* LP

22 FEBRUARY 1969
'Who Am I' – *You'll Never Walk Alone* LP

MARCH 1969
'Have A Happy' – *Let's Be Friends* LP
'Let's Be Friends' – *Let's Be Friends* LP

'Change Of Habit' – *Let's Be Friends* LP
'Let Us Pray' – *You'll Never Walk Alone* LP
'Let Us Pray' – unissued

21 AUGUST 1969
'Yesterday'/'Hey Jude' (live) – unissued
'In The Ghetto' (live) – unissued
'Suspicious Minds' (live) – unissued
'What'd I Say' (live) – unissued
'Can't Help Falling In Love' (live) – unissued

22 AUGUST 1969
'I Got A Woman' (live) – unissued
'All Shook Up' (live) – *From Memphis To Vegas* LP
'Love Me Tender' (live) – *Collectors Gold* box set
'Suspicious Minds' (live) – *From Memphis To Vegas* LP
'Words' (live) – *From Memphis To Vegas* LP
'Johnny B. Goode' (live) – *From Memphis To Vegas* LP
'Runaway' (live) – unissued
'Are You Lonesome Tonight' (live) – *From Memphis To Vegas* LP
'Jailhouse Rock'/'Don't Be Cruel' (live) – *Collectors Gold* box set
'Mystery Train'/'Tiger Man' (live) – *Collectors Gold* box set

23 AUGUST 1969
'Love Me Tender' (live) – *Collectors Gold* box set
'Reconsider Baby' (live) – *Collectors Gold* box set
'What'd I Say' (live) – *Collectors Gold* box set

24 AUGUST 1969
'Rubberneckin'' (live) – unissued
'This Is The Story' (live) – unissued
'Can't Help Falling In Love' (live) – *From Memphis To Vegas* LP
'Heartbreak Hotel' (live) – *Collectors Gold* box set
'My Babe' (live) – *From Memphis To Vegas* LP
'Funny How Time Slips Away' (live) – unissued

25 AUGUST 1969
'Blue Suede Shoes' (live) – *Collectors Gold* box set
'I Got A Woman' (live) – *Collectors Gold* box set
'Jailhouse Rock'/'Don't Be Cruel' (live) – unissued
'Yesterday'/'Hey Jude' (live) – *On Stage* LP
'Memories' (live) – *Collectors Gold* box set
'I Can't Stop Loving You' (live) – *From Memphis to Vegas* LP
'In The Ghetto' (live) – *From Memphis To Vegas* LP
'What'd I Say' (live) – unissued
'Inherit The Wind' (live) – unissued
'Funny How Time Slips Away' (live) – *Collectors Gold* box set

26 AUGUST 1969
'Blue Suede Shoes' (live) – *From Memphis To Vegas* LP
'Hound Dog' (live) – *From Memphis To Vegas* LP
'Baby What You Want Me To do' (live) – *Collectors Gold* box set
'Mystery Train'/'Tiger Man' (live) – *From Memphis To Vegas* LP
'Runaway' (live) – *Collectors Gold* box set
'Surrender'/'Are You Lonesome Tonight' (live) – *Collectors Gold* box set
'Rubberneckin'' (live) – *Collectors Gold* box set
'Inherit The Wind' (live) – *Collectors Gold* box set
'This Is The Story' (live) – *Collectors Gold* box set

27 AUGUST 1969
'Are You Lonesome Tonight' (live) – *Elvis Aron Presley* box set
'My Babe' (live) – *Elvis Aron Presley* box set
'In The Ghetto' (live) – *Elvis Aron Presley* box set
'Yesterday'/'Hey Jude' (live) – *Elvis Aron Presley* box set
'What'd I say' (live) – *Greatest Hits Volume One* LP

16 FEBRUARY 1970
'Yesterday'/'Hey Jude' (live) – *A Legendary Performer Vol. 3* LP
'Let It Be Me' (live) – unissued
'All Shook Up' (live) – unissued
'In The Ghetto' (live) – unissued
'Suspicious Minds' (live) – unissued

17 FEBRUARY 1970

'Proud Mary' (live) – *On Stage* LP

'See See Rider' (live) – *On Stage* LP

'Let It Be Me' (live) – *On Stage* LP

'Don't Cry Daddy' (live) – *Greatest Hits Volume One* LP

18 FEBRUARY 1970

'Sweet Caroline' (live) – *On Stage* LP

'Release Me' (live) – *On Stage* LP

'Kentucky Rain' (live) – *Elvis Aron Presley* box set

'Long Tall Sally' (live) – unissued

'Walk A Mile In My Shoes' (live) – *On Stage* LP

'Polk Salad Annie' (live) – *On Stage* LP

'I Can't Stop Loving You' (live) – unissued

19 FEBRUARY 1970

'The Wonder Of You' (live) – single A-side

'Polk Salad Annie' (live) – unissued

'Kentucky Rain' (live) – unissued

'Suspicious Minds' (live) – unissued

'I Got A Woman' (live) – unissued

4 JUNE 1970

'Twenty Days & Twenty Nights' – *That's The Way It Is* LP

'I've Lost You' – single A-side

'I Was Born About 10,000 Years Ago' – *Elvis Now* LP

'The Sound Of Your Cry' – single B-side

'The Fool' – *Elvis Country* LP

'Little Cabin On The Hill' – *Elvis Country* LP

'Cindy, Cindy' – *Love Letters* LP

5 JUNE 1970

'Bridge Over Troubled Water' – *That's The Way It Is* LP

'Got My Mojo Working' – *Love Letters* LP

'How The Web Was Woven' – *That's The Way It Is* LP

'It's Your Baby, You Rock It' – *Elvis Country* LP

'Stranger In The Crowd' – *That's The Way It is* LP

'I'll Never Know' – *Love Letters* LP
'Mary In The Morning' – *That's The Way It Is* LP

6 JUNE 1970
'It Ain't No Big Thing' – *Love Letters* LP
'You Don't Have To Say You Love Me' – single A-side
'Just Pretend' – *That's The Way It Is* LP
'This Is Our Dance' – *Love Letters* LP
'Life' – single A-side
'Heart Of Rome' – *Love Letters* LP

7 JUNE 1970
'When I'm Over You' – *Love Letters* LP
'I Really Don't Want To Know' – single A-side
'Faded Love' – *Elvis Country* LP
'Tomorrow Never Comes' – *Elvis Country* LP
'The Next Step Is Love' – single B-side
'Make The World Go Away' – *Elvis Country* LP
'Make The World Go Away' – *Welcome To My World* LP
'Funny How Time Slips Away' – *Elvis Country* LP
'I Washed My Hands In Muddy Water' – *Elvis Country* LP
'Love Letters' – *Love Letters* LP

8 JUNE 1970
'There Goes My Everything' – single B-side
'If I Were You' – *Love Letters* LP
'Only Believe' – single B-side
'Sylvia' – *Elvis Now* LP
'Patch It Up' – single B-side

AUGUST 1970
'You've Lost That Lovin' Feelin'' – *Elvis Aron Presley* box set
'Sweet Caroline' – *Elvis Aron Presley* box set
'That's All Right, Mama' (live) – unissued
'Mystery Train'/'Tiger Man' (live) – unissued
'Sweet Caroline' (live) – unissued
'Tiger Man' (live) – unissued

'Polk Salad Annie' (live) – unissued
'Heartbreak Hotel' (live) – unissued
'One Night' (live) – unissued
'Blue Suede Shoes' (live) – unissued
'All Shook Up' (live) – unissued
'Suspicious Minds' (live) – unissued
'Can't Help Falling In Love' (live) – unissued
'I've Lost You' (live) – unissued
'Patch It Up' (live) – *That's The Way It Is* LP
'Love Me Tender' (live) – unissued
'You've Lost That Lovin' Feelin'' (live) – unissued
'I Just Can't Help Believing' (live) – *That's The Way It Is* LP
'Little Sister'/'Get Back' (live) – *Elvis Aron Presley* box set
'Bridge Over Troubled Water' (live) – unissued
'I've Lost You' (live) – *That's The Way It Is* LP
'You've Lost That Lovin' Feelin'' (live) – *That's The Way It Is* LP
'Bridge Over Troubled Water' (live) – unissued
'Polk Salad Annie' (live) – *Elvis Aron Presley* box set

22 SEPTEMBER 1970
'Snowbird' – *Elvis Country* LP
'Where Did They Go, Lord' – single B-side
'Whole Lotta Shakin' Goin' On' – *Elvis Country* LP
'Rags To Riches' – single A-side

15 MARCH 1971
'The First Time Ever I Saw Your Face' – single B-side
'Amazing Grace' – *He Touched Me* LP
'Early Morning Rain' – *Elvis Now* LP
'For Lovin' Me' – *Elvis* LP

15 MAY 1971
'Miracle Of The Rosary' – *Elvis Now* LP
'It Won't Seem Like Christmas' – *The Wonderful World Of Christmas* LP
'If I Get Home On Christmas Day' – *The Wonderful World Of Christmas* LP
'Padre' – *Elvis* LP
'Holly Leaves And Christmas Trees' – *The Wonderful World Of Christmas* LP

'Merry Christmas Baby' – *The Wonderful World Of Christmas* LP
'Silver Bells' – *The Wonderful World Of Christmas* LP

16 MAY 1971
'I'll Be Home On Christmas Day' – *The Wonderful World Of Christmas* LP
'I'll Be Home On Christmas Day' – *Memories of Christmas* LP
'On A Snowy Christmas Night' – *The Wonderful World Of Christmas* LP
'Winter Wonderland' – *The Wonderful World Of Christmas* LP
'Don't Think Twice It's Alright' – *Elvis* LP
'O Come All Ye Faithful' – *The Wonderful World Of Christmas* LP
'O Come All Ye Faithful' – *Memories Of Christmas* LP
'The First Noel' – *The Wonderful World Of Christmas* LP
'The Wonderful World Of Christmas' – *The Wonderful World Of Christmas* LP
'Help Me Make It Through The Night' – *Elvis Now* LP

17 MAY 1971
'Until It's Time For You To Go' – single A-side
'Lead Me, Guide Me' – *He Touched Me* LP

18 MAY 1971
'Fools Rush In' – *Elvis Now* LP
'He Touched Me' – single B-side
'I've Got Confidence' – *He Touched Me* LP
'An Evening Prayer' – *He Touched Me* LP

19 MAY 1971
'Seeing Is Believing' – *He Touched Me* LP
'A Thing Called Love' – *He Touched Me* LP
'It's Still Here' – *Elvis* LP
'I'll Take You Home Again, Kathleen' – *Elvis* LP
'I Will Be True' – *Elvis* LP

20 MAY 1971
'I'm Leavin'' – single A-side
'We Can Make The Morning' – single B-side

21 MAY 1971
'It's Only Love' – single A-side
'Love Me, Love The Life I Lead' – *Elvis* LP

8 JUNE 1971
'Until It's Time For You To Go' – unissued
'Put Your Hand In The Hand' – *Elvis Now* LP
'Reach Out To Jesus' – *He Touched Me* LP

9 JUNE 1971
'He's My Everything' – *He Touched Me* LP
'There Is No God But God' – *He Touched Me* LP
'I, John' – *He Touched Me* LP
'Bosom of Abraham' – single A-side
'I'll Be Home On Christmas Day' – unissued
'The First Time Ever I Saw Your Face' – unissued

FEBRUARY 1972
'An American Trilogy' (live) – *Elvis Aron Presley* LP
'Never Been To Spain' (live) – unissued
'You Gave Me A Mountain' (live) – unissued
'A Big Hunk O' Love' (live) – *Greatest Hits Volume One* LP
'It's Impossible' (live) – *Elvis* LP
'The Impossible Dream' (live) – *He Walks Beside Me* LP
'An American Trilogy' (live) – single A-side
'It's Over' (live) – unissued

27 MARCH 1972
'Separate Ways' – single A-side
'For The Good Times' – unissued
'Where Do I Go From Here' – *Elvis* LP

28 MARCH 1972
'Burning Love' – single A-side
'Fool' – single B-side

29 MARCH 1972
'Always On My Mind' – single B-side
'Always On My Mind' – *This Is Elvis* LP
'It's A Matter Of Time' – single B-side

APRIL 1972
'An American Trilogy' (live) – *This Is Elvis* LP
'For The Good Times' – unissued

10 JUNE 1972
'Reconsider Baby' (live) – *A Legendary Performer Vol. 4* LP
'I'll Remember You' (live) – *A Legendary Performer Vol. 4* LP
'I Can't Stop Loving You' (live) – *Welcome To My World* LP
'That's All Right, Mama' (live) – *As Recorded At Madison Square Garden* LP
'Proud Mary' (live) – *As Recorded at Madison Square Garden* LP
'Never Been To Spain' (live) – *As Recorded at Madison Square Garden* LP
'You Don't Have To Say You Love Me' (live) – *As Recorded at Madison Square Garden* LP
'You've Lost That Lovin' Feelin'' (live) – *As Recorded at Madison Square Garden* LP
'Polk Salad Annie' (live) – *As Recorded at Madison Square Garden* LP
'Love Me' (live) – *As Recorded at Madison Square Garden* LP
'All Shook Up' (live) – *As Recorded at Madison Square Garden* LP
'Heartbreak Hotel' (live) – *As Recorded at Madison Square Garden* LP
'Teddy Bear'/'Don't Be Cruel' (live) – *As Recorded at Madison Square Garden* LP
'Love Me Tender' (live) – *As Recorded at Madison Square Garden* LP
'The Impossible Dream' (live) – *As Recorded at Madison Square Garden* LP
'Hound Dog' (live) – *As Recorded at Madison Square Garden* LP
'Suspicious Minds' (live) – *As Recorded at Madison Square Garden* LP
'For The Good Times' (live) – *As Recorded at Madison Square Garden* LP
'An American Trilogy' (live) – *As Recorded at Madison Square Garden* LP
'Funny How Time Slips Away' (live) – *As Recorded at Madison Square Garden* LP
'I Can't Stop Loving You' (live) – *As Recorded at Madison Square Garden* LP
'Can't Help Falling In Love' (live) – *As Recorded at Madison Square Garden* LP

12 JANUARY 1973
'See See Rider' (live) – *The Alternate Aloha* LP
'Burning Love' (live) – *The Alternate Aloha* LP
'Something' (live) – *The Alternate Aloha* LP
'You Gave Me A Mountain' (live) – *The Alternate Aloha* LP
'Steamroller Blues' (live) – *The Alternate Aloha* LP
'My Way' (live) – *The Alternate Aloha* LP
'Love Me' (live) – *The Alternate Aloha* LP
'It's Over' (live) – *The Alternate Aloha* LP
'Blue Suede Shoes' (live) – *The Alternate Aloha* LP
'I'm So Lonesome I Could Cry' (live) – *The Alternate Aloha* LP
'Hound Dog' (live) – *The Alternate Aloha* CD
'What Now My Love' (live) – *The Alternate Aloha* LP
'Fever' (live) – *The Alternate Aloha* LP
'Welcome To My World' (live) – *The Alternate Aloha* LP
'Suspicious Minds' (live) – *The Alternate Aloha* LP
'I'll Remember You' (live) – *The Alternate Aloha* LP
'An American Trilogy' (live) – *The Alternate Aloha* LP
'A Big Hunk O' Love' (live) – *The Alternate Aloha* LP
'Can't Help Falling In Love' (live) – *The Alternate Aloha* LP

14 JANUARY 1973
'See See Rider' (live) – *Aloha From Hawaii Via Satellite* LP
'Burning Love' (live) – *Aloha From Hawaii Via Satellite* LP
'Something' (live) – *Aloha From Hawaii Via Satellite* LP
'You Gave Me A Mountain' (live) – *Aloha From Hawaii Via Satellite* LP
'Steamroller Blues' (live) – *Aloha From Hawaii Via Satellite* LP
'My Way' (live) – *Aloha From Hawaii Via Satellite* LP
'Love Me' (live) – *Aloha From Hawaii Via Satellite* LP
'Johnny B. Goode' (live) – *Aloha From Hawaii Via Satellite* LP
'It's Over' (live) – *Aloha From Hawaii Via Satellite* LP
'Blue Suede Shoes' (live) – *Aloha From Hawaii Via Satellite* LP
'I'm So Lonesome I Could Cry' (live) – *Aloha From Hawaii Via Satellite* LP
'I Can't Stop Loving You' (live) – *Aloha From Hawaii Via Satellite* LP
'Hound Dog' (live) – *Aloha From Hawaii Via Satellite* LP
'What Now My Love' (live) – *Aloha From Hawaii Via Satellite* LP
'Fever' (live) – *Aloha From Hawaii Via Satellite* LP

'Welcome To My World' (live) – *Aloha From Hawaii Via Satellite* LP
'Suspicious Minds' (live) – *Aloha From Hawaii Via Satellite* LP
'I'll Remember You' (live) – *Aloha From Hawaii Via Satellite* LP
'Long Tall Sally'/'Whole Lotta Shakin' Goin' On' (live) – *Aloha From Hawaii Via Satellite* LP
'An American Trilogy' (live) – *Aloha From Hawaii Via Satellite* LP
'A Big Hunk O' Love' (live) – *Aloha From Hawaii Via Satellite* LP
'Can't Help Falling In Love' (live) – *Aloha From Hawaii Via Satellite* LP
'Blue Hawaii' – *A Legendary Performer Vol. 2* LP
'Ku-u-i-po' – *Mahalo From Elvis* LP
'No More' – *Mahalo From Elvis* LP
'Hawaiian Wedding Song' – *Mahalo From Elvis* LP
'Early Morning Rain' – *Mahalo From Elvis* LP

21 JULY 1973
'If You Don't Come Back' – *Raised On Rock* LP
'Three Corn Patches' – *Raised On Rock* LP
'Take Good Care Of Her' – single B-side

22 JULY 1973
'Find Out What's Happening' – *Raised On Rock* LP
'I've Got A Thing About You Baby' – single A-side
'Just A Little Bit' – *Raised On Rock* LP

23 JULY 1973
'Raised On Rock' – single A-side
'For Ol' Times Sake' – single B-side

24 JULY 1973
'Girl Of Mine' – *Raised On Rock* LP

24 SEPTEMBER 1973
'Sweet Angeline' – *Raised On Rock* LP
'I Miss You' – *Raised On Rock* LP
'Are You Sincere' – *Raised On Rock* LP
'Are You Sincere' – *Our Memories Of Elvis* LP

10 DECEMBER 1973
'I Got A Feelin' In My Body' – *Good Times* LP
'It's Midnight' – single B-side

11 DECEMBER 1973
'You Asked Me To' – *Promised Land* LP
'If You Talk In Your Sleep' – single A-side

12 DECEMBER 1973
'Mr Songman' – *Promised Land* LP
'Thinking About You' – *Promised Land* LP
'Love Song Of The Year' – *Promised Land* LP
'Help Me' – single B-side

13 DECEMBER 1973
'My Boy' – *Good Times* LP
'Loving Arms' – *Good Times* LP
'Loving Arms' – *Guitar Man* LP
'Good Time Charlie's Got The Blues' – *Good Times* LP

14 DECEMBER 1973
'Talk About The Good Times' – *Good Times* LP

15 DECEMBER 1973
'Promised Land' – single A-side
'Your Love's Been A Long Time Coming' – *Promised Land* LP
'There's A Honky Tonk Angel' – *Promised Land* LP

16 DECEMBER 1973
'If That Isn't Love' – *Good Times* LP
'Spanish Eyes' – *Good Times* LP
'She Wears My Ring' – *Good Times* LP

20 MARCH 1974
'See See Rider' (live) – *As Recorded Live On Stage In Memphis* LP
'I Got A Woman' (live) – *As Recorded Live On Stage In Memphis* LP
'Love Me' (live) – *As Recorded Live On Stage In Memphis* LP

'Trying To Get To You' (live) – *As Recorded Live On Stage In Memphis* LP
'Rock 'n' Roll Medley' (live)* – *As Recorded Live On Stage In Memphis* LP
'Why Me Lord' (live) – *As Recorded Live On Stage In Memphis* LP
'How Great Thou Art' (live) – *As Recorded Live On Stage In Memphis* LP
'Blueberry Hill'/'I Can't Stop Loving You' (live) – *As Recorded Live On Stage In Memphis* LP
'Help Me' (live) – *As Recorded Live On Stage In Memphis* LP
'An American Trilogy' (live) – *As Recorded Live On Stage In Memphis* LP
'Let Me Be There' (live) – *As Recorded Live On Stage In Memphis* LP
'My Baby Left Me' (live) – *As Recorded Live On Stage In Memphis* LP
'Lawdy Miss Clawdy' (live) – *As Recorded Live On Stage In Memphis* LP
'Can't Help Falling In Love' (live) – *As Recorded Live On Stage In Memphis* LP

10 MARCH 1975
'Fairytale' – *Today* LP

11 MARCH 1975
'Green Green Grass Of Home' – *Today* LP
'I Can Help' – *Today* LP
'And I Love You So' – *Today* LP
'Susan When She Tried' – *Today* LP

12 MARCH 1975
'T-R-O-U-B-L-E' – single A-side
'Woman Without Love' – *Today* LP
'Shake A Hand' – *Today* LP
'Bringin' It Back' – *Today* LP

13 MARCH 1975
'Pieces Of My Life' – *Today* LP

6 JUNE 1975
'I Got A Woman'/'Amen' (live) – *Elvis Aron Presley* box set
'Love Me' (live) – *Elvis Aron Presley* box set

* The medley consists of 'Long Tall Sally', 'Whole Lotta Shakin' Goin' On', 'Your Mama Don't Dance', Flip, Flop And Fly', 'Jailhouse Rock' and 'Hound Dog'.

'If You Love Me' (live) – *Elvis Aron Presley* box set
'Love Me Tender' (live) – *Elvis Aron Presley* box set
'All Shook Up' (live) – *Elvis Aron Presley* box set
'Teddy Bear'/'Don't Be Cruel' (live) – *Elvis Aron Presley* box set
'Hound Dog' (live) – *Elvis Aron Presley* box set
'The Wonder Of You' (live) – *Elvis Aron Presley* box set
'Burning Love' (live) – *Elvis Aron Presley* box set
'Johnny B. Goode' (live) – *Elvis Aron Presley* box set
'Long Live Rock 'n' Roll' (live)* – *Elvis Aron Presley* box set
'T-R-O-U-B-L-E' (live) – *Elvis Aron Presley* box set
'How Great Thou Art' (live) – *Elvis Aron Presley* box set
'Let Me Be There' (live) – *Elvis Aron Presley* box set
'An American Trilogy' (live) – *Elvis Aron Presley* box set
'Funny How Time Slips Away' (live) – *Elvis Aron Presley* box set
'Little Darlin'' (live) – *Elvis Aron Presley* box set
'Mystery Train'/'Tiger Man' (live) – *Elvis Aron Presley* box set
'Can't Help Falling In Love' (live) – *Elvis Aron Presley* box set
'See See Rider' (live) – *Elvis Aron Presley* box set
'Why Me Lord' (live) – *Elvis Aron Presley* box set

13 DECEMBER 1975
'Softly As I Leave You' (live) – single A-side
'America The Beautiful' (live) – single B-side

2 FEBRUARY 1976
'Bitter They Are, Harder They Fall' – *From Elvis Presley Boulevard* LP
'She Thinks I Still Care' – single B-side
'She Thinks I Still Care' – *Guitar Man* LP
'The Last Farewell' – *From Elvis Presley Boulevard* LP

3 FEBRUARY 1976
'Solitaire' – *From Elvis Presley Boulevard* LP

4 FEBRUARY 1976
'Moody Blue' – single A-side
'I'll Never Fall In Love Again' – *From Elvis Presley Boulevard* LP

* This song is actually Chuck Berry's 'School Day' mistitled.

5 FEBRUARY 1976
'For The Heart' – single B-side
'Hurt' – single A-side
'Danny Boy' – *From Elvis Presley Boulevard* LP

6 FEBRUARY 1976
'Never Again' – *From Elvis Presley Boulevard* LP
'Love Comin' Down' – *From Elvis Presley Boulevard* LP

8 FEBRUARY 1976
'Blue Eyes Crying In The Rain' – *From Elvis Presley Boulevard* LP

29 OCTOBER 1976
'It's Easy For You' – *Moody Blue* LP
'Way Down' – single A-side
'Pledging My Love' – single B-side

31 OCTOBER 1976
'He'll Have To Go' – *Moody Blue* LP

24 APRIL 1977
'Unchained Melody' (live) – *Moody Blue* LP
'Little Darlin'' (live) – *Moody Blue* LP

25 APRIL 1977
'If You Love Me' (live) – *Moody Blue* LP

19 JUNE 1977
'Teddy Bear'/'Don't Be Cruel' (live) – *Elvis In Concert* LP
'How Great Thou Art' (live) – *Elvis In Concert* LP
'Can't Help Falling In Love' (live) – *Elvis In Concert* LP
'Fairytale' (live) – *Elvis In Concert* LP
'Little Sister' (live) – *Elvis In Concert* LP
'And I Love You So' (live) – *Elvis In Concert* LP
'What'd I Say' (live) – *Elvis In Concert* LP
'Johnny B. Goode' (live) – *Elvis In Concert* LP
'I Really Don't Want To Know' (live) – *Elvis In Concert* LP

21 JUNE 1977
'See See Rider' (live) – *Elvis In Concert* LP
'I Got A Woman'/'Amen' (live) – *Elvis In Concert* LP
'That's All Right, Mama' (live) – *Elvis In Concert* LP
'Are You Lonesome Tonight' (live) – *Elvis In Concert* LP
'Love Me' (live) – *Elvis In Concert* LP
'If You Love Me' (live) – *Elvis In Concert* LP
'You Gave Me A Mountain' (live) – *Elvis In Concert* LP
'Jailhouse Rock' (live) – *Elvis In Concert* LP
'It's Now Or Never' (live) – *Elvis In Concert* LP
'Trying To Get To You' (live) – *Elvis In Concert* LP
'Hawaiian Wedding Song' (live) – *Elvis In Concert* LP
'My Way' (live) – *Elvis In Concert* LP
'Early Morning Rain' (live) – *Elvis In Concert* LP
'Hurt' (live) – *Elvis In Concert* LP
'Hound Dog' (live) – *Elvis In Concert* LP
'Unchained Melody' (live) – single B-side

Index